FINANCIAL ASPECTS OF MARKETING

Financial Aspects of Marketing

Ruth A. Schmidt

and

Helen Wright

palgrave

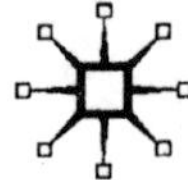

Published by
PALGRAVE
Houndmills, Basingstoke, Hampshire RG21 6XS and
175 Fifth Avenue, New York, N. Y. 10010
Companies and representatives throughout the world

PALGRAVE is the new global academic imprint of
St. Martin's Press LLC Scholarly and Reference Division and
Palgrave Publishers Ltd (formerly Macmillan Press Ltd).

ISBN-10: 0–333–63781–X hardcover ISBN-13: 978–0–333–63781–4 hardcover
ISBN-10: 0–333–63782–8 paperback ISBN-13: 978–0–333–63782–1 paperback

This book is printed on paper suitable for recycling and made from fully managed and sustained forest sources.

A catalogue record for this book is available from the British Library.

14 13 12 11
09 08 07 06

Typeset in Great Britain by
Aarontype Limited, Easton, Bristol

Printed and bound in Great Britain by
Biddles Ltd, King's Lynn, Norfolk

Contents

List of Figures

List of Tables

Acknowledgements

The authors and publishers acknowledge with thanks permission from the following to reproduce data:

Claudio Vignali and Barry J. Davies of the Manchester Metropolitan University for the data in Case Study 2.

Neville Atkinson of Allied Domecq plc for the data in Case Study 4.

Economic Trends.

The following information sources were used in compiling the raw data which were reworked into simplified examples and exercises in the text:

Allied-Lyons plc, *Annual Report and Accounts,* 1993–1995.

MFI plc, *Annual Report and Accounts,* 1988–1995.

J Sainsbury plc, *Annual Report and Accounts,* 1989–1995.

Kwik Save plc, *Annual Report and Accounts,* 1993–1995.

The share performance data on Wimpey, Barratt, Banner and Beazer Homes and Sainsbury and Kwik Save were extracted from publicly available information sources on 16 May 1995.

The price comparison in Table 25.1 serves to illustrate a point of principle only. It is loosely based on an ad hoc collection of prices during a shopping trip and the prices presented may bear no resemblance to real prices currently charged.

1

Introduction to the Finance and Marketing Interface

1.1 Background and target readership

Modern business needs managers who are versatile, with a good understanding of the basics of all the various business functions. Such a manager can work easily in a team which consists of people who have specialised in different areas. Business structures are increasingly becoming flatter. There is a need for clear communication and decision-making at all levels. The effectiveness of teams depends on team members' understanding of how their own areas' aims and priorities relate to the objectives set by the organisation's mission statement. Increasingly there is a recognition that a range of financial and other objectives must be balanced to ensure the long-term success of the business. This means that it is important that everybody in the business can speak the language of finance, at least to the extent that they can use financial information to inform their own decisions and to assess its relevance and use under different circumstances.

Increasingly these trends are reflected in the structure of marketing and management courses, which aim to provide a thorough grounding in the various functional disciplines in order to allow marketing managers to work with other functional specialists and to communicate effectively.

This text aims to provide an introduction to the use of financial information for students of marketing and other business disciplines which are not primarily financially based.

The basis for writing this text was our work with students on marketing and retail programmes who had already had substantial exposure to the working environment in modern business organisations, but had only a limited academic background. Many of these students are working managers who are studying part-time in company sponsored programmes. In this text, we are attempting to meet the challenge of making our material relevant and interesting to such people, who have an excellent grasp of how financial information is used in their specific work place, but who need to be able to stand back from this and understand the general principles involved.

In recent years, there has been a shift in the UK economy and a decline in much of the traditional manufacturing sector has been going hand in hand with growth in the retail and service sector. This is reflected throughout the text in a greater emphasis on examples from the retail and service sector than you might find in the long-established standard accountancy texts. This difference in balance is intended to make the material interesting and relevant to you, whatever your current or future work place may be.

1.2 Additional equipment required

There can be no doubt that in virtually all medium to large business organisations financial information is produced and processed using information technology, namely spreadsheets. In fact, most managers will be required to master the use of the spreadsheet at some stage in their careers, regardless of their functional specialism. In other words, just as a manager needs a sound grasp of basic finance, so a good grounding in the use of computer software is required. This is also reflected in the structure of most marketing management related courses.

Again, this trend is reflected in the approach used in this text. Whilst for the most part of the text you will require only a calculator which has the basic functions to complete the calculations, it is desirable to have access to a scientific calculator and a personal computer with spreadsheet software if you wish to make full use of all the exercises in this book. Having said that, we do not take spreadsheet skills for granted, but provide an introductory chapter which takes you through the basics of spreadsheet applications, using Microsoft Excel as an example of the kind of software you might use.

1.3 Structure

In overview, the text is subdivided into five parts which deal with the key areas of interest to the user of financial information.

For students who need to become proficient users of financial information in a management context, the first step inevitably has to be to gain a grounding in the language of accountancy and to acquire a basic understanding of the principles and layout of the key financial statements. Part I therefore covers the elementary aspects of financial accounting as a record keeping system. The balance sheet, the profit and loss account and the cash flow statement are introduced. Depreciation and stock valuation methods are discussed to illustrate the principles involved. Chapter 6 provides an introduction to the use of spreadsheets. This lays the foundation for the remaining parts of the book where the focus is on the manager as end user of financial information and the emphasis is on interpretation.

In Part II, ratio analysis is introduced as a management tool for the interpretation of historical financial data. Whilst the focus is still on the past, such data are now used in the context of a wider analysis of the strategic strengths and weaknesses of the business and in a comparison over time and with industry averages. Performance is viewed from an investor's perspective on the one hand and linked to operational activities on the other. This emphasises the integrated nature of all business activity.

Part III introduces the application of a range of forecasting techniques to financial data in order to reduce future uncertainty and to facilitate planning. This Part illustrates how quantitative techniques such as correlation analysis can be used to represent links between marketing activities and financial performance.

In Part IV, management approaches to the budgetary planning and control process are discussed. This Part builds on an introduction to costing systems, placing emphasis on the need for an integrated approach towards costing throughout the value chain. In this way, efficiency is maximised for both manufacturing and retailing organisations, resulting in a better offering to the end consumer.

Part V looks at a range of techniques used in managerial decision-making. This includes break-even analysis, short-term decision-making techniques and discounted cash flow (DCF) techniques for long-term capital investment decisions. The need to integrate the use of financial data with other relevant information is emphasised and illustrated.

1.4 Progression through the text

Throughout the text, learning objectives are set out at the beginning of each chapter. Wherever new material is introduced, this is first defined, explained and illustrated in a worked example. Exercises are then used to reinforce the learning. Once you have mastered each of the techniques introduced, further examples and exercises are provided where you can make use of spreadsheet software to apply the techniques in a more realistic businesslike manner. In order to assist you in checking your own progress, answers to the exercises are provided at the end of the book.

Each of the five Parts ends in a Case Study. The case studies are based on material from real business organisations and provide integrated examples of the business application of the material covered in the preceding Part of the book. They enable you to practise the skills you have acquired in working with financial information and spreadsheets and to bring these together with information from other relevant sources in order to make strategic and marketing decisions. There are no model answers for the case studies, as it is intended that these should be used as assessed work by lecturers using the text in class.

The language of accountancy often acts as a barrier to students who feel that they have to learn a whole new vocabulary before they can be comfortable dealing with financial statements. We have therefore provided a glossary of terms at the end of the book, which can be used as a reference source and also as a quick revision aid.

Terms defined in the Glossary appear in the text as SMALL CAPITALS.

We have also put together a list of references to guide and encourage further reading for the topic areas covered in each of the five parts. Hopefully this introductory text will leave you interested in learning more and ready to move on to more specialist books.

We wish you every success working through the book and we are always interested in hearing from readers who can add to our pool of up-to-date business examples of any of the techniques covered.

Part I
Introduction to Financial Statements

2

The Balance Sheet

2.1 Learning objectives

When you have finished working through this chapter you should be able to

- Give a brief explanation of the **BALANCE SHEET**
- Define the term **ASSET**
- Distinguish between a **FIXED ASSET** and a **CURRENT ASSET** and give examples of both
- Define and contrast the terms **DEBTOR** and **CREDITOR**
- Define the term **LIABILITY**
- Explain the difference between a **LONG-TERM LIABILITY** and a **CURRENT LIABILITY**, giving examples of both
- Explain what is meant by the **CAPITAL** of a business, and appreciate the difference between cash and capital
- Understand why the two parts of the balance sheet must always balance
- Draw up a balance sheet in the context of a simple exercise
- Calculate and explain the impact of simple business transactions on a balance sheet
- Explain what is meant by **DUALITY**

2.2 Introduction

In the UK, most of the turnover generated from business activities every year comes from large business organisations which are owned publicly by shareholders. This implies that there is a division between ownership and control – the managers and the owners of the business are different groups of people who need to communicate with each other concerning the objectives and financial performance of the business. Such communication is facilitated formally through the production of an annual set of final accounts, consisting of a *BALANCE SHEET* and *PROFIT AND LOSS ACCOUNT* for the business. Since these financial statements form the cornerstone of the business's external communications about its results, it is important for any user of financial information to be able to read and understand such statements.

Part I therefore lays the foundation for this book by introducing you to the language of finance and accountancy and showing you how to draw up a set of final accounts. This chapter covers the terminology and logic of the balance sheet. Chapters 3 and 4 look at the profit and loss account and the cash flow statement and Chapter 5 draws the material together to produce an integrated set of final accounts. Chapter 6 provides a basic introduction to the use of spreadsheets in the production of financial information for a range of users.

2.3 Defining the balance sheet

Because of the division between ownership and control, all large business organisations are legally obliged to provide their owners with a statement of their financial position on an annual basis to let them know what has happened to their investment and what the business has got to show for it at that point in time. Such a statement is known as a *BALANCE SHEET.*

The balance sheet basically shows *two* things: where the money invested in the business has come from and what the business has got to show for that money at the point in time when the balance sheet is drawn up. The principle of stewardship means that, assuming management has been trustworthy and kept accurate records then the two should always be equal. For every penny invested in the business the business should have something of equal value to show the owners. This can be summarised in the *BALANCE SHEET EQUATION.*

The balance sheet equation

CAPITAL	=	*ASSETS – LIABILITIES*
Original investment		Value of everything owned by the business after all debts are settled

Example

Figure 2.1 shows a simplified version of the 199X balance sheet of a small toy manufacturer and retailer.

The balance sheet represents a snapshot of the activities of the business at *only one point in time.* Any transactions carried out in the normal course of business activities affect this picture. This means that it is important to put a *date* on the balance sheet, otherwise it is meaningless.

FIGURE 2.1

TOY COMPANY:
BALANCE SHEET AS AT 31 DECEMBER 199X

	£	£
Fixed Assets		
Fixtures and Fittings		60 000
Computers		23 000
Vans		17 000
		100 000
Current Assets		
Stock	12 000	
Debtors	5 000	
Cash and Bank	2 000	
	19 000	
Creditors (due within one year)		
Trade Creditors	17 000	
Net Current Assets		2 000
Total Assets *less* Current Liabilities		102 000
Creditors (due after one year)		
Bank Loan		20 000
		82 000
Capital		
Share Capital		75 000
Retained Profit		7 000
		82 000

2.4 Assets

The top part of the balance sheet deals with everything of monetary value owned by the business, the so-called *ASSETS.* Assets can be *tangible* or *intangible.*

Tangible means that the business holds the property in something that can be seen and touched, for example a computer, display shelves, a machine, stock of raw material. *Intangible* refers to the ownership of a right, as in the case of a patent, or entitlement to a future benefit, for instance money owed by a customer who bought goods on credit.

Note that all assets listed are items which can be assigned an objective money value. There may well be other aspects of a business organisation which are very important to its future success, such as staff motivation, a reputation for strong environmental values and many others. However, these cannot be included in the balance sheet, as their potential monetary value is far too vague.

Exercise 2.1

For each of the businesses below, list *three* types of assets (other than cash) you would expect them to have:

(a) Ice cream manufacturer
(b) Building society
(c) Fairground ride operator

Looking at the balance sheet provided in Figure 2.1 you notice that the assets are divided into *fixed* and *current* assets.

> *FIXED ASSETS* are of relatively high value and of permanent use in the business. *CURRENT ASSETS* include cash and other items which are easily and rapidly turned into cash, such as the *STOCK* of goods for sale and amounts of money owed by customers, the so-called *DEBTORS*.

Exercise 2.2

The assets listed below are found in the KoolKurls hairdressing salon. Sort them into fixed and current assets.

- Set of professional styling scissors
- Shampoo
- Electric hairdryers
- Electronic till
- £10 owed by a customer
- £15 in the till

2.5 Liabilities

Just as the business can hold a right or entitlement to some future benefit, so it can be under an obligation to an outside party. Such obligations are known as *LIABILITIES*. Liabilities arise where the business uses credit or a loan as a source of finance and they can be either of a current or a long-term nature.

> *CURRENT LIABILITIES* are those financial obligations which have to be met in the short-term, which is often defined as less than the next financial year. Because of this they are listed under *CREDITORS (DUE WITHIN ONE YEAR)*. These may include amounts owing to trade suppliers, the so-called *TRADE CREDITORS*. A bank overdraft, to the extent to which it is actually used, is also a current liability, as the bank has the right to call it in at any time.
>
> In contrast, *LONG-TERM LIABILITIES* or *CREDITORS (DUE AFTER ONE YEAR)* are items of longer-term loan finance which do not have to repaid within the next financial year.

Exercise 2.3

Are the following liabilities of Paws&Claws Petshop? Explain your answer.

- £50 wages of Lenny, the part-time shop assistant, for work he did during the previous week
- £300 owed to the wholesaler for cages and petfood purchased and delivered last month
- £15 for stationery ordered but not yet delivered
- £300 overdraft facility agreed with the bank manager but not yet used

2.6 Capital

As you can see from the above, at any one point in time, the business holds a number of items of value, the assets. However, it also *owes* money to various parties, the liabilities. To determine the net value of the business, that is to show how much the assets of the business are really worth after all the liabilities have been met and paid for, you have to take away the liabilities from the assets:

FIXED ASSETS + CURRENT ASSETS
− CURRENT LIABILITIES
− LONG-TERM LIABILITIES = CAPITAL

The balance sheet equation tells us that this should be equal to the owners' investment, the CAPITAL.

The capital to date consists of two parts, the owners' original investment *plus* any profits reinvested during the life of the business, the so-called RETAINED PROFIT.

Exercise 2.4

The founder of the toy company in Figure 2.1 discusses the company's balance sheet with the company accountant.

> 'In this balance sheet you have prepared for the last financial year, our capital is listed as £82 000, but we only seem to have £2000 in cash. I don't mean to complain, but where has all the rest of the money gone?'

Can you think of an explanation?

It is very important to understand that capital is not the same as *cash*. True, a typical business starts its life when the owner opens a business bank account and puts a sum of money into it. However, the whole point of having a business is putting this cash to work. So it does not stay in the form of a bank balance for very long, but soon gets transformed into other forms of value. It changes shape as the money gets spent on stock, which in turn gets sold to customers who pay more cash, or it is turned into furniture, plant, computers and other fixed assets. These are necessary for running the business, and whilst they are not cash they are of equal value to the cash spent on them. So the value if not the form of the original capital is preserved, and even increased if the transactions result in profit which is reinvested in the business.

When you look at the balance sheet, the sum of the original capital and the profit reinvested reflects the minimum amount the owners would have to get back, were they to sell the business's net assets. In this sense, you could look on the capital as the business's 'debt' to the owners, although no legal entitlement exists.

Exercise 2.5

The following information is based on a simplified version of the balance sheet of Allied Domecq plc, a large holding company trading in spirits, public house and fast food retailing worldwide. Using the example given in Figure 2.1 as a model, re-present the information given here in the format of a balance sheet as at 5 March 199X, classifying assets and liabilities under appropriate headings.

	£m
Cash	150
Buildings	2400
Retained profit	250
Furniture and fittings	300
Debtors	1000
Trade creditors	1700
Stock	1000
Long-term bank loan	2700
Plant and machinery	1300
Share capital	1500

2.7 Impact of business transactions on the balance sheet

All business activity is really concerned with turning the resources of the business from one form into another. As a result, the balance sheet is like a snapshot of a moving target. It keeps changing every time a business transaction is undertaken and to stay accurate you would have to draw up a new balance sheet after each transaction.

The following example demonstrates this impact of business transactions on the balance sheet in principle. Note that for balance sheet purposes, transactions are recognised when they become legally binding.

Example

Transaction 1

On 1 January 199X Nico starts a new business venture designing and laminating business cards by opening a

FIGURE 2.2

NICO'S BUSINESS: BALANCE SHEET AS AT 1 JANUARY 199X	
Current Assets	£
Bank and Cash	2500
Capital	2500

business bank account and depositing the initial capital of £2500.

At the end of that day the balance sheet for Nico's business card business looks as presented in Figure 2.2.

Explanation

The birth of the business is marked by the capital investment of £2500. In concrete terms, this is shown by the fact that there is now a sum of £2500 in the new business bank account.

Transaction 2

On 2 January 199X Nico buys a laminating machine for £60, a computer with printer and desktop publishing software for £2000 and a stock of business cards for £30.

For the end of that day the balance sheet for Nico's business card business is shown in Figure 2.3.

FIGURE 2.3

NICO'S BUSINESS: BALANCE SHEET AS AT 2 JANUARY 199X	
Fixed Assets	£
Computer Equipment	2000
Laminating Machine	60
Current Assets	
Stock	30
Bank and Cash	410
	2500
Capital	2500

Explanation

To make the purchases of the computer equipment, the laminating machine and the stock of cards, Nico has to use up most of the cash he had put into the bank. In consequence, his Current Asset (cash) entry is reduced to £410; however, the cash is not lost, it is just transformed. So the apparent shortfall of £2090 is now represented by £30 Current Assets (Stock) and £2060 Fixed Assets (computing equipment and laminating machine). The overall value of Nico's investment in the business remains unchanged, therefore the capital entry is still £2500.

Transaction 3

On 3 January 199X Nico designs, produces and laminates a set of business cards for a customer. The cards had initially cost £10 and the customer pays £40 cash. Nico decides to reinvest all profits into the business.

The balance sheet for Nico's business card business at the end of that day is shown in Figure 2.4.

Explanation

Nico has made a sale and cleared £30 more than the initial cost of the cards. In other words he has made some *profit*. This means that as the value of his stock

FIGURE 2.4

NICO'S BUSINESS: BALANCE SHEET AS AT 3 JANUARY 199X	
Fixed Assets	£
Computer Equipment	2000
Laminating Machine	60
Current Assets	
Stock	20
Bank and Cash	450
	2530
Capital	2500
Retained Profit	30
	2530

of cards declines by £10, the value of his cash holding has increased by £40, an overall increase in Current Assets of £30. Since he has decided to reinvest all profits in the business – this also means that his overall investment has gone up by £30, in other words the retained profit is added on to the capital. This example shows that the capital of the business changes when there is a change in the overall investment levels in the business, that is, when a profit is made and the investment goes up, or, when a loss is made and the investment is eroded by that amount.

Transaction 4

On 4 January 199X Nico buys a further supply of business cards from a local wholesaler. The cards cost £40, but he does not have to pay until 4 February 199X.

At the end of that day the balance sheet for Nico's business card business looks like the one shown in Figure 2.5.

Explanation

The business gains Current Assets (Stock) worth £40, but since these are financed through trade credit, there is a corresponding increase on the liability side in Creditors: due within one year (Trade Creditors). The overall capital investment in the business remains unchanged.

The above example demonstrates the principle of *DUALITY*, every transaction has at least two matching effects on the balance sheet.

> As a result, the two halves always remain in balance.

FIGURE 2.5

NICO'S BUSINESS: BALANCE SHEET AS AT 4 JANUARY 199X	
Fixed Assets	£
Computer Equipment	2000
Laminating Machine	60
+	
Current Assets	
Stock	60
Bank and Cash	450
–	
Creditors: due within one year	
Trade Creditors	40
	2530
=	
Capital	2500
Retained Profit	30
	2530

Exercise 2.6

Figure 2.6 represents the opening balance sheet of a small manufacturing business.

The balance sheets shown in Figures 2.7–2.9 were drawn up after a number of single or multiple transactions had taken place. Each balance sheet follows on from the previous one. Indicate which transaction(s) has (have) taken place by circling the letter next to the correct answer.

FIGURE 2.6

MANUFACTURING BUSINESS: BALANCE SHEET AS AT 6 JUNE 199X	
Fixed Assets	£
Plant and Machinery	6 000
Vehicles	3 000
+	
Current Assets	
Stock	1 000
Debtors	2 000
Bank and Cash	300
–	
Creditors: due within one year	
Trade Creditors	1 500
	10 800
=	
Capital	10 800

FIGURE 2.7

MANUFACTURING BUSINESS:
BALANCE SHEET AS AT 7 JUNE 199X

Fixed Assets	£
Plant and Machinery	6 000
Vehicles	3 000
+	
Current Assets	
Stock	1 000
Debtors	2 000
Bank and Cash	1 300
–	
Creditors: due within one year	
Trade Creditors	1 500
Creditors: due after one year	1 000
	10 800
=	
Capital	10 800

(a) Refer to Figure 2.7.
  (A) Introduced more capital in the form of £1000 cash
  (B) Took out a long-term loan in the form of £1000 cash
  (C) Sold stock for £1000 cash
  (D) Received £1000 cash owed by a customer

(b) Refer to Figure 2.8.
  (A) Invested profit in stock worth £1000
  (B) Took out a long-term loan for £1000 to buy stock
  (C) Bought stock to the value of £1000 for cash
  (D) Bought stock to the value of £1000 for credit

(c) Refer to Figure 2.9.
  (A) Sells stock valued at £1000 and gets paid £500 by a debtor
  (B) Invests an additional £500 in the business and buys stock to the same value
  (C) Sold stock which had originally cost £1000 for £1500, making £500 profit which is reinvested in the business
  (D) None of the above

FIGURE 2.8

MANUFACTURING BUSINESS:
BALANCE SHEET AS AT 8 JUNE 199X

Fixed Assets	£
Plant and Machinery	6 000
Vehicles	3 000
+	
Current Assets	
Stock	2 000
Debtors	2 000
Bank and Cash	1 300
–	
Creditors: due within one year	
Trade Creditors	2 500
Creditors: due after one year	1 000
	10 800
=	
Capital	10 800

FIGURE 2.9

MANUFACTURING BUSINESS:
BALANCE SHEET AS AT 9 JUNE 199X

Fixed Assets	£
Plant and Machinery	6 000
Vehicles	3 000
+	
Current Assets	
Stock	1 000
Debtors	2 000
Bank and Cash	2 800
–	
Creditors: due within one year	
Trade Creditors	2 500
Creditors: due after one year	1 000
	11 300
=	
Capital	10 800
Retained Profit	500
	11 300

2.8 Summary

This chapter introduced you to the balance sheet, a financial statement showing the financial position of the business at one point in time. The balance sheet lists what the business owns, the assets, and what the business owes, the liabilities. The balance sheet equation states that the value of the investment the owners have made in the business, in other words, the capital, must always be equal to the net worth of the assets, once all the liabilities have been met. The impact of business transactions on the balance sheet was shown and the principle of duality demonstrated.

3

The Cash Flow Statement and the Profit and Loss Account

3.1 Learning objectives

When you have finished working through this chapter you should be able to

- Identify a number of important objectives in a modern business organisation
- Discuss the relationship between financial and marketing objectives
- Broadly define the concept of **PROFIT**
- Appreciate the difference between profit and **CASH FLOW**
- Explain the **MATCHING CONCEPT**
- Define, contrast and illustrate with examples the terms **SALES REVENUE** and **RECEIPT**
- Define, contrast and illustrate with examples the terms **EXPENSE** and **PAYMENT**
- Explain and calculate **GROSS PROFIT**
- Explain and calculate **TRADING PROFIT** and **RETAINED PROFIT**
- Using the standardised layout provided, draw up a **CASH FLOW STATEMENT** in the context of a simple example
- Using the standardised layout provided, draw up a **PROFIT AND LOSS ACCOUNT** in the context of a simple example

3.2 The cash flow statement

The balance sheet tells you only the financial position of the business at one point in time. It does not tell you how the business got there or how well it is likely to do in the future. What is required is a communication tool which shows the *changes* in the financial position of the business *over time*. Many people find looking at the cash position of the business a useful starting point.

Example

Jean Bean wants to take out a loan to expand her exporting business. She started her business on 1 March 199X with redundancy money to the value of £1000. The balance sheet for the business at that point in time looked as represented in Figure 3.1.

During March her workshop was operating at full capacity, making pewter brooches and earrings to the value of £1600 for a wholesale order from the Netherlands. During this time she had to make cash payments for raw materials £500 (all used up for this order), labour £100, packaging and postage £100 and

FIGURE 3.1

JEAN BEAN'S BUSINESS: BALANCE SHEET AS AT 1 MARCH 199X	
	£
Current Assets	
Cash and Bank	1000
Capital	1000

workshop rent £200 for the months March and April, which altogether came to £900. The order has now been completed and posted. Unfortunately Jean had to give two months' credit, so her customer will be paying her only in May.

At the end of March, she has a meeting with her accountant who has drawn up a provisional balance sheet in preparation for her meeting with the bank. The balance sheet for Jean Bean's business as at 31 March 199X is shown in Figure 3.2.

FIGURE 3.2

JEAN BEAN'S BUSINESS: BALANCE SHEET AS AT 31 MARCH 199X	
	£
Current Assets	
Debtors	1600
Prepayment Rent	100
Cash	100
	1800
Capital	1000
Retained Profit	800
	1800

Clearly Jean needs more cash to be able to take on additional orders. She realises that the balance sheet on its own does not provide sufficient information for the bank and she is concerned that the bank manager will be put off by the poor cash position. So, first of all let us consider the cash flow position of Jean Bean's business.

> *CASH FLOW* is to do with the actual physical exchange of cash (or cash equivalents, such as cheques or Switch).
>
> A business's cash flows are shown in the *CASH FLOW STATEMENT*.

Figure 3.3 shows what a cash flow statement looks like in the case of Jean's business.

FIGURE 3.3

JEAN BEAN'S BUSINESS: CASH FLOW STATEMENT 1 MARCH TO 31 MARCH 199X		
		£
	Opening Balance	1000
+	Receipts	0
−	Payments	900
=	Closing Balance	100

As the cash flow statement is about changes in the *cash position* of the business over a period of time, it is important to put the *start* and *end dates* for this period on top of the statement. The *OPENING BALANCE* is the amount of cash held by the business on the start date. The cash flow statement is only concerned with actual cash, not with anything else of value the business may own or do. So when you are trying to decide whether a transaction has an impact on the cash flow statement, simply ask:

> 'Does a physical amount of money change hands?'

Only include the transaction if the answer is 'Yes'. In business, cash can only go in two directions, it can either come into the business or it can go out. If it flows in, then it is called a *RECEIPT*, if it goes out it is known as a *PAYMENT*. In the case of Jean's business, there have been a number of payments, but as yet no receipts. The *CLOSING BALANCE* is the amount of cash held by the business at the end date. This is calculated by applying the following formula:

	Cash flow calculations
	Opening Balance
+	Receipts
−	Payments
=	Closing Balance

Now check your understanding so far by drawing up a cash flow statement for the business described in Exercise 3.1.

Exercise 3.1

Jonathan runs a business selling sweets from a warehouse. He supplies market traders who run market stalls on the weekend outdoor markets and shows in the Derbyshire mining villages. His business starts on 1 May 199X with a cash balance of £50. During the month his trade suppliers deliver sweets to the value of £600 to his warehouse. However, he is given six weeks' credit. He also picks up further sweets from a new supplier for £500 cash. He pays rent on his warehouse for the month, £300 cash. During the month he sells sweets to customers for £1100 cash and £1500 on four weeks' credit (altogether these had initially cost him £1100). In addition he pays £360 for casual part-time staff and his own director's salary of £500 for the month.

Using the layout provided in Figure 3.4, draw up a cash flow statement for the business and comment on the business's cash position.

FIGURE 3.4

JONATHAN'S SWEETS:
CASH FLOW STATEMENT 1 MAY TO 31 MAY 199X

		£
	Opening Balance	
+		
	Receipts	
	Cash Sales	
−		
	Payments	
	New Supplier	
	Rent Warehouse	
	Wages – Staff	
	Salary – Director	
=	Closing Balance	

3.3 Business objectives

For both the businesses of Jean Bean and Jonathan, the sweets wholesaler, it could be argued that the cash flow statement does not tell the full story. Both companies seem to suffer from a temporary cash flow problem, but both are working on profitable orders – the problem lies in the *timing of cash flows.*

It follows then that there is an important difference between profit and cash flow.

When you are drawing up a cash flow statement you are simply keeping accurate records of one of the resources of the business, its cash holding. However, when you are working out *PROFIT*, you are assessing the company's income for a specific time period which has been generated as a result of the business transactions of that period.

Every successful business organisation has to pursue a range of objectives, maintaining a balance between the interests of the different stakeholder groups. Not all the objectives are financial in nature. However, as they all affect the business's standing and reputation in the City and wider community, they have at the very least an indirect bearing on the short- and long-term success of the business. As explained in Chapter 2, the idea of stewardship implies that the managers of the business have the task of balancing these objectives in the best interest of the owners to whom they are ultimately accountable on the financial side. It is therefore important to define the *goals* of the firm very clearly, to establish what finance is needed to achieve them and to have standardised ways of communicating the returns to the owners.

When we looked at the impact of business transactions on the balance sheet in the example given in Section 2.7, you noticed that the overall capital invested in the business increased by £30, the retained profit. Profit is often seen as one of the key objectives of business and is included in the mission statement of many large companies. Goods are bought and sold to make a profit, resulting in the growth of the business.

Exercise 3.2

The United States based ice cream company Ben & Jerry has built its success on projecting an image as a caring company of the 1990s. It aims to create an association between its product lines and new age philosophy and the green movement by using names such as 'Rainforest Crunch'. In a TV appearance the owners stated the three-part mission of their business as being to make the highest quality product, to make a profit and to work to improve the quality of life in the community.

For each of the stakeholder groups listed below, explain how they are potentially benefited if the Ben & Jerry ice cream business has sufficient cash and operates at a profit:

(a) Customers
(b) Staff
(c) The wider community

It follows that profit is an important objective of the business. It relates to and imposes constraints on the other objectives. However, bear in mind that a business can only succeed in being profitable if it has first succeeded in formulating a successful marketing strategy which meets the needs and desires of consumers. Ben & Jerry did this by successfully countering the 1980s' sensual Yuppie image of their nearest competitor Haägen-Dazs.

3.4 The profit and loss account

On successive balance sheets, profit is only shown in an indirect way. Also you find out only how much profit has been kept in the business – the owners may have taken some out. Furthermore, the cash flow statement can be very misleading as a source of information on profitability. Many cash transactions do not have a bearing on profit at all. For example, when Jean in Section 3.2 spends £500 on raw materials, this simply means that the resources of the business change form as a result of the transaction. Instead of £500 cash the business now owns £500 worth of stock. No value is gained or lost.

Clearly, for communication purposes, a further statement is required which shows the business's profit *over a time period*. Such a statement is the *PROFIT AND LOSS ACCOUNT*.

Profit is the result of trading activity. To calculate profit, you are matching up the *SALES REVENUE* (this is how much the customers have paid for the goods) with the *COST OF GOODS SOLD* (this is how much it cost to make or buy these same goods) and the *EXPENSES* (this is how much it cost to undertake the business operations necessary to bring about the sale of those goods in the first place, including rent, wages and other similar cost items).

The calculation of profit is based on the *MATCHING PRINCIPLE*. This principle can be split into two parts. First, each transaction is recognised as soon as the *legal obligation to pay* arises (regardless of whether or not a physical amount of money has changed hands). Secondly, only that amount is charged to the profit and loss account which can actually be related to the *trading activities of the period*.

Example

The profit and loss account for Jean Bean's business as introduced in the example used in Section 3.2 is shown in Figure 3.5.

As with the cash flow statement it is important to put the *start* and *end date* of the period on top of the statement. The profit and loss account can be divided into three parts.

The top part deals with the calculation of *gross profit*. This section is about the core of business activity, the buying and selling of products. Note the application of the matching concept. The full value of sales is

FIGURE 3.5

JEAN BEAN'S BUSINESS: PROFIT AND LOSS ACCOUNT 1 MARCH TO 31 MARCH 199X

		£
	Sales	1600
–	Cost of Goods Sold	500
=	Gross Profit	1100
–	Expenses:	
	Wages	100
	Packaging and Postage	100
	Rent	100
=	Trading Profit	800

included, even though no cash has been received yet. This is because the goods have changed hands and a contract exists with the Dutch firm which places it under a legal obligation to pay at a future date.

GROSS PROFIT is calculated by applying the following formula:

	Gross profit calculations
	Sales
–	Cost of Goods Sold
=	Gross Profit

The middle section of the profit and loss account deals with all the overhead costs incurred in the course of generating the sales of the period. The formula for calculating trading profit is:

	Trading profit calculations
	Gross Profit
–	Expenses
=	Trading Profit

Note again that the matching principle is applied. As the full amount paid in cash for the rent related to two months, only half of it, or £100, can be placed in this profit and loss account, because this is the amount that *belongs to the month of March*. The remainder will go into the profit and loss account of the next month. (In the meantime, the prepayment is listed as a current asset in the balance sheet.)

Last not least, in real life a third section must be added which deals with the distribution of the company's earnings. Corporation tax must be paid and the shareholders are likely to expect the payment of a dividend if the company has had a profitable period. However, for the purposes of these examples we will ignore the distribution of income for now.

Exercise 3.3

Using the layout provided in Figure 3.6, draw up a profit and loss account for the month of May for the business of Jonathan, the sweets wholesaler in Exercise 3.1.

FIGURE 3.6

JONATHAN'S SWEETS: PROFIT AND LOSS ACCOUNT 1 MAY TO 31 MAY 199X

		£
	Sales	
–	Cost of Goods Sold	
=	Gross Profit	
–	Expenses:	
	Rent	
	Wages – Staff	
	Salary – Director	
=	Trading Profit	

Exercise 3.4

On 1 September 199X Janine Swift starts a driving school. She brings £300 cash and a nearly new Vauxhall Corsa worth £7000 into the business.

On 2 September 199X she buys a stock of copies of the Highway Code for sale to her customers, for which she pays £5 cash. She also fills up with petrol and pays £25 cash for this. She puts an advertisement in the paper which costs £15 and will run the following week.

On 3 September 199X she spends the day giving driving lessons to new customers. She sells all the copies of the Highway Code for cash, £10 in total, and her customers pay her £100 cash in total for the lessons. At the end of the day she spends another £30 on petrol which is likely to last her for the next day.

(a) At the end of the day (3 September 199X) the cash closing balance of Janine Swift's driving school is:
- **(A)** £1035
- **(B)** £80
- **(C)** £335
- **(D)** £50

(b) The net trading profit of the business for the period 1 September to 3 September 199X is:
- **(A)** £50
- **(B)** £80
- **(C)** £335
- **(D)** No profit has been made

3.5 Summary

Against the background of the numerous objectives of business organisations, the need for two further financial statements – the cash flow statement and the profit and loss account – as record-keeping and communication devices was discussed. Both reflect the changing financial position of the business over a time period. However, they serve different and complementary functions. The cash flow statement records the physical movements of cash as it comes into the business as cash receipts and leaves the business in the form of cash payments. The profit and loss account applies the matching principle to bring together the sales revenues and expenses belonging to a particular financial period in order to calculate profit. Standardised layouts for both the cash flow statement and the profit and loss account were introduced and applied in the context of a simple exercise.

4

The Matching Concept: Stock Valuation and Depreciation

4.1 Learning objectives

When you have finished working through this chapter you should be able to

- Understand the **MATCHING CONCEPT** and its meaning in the context of the computation of profit
- Appreciate the need for stock valuation and link it to the matching concept
- In the context of an example, calculate **COST OF GOODS SOLD** and **GROSS PROFIT**
- Contrast and compare a range of different possible stock valuation methods
- Define and apply in the context of an example, the stock valuation methods **FIRST IN FIRST OUT (FIFO)**, **LAST IN FIRST OUT (LIFO)** and **WEIGHTED AVERAGE COST (WAC)**
- Appreciate the need for **DEPRECIATION** and link it to the matching concept
- Contrast and compare a number of different depreciation methods
- Define and apply in the context of an example, the **STRAIGHT LINE** and **REDUCING BALANCE** depreciation methods
- Discuss the advantages and disadvantages of different stock valuation and depreciation methods under conditions of changing prices

4.2 The matching concept

So far, we have made the assumption that in our profit calculations we can always easily match up the goods sold with their purchase costs and the corresponding expenses of the period. However, this may not always be the case. At some times during the year, a business may build up stock far beyond what is currently being sold. Also we have already come across the case of expenses which have to be spread over more than one financial period to match them up with the corresponding sales revenue. A special case of this kind arises where the business invests in fixed assets which will be of use for a number of years. Clearly you cannot charge the whole amount to the financial period when the asset is purchased, that would go against the matching concept. This chapter addresses some of the issues arising from these points and shows you how to deal with matching up the cost of stock and that of fixed assets to the appropriate time periods, so a realistic profit figure can be calculated.

4.3 Stock valuation

Where there is a strong seasonal effect, such as Christmas trade, stocks at the beginning of November may be much lower than at the end of November. In order to apply the matching concept properly, it is therefore necessary to adjust the calculation of *COST OF GOODS SOLD*, taking both purchases and stock levels at the beginning and end of the period into account.

Example

At the beginning of May a sports shop valued its stock of swimwear at £3500. During May, swimwear was purchased at a cost of £10 500. During the month, sales of swimwear came to £20 340 (at selling prices). At the end of May, the remaining stock of swimwear was valued at £5600.

To calculate cost of goods sold, you need to apply the following formula:

	Stock calculations
	Opening Stock (at valuation)
+	Purchases (at cost)
–	Closing Stock (at valuation)
=	Cost of Goods Sold

In this case the application of the formula results in the workings set out in Figure 4.1.

We can now work out gross profit in the same way as we did in Chapter 3. This is demonstrated in Figure 4.2.

Thus the company has made a gross profit of £11 940 during the month of May. This part of the profit and loss account which deals with the calculation of gross profit is known as the *TRADING ACCOUNT*.

FIGURE 4.1

SPORTS SHOP: STOCK CALCULATIONS

		£
	Opening Stock (at valuation)	3 500
+	Purchases (at cost)	10 500
–	Closing Stock (at valuation)	5 600
=	Cost of Goods Sold	8 400

FIGURE 4.2

SPORTS SHOP: GROSS PROFIT CALCULATIONS

		£
	Sales (at selling price)	20 340
–	Cost of Goods Sold (as above)	8 400
=	Gross Profit	11 940

Exercise 4.1

At the beginning of the month of July the 'White Lion' public house holds a stock of beer valued at £1100. During July more beer is purchased from the brewery at a cost of £5640. Sales of beer (at selling prices) come to £7520. At the end of July a stock of beer remains which is valued at £576.

Calculate the cost of goods sold and the gross profit for the 'White Lion' for the month of July.

In the above examples the accurate calculation of the cost of goods sold relied on an accurate valuation of stock both at the beginning and end of the period. This raises the question how best to go about *valuing stock*. Since one of the principles of accountancy is that of prudence, it is the norm to use whichever is lowest of the following two: either *cost* (that is, how much it cost to purchase the item from the supplier) or *net realisable value* (that is, how much the business would be able to get for it if it were to be sold now). This means that most items would be valued at cost. Net realisable value would be applied in unusual cases, for example where items have to be marked down because they are damaged or have become unfashionable.

However, this does not provide a perfect solution. The business may hold a very large quantity of the same kind of goods in stock and these may not all have been purchased at the same time and at the same price. It may therefore be very difficult, if not impossible, to attach a cost to each item. In times of changing prices the company is faced with a challenging task. The aim is that the profit and loss account should bring together current costs and revenues to show a realistic profit. Also the stock entry in the balance sheet should reflect a valuation which is based on current cost prices. Most methods of stock valuation have to settle for a trade-off between these two aims.

Currently there are three main stock valuation methods in use worldwide, these are known as *FIRST IN FIRST OUT (FIFO), WEIGHTED AVERAGE COST (WAC)* and *LAST IN FIRST OUT (LIFO)*. Of these methods, the first two may be used in the UK context. The following sections set out the principles and calculations involved in all three methods.

First In First Out (FIFO)

Under the FIFO method of stock valuation, calculations are based on the assumption that the *first* items to come into stock are also the *first* ones to be sold again. This is illustrated in the following example.

Example

Beanstalk Ltd starts in business selling compact disks by mail order at the beginning of January 199X. During the first six months of operations the stock movements shown in Table 4.1 were recorded.

The calculation of the value of closing stock using FIFO is shown in Table 4.2.

Using the FIFO method of stock valuation, closing stock is valued at £3080.

Note that under the FIFO method of stock valuation all stock purchased is recorded at *cost price*. As stock is sold, the assumption is made that the stock which was *first* acquired by the business is the *first* to be sold. The number of items sold is therefore deducted from those items in stock purchased at the earliest cost price. This method is very popular, as it seems very logical. The calculations on paper correspond to the physical rotation of stock in the warehouse and on the shelves. Using this method also makes it very easy to calculate closing stock values. It is just a matter of keeping accurate records.

TABLE 4.1

BEANSTALK LTD: STOCK RECORDS

Compact disks

January	Bought	600 @ £ 7.00	(cost price)
February	Bought	200 @ £ 7.50	(cost price)
March	Sold	300 @ £14.00	(selling price)
April	Bought	400 @ £ 7.70	(cost price)
May	Sold	300 @ £14.50	(selling price)
June	Sold	200 @ £14.80	(selling price)

TABLE 4.2

BEANSTALK LTD: FIFO STOCK CALCULATIONS

Month	Purchases (at cost)	Stock issued for sale (at valuation)	Stock after transaction (at valuation)
January	600 @ £7.00		600 @ £7.00
February	200 @ £7.50		600 @ £7.00
			200 @ £7.50
March		300 @ £7.00	300 @ £7.00
			200 @ £7.50
April	400 @ £7.70		300 @ £7.00
			200 @ £7.50
			400 @ £7.70
May		300 @ £7.00	200 @ £7.50
			400 @ £7.70
June		200 @ £7.50	400 @ £7.70

Closing Stock = 400 * £7.70 = £3080

Weighted Average Cost (WAC)

In contrast, the WAC method of stock valuation is based on a calculation of the *average cost* of all goods in stock. A weighting is given to the quantities purchased at the different cost prices. Table 4.3 contains a demonstration of the WAC stock calculations in the context of the example given above.

Using the WAC method of stock valuation, closing stock is valued at £2952.

Note that in calculating the average stock values you cannot just work out a simple average for the whole period. The average is *weighted* according to how many items were purchased at the respective prices. That means that if a large consignment of stock comes in at a new price, then this has greater impact on stock valuation than a smaller batch would. WAC is popular for businesses dealing with large quantities of relatively small, indistinguishable items, where each

TABLE 4.3

BEANSTALK LTD: WAC STOCK CALCULATIONS			
Month	**Purchases (at cost)**	**Stock issued for sale (at valuation)**	**Stock after transaction (at valuation)**
January	600 @ £7.00		600 @ £7.00
February	200 @ £7.50		800 @ $\frac{600 * 7.00 + 200 * 7.50}{800}$
			or 800 @ £7.13
March		300 @ £7.13	500 @ £7.13
April	400 @ £7.70		900 @ $\frac{500 * 7.13 + 400 * 7.70}{900}$
			or 900 @ £7.38
May		300 @ £7.38	600 @ £7.38
June		200 @ £7.38	400 @ £7.38
Closing Stock = 400 * £7.38 = £2952			

item has a low value in its own right and cannot easily be identified with a particular cost price anyway, for example, tins of soup or bags of nails.

Last In First Out (LIFO)

For purposes of applying the LIFO method, the assumption underlying the calculations is that the *last* item to come into stock is the *first* one to be sold. Naturally this does not mean that no physical stock rotation takes place, the assumption of last in first out is made on paper only. The advantage of doing this is that the *most current cost prices* are applied to the profit calculation. The use of LIFO in the context of the example used previously is shown in Table 4.4.

Using the LIFO method of stock valuation, closing stock is valued at £2800.

LIFO basically follows the same principle as FIFO, only in reverse. This time the assumption is made that the *first* items to be sold are the *last* to come into the business. Thus stock sold is always valued at the latest cost prices, leaving the earlier prices to be applied to closing stock valuation. This method is not used in the UK; however, you may come across it when looking at US business accounts.

TABLE 4.4

BEANSTALK LTD: LIFO STOCK CALCULATIONS			
Month	**Purchases (at cost)**	**Stock issued for sale (at valuation)**	**Stock after transaction (at valuation)**
January	600 @ £7.00		600 @ £7.00
February	200 @ £7.50		600 @ £7.00 200 @ £7.50
March		200 @ £7.50 100 @ £7.00	500 @ £7.00
April	400 @ £7.70		500 @ £7.00 400 @ £7.70
May		300 @ £7.70	500 @ £7.00 100 @ £7.70
June		100 @ £7.70 100 @ £7.00	400 @ £7.00
Closing Stock = 400 * £7.00 = £2800			

4.4 Profit calculation: the impact of stock valuation

A knowledge of the different methods of stock valuation and their respective impact on the calculation of gross and net profit is very useful when you wish to compare the accounts of companies, within the UK or across different countries, as it will allow you to adjust your calculations for the differences in accounting practice.

Figure 4.3 sets out the calculation of gross profit for the example used so far, showing the differences resulting from the choice in valuation method.

FIGURE 4.3

BEANSTALK LTD: TRADING ACCOUNT
1 JANUARY TO 30 JUNE 199X

		FIFO	WAC	LIFO
		£	£	£
	Sales	11 510	11 510	11 510
	Opening Stock	0	0	0
+	Purchases	8 780	8 780	8 780
–	Closing Stock	3 080	2 952	2 800
=	Cost of Goods Sold	5 700	5 828	5 980
	Gross Profit	5 810	5 682	5 530

The example illustrates that in times of changing prices the three methods can give you really quite different values for closing stock, cost of goods sold and therefore gross profit. This in turn filters through to the net profit calculation and therefore has an impact on the tax liability of the business. Although this evens out in the long run, in the short run it can make a difference.

From an accountant's point of view, the ideal method of stock valuation is that which meets the criterion of the matching principle best. It should attach a realistic current value to the stock figure in the balance sheet. It should also match current costs and current sales revenues in the profit and loss account in order to state a realistic profit figure. As you can see from the above, in times of changing prices there is normally a trade-off between the two. Under conditions of rising prices (that is, inflation), the application of FIFO results in a higher gross profit figure than LIFO, as it relies more strongly on earlier, and therefore lower, prices. In the profit and loss account, the match is therefore less than ideal – historic costs are matched with current sales revenues. However, in balance sheet terms FIFO is highly accurate, the very latest prices are applied to closing stock valuation. Under conditions of falling prices (that is, deflation) the opposite is true. The use of WAC always results in figures in between those derived from the use of FIFO and LIFO.

Exercise 4.2

After their initial success in the compact disk mail order business, Beanstalk Ltd set up a subsidiary, Vineleaves Ltd, which sells videos through the established mail order channels. Table 4.5 shows a record of the stock transactions of this subsidiary for the period July to October 199X.

TABLE 4.5

VINELEAVES LTD: STOCK RECORDS

Videos			
July	Bought	900 @ £6.00	(cost price)
August	Sold	700 @ £17.00	(selling price)
September	Bought	500 @ £8.00	(cost price)
October	Sold	400 @ £16.00	(selling price)

(a) Making the assumption that there is no opening stock, calculate the closing stock at the end of October, using FIFO, LIFO and WAC in turn

(b) Calculate the respective cost of goods sold and gross profit figures for the business, applying the three methods in turn; Comment on your findings

Exercise 4.3

The stock of musical birthday cards held by CardsRUs Stationery Ltd at 1 January was 400 cards. These had cost £0.50 each. On 2 January 650 cards were purchased at a cost of £0.65 each. On 3 January, 100 cards were sold, charging a selling price of £1.75

each. In each of the following, indicate the correct statement by circling the appropriate letter.

(a) Using the FIFO method of stock valuation, the cost of goods sold is:
(A) £572.50
(B) £422.50
(C) £50.00
(D) None of the above

(b) Using the WAC method of stock valuation, closing stock will be valued at:
(A) £12 less than using FIFO
(B) £12 more than using FIFO
(C) £3 less than using FIFO
(D) £3 more than using FIFO

(c) During a period of rising prices, the method of stock valuation which will result in the highest stated gross profit figure is:
(A) WAC
(B) FIFO
(C) LIFO
(D) The choice of method does not affect gross profit

4.5 Depreciation

A similar issue as with the valuation of stock arises in the treatment of the cost of fixed assets. As you know, the matching concept implies that the profit and loss account should bring together the sales revenues of a financial period with those costs that have gone into generating those sales.

Example

During the 199X financial year a clothes manufacturer acquires a new sewing machine at a cost of £600. The average useful life of such a machine is five years. After this time it is likely that the machine can be sold for £100. This is the scrap value of the machine.

At the end of the financial year the question arises how the cost of this new fixed asset should be treated in the accounts. Clearly the asset has already been used and therefore has made some contribution to generating the sales revenue of the period. However, much of the initial value of the asset remains, as it is still expected to have a useful life of another four years. Because of the matching concept it would therefore not be right to put down the whole cost of the asset in the profit and loss account. Besides, if businesses were allowed to treat the whole cost as an immediate expense, then obviously all profits would be reinvested in new fixed assets immediately and no tax would ever be paid. So what is needed is a way of spreading the cost of the sewing machine over the life of the asset.

> DEPRECIATION is defined as the spreading of the initial cost of a fixed asset over its useful life in a logical manner which takes into account any remaining scrap value at the end.

There are two main methods of calculating depreciation, the STRAIGHT LINE method and the REDUCING BALANCE method. They will now be explained and the calculations demonstrated.

Straight line method

The straight line method is based on the assumption that the business gets *equal value* out of the asset *at all times* during the course of its life.

The calculation of the annual depreciation charge is carried out applying the following formula:

Straight line method: annual depreciation charge formula

Annual depreciation charge

$$= \frac{\text{Cost} - \text{Scrap value}}{\text{Number of years of expected useful life}}$$

If this method were to be applied in the above example then the calculation of the annual depreciation charge would be:

Sewing machine: annual depreciation charge

Annual depreciation charge

$$= \frac{£600 - £100}{5} = £100 \text{ per year}$$

This means that a charge of £100 would be listed under the heading 'expenses' in the profit and loss

TABLE 4.6

SEWING MACHINE: STRAIGHT LINE DEPRECIATION SCHEDULE

Year	Initial Cost	Depreciation Charge to Profit and Loss	Cumulative Depreciation	Year End Balance Sheet Value
	£	£	£	£
1	600	100	100	500
2	600	100	200	400
3	600	100	300	300
4	600	100	400	200
5	600	100	500	100

account for the five years of the sewing machine's life. To work out the remaining balance sheet value of the asset at the end of each year, you need to *deduct* depreciation up to that balance sheet date from the original cost of the asset, as shown in Table 4.6.

Note that the cash flow statement is unaffected by depreciation, the cash involved has changed hands when the asset is first purchased, after that no further cash is exchanged.

The straight line method is most suitable for assets the business gets value from in a steady stream, for example, patents and leases. However, it is a very popular method all round because it is so easy to understand and the calculations can be carried out very quickly and by non-experts.

Reducing balance method

For some assets it is very clear from the start that the business will get most use out of them during the *early days* of their lives. This is often the case with assets where there is new technology involved, for example, computer equipment and cars. Because of the idea of the matching concept it would not be right to apply depreciation in equal chunks in such cases. However, once again the cost of the asset (taking the scrap value into consideration) is spread over its useful life, but this time a *percentage rate* is applied which ensures that a high amount of depreciation is charged early on and then declines steadily over the course of the asset's life.

The formula for working out the percentage rate to be applied to calculate the annual depreciation charge is:

Reducing balance method: percentage rate depreciation formula

Percentage rate of depreciation

$$= (1 - \sqrt[n]{(\text{Scrap value}/\text{Cost})}) * 100$$

(with **n** = the number of years of useful life of the asset)

In the context of the example used above, the application of this method would work as follows:

Sewing machine: percentage rate

Percentage rate of depreciation

$$= (1 - \sqrt[5]{(£100/£600)}) * 100$$

Percentage rate of depreciation = 30.1%

Having worked out the percentage to be applied, the depreciation charge for the profit and loss account for each of the five years can now be calculated. In the first year the percentage is applied to the original cost of the asset to give you the depreciation charge for that year. To work out the depreciation charge for the second year you first *deduct* the charge for the

TABLE 4.7

SEWING MACHINE: REDUCING BALANCE DEPRECIATION SCHEDULE

Year	Initial Cost	Depreciation Charge to Profit and Loss	Cumulative Depreciation	Year End Balance Sheet Value
	£	£	£	£
1	600	180.60	180.60	419.40
2	600	126.24	306.84	293.16
3	600	88.24	395.08	204.92
4	600	61.68	456.76	143.24
5	600	43.12	499.88	100.12

first year from the original cost. This gives you the remaining balance sheet value of the asset at the end of the first year. You then apply the above percentage again to what is left, to give you the second year's depreciation charge. Follow the same steps for subsequent years as shown in Table 4.7.

You will have noticed that the end book value differs very slightly from that given by the straight line method. This is due to rounding error and is no cause for concern.

Exercise 4.4

A small brewery has recently invested in a basic EPOS (Electronic Point Of Sale) system to control stock management and sales budgets in its twenty public houses. The equipment was acquired at an initial cost of £14 000. It is expected that the equipment will match the needs of the organisation for at least six years, after that major replacements are likely. However, as there is a second hand market for small-scale EPOS systems, the equipment will probably have a scrap value of £2000. Using the layout provided in Table 4.8, take the straight line and reducing balance method of calculating depreciation in turn. For each method, calculate the depreciation charge to the profit and loss account for each of the six years, as well as the balance sheet value of the equipment at the end of each year. Contrast and compare your results for the two methods. Make a reasoned recommendation as to which one would be most appropriate to use in this case.

TABLE 4.8

BREWERY: COMPARISON OF THE TWO DEPRECIATION METHODS

	Straight line		Reducing balance	
	Depreciation Charge to Profit and Loss	Balance Sheet Entry	Depreciation Charge to Profit and Loss	Balance Sheet Entry
Initial Cost				
Year 1				
Year 2				
Year 3				
Year 4				
Year 5				
Year 6				

4.6 Impact of depreciation method on net profit

It follows from the above that the choice of depreciation method has an impact on the stated *net profit* of the business for the financial period. Clearly, where the reducing balance method is chosen, the higher charge applied to the early periods means that the total charge for expenses is higher and therefore net profit and resulting tax liability are lower. Whilst this evens out over the life of the asset, it may be a consideration when making the choice.

Exercise 4.5

On 1 January 199X, Tania Stopher starts her business with £20 000 capital. She makes arrangements to rent a 800 sq ft T-shirt store in a good shopping centre location for £15 000 a year. She intends to stock a large range of T-shirts in different colours and sizes plus hundreds of designs for heat-embossing onto the shirts. To get started she acquires a heat-embossing machine at a cost of £3000. It is expected that the machine will have a useful life of five years and a scrap value of £500 at the end of it.

Complete the following statement correctly by circling the appropriate letter:

If the depreciation charge for the heat-embossing machine was worked out using the reducing balance method, at a rate of 30.1 per cent, the charge to expenses in the profit and loss account for the year ending 31 December 199X would be:

(A) £403 lower than using the straight line method
(B) The same as using the straight line method
(C) £403 higher than using the straight line method
(D) It cannot be worked out as it depends on the inflation rate

Exercise 4.6

During the 199X financial year, Tania's business also undertakes the transactions summarised in Table 4.9.

TABLE 4.9

TANIA'S BUSINESS: STOCK TRANSACTIONS

January	1500 T-shirts bought	cost price	£3.50 each
February	4000 T-shirts bought	cost price	£4.00 each
April	3000 T-shirts sold	selling price	£7.50 each
July	3500 T-shirts bought	cost price	£4.10 each
November	4000 T-shirts sold	selling price	£7.50 each

All purchases and sales are for cash
Wages are paid in cash to the shop assistant for work done during the year, £9000
Rent is paid for the year, £15 000 cash

Using the FIFO method of stock valuation and the straight-line method of charging depreciation, draw up the cash flow statement and profit and loss account for Tania's business for the year, as well as the balance sheet as at the end of the year. You may use the layouts provided in Figures 4.4, 4.5 and 4.6, respectively.

FIGURE 4.4

TANIA'S BUSINESS: CASH FLOW STATEMENT
1 JANUARY TO 31 DECEMBER 199X

		£
	Opening Balance	
+	Receipts:	
	Sales	
–	Payments:	
	Heat-embossing Machine	
	Purchases of Stock	
	Wages	
	Rent	
=	Closing Balance	

FIGURE 4.5

TANIA'S BUSINESS:
PROFIT AND LOSS ACCOUNT FOR THE YEAR
1 JANUARY TO 31 DECEMBER 199X

		£
	Sales	
–	Cost of Goods Sold	
=	Gross Profit	
–	Expenses:	
	Depreciation	
	Wages	
	Rent	
=	Net Trading Profit	

FIGURE 4.6

TANIA'S BUSINESS:
BALANCE SHEET AS AT 31 DECEMBER 199X

	Cost	Depreciation	Net Book Value
	£	£	£
Fixed Assets:			
Heat-embossing Machine			
Current Assets:			
Stock			
Cash			
Net Total Assets			
Capital			
Retained Profit			

4.7 Summary

This chapter has built on your understanding of the matching concept and shown you how it is applied to the valuation of stocks of goods for resale and the treatment of the cost of fixed assets.

Three different methods of stock valuation (FIFO, LIFO and WAC) and two methods of calculating depreciation (straight line and reducing balance) were introduced and their impact on the calculation of gross and net profit, respectively, compared.

This discussion served to illustrate that the idea of profit is *relative* and based on a number of assumptions guided by the matching concept.

5 Reconciliation of Financial Statements

5.1 Learning objectives

When you have finished working through this chapter you should be able to carry out the following tasks in the context of a simple integrated example providing summary information on all the business transactions of an accounting period

- Apply the matching concept in order to calculate profit, making use of a given stock valuation and depreciation method
- Draw up a profit and loss account
- Draw up a cash flow statement
- Calculate debtor and creditor balances as at the end of the accounting period
- Draw up a balance sheet as at the end of the accounting period by bringing together the end balances of the depreciation and stock calculations, the cash flow statement, the debtors' and creditors' workings and the retained profit from the profit and loss account
- Demonstrate your competence in the area of financial accounts by combining all the above skills in drawing up a set of financial statements in the context of a case study which is presented at the end of Part I

5.2 Recording the movements of working capital

Businesses are under a legal obligation to produce a set of financial statements at regular intervals in order to provide information to their shareholders and to the Inland Revenue. The annual reports of large public limited companies include a balance sheet and a profit and loss account for the financial year. This is simply a summary of all the records kept in the accounting system during the year. This section shows you the principles involved in drawing up such statements on the basis of a record of the transactions undertaken during the financial period.

Example

A digital watch wholesaler's balance sheet at the beginning of a financial year is shown in Figure 5.1.

The transactions undertaken during the 199X financial year are listed:

Opening stock from the balance sheet came to 5000 watches valued at £1 each

Cash receipts from debtors came to £55 000

Cash payments to trade creditors were £17 000

FIGURE 5.1

WATCH WHOLESALER: BALANCE SHEET AS AT 1 JANUARY 199X

	Cost	Depreciation to Date	Net Book Value
	£	£	£
Fixed Assets			
Car	14 000	4 000	10 000
Fixtures and Fittings	21 000	12 000	9 000
			19 000
Current Assets			
Stock	5 000		
Debtors	4 600		
Cash and Bank	0		
		9 600	
Creditors: due within one year			
Trade Creditors	8 600		
Bank Overdraft	500		
		9 100	
Net Current Assets			500
Total Assets *less* Current Liabilities			19 500
Capital			
Share Capital			15 000
Retained Profit			4 500
			19 500

Depreciation was charged using the straight line method, assuming an asset life of seven years and no scrap value at the end

Staff wages were paid in cash for all the work carried out during the year and came to £40 000

Rent of £25 000 was paid in cash

Stock transactions over the period are shown in Table 5.1.

TABLE 5.1

WATCH WHOLESALER: STOCK TRANSACTIONS

February	6000 watches bought for cash, cost price £1.20 each
May	9000 watches sold for cash, selling price £6.50 each
August	10 000 watches bought on credit, cost price £1.10 each
November	11 000 watches sold on credit terms, selling price £6.50 each
December	3000 watches bought on credit, cost price £1.30 each

First of all, let us review what you have already practised in Chapters 3 and 4. Using the above information you can calculate the value of closing stock (on this occasion applying the WAC method, due to the relatively small value of individual items), you can work out the depreciation charge for the financial year (based on the straight line method) and you can then draw up a profit and loss account and a cash flow statement for the period. If you would like the practice, you may wish to attempt doing this by yourself before reading on to check your calculations.

The end result should look similar to the workings shown in Figures 5.2 and 5.3 and Table 5.2.

This then feeds into the profit and loss account as shown in Figure 5.4.

Whereas the profit and loss account made use of the matching concept to calculate profit, the cash flow statement is simply concerned with keeping accurate records of all cash transactions. This is shown in Figure 5.5.

Note that in drawing up the cash flow statement you make use of the initial balance sheet to get the opening balance, this is how much cash the business has at the beginning of the accounting period. The

FIGURE 5.2

WATCH WHOLESALER: DEPRECIATION CALCULATION

Car

$$\text{Annual depreciation charge} = \frac{£14\,000}{7} = £2000$$

Fixtures and Fittings

$$\text{Annual depreciation charge} = \frac{£21\,000}{7} = £3000$$

TABLE 5.2

WATCH WHOLESALER:
STOCK CALCULATION FOR THE PERIOD – WAC

Month	Purchases (at cost)	Stock issued for sale (at valuation)	Stock after transaction (at valuation)
January			Opening Stock 5000 @ £1
February	6000 @ £1.20		$\frac{5000*1+6000*1.20}{11\,000}$ i.e. 11 000 @ £1.11
May		9000 @ £1.11	2000 @ £1.11
August	10 000 @ £1.10		$\frac{2000*1.11+10\,000*1.1}{12\,000}$ i.e. 12 000 @ £1.10
November		11 000 @ £1.10	1000 @ £1.10
December	3000 @ £1.30		$\frac{1000*1.1+3000*1.3}{4000}$ i.e. 4000 @ £1.25

Closing stock is valued at 4000 * £1.25 = £5000

FIGURE 5.3

WATCH WHOLESALER:
CALCULATING THE COSTS OF GOODS SOLD

	Opening Stock (from start balance sheet) £ 5000
+	Purchases (at cost) £22 100
–	Closing Stock (at valuation) (to end balance sheet) £ 5000
=	Cost of Goods Sold (to profit and loss account) £22 100

FIGURE 5.4

WATCH WHOLESALER:
PROFIT AND LOSS ACCOUNT FOR THE PERIOD

	£
Sales	130 000
Cost of Goods Sold	22 100
Gross Profit	107 900
Expenses	
Wages	40 000
Rent	25 000
Depreciation Car	2 000
Depreciation Fixtures and Fittings	3 000
Trading Profit	37 900

FIGURE 5.5

WATCH WHOLESALER:
CASH FLOW STATEMENT FOR THE PERIOD

	Opening Balance (from start balance sheet)	
	Bank Overdraft	(£500)
+	Receipts	
	Cash Sales	£58 500
	Debtors	£55 000
–	Payments	
	Cash Purchases	£ 7200
	Creditors	£17 000
	Wages	£40 000
	Rent	£25 000
=	Closing Balance (to end balance sheet)	
		£23 800

closing balance is the figure which goes into the balance sheet at the end of the period. If the balance is positive, it is listed under Current assets: cash and bank. If it is negative, then this implies that the business bank account is overdrawn and the balance is listed under Current liabilities: overdraft.

The calculations required to work out the debtors' and creditors' balances at the end of the accounting period are very similar to the cash flow statement. Again, we are simply concerned with summarising the records of a particular type of transaction. You can therefore use the same kind of layout, as shown in Figure 5.6.

FIGURE 5.6

WATCH WHOLESALER:
CALCULATING THE DEBTORS' BALANCE

	Opening Balance Debtors (from start balance sheet) £ 4600
+	Credit Sales (at selling prices) £71 500
–	Receipts from Debtors £55 000
=	Closing Balance Debtors (to end balance sheet) £21 100

The debtors' calculation is only concerned with those transactions where either credit was given to customers or where customers who had bought goods on credit settle their debts. The opening balance comes from the first balance sheet, the calculated closing balance feeds into the balance sheet at the end of the financial period.

> The closing balance of the debtors' calculation shows the exact amount owed to the business by its customers at the new balance sheet date.

The calculation of the creditors' figure for the new balance sheet follows a similar logic, and is shown in Figure 5.7.

Here the concern is with all those transaction where either goods are purchased on credit terms or suppliers who had granted credit are paid amounts of money outstanding for goods previously received.

> The closing balance of the creditors' calculation shows the exact amount the business owes to its trade suppliers at the new balance sheet date.

Having calculated the profit for the financial period, as well as all the new balances in the working capital section of the balance sheet, you are now in a position to draw up the new balance sheet as at the end of the financial year. You do this by simply inserting all the

FIGURE 5.7

WATCH WHOLESALER:
CALCULATING THE CREDITORS' BALANCE

	Opening Balance Creditors (from start balance sheet) £ 8600
+	Credit Purchases (at cost prices) £14 900
–	Payments to Creditors £17 000
=	Closing Balance Creditors (to end balance sheet) £ 6500

new closing balances you have calculated. If you have carried out all the above calculations correctly, you will find that this final task is really quite easy. It is like a jigsaw puzzle, all the pieces should fit together quite nicely. When you total up the Net Total Assets on one hand and the Capital section on the other, you will find the final confirmation of your calculation as they should balance again.

In the example, the new balance sheet looks like the one presented in Figure 5.8.

FIGURE 5.8

WATCH WHOLESALER:
BALANCE SHEET AS AT 31 DECEMBER 199X

	Cost	Depreciation to Date	Net Book Value
Fixed Assets	£	£	£
Car	14 000	6 000	8 000
Fixtures and Fittings	21 000	15 000	6 000
Current Assets			14 000
Stock	5 000		
Debtors	21 100		
Cash and Bank	23 800		
		49 900	
Creditors:			
due within one year			
Trade Creditors	6 500		
Bank Overdraft	0		
		6 500	
Net Current Assets			43 400
Total Assets *less* Current Liabilities			57 400
Capital			
Share Capital			15 000
Retained Profit			42 400
			57 400

Exercise 5.1

On 1 January 199X, Joey starts his business with capital of £20 000 and acquires a van for use in his business at a cost of £2500. He pays fully in cash. It is expected to have a useful life of seven years, at the end of which it is likely that it can be sold for £400.

During the 199X accounting year, Joey's business also undertakes the following additional transactions:

- In January, goods for resale are purchased: 1000 items at a cost of £3.00 each
- In March, further stock is purchased: 3000 items at a cost of £3.30 each
- In May, goods are sold to customers: 2000 items at a selling price of £6.50 each
- In October, stock is purchased: 4000 items at 3.20 each
- In December, stock is sold to customers: 3500 items at a selling price of 12.00 each
  (All purchases and sales are for cash.)
- Wages for work done during the year are paid in cash £10 000
- Rent for the year is paid in cash £9000

(a) Indicate which of the following statements is true, by circling the appropriate letter:

If the depreciation charge for the van was worked out using the reducing balance method, at a rate of 25 per cent, the charge to expenses in the profit and loss account for the year 1 January 199X to 31 December 199X would be:

(A) £225 higher than under the straight line method
(B) £325 higher than under the straight line method
(C) £225 lower than under the straight line method
(D) The same as for the straight line method

(b) Using the FIFO method of stock valuation and the straight line method of charging depreciation, draw up the cash flow statement, the profit and loss account for the year and the balance sheet at the year end, using the layouts provided in Figures 5.9–5.11.

FIGURE 5.9

**JOEY'S BUSINESS:
CASH FLOW STATEMENT FOR THE PERIOD
1 JANUARY TO 31 DECEMBER 199X**

		£
	Opening Balance	
+	Receipts:	
	Sales	
–	Payments:	
	Van	
	Stock	
	Wages	
	Rent	
=	Closing Balance	

FIGURE 5.10

**JOEY'S BUSINESS:
PROFIT AND LOSS ACCOUNT FOR THE PERIOD
1 JANUARY TO 31 DECEMBER 199X**

		£
	Sales	
–	Cost of Goods Sold	
=	Gross Profit	
–	Expenses:	
	Depreciation	
	Van	
	Wages	
	Rent	
=	Net Trading Profit	

FIGURE 5.11

**JOEY'S BUSINESS:
BALANCE SHEET AS AT 31 DECEMBER 199X**

	Cost	Depreciation to Date	Net Book Value
	£	£	£
Fixed Assets			
Van			
Current Assets			
Stock			
Cash			
Net Total Assets			
Capital			
Retained Profit			

5.3 Summary

In this chapter you learnt how the records kept in the firm's accounting systems can be used to summarise the transactions carried out during the financial year in the form of a set of final accounts, showing a profit and loss account for the period and a new balance as at the end of the period. Starting with the balance sheet at the beginning of the year and information about the transactions carried out during the year you learned to draw up separate balances for cash, stock, debtors and creditors, which were used to put together the new balance sheet.

All the skills introduced and practised up to this point are brought together in drawing up a set of final accounts in the context of Case Study 1, which follows on from Chapter 6 and completes Part I.

6

Introduction to Spreadsheets: Calculations and Charts

6.1 Learning objectives

When you have finished working through this chapter you should be able to

- Understand what a **SPREADSHEET** is, and how it can be used for financial purposes
- Be aware that a spreadsheet **CELL** may contain **TEXT**, a **NUMBER**, or a **FORMULA**
- Set up a worksheet to perform calculations using numbers, formulae, **OPERATORS** and **FUNCTIONS**
- Understand the difference between an **ABSOLUTE** and a **RELATIVE CELL REFERENCE**
- Know how to enhance the appearance of a worksheet by changing column widths, selecting appropriate fonts and styles, formatting to an appropriate number of decimal places, inserting extra rows, columns or page breaks
- Display a worksheet showing the formulae
- Print out and save a worksheet
- Construct a spreadsheet **TEMPLATE** to use repeatedly for different versions of the same procedure
- Use a spreadsheet to draw a **BAR CHART**, a **PIE CHART**, a **LINE CHART** and an **XY CHART** and to print them out

6.2 What is a spreadsheet?

The word *SPREADSHEET* was originally used by accountants to describe their very large sheets of paper, ruled in rows and columns, on which they entered financial information and performed calculations. Every price, cost, commission and tax rate relevant to running a business would appear somewhere on these financial records. Some were used for preparing forecasts and budgets and if there were any changes in prices or costs, the whole spreadsheet needed to be altered, a process that involved lavish use of an eraser. Once it was realised that a computer could be programmed to perform such tasks much more efficiently, the name *spreadsheet* was given to any computer package that displays words and numbers in rows and columns and enables calculations to be performed. Of course, spreadsheets today have become much more sophisticated and offer, for example, chart-drawing facilities as standard.

In order to be able to work through the rest of this book fully and then be able to apply your learning in practice, you need to have access to a spreadsheet package. Although we shall use a calculator to carry out small-scale calculations, in business today all financial calculations are done on a spreadsheet so it is important that you get to know how to use one.

There are several spreadsheet packages on the market such as Excel, Lotus 1-2-3, Works and Quattro Pro. In this book, our printouts are made using Excel but as far the applications in this book are concerned, you can perform almost all the procedures on any spreadsheet. Some of the commands and functions differ slightly between packages but your spreadsheet manual or the on-screen Help facility should enable you to make any minor changes necessary to the instructions given in this chapter.

If you are using a Windows package such as Excel for the first time, you will find it helpful to work through the on-screen Windows tutorial. You gain access to this from the Windows Program Manager screen by moving the mouse arrow to **Help** on the menu bar and clicking the left mouse button once to display the drop-down menu. Move the mouse arrow down to the Windows Tutorial line and click once. Then follow the tutorial instructions to learn about using the mouse and the basics of Windows.

6.3 Input, calculations and formulae

To enter Excel, double-click on its icon in the Program Manager screen. When the Excel screen appears, you will notice that underneath the Menu Bar there is a standard toolbar containing icons for commonly used commands and beneath that a formatting toolbar. If you move the mouse arrow over each of the toolbar buttons in turn, you will discover that the name of the button appears in a yellow box and a brief description is given in a Status Bar at the foot of the screen.

In a spreadsheet package, all input is made on a *worksheet*. The layout of a new worksheet is shown in Figure 6.1. You can see that it consists of rows, numbered **1**, **2**, **3**..., and columns labelled **A**, **B**, **C**.... These form a grid of *CELLS*. Each cell has a unique *REFERENCE*. For example, cells **A3** and **D7** are shaded in Figure 6.1.

FIGURE 6.1

WORKSHEET LAYOUT

	A	B	C	D	E	F
1						
2						
3	//////////////					
4						
5						
6						
7				//////////////		
8						
9						
10						
11						
12						
13						
14						
15						
16						
17						
18						
19						
20						

Inputs can be made to a cell when that cell is *active*. To make a cell active, you highlight it by clicking on the cell with the mouse. The currently active cell reference is indicated on the display.

You can input either *TEXT* (words or a string of characters from the keyboard), a *NUMBER* or a *FORMULA* into the active cell. Type the input you want and press the **Enter (Return)** key. By convention, words are justified to the left and numbers to the right in the default setting.

Initially the worksheet columns are set to a standard width, usually 10 characters. If your cell entry is too long to fit in the space, you can widen a column by dragging with the mouse on the right hand boundary of the column label. It is only necessary to do this if you have overlapping entries in adjacent columns. If you have no other entries nearby on a given row, the spreadsheet will show the complete entry, even if it overlaps other, empty, cells.

Example

Figure 6.2 shows the entries on a worksheet used by the Fast Forward Video Company to calculate the wages due to its sales workforce. The employees get basic pay of £50 per week plus a percentage commission on the value of the videos they sell. The employees who have been with the company longer and proved their selling ability get a higher rate of commission.

You may find it useful to set up the payroll data on a worksheet of your own. Type the company name in cell **A1**, COMMISSION PAYROLL in cell **A2** and Calculations of gross pay in cell **A3**.

Widen column **A** to 15 characters so that it can accommodate long names. Then type the column heading EMPLOYEE in **A5** followed by the employee names in cells **A7–A11**. Move to **B5** and type SALES (£). Enter the given amounts in cells **B7–B11**. Do not put any commas or spaces to indicate thousands at this stage. Fill in the other column headings and cell values in a similar way.

Every employee gets the same basic wage so we want to enter the amount 50 in every cell of column **D**. First type 50 in cell **D7**. Next highlight the range of cells **D7–D11**. Do this by making cell **D7** active and then drag the mouse to **D11**. Finally, click on the **Copy** icon on the standard toolbar.

To calculate gross pay we need to work out each employee's commission and add it on to the basic pay. We accomplish this using a *FORMULA*. A formula is a sequence of numbers or cell addresses and *OPERATORS* such as + (plus), − (minus), * (times), / (divided by).

Move to cell **E7** for the first calculation. We need to work out

3 per cent of 5700 and add it to 50

FIGURE 6.2

PAYROLL DATA

	A	B	C	D	E
1	FAST FORWARD VIDEO COMPANY				
2	COMMISSION PAYROLL				
3	Calculations of gross pay				
4					
5	EMPLOYEE	SALES (£)	COMMISSION	BASIC PAY(£)	GROSS PAY (£)
6			RATE		
7	Arnold	5700	3%	50	
8	Chalmers	7500	4%		
9	Michaelson	8500	2%		
10	Pratt	8000	4%		
11	Wilson	4200	3%		

Instead of using the actual numbers, we use the cell addresses

C7∗B7+D7

The usual rules of arithmetic apply so multiplication and division take precedence over addition and subtraction. This means we do not need to put brackets round (**C7∗B7**) but we can if we wish.

To alert the spreadsheet to the fact that we are entering a formula rather than text, we first type = so the complete entry in cell **E7** is

=C7∗B7+D7

followed by **Enter**. Note that there must be no spaces between successive symbols. The result of the calculation appears in the cell but the actual formula is displayed immediately above the column headings on the worksheet.

Now we want to repeat this calculation for all the employees so we simply highlight cells **E7–E11** and use the **Copy** command as before. Your worksheet should look like Figure 6.3.

Move the cursor to cell **E8**. You will see that the formula displayed for cell **E8** is

=C8∗B8+D8

In the copying process, the spreadsheet uses *RELATIVE REFERENCES*. Our initial formula went in **E7** but we have copied to **E8** so all the sevens are automatically changed to eights by the spreadsheet. Similarly, if you move further down column **E**, you will see that for every row you move, the row number in the cell addresses in the formula also increases by one.

The company wants to know both the total sales and its total payroll bill so we need to add this information to the worksheet.

Type totals in **A12** and then move to **B12**. This time we need to use one of the *FUNCTIONS* that are built into spreadsheet packages. These functions encompass mathematical, statistical and financial operations such as finding totals, averages and rates. The function we require here is SUM so in **B12** we type

=SUM(**B7**:**B11**)

and the total is calculated. Note that we again typed = to show that a formula was to follow. To show the range of cells to be included, we simply type the first cell and the last cell separated by the colon symbol : .

We still need to calculate the total in the gross pay column. Cell **B12** is currently highlighted. If you click on the **Copy** icon on the standard toolbar, move to cell **E12** and click on the **Paste** icon, you will find that the required total appears. Again relative referencing has automatically changed the column labels. We copied from cell **B12** to **E12** so the formula has become

=SUM(**E7**:**E11**)

FIGURE 6.3

CALCULATION OF GROSS PAY

	A	B	C	D	E
1	FAST FORWARD VIDEO COMPANY				
2	COMMISSION PAYROLL				
3	Calculations of gross pay				
4					
5	EMPLOYEE	SALES (£)	COMMISSION	BASIC PAY(£)	GROSS PAY (£)
6			RATE		
7	Arnold	5700	3%	50	221
8	Chalmers	7500	4%	50	350
9	Michaelson	8500	2%	50	220
10	Pratt	8000	4%	50	370
11	Wilson	4200	3%	50	176

6.4 Enhancing the appearance of a worksheet

We can enhance the appearance of the worksheet in several different ways using the icons on the formatting toolbar or, for a greater choice of options, using commands from the Menu Bar.

For example, if you want to centre all the entries in the table, highlight the appropriate cells and click on the **Centre** icon.

The gross pay may not always work out exactly to a whole number of pounds. We should really allow for two decimal places so that we can display the values to the nearest penny. To do this highlight cells **E7–E11**, click on **Format** in the Menu Bar, then Cells Number 0.00. If you are desperate to show the commas to indicate thousands in the sales figures, highlight column **B** and click on the **Comma** icon on the formatting toolbar.

If you wish to show the worksheet headings in a bold typeface, highlight these cells and click on the **Bold** icon. You can use underlining or italics if you prefer. Your table should have the appearance of Figure 6.4.

You may decide you would like to space out your worksheet by adding an extra row or column. For example, it might look better if there is an empty row between the company name FAST FORWARD VIDEO COMPANY and the heading COMMISSION PAYROLL. To do this, move to cell **A2**, click on **Insert** in the Menu Bar, then click on **Row** and the extra row appears. The remaining entries in the table are moved down a row and any formulae are automatically changed to the new cell references.

6.5 Printing and saving a worksheet

To print out a worksheet, you should first check that your desired printer is selected and recognised by the spreadsheet. You can highlight just a range of cells you wish to print or you can print the whole worksheet. You must remember when you start producing large worksheets that they will not fit on to one side of A4 paper. If you click on **File** in the Menu Bar, then **Print Preview**, you will be able to view the arrangement of the pages. If the splits are not to your liking, there are several options open to you:

- landscape orientation instead of portrait orientation
- insert one or more page breaks
- use a smaller size font

Some spreadsheets have commands that fit a selected range of cells to a page or allow you to centre the printout horizontally or vertically on the page so it

FIGURE 6.4

CALCULATION OF TOTALS

	A	B	C	D	E
1	**FAST FORWARD VIDEO COMPANY**				
2	**COMMISSION PAYROLL**				
3	**Calculations of gross pay**				
4					
5	EMPLOYEE	SALES (£)	COMMISSION	BASIC PAY(£)	GROSS PAY (£)
6			RATE		
7	Arnold	5,700	3%	50	221.00
8	Chalmers	7,500	4%	50	350.00
9	Michaelson	8,500	2%	50	220.00
10	Pratt	8,000	4%	50	370.00
11	Wilson	4,200	3%	50	176.00
12	TOTALS	33,900			1337.00

is straightforward to obtain a printout in the form you desire.

In many packages, you have further options, such as whether to show the gridlines or not, shading of cells, putting borders round a selected range, including the row and column headings or not and choice of colour, assuming you have access to a colour printer.

When you have checked the **Print Preview**, click on **Print** and your worksheet will be printed out.

You should get into the habit of saving your work regularly, perhaps every quarter of an hour, so that if the computer system breaks down for whatever reason, you do not have to repeat too much work.

Click on **File**, then **Save As** if it is the first time you are saving the worksheet. Indicate which drive you want to save to, give the file a name and then click on the **OK** button. When you want to save the file again, click on **File**, then **Save**.

When you are finishing work on a worksheet, click on **File** then **Close**. You will be prompted to save the file if you have not done so already. Next click on **File** then **Exit** and you will be returned to the Windows Program Manager screen. Double click on the Control Menu box in the top left-hand corner of the screen to exit from Windows.

There may be a quick key that you can click on to activate functions on your spreadsheet. You will find that the more modern the spreadsheet you are using the more ways there are of carrying out the same calculation. Once you get used to your spreadsheet package you will find that there are often short-cut keys that save time.

6.6 Absolute cell references

In Section 6.3, we noted that a spreadsheet assumes that relative references are wanted when a formula is copied from one cell to another on the worksheet. In some calculations, this is not appropriate and we have to use an *ABSOLUTE CELL REFERENCE* which remains fixed when we copy it to another cell.

Example

The Fast Forward Video Company wants to know what percentage of its total sales were made by each employee.

FIGURE 6.5

CALCULATION OF PERCENTAGES

	A	B	C
1	**FAST FORWARD VIDEO COMPANY**		
2	**COMMISSION PAYROLL**		
3	**Calculation of sales percentages**		
4			
5	EMPLOYEE	SALES (£)	SALES
6			PERCENTAGE
7	Arnold	5,700	16.81
8	Chalmers	7,500	22.12
9	Michaelson	8,500	25.07
10	Pratt	8,000	23.60
11	Wilson	4,200	12.39
12	TOTALS	33,900	100.00

Figure 6.5 shows the employees and their sales.

The sales percentages have been calculated in column **C**. In cell **C7**, we want to work out 5700 as a percentage of 30 900, which is

5700/30 900∗100

or using cell addresses and indicating it is a formula

=**B7/B12**∗100

If we enter this in cell **C7**, it will give the correct percentage but if we copy it down the column for the remaining employees, an error message appears.

Because the spreadsheet assumes that relative referencing is required when we move to cell **C8** from **C7**, it updates all the row numbers in the formula to give

=**B8/B13**∗100

As there is no entry in cell **B13**, the error message is triggered. Of course what we want is for **B8** to be calculated as a percentage of the total sales which are always in **B12** so we must make **B12** an absolute reference.

To do this we have to use the **$** symbol and the formula to type in **C7** becomes

=**B7/$B$12**∗100

We then copy this down column **C** to **C12** and we obtain the results in Figure 6.5, formatted to 2 decimal places.

In a spreadsheet, you have the option of displaying the *formula* in a *cell* rather than the result of the calculation. Figure 6.6 displays the result of using the Menu Bar commands **Tools, Options, View Formulas** on Figure 6.5 and you can see the absolute references clearly.

Using the **View Formulas** option affects the formatting of the spreadsheet and you may need to adjust the column widths before printing out. It is a good idea to save two versions of the worksheet, one with the formulae and one with the actual calculations.

Exercise 6.1

Reproduce the worksheet we developed in Figure 6.4 using your own spreadsheet package. Then make the following changes, one after the other:

(a) Insert two new employees in the correct alphabetic order
Hobart Sales = £6500 Rate = 4% Basic pay £50
Smith Sales = £7600 Rate = 2% Basic pay £50
and work out their gross pay.
Hint:
Either:
Move to **A9** and use the command **Insert Row** to use for Hobart. Type in Hobart's details and note what happens in column **E** and to the totals.
Or:
Insert Hobart and Smith on rows **12** and **13**. Then highlight the names in column **A** and extend the highlight across all columns. Choose **Data Sort** in ascending order of column **A** or click on the **A** to **Z** sort icon.

(b) Michaelson's commission is upgraded to 3%.

(c) The basic pay changes to £60.

(d) Print out the final worksheet in the standard and in the View Formula versions.

6.7 Spreadsheet templates

When you worked through the examples and exercises in Chapters 4 and 5, you probably began to realise that the calculations involved in drawing up a set of final accounts are really quite simple. They just require accuracy, concentration and attention to detail. So why not solve the problem once and for all by designing a worksheet that can carry out the calculations for you? The best way to approach this is to think through all the calculations involved in principle and to set out a worksheet which contains only the headings and formulae which you would always use in these calculations. Such a general worksheet is called a *TEMPLATE*.

Exercise 6.2

Design and set up a worksheet which will carry out all the calculations we did manually in working through the example in Chapter 5. The worksheet

FIGURE 6.6

FORMULAE FOR CALCULATION OF PERCENTAGES

	A	B	C
1	**FAST FORWARD VIDEO COMPANY**		
2	**COMMISSION PAYROLL**		
3	**Calculation of sales percentages**		
4			
5	EMPLOYEE	SALES (£)	SALES
6			PERCENTAGE
7	Arnold	5700	=B7/$B$12*100
8	Chalmers	7500	=B8/$B$12*100
9	Michaelson	8500	=B9/$B$12*100
10	Pratt	8000	=B10/$B$12*100
11	Wilson	4200	=B11/$B$12*100
12	TOTALS	=SUM(B7:B11)	=B12/$B$12*100

should contain layouts and formulae for the stock, debtors' and creditors' calculations, the cash flow statement, the profit and loss account and the balance sheet. It should also make use of the spreadsheet's facilities in order to draw the closing balances from all the other statements into the balance sheet.

You may want to sketch out your worksheet design in rough on paper before putting it onto the screen. Input and save the worksheet in this form before trying it out on the above example. Then key in the figures relating to the example to see if it works. If you are satisfied with the outcome, save the worksheet again, but this time under a different name, relating to the example. You have now got two worksheets, a general one, containing only headings and formulae and an example-specific one, containing the actual figures. That way the first worksheet remains independent from a particular example and you can use it over and over again.

6.8 Drawing charts

Using a spreadsheet it is possible to produce many different types of charts. It is often much easier to get an understanding of a set of figures from a chart than from a report or a table. Of course, we cannot always show every detail on a chart but we can gain a quick overall impression. In this section we will look at some of the types of charts that are particularly helpful to use when interpreting financial data. The data in this section have been taken from the MFI Furniture Group plc report for 1994.

Bar chart

This is the simplest and most widely applicable of all charts. It shows the actual number of items (the fre-

FIGURE 6.7

BAR CHART: MFI GROUP (1994), AVERAGE NUMBER EMPLOYED

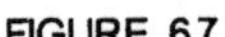

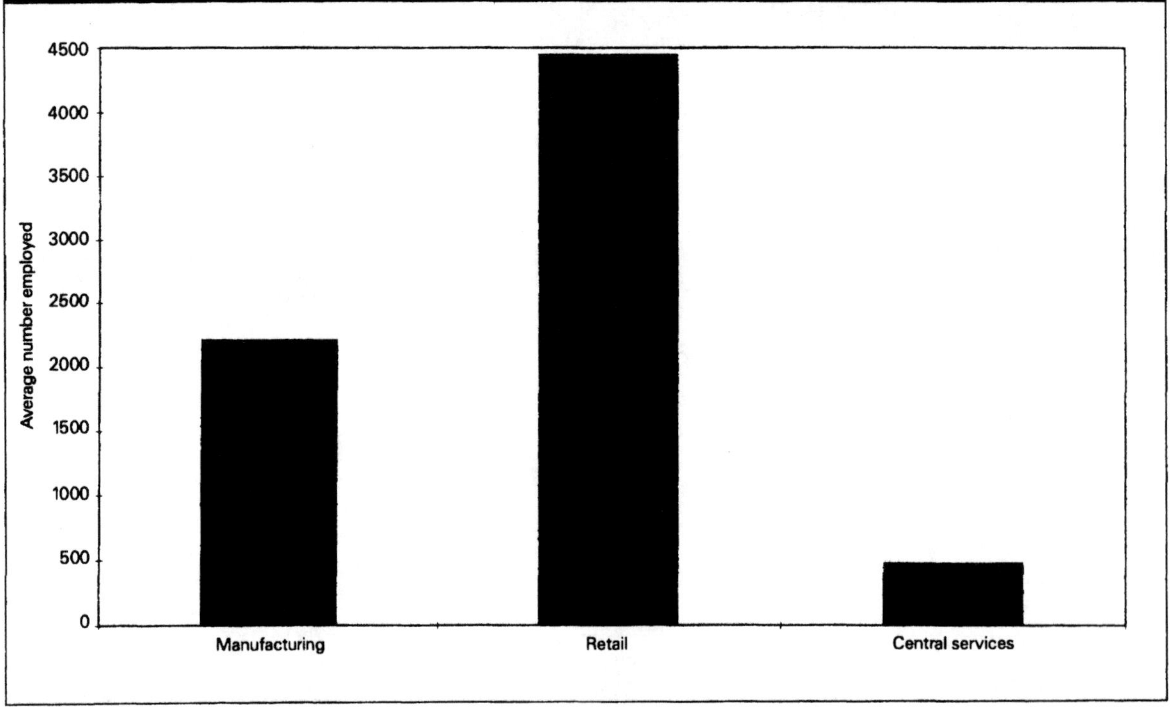

quency) in various different categories. These categories may be purely descriptive as in Figure 6.7 or they may be numerical and have some order as in Figure 6.9. Bar charts can be drawn with either horizontal or *vertical* bars. For obvious reasons, vertical bar charts are also referred to as *column* charts and would be the preferred choice for data showing changes over time such as displayed in Figure 6.9.

Figure 6.7 shows the average number of persons employed by the MFI Group in 1994.

To draw this chart, we first need to enter the data into adjacent columns of the worksheet as shown in Figure 6.8.

FIGURE 6.8

WORKSHEET LAYOUT FOR CHART DRAWING

	A	B	C	D
1	MFI GROUP 1994			
2		Average number employed		
3	Manufacturing	2212		
4	Retail	4445		
5	Central services	477		

Next highlight these two columns, including the headings and select the **Chart** option on your worksheet by clicking the **ChartWizard** icon on the standard toolbar. Move the pointer to a clear part of the worksheet, (**A7**), and then drag to **F22**, say, to outline a rectangle of an appropriate size. When you release the mouse, step 1 of 5 of the **ChartWizard** dialog box appears. First check that, in the highlighted box, the desired range of cells has indeed been selected. If the range is incorrect, type the correct version in the **Range** box. Click on **Next** to move to step 2 of 5 dialog box. Then select the type of chart, **Column**, as we require vertical bars and click on **Next**. You are presented with various different formats for column charts in the step 3 of 5 dialog box. To draw Figure 6.7 we have selected option 1 which has a single bar for each category. When you click on **Next**, a sample chart is displayed in the step 4 of 5 dialog box. Check that you have told the spreadsheet that the data series are in columns and that the first column contains the category **(X)** axis labels. Click on **Next** and in the step 5 of 5 dialog box, you are given the opportunity to add a legend or key to the different categories. This is not needed in a simple bar chart but is important in line charts and pie charts to distinguish categories or cases. Finally, we add a chart

FIGURE 6.9

BAR CHART OF TIME SERIES DATA: MFI GROUP (1988–94)

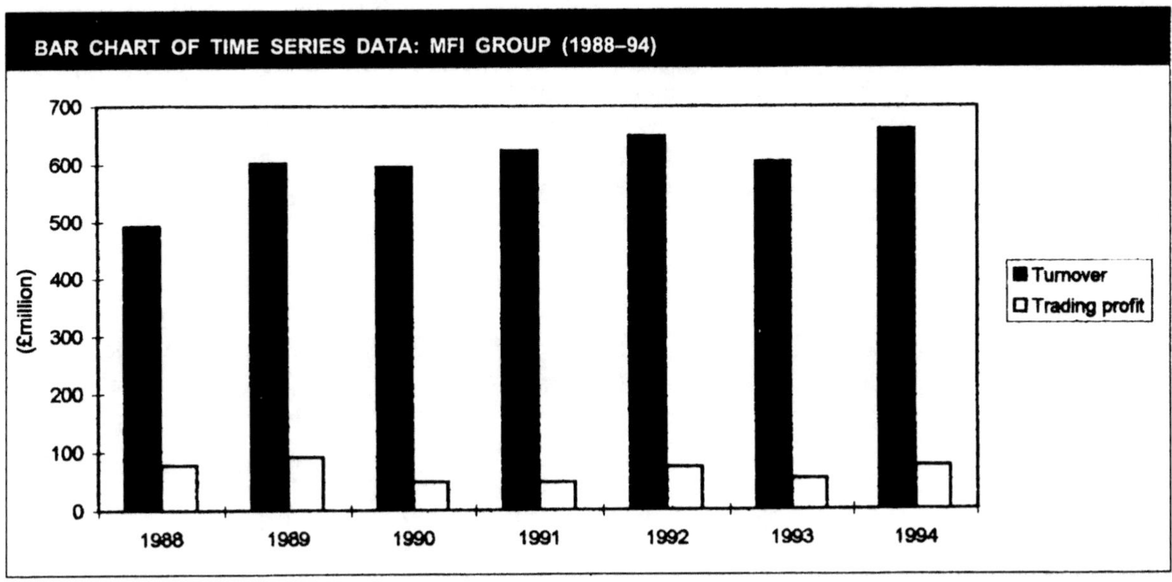

title and axis titles. First click in the **Chart Title** box and type MFI Group Average number employed. Then click in the **Value (Y)** box and type Average number employed. **Click Finish**.

A chart will then appear in the worksheet. It may not look quite as you expected but it is easy enough to alter it in almost any respect. If the chart is surrounded by a rectangle without handles (8 black squares), click once anywhere within the chart to select it and then you can start work.

To size the chart, direct the pointer to the middle handle on the right-hand side of the chart. It will change to a double-headed arrow and you can then drag this side of the chart and make it as large or small as you wish. Similarly, you can use any of the other handles to change the size.

To change other elements of the chart, position the mouse pointer anywhere within the chart and double-click to activate the chart. A thick blue rectangle surrounding the chart area indicates that it has been activated. To edit any element of the chart, such as the title or the Category axis, simply double-click on it to select it. Handles will appear round the item and you will be presented with a Format box. You can change font sizes and styles, shading, patterns, gridlines, the position of tick marks on the scales and so on. The main thing to remember as you alter the chart is to keep everything as clear and simple as possible. You are trying to produce an aid to understanding not a work of art.

When the chart is to your liking, save the worksheet and the chart will be saved with it. If at a later stage, you alter any of the data on which the chart is based, the chart on the screen will be changed appropriately. If you want to keep both your original chart and the modified version, use the **File Save As** command to create a new file for the modified worksheet. Of course, if you want only the modified version, you can use the **File Save** command to overwrite the original worksheet.

Exercise 6.3

Put the data shown in Table 6.1 into a worksheet and use the chart options available within your spreadsheet package to produce a chart similar to Figure 6.9.

Comment on what the chart shows.

Pie chart

In Figure 6.7, the bar chart presentation emphasises the actual numbers of employees in the different areas of the business and clearly shows that the Retail area has far more employees than the other categories. An alternative form of presentation of the data is as a *PIE CHART* as in Figure 6.10.

This shows clearly what proportion or percentage of the group's employees work in the different areas of the business. We can see that more than half of the group's workforce are working in Retail. The pie chart and the bar chart are complementary to each other and it is often useful to display the same data in both ways.

To draw the pie chart, we return to the worksheet where the MFI data are entered, Figure 6.8. As before, we highlight cells **A3–B5** and click on the **ChartWizard** icon. Move the pointer to a clear part of the worksheet, say, cell **A30**, and drag the pointer to outline a rectangle. Once again when you release the mouse, step 1 of 5 of the **ChartWizard** dialog box appears. Proceed through the five steps as before but at step 2 select the option **Pie chart**. At step 3 you

TABLE 6.1

DATA FOR EXERCISE 6.3

MFI GROUP Seven year record of key financial statistics							
YEAR	1988	1989	1990	1991	1992	1993	1994
Turnover (£m)	491.8	601.7	594.9	623.1	647.4	603.9	659.4
Trading profit (£m)	77.1	91.4	48.5	47.4	72.7	52.1	74.5
Average number of employees	6245	7610	8025	8222	7848	7579	7134
(full-time equivalent)							

FIGURE 6.10

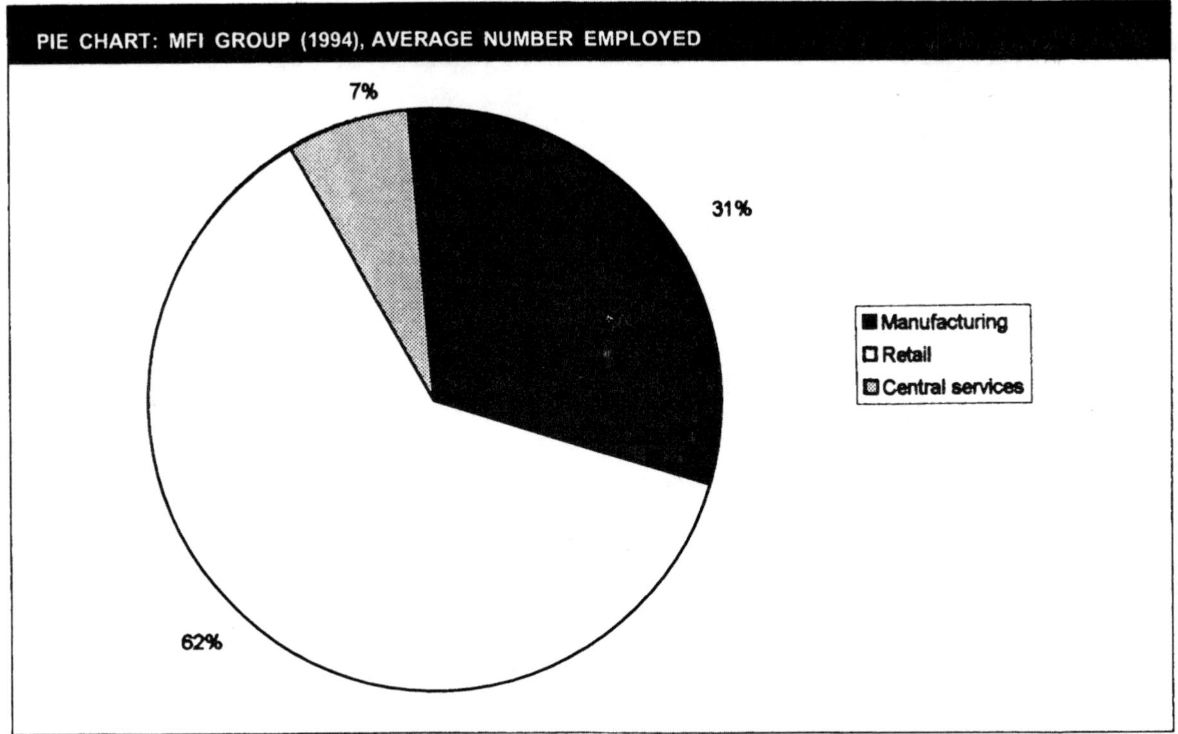

have the choice of different versions. Figure 6.10 is option 6, which prints the category percentages. When you have finished step 5, double-click to activate the chart and format the titles, labels, patterns and so on as you wish.

When the chart is acceptable, save the worksheet again.

Line chart

When we need to look at trends over time, instead of drawing a bar chart as in Figure 6.9, we can give a greater impression of continuity by drawing a line chart as shown in Figure 6.11.

This clearly show the fluctuations in Turnover and Trading profit over time and it is easy to see whether they have moved in the same or in opposite directions from year to year.

To draw this line chart, return to the worksheet where you have entered the data in Table 6.1. Highlight the rows containing the Year, Turnover, Trading profit and Average number of employees. Use the **ChartWizard** icon to outline where you want the chart to go. Work through the five steps of the **ChartWizard** dialog box as before. At step 2, select the **Line chart** option. There are several possible formats for the line chart shown at step 3. Select option 1 which shows the data points with symbols, joins them with straight lines and displays them on a plain background. Again it is important to include a legend to distinguish each line and always check the chart and its axes are appropriately titled at step 5. When you have finished step 5, the line chart appears in the worksheet and you may wish to format it using the same procedures as with the bar and pie charts. Remember to save the worksheet and the chart when you are satisfied with the result.

XY chart (scatter diagram)

When we want to investigate the relationship, if any, between two variables, there is a special type of chart that we can draw called a *SCATTER DIAGRAM*, although on many of the spreadsheet packages you will find it

FIGURE 6.11

LINE CHART: MFI GROUP (1988–94)

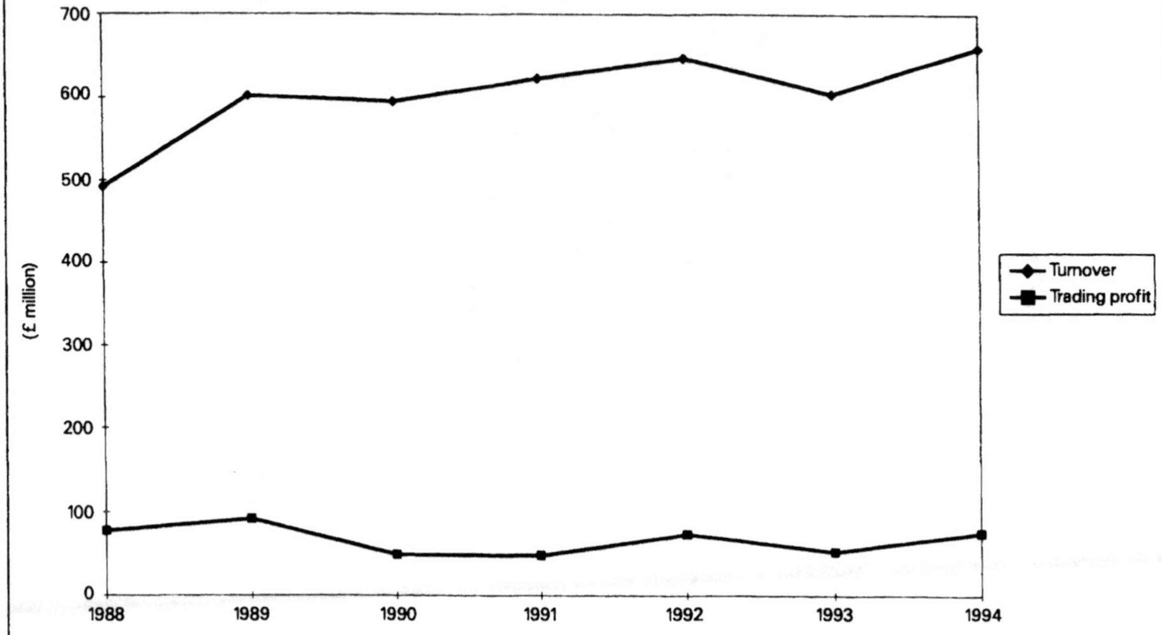

700
600
500
400
300
200
100
0
(£ million)
1988
1989
1990
1991
1992
1993
1994
Turnover
Trading profit

FIGURE 6.12

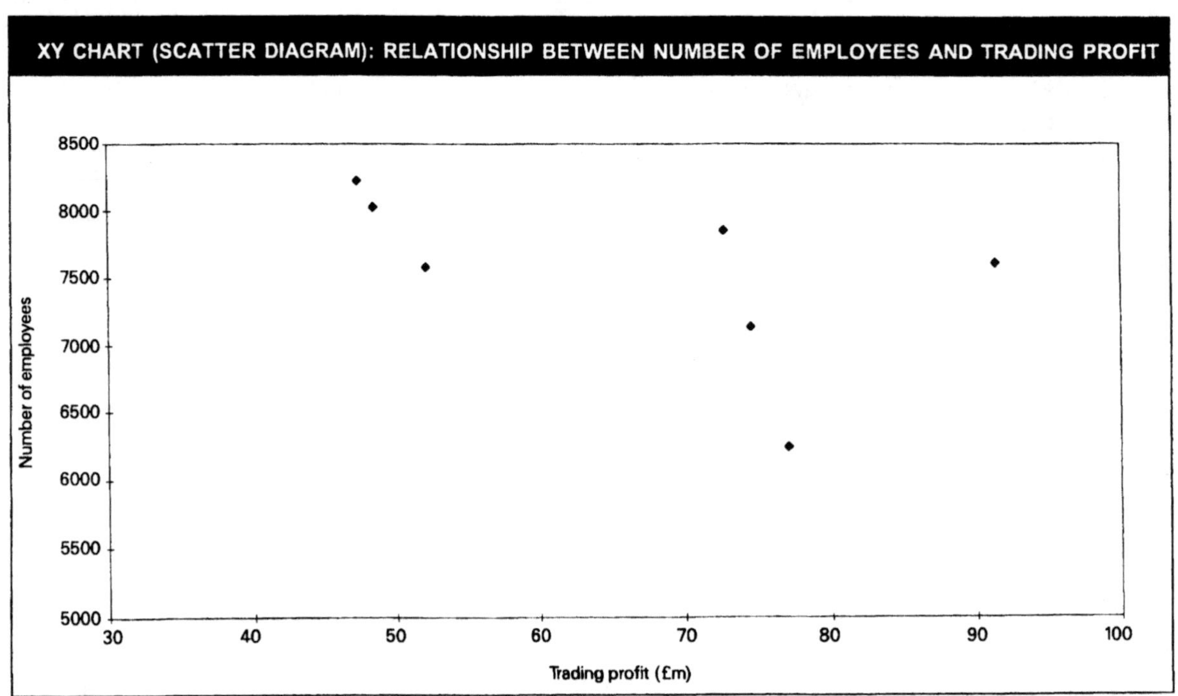

XY CHART (SCATTER DIAGRAM): RELATIONSHIP BETWEEN NUMBER OF EMPLOYEES AND TRADING PROFIT

8500
8000
7500
7000
6500
6000
5500
5000
Number of employees
30
40
50
60
70
80
90
100
Trading profit (£m)

referred to as an *XY CHART*. Figure 6.12 shows a scatter diagram relating the Number of employees each year to the Trading profit.

The horizontal axis (the **X** axis) of the graph shows values for the Trading profit and the vertical axis (the **Y** axis) of the graph shows the Number of employees. For each of the seven years' data in Table 6.1, we obtain one point on the scatter diagram. For example, in 1988, the Trading profit was 77.1 (£m) and there were 6245 employees. Therefore, the point for 1988 is plotted corresponding to 77.1 on the **X** axis and 6245 on the **Y** axis and similarly for the other years. You can see how the chart gets its name because the points, in general, are scattered over the page. We shall look at scatter diagrams in more detail in Chapter 14 but you will probably notice in Figure 6.12 that there is a tendency, although not very strong, for higher trading profits to be associated with lower numbers of employees.

To draw one of these charts on the spreadsheet, return to the worksheet where you have entered the data from Table 6.1. Highlight the two rows containing the variables of interest, Trading profit and Average number of employees. Click on the **ChartWizard**, outline the chart area in the worksheet and this time select the option **XY Chart (Scatter diagram)** in step 2 of the **ChartWizard** dialog box. Various formats are proposed at step 3 but the one to choose is option 1 which shows only the points. No legend is required at step 5 but the chart and axes do need titles.

There is one further point to note about Figure 6.12 – it has been drawn so that the scales on the axes do not start at zero. This can be achieved by activating the chart, double-clicking each scale in turn and specifying the minimum scale mark required. This is appropriate when drawing scatter diagrams because we are interested in the positions of the points relative to each other rather than in their absolute values. It is misleading in a bar chart or a line chart if the vertical scale starts at anything other than zero because our perception of the actual values displayed is altered.

Save the worksheet again once your chart is completed.

6.9 Printing out charts

To print out a chart, return to the worksheet containing the chart. Double-click on the chart to activate it. Click on the **File** command in the Menu Bar and then click on the **Print** option. You will need to go into **Page setup** where you can select **Portrait** or **Landscape** view, add a **Header** and/or **Footer**, specify the position and size on the page and the colour. Use the **Print preview** to check everything is as you require and then click on **Print**. You may need to consult your printer manual if everything appears correctly on the screen but you cannot get a copy on paper.

If you are using an integrated package, such as MS Office, Lotus Smartsuite or Works, you can easily insert a chart into a word-processed document. Open your document and position the cursor where you want the chart to appear, open the worksheet, select the chart, cut or copy it to the clipboard, return to the document and paste the chart from the clipboard. For further instructions refer to your manual.

Exercise 6.4

Reproduce Figures 6.10–6.12 using your spreadsheet package and print them out.

6.10 Summary

In this chapter you have learned how to enter text, numbers and formulae into a spreadsheet. You are able to perform calculations using formulae, operators and functions. You have practised drawing a bar chart, pie chart, line chart and a scatter diagram. You can enhance the appearance of your worksheet and charts and can print them out.

Case Study 1

McTucky's Ltd: Final Accounts

1 A business startup

Having made redundant from his job in a fast food restaurant, Jim Tucker starts a business selling stuffed pancakes from a mobile stand on fairgrounds in the North of England. He goes into business on 1 January 199X, investing £1000 redundancy money in cash and trading under the name of McTucky's Ltd. All the cash is put into a newly opened business bank account. In addition to his cash investment he also brings a van into the business which is a gift from his old uncle Florian and which is worth £6000 when Jim receives it. The van will only be used for business purposes. Jim expects the business to make a loss for the first few weeks and arranges an overdraft facility up to the amount of £3000 with his bank manager.

2 Initial business transactions

During the first week of January, Jim acquires a computer to be used for stock control and accounting purposes (cost £1000) and a second hand mobile unit, which combines a small freezer, an oven and a display counter, to be used on the fairs (cost £2000). Both are paid for in cash at the time of purchase. Jim will be buying the stuffed pancakes frozen from a local wholesaler and the equipment will be used to heat them up at the point of sale.

The transactions taking place during the first month of trading are summarised in Tables C1.1 and C1.2.

Wages for casual staff are paid on the day the work is done and come to £250 for the month. Jim's own salary as a director of the company comes to £1000.

The rent of the pitch on the fair grounds visited comes to £300 for the month. Van expenses are £210. All these expenses are paid at the time when they are incurred.

The business's fixed assets are to be depreciated using the assumptions summarised in Table C1.3.

TABLE C1.1

MCTUCKY'S LTD:
PURCHASE OF GOODS FOR RESALE

Date	Number of Units	Cost Price/Unit	Cash or Credit
2 Jan 199X	300	£1.20	Cash paid
10 Jan 199X	500	£1.30	Cash paid
15 Jan 199X	400	£1.25	Credit (1 month)
25 Jan 199X	600	£1.35	Credit (1 month)

TABLE C1.2

MCTUCKY'S LTD: SALE OF GOODS			
Date	**Units Sold**	**Selling Price/Unit**	**Cash or Credit**
5 Jan 199X	200	£2.50	Cash
16 Jan 199X	400	£2.50	Cash
20 Jan 199X	500	£2.50	Cash
27 Jan 199X	300	£3.00	Cash

TABLE C1.3

MCTUCKY'S LTD: FIXED ASSETS		
Asset	**Life (years)**	**Expected Scrap Value**
Van	6	£600
Computer	8	£200
Mobile Unit	5	£200

Tasks

Acting as an advisor to Jim Tucker you are required to carry out the following tasks.

Task 1

Calculate the value of closing stock, using FIFO, LIFO and WAC. Select the most appropriate method, briefly contrasting the three methods and discussing the reasons behind your choice.

Task 2

Calculate the depreciation charge for the fixed assets, using two methods each. (In the case of the reducing balance method, the percentages to be applied annually are 32 per cent for the van, 18 per cent for the computer and 37 per cent for the mobile unit.) Briefly contrast the two methods and discuss which method of charging depreciation would be most suitable in this case.

Task 3

For the McTucky business, draw up

(a) A cash flow statement for the period 1 to 31 January 199X
(b) A profit and loss account for that period
(c) A balance sheet as at 31 January 199X

(For the purpose of your calculations use the method of stock valuation selected in Task 1 and the method of charging depreciation selected in Task 2.)

Clearly show your calculations of the stock and creditor balances which go into the balance sheet as at the end of the period.

Task 4

Transfer the work carried out in Task 3 onto a spreadsheet. (The emphasis should be on designing the spreadsheet well – ensure that you make efficient use of formulae, so that the spreadsheet does the work for you wherever possible.)

Produce two printouts of your work; one showing the statements as in Task 3, the other showing the formulae.

Part II
Ratio Analysis

7

Introduction to Ratio Analysis

7.1 Learning objectives

When you have finished working through this chapter you should be able to

- Understand why there is a need for all business managers to be able to read and interpret financial statements
- Define the term **RATIO** in a business context
- Explain the term **RATIO ANALYSIS**
- Appreciate the reasons for using ratio analysis in the interpretation of financial statements
- Identify the key areas on which ratio analysis focuses

7.2 Interpretation of financial statments

In Part I of this book you learned to draw up a set of final accounts in the context of a simple exercise, both manually and on a spreadsheet. This entailed bringing together financial information in the format of a cash flow statement, a profit and loss account and a balance sheet and carrying out calculations of stock values and depreciation charges as appropriate. In the course of working through Chapters 2–5 you have gained a basic appreciation of a number of concepts and principles which guide business organisations in drawing up their accounts, such as the ideas of *DUALITY*, *BUSINESS ENTITY* and the *MATCHING PRINCIPLE*.

All the statements you have drawn up so far were based on historical data, drawn from the company's record-keeping system. Because businesses have to follow strict guidelines in drawing up these statements, they are possibly the most objective source of information about the organisation and its performance publicly available to managers, investors and competitors alike. As such, they are used widely.

Externally, City analysts make use of financial statements as an important information source in assessing whether or not to invest in a company's shares. In this they will consider a range of criteria, such as the sales volume and profitability generated from shareholders' investment, the company's ability to pay its debtors, as well as the company's standing relative to the competition. For competitors, the published accounts are a legitimate information source which helps them assess the relative standing of companies in their industry. This kind of analysis has been made particularly easy, and therefore popular, since the advent of sophisticated information systems for financial analysis, such as FAME (Financial Analysis Made Easy), which is a CD-ROM system available at most university libraries.

nally, company management makes use of his- al financial statements to assess the financial engths and weaknesses of the business and to see how well matched they are to the opportunities and threats arising in the wider business environment and whether their results match those required by investors. Almost inevitably, this also entails a comparison with near competitors and industry standards. Such an analysis of historical performance forms the logical first step in determining the business's financial strategy and setting clear targets for future financial performance, thus gaining a degree of control over future activities. Whilst the broad strategic planning process may be in the hands of the board of directors, it can only become reality if all line management have a clear understanding of how the overall targets translate into concrete and measurable performance targets in the context of their own individual workplaces. Such targets can then serve as a yardstick for each manager against which individual performance can be assessed. To give such targets credibility, it is important that each manager can read, analyse and interpret financial statements correctly, so he or she can understand where the financial measures and targets come from and why they are necessary.

Unfortunately, when confronted with a full set of published accounts, people often feel overwhelmed by the amount of information presented and the terminology used often appears alien and daunting. Also, many people are not comfortable working with numbers in the first place. Having worked through Part I of this book, in theory you should now be in a position where you can read such financial information quite easily and explain to others what it all means.

Exercise 7.1

Imagine that the Institute of Grocery Distribution is compiling a report on the performance of grocery discount retailers operating in the European Union (EU). For the German based discounters DALI, the sales data presented in Table 7.1 are available from the profit and loss accounts compiled by the company.

(a) From the data shown in Table 7.1, what can you say about the company's overall performance over the three years, as well as about its comparative performance in the three countries it operates in?

TABLE 7.1

DALI: EUROPEAN SALES DATA

	Year 1	Year 2	Year 3
UK			
Sales	£15m	£17m	£20m
Net Profit	£1.2m	£1.1m	£1.2m
Germany			
Sales	DM10m	DM11m	DM12m
Net Profit	DM0.1m	DM0.13m	DM0.13m
France			
Sales	F25m	F30m	F30m
Net Profit	F0.6m	F0.7m	F0.68m

(b) List **three** items of additional information which you would require to be able to offer a more accurate interpretation.

As you can see, even if you are familiar with financial information, the interpretation of financial figures can be far from straightforward. Sales information must be seen in conjunction with the resulting cost and profit figures to be meaningful. When looking at trends over time, inflation rates must be taken into account. For multinational operators, a knowledge of the exchange rates used becomes vital.

For the above reasons, a simple tool or measure is needed which enables you to focus on the important areas and to present the data in such a way that comparisons over time and between companies and countries are made easy.

7.3 An overview of ratio analysis

One such tool is *RATIO ANALYSIS*. Here, instead of looking at the figures as they are presented in the full financial statements, the focus is on the *relationship* between a small number of key figures extracted from the statements, for example, between net profit and sales or between sales and the number of staff currently employed.

Where you express one figure in relation to another, this is called a *RATIO*. Thus, if in Exercise 7.1 you want to express the Year 1 DALI German net profit in relation to sales, you might calculate the ratio of net profit to sales, in this case that would work out as DM0.1m : DM10m, or 1:100. Please note that ratios can be written in a number of different ways, all of which mean the same thing. So in the example above, the ratio can be written as 1:100; 1/100; 0.01; or even 1 per cent, all four express the same relationship. Because of this, the different ways of writing out a ratio will be treated as interchangeable in the rest of the book.

Since ratios focus on the relationship between figures, they get round the problems encountered in Exercise 7.1. As demonstrated, you can carry out a straightforward comparisón between the relationship between net profit and sales for all three countries without having to worry about exchange rates or inflation rates since both elements of the ratio would be affected in the same proportion.The calculation of financial ratios focuses mainly on three key areas:

- *profitability*, or the management of the selling and buying process – this is introduced in Chapter 8
- *resource utilisation*, or the management of assets – this is discussed in detail in Chapter 8
- returns to investors – this is treated in Chapter 9.

> *RATIO ANALYSIS* is a technique which makes use of the calculation of financial ratios as a starting point in the interpretation of financial statements. This is used in the strategic planning process to monitor performance, to identify strengths and weaknesses compared to the competition and to plan and control changes in the business's operations in view of their projected impact on future performance.

Chapter 10 brings all the ratios together into an integrated model which facilitates analysis and interpretation by showing how the various ratios are linked and how the overall performance of the business can be influenced by improving individual areas of operating performance. This is supported by a spreadsheet application of the model. Part II concludes with Case Study 2, which allows you to practise the ratio analysis skills acquired by applying them to a business case.

7.4 Summary

This chapter has provided an overview of Part II and set out the structure for this part. The need for management to be able to read and interpret financial statements was highlighted and the difficulties of interpreting and comparing financial information from different years and countries examined. The concept of financial ratios was explained. Ratio analysis was identified as a tool for making key financial information readily accessible and for analysing a business's strengths and weaknesses, both over time and by comparison to the competition. This was presented as an important part of the strategic planning process, as ratios can be used to relate different areas of operating performance to each other and to overall company objectives, which can then be translated into clear objectives for individual line managers.

8

Analysis of Asset Utilisation, Profitability and Performance

8.1 Learning objectives

When you have finished working through this chapter you should be able to

- Identify the key components which make up business performance
- Describe and illustrate with examples what is meant by the terms **PERFORMANCE**, **RESOURCE UTILISATION**, **LIQUIDITY** and **PROFITABILITY**
- Identify the key business ratios used to assess performance, resource utilisation, liquidity and profitability
- In the context of a simple example, calculate and interpret the following ratios: **ASSET TURNOVER**, **CURRENT RATIO**, **ACID TEST**, **STOCK TURNOVER**, **CREDITORS' PAYMENT PERIOD**, **DEBTORS' COLLECTION PERIOD**, **FIXED ASSET RATIO**, **SALES PER SQUARE FOOT**, **SALES PER EMPLOYEE**, **NET MARGIN**, **GROSS MARGIN** and **RETURN ON CAPITAL EMPLOYED (ROCE)**
- Discuss and illustrate with an example the trade-off between resource utilisation and profitability
- Assess the likely impact of changes in the above ratios on overall business performance

8.2 Business performance objectives

In its simplest form, the business organisation could be viewed as a black box, where the investors put in money at one end and profit comes out at the other. What take place inside the black box are the activities involved in producing and selling goods and services to the consumer.

Naturally, investors are concerned with identifying those business opportunities which generate high *PERFORMANCE*, in other words, which involve the highest possible returns for the lowest possible investment, at a reasonable risk. Using ratio analysis, this can be assessed by looking at two key aspects of business. First, you need to investigate the sales volume that has been generated from a given capital investment base – this area is known as *RESOURCE UTILISATION*. Secondly, it is also necessary to ask how profitable each sale has been – this area of investigation is called *PROFITABILITY*.

8.3 Resource utilisation

In assessing resource utilisation we are asking the question: for every pound the investors have put into the business, how many pounds worth of sales has the business generated during the financial period in question? The ratio used to examine this relationship is the *ASSET TURNOVER* ratio.

Asset turnover

Asset turnover is calculated using the following formula.

Asset turnover formula

$$\text{Asset turnover} = \frac{\text{Sales}}{\text{Net total assets}}$$

with Net total assets = Fixed assets
+ Current assets
− Current liabilities

Example

At the end of the financial year, the entry for Net Total Assets in the balance sheet of a small manufacturing company is £250 000. During the financial year preceding the balance sheet date, total sales came to £1 000 000.

The calculation of the asset turnover ratio is shown in Figure 8.1.

FIGURE 8.1

MANUFACTURING COMPANY:
ASSET TURNOVER CALCULATIONS

$$\text{Asset turnover} = \frac{£1\,000\,000}{£250\,000} = 4 \text{ times}$$

This means that for every £1 invested in the business, £4 worth of sales have been generated during the financial year. In other words, the value of sales was four times the value of net total assets.

Exercise 8.1

A retailer's balance sheet shows an entry for net total assets of £150 000. For the financial year leading up to the balance sheet date, total sales came to £900 000. Calculate asset turnover and explain your answer.

If you compare the answer to Exercise 8.1 to the answer calculated in the example above, you can see that a retailer often has a higher asset turnover figure than a manufacturer. The reason for this is that since manufacturers make goods, they need to invest in expensive machines and equipment, whereas retailers are only concerned with the distribution and selling of goods which have been produced elsewhere. This implies that manufacturing is more ***capital intensive***, and this is reflected in the asset turnover figure.

It follows from the above formula that asset turnover can be influenced in two ways: either the level of sales is changed or the net total assets change. Whilst sales volume can be affected by marketing activity, the net total assets are altered either by a change in the short-term working capital position of the business, its *LIQUIDITY*, or through a change in the investment in fixed assets.

Investment in fixed assets

It is virtually impossible to generate sales without investing in fixed assets in the form of additional floorspace, plant and machinery and the updating and maintenance of existing assets. There is often a lag between the time when the original investment is made and the time when the additional sales finally materialise. In retail businesses the link between the investment in expensive key resource areas, such as selling space and staff, is carefully monitored and measured through the use of ratios such as *SALES PER SQUARE FOOT* and *SALES PER EMPLOYEE*.

Liquidity

LIQUIDITY is concerned with the management of working capital. It is a measure of a business organisation's ability to pay amounts due in the short term out of current assets. A company can be described as liquid, if there are more than sufficient current assets to cover all short-term debt (or, in other words, to match all current liabilities).

Example

The concept of liquidity is illustrated by the comparison of the working capital position of two companies shown in Figure 8.2.

FIGURE 8.2

LIQUIDITY

Company X		**Company Y**	
Current Assets	£	Current Assets	£
Stock	10 000	Stock	15 000
Debtors	8 000	Debtors	11 000
Cash	900	Cash	1 000
	18 900		27 000
Current Liabilities		Current Liabilities	
Creditors	15 000	Creditors	29 000
		Bank Overdraft	5 000
	15 000		34 000
Net Current Assets	3 900	Net Current Liabilities	(7 000)

Company **X** is *LIQUID* Its *WORKING CAPITAL* is a positive figure The amount that could be raised almost immediately by selling off stock, calling on debtors and using cash currently held, is higher than the amount owed to suppliers	Company **Y** is *ILLIQUID* Its *WORKING CAPITAL* is a negative figure The amount owed to trade suppliers and the bank exceeds that which could be raised quickly by turning current stock and debtors into cash and using the cash held

The two key ratios used to analyse liquidity are the *CURRENT RATIO* and the *ACID TEST.*

The current ratio is defined as the relationship of current assets to current liabilities and is calculated using the following formula:

Current ratio formula

$$\text{Current ratio} = \frac{\text{Current assets}}{\text{Current liabilities}}$$

This ratio assesses the relationship between the value of those assets which are liquid, in the sense that they will be turned into cash within the next financial year, and the value of the debts which will fall due within the same time period.

The optimum level of liquidity varies depending on the nature of the business organisation concerned. For many manufacturing organisations the current ratio is at a relatively high level, since stock is made up of raw materials and partly finished items as well as finished products and may therefore be difficult to sell at full value should it become necessary at very short notice. On the other hand, many retail organisations only hold stock for a very short time and can get excellent credit terms from the manufacturers supplying them. As a result, current ratios well below one are not uncommon and no cause for concern in the average retail organisation, unless there are other reasons to suspect that the business may have a cash flow problem.

The acid test assesses what percentage of the outstanding debt in the short run could be paid out of current assets if no stock could be turned into cash. Especially in the context of manufacturing organisations, where often much of current stock is in the form of raw materials and work in progress, this is not an unreasonable assumption to make, and in such situations the acid test is a useful ratio to calculate as a measure of immediate liquidity. The acid test ratio is calculated using the following formula:

Acid test formula

$$\text{Acid test} = \frac{\text{Current assets} - \text{Stock}}{\text{Current liabilities}}$$

In retail organisations selling fast moving consumer goods, such as groceries, this ratio is less relevant, as stock is very easily turned into cash. However, for retailers of high value items, this ratio is also relevant as it may be difficult to sell such stock at short notice without making a substantial loss.

Example

Figure 8.3 shows two extracts which were taken from the balance sheets of two competing retailers in order to analyse their respective liquidities.

The calculation of the current ratio, as shown in Figure 8.4, allows you to compare the two in terms of liquidity.

FIGURE 8.3

BALANCE SHEET EXTRACTS

Retailer A		**Retailer B**	
Current Assets	£	Current Assets	£
Stock	25 000	Stock	19 000
Debtors	17 000	Debtors	15 000
Cash	3 000	Cash	4 000
	45 000		38 000
Current Liabilities		Current Liabilities	
Creditors	60 000	Creditors	40 000
	60 000		40 000

FIGURE 8.4

COMPARISON OF LIQUIDITY

Retailer A

$$\text{Current ratio} = \frac{£45\,000}{£60\,000} = 0.75$$

Retailer B

$$\text{Current ratio} = \frac{£38\,000}{£40\,000} = 0.95$$

You can now rank the two companies, with **B** being the most liquid and **A** the least liquid. Strictly speaking both companies are illiquid, as they would both need to raise extra funds from sources other than the liquidation of their current assets, should the need arise to pay all the short-term creditors at once. The meaning of the ratios is that, in such a case, for every £1 owed to short-term creditors, Retailer **B** would be able to raise funds of £0.95 immediately, just by selling off stock, calling in debtors and using cash currently owned. Retailer **A** would only be able to raise £0.75 in that manner. This implies that Retailer **A** would have to find another £0.25 for every £1 owed to creditors, whereas Retailer **B** would only need to find another £0.05.

The calculation of the acid test, as shown in Figure 8.5, provides some further information.

These figures mean that if for some reason the two retailers could not sell their stock and still had to pay off all their creditors, they would only be able to find £0.33 and £0.48 respectively for every £1 owed. This illustrates the important role stockholding plays in the working-capital management of both retailers.

FIGURE 8.5

COMPARISON OF IMMEDIATE LIQUIDITY

Retailer A

$$\text{Acid test} = \frac{£45\,000 - £25\,000}{£60\,000} = \frac{£20\,000}{£60\,000} = 0.33$$

Retailer B

$$\text{Acid test} = \frac{£38\,000 - £19\,000}{£40\,000} = \frac{£19\,000}{£40\,000} = 0.48$$

You may think that these findings are rather alarming and that both should make sure that they have sufficient cash to match all their debts. However, that would not make good business sense, as the cash could be working for them in the businesses. In reality, for a going concern with an established reputation and long-lasting relationships of trust with its suppliers, the need to pay off all creditors at once is very unlikely to arise. As long as a business is profitable and generally financially sound, management could also quite easily borrow some additional cash from the bank to tide them over, should this become necessary. Under those circumstances it makes sense to make as much use of trade credit as a cheap source of short-term finance as the suppliers will allow. Last not least, it is impossible to judge whether a given set of ratios is 'good' or 'bad', unless you are in a position to carry out a detailed comparison over time and with industry standards. So always be very careful not to go too far in your discussion of the meaning of ratios and remain tentative in your conclusions unless you really know a great deal about the business and industry in question.

Exercise 8.2 allows you to practise the calculation and interpretation of the liquidity ratios covered so far.

Exercise 8.2

On the basis of the information provided in Table 8.1:

(a) Calculate the working capital (or Net current assets/liabilities) figure for each of the three companies

TABLE 8.1

COMPARISON OF THREE COMPANIES: DATA ON LIQUIDITY

Company A		**Company B**		**Company C**	
Current Assets		*Current Assets*		*Current Assets*	
Stock	£30 000	Stock	£10 000	Stock	£15 000
Debtors	£10 000	Debtors	£ 9 000	Debtors	£11 000
Cash	£ 1 000	Cash	£ 2 000	Cash	£ 1 000
Current Liabilities		*Current Liabilities*		*Current Liabilities*	
Creditors	£40 000	Creditors	£12 000	Creditors	£15 000

(b) Calculate the current ratio for each company and on the basis of your calculations rank the companies in order of liquidity; explain your findings

(c) For each company, calculate the acid test ratio
Rank the three companies in terms of immediate liquidity as expressed by the acid test
Compare your results with the findings in **(b)** and discuss the results.

Impact of operations on liquidity

So far, you have learned how to assess the state of liquidity of a company, using information drawn from the balance sheet. In addition, we also need to consider how liquidity can be managed through the organisation of a firm's operations.

Exercise 8.3

Briefly note **two** advantages of high liquidity, as well as **two** advantages of low liquidity.

You have probably noted that whilst it is advantageous to have cash or near cash resources in case of sudden demands from the creditors, under normal trading circumstances it makes sense to keep liquidity as low as possible. Low liquidity implies that only a small amount of resources is tied up in working capital and good use is made of trade credit as a 'free' source of short-term finance.

As the management of working capital is all about the efficiency of the day-to-day operations of the business, management can influence this by making sure that well designed and effective systems are in place in the area of stock management and debtor control, as well as by building good relations with trade creditors.

Success in these areas of operational management can also be measured through the use of ratios, namely *STOCK TURNOVER*, *DEBTORS' COLLECTION PERIOD* and *CREDITORS' PAYMENT PERIOD*.

The formulae for calculating these ratios are as follows:

Stock turnover formula

$$\text{Stock turnover} = \frac{\text{Cost of goods sold}}{\text{Average stock}}$$

The speed of stock turnover is related to the nature of the product. Naturally a grocer can expect to have a much higher stock turnover than a manufacturer of furniture. In addition, within the grocery trade, each operator may try to gain a further competitive advantage by implementing a more sophisticated electronic stock control system than the competition with the aim of increasing stock turnover even further and reducing the amount of resources tied up in stock.

Debtors' collection period formula

$$\text{Debtors' collection period (days)} = \frac{\text{Debtors}}{\text{Credit sales}} * 365$$

Clearly, every business would prefer to have as little money as possible tied up with debtors. However, whilst retailers mainly sell their goods for cash, manufacturers often need to offer generous trade credit in order to compete for key retail and wholesale accounts. In such cases, it is important to manage the collection period tightly by offering incentives for early payment and sending reminders when payments are due.

Creditors' payment period formula

Creditors' payment period (days)

$$= \frac{\text{Creditors}}{\text{Credit purchases}} * 365$$

Seen from the other side, the retailer in receipt of the manufacturer's offer of trade credit will try to negotiate as long a payment period as possible as trade creditors are a very important source of short-term finance. Why pay the high interest rates a bank would charge on an overdraft if you can get the suppliers to finance your retail operations for you? However, delaying payment too long can cause problems, especially if it is a reflection of financial difficulties on the retailer's part rather than effective use of trade credit.

The optimum levels for all these ratios are very much influenced by the industry in which the business operates as well as by the management systems in place.

Example

Figure 8.6 shows balance sheet extracts from two different financial years.

For the first year the ratios are worked out as presented in Figure 8.7.

The stock turnover figure means that during Year 1 stock was turned round five times.

The debtors' collection ratio calculated implies that, on average, debtors took 55 days before settling their accounts with the company during Year 1.

The creditors' payment period ratio indicates that, on average, during Year 1, 91 days passed before trade creditor accounts were settled.

Exercise 8.4

You can now carry out the rest of the calculations for the figures in Figure 8.6 unaided.

FIGURE 8.6

CHANGES IN THE FINANCIAL POSITION

Extract from Balance Sheet at End of Year 1		**Extract from Balance Sheet at End of Year 2**	
Current Assets	£	Current Assets	£
Stock	2 000	Stock	1 500
Debtors	150	Debtors	1 000
Cash	500	Cash	500
Current Liabilities		Current Liabilities	
Creditors	1 500	Creditors	700
Additional Information for Year 1		**Additional Information for Year 2**	
Cash Sales	20 000	Cash Sales	15 000
Credit Sales	1 000	Credit Sales	6 000
Cash Purchases	4 000	Cash Purchases	7 000
Credit Purchases	6 000	Credit Purchases	5 000
Cost of Goods Sold	10 000	Cost of Goods Sold	10 000

FIGURE 8.7

CALCULATION OF RATIOS FOR YEAR 1

$$\text{Stock turnover} = \frac{£10\,000}{£2\,000} = 5 \text{ times}$$

$$\text{Debtors' collection period} = \frac{£150}{£1\,000} * 365 = 55 \text{ days}$$

$$\text{Creditors' payment period} = \frac{£1\,500}{£6\,000} * 365 = 91 \text{ days}$$

(a) Calculate the ratios for stock turnover, debtors' collection period and creditors' payment period for the second year and compare the two years. Interpret your findings and comment on the overall impact of changes in the ratios on working-capital requirements.

(b) Using the layout provided in Table 8.2, match the changes in the ratios with the appropriate causes.

TABLE 8.2

INTERPRETING CHANGES IN RATIOS	
Cause	**Ratio Affected**
Implementation of new sales based ordering system	
Acquisition of large new wholesale account	
Unexpected bankruptcy of a key supplier	

Please note that whilst the use of these ratios is invaluable to middle management in setting targets and controlling the management of these three areas, the calculation of these ratios is often impossible for anybody external to the organisation, as the information is simply not made available. Because of stock fluctuations throughout the year, the balance sheet entry for stock can be seen only as a crude approximation to a true average stock figure. The published profit and loss account does not tell you the proportion of purchases made on credit, nor does it give you information about the relative percentages of cash and credit sales. For these reasons, any external assessment of the ratios must be interpreted with a great deal of caution.

In summary, resource utilisation, as measured by the asset turnover ratio, is monitored and controlled by managing the relationship between the overall investment in the business and the level of sales generated through that investment. In particular, middle management is responsible for controlling the working-capital position, or liquidity, of the business. This is achieved through the implementation of effective systems of stock, debtor and creditor control.

8.4 Profitability

Just as important as the question concerning the level of sales generated from an existing resource base is the question how profitable each sale actually is. In other words, we want to know, for each pound spent by the customers, how many pence are needed to cover costs and how many are left over as profit to be distributed or reinvested in the business?

A business organisation's *PROFITABILITY* is defined as the relationship of the volume of sales activity generated to the actual profits obtained through this.

As you know from studying Chapter 3, the profitability of a business can be assessed by looking at the profit and loss account. Making use of the figures provided there, two key profitability ratios can be calculated, the *NET MARGIN* and the *GROSS MARGIN*. This section is concerned with the calculation and interpretation of these ratios and discusses how profitability can be influenced through pricing policy and efficient cost management.

Net margin

The net margin ratio allows an assessment of the overall profitability of a business over a given time period by comparing the level of net trading profit achieved to the level of sales volume. The formula used is:

Net margin formula

$$\text{Net margin} = \frac{\text{Net profit}}{\text{Sales}} * 100$$

The meaning of this is that for a business where the net margin is 10 per cent, for every £100 worth of sales, £10 are pure profit after the cost of goods and all operating expenses have been paid for. This also indicates how much profitability could be allowed to decline before the business would make a loss.

Net margin is influenced by the pricing policy of the business (as measured through gross margin and *MARK-UP*) and through the control of expenses.

Gross margin

The gross margin ratio expresses, as a percentage, the gross profit in relation to sales. The formula used to calculate this ratio is:

Gross margin formula

$$\text{Gross margin} = \frac{\text{Gross profit}}{\text{Sales}} * 100$$

For example, a gross margin of 30 per cent means that for every £100 of sales, the business made £30 gross profit.

Gross margins vary considerably between industries and there is often a trade-off between stock turnover and gross margin. Thus a retailer of designer fashion items would obtain a relatively low stock turnover, but very high gross margins, whereas a grocer's ratios would be the other way round. Likewise, manufacturers often need to achieve higher gross margins than retailers, as the goods are tied up for longer in the production process.

More generally, gross margin is determined by the company's pricing policy, its ability to obtain discounts for bulk buying and generally the buyers' negotiating skills.

Buyers often make use of the mark-up ratio as a pricing tool. This ratio is very closely related to the gross margin and you must take care not to confuse the two. It is calculated using the following formula:

Mark-up formula

$$\text{Mark-up} = \frac{\text{Gross profit}}{\text{Cost of goods sold}} * 100$$

When determining the appropriate mark-up, the buyer must take into account the desired *strategic positioning* of the business's offering relative to the competition. Quite often there is a trade-off between prices charged and sales volumes obtainable. At one end of the market there may be high quality image operators charging premium prices and selling relatively small volumes; at the other end there will be discounters selling very high quantities at low prices. This relationship is discussed in greater detail in Chapter 10.

Example

Figure 8.8 further illustrates the differences in profitability ratios commonly found when comparing different types of business organisations.

The calculations of the profitability ratios are set out in Figure 8.9.

The ratios in Figure 8.9 can be interpreted as follows. In this example both businesses have achieved the same level of sales. However, the manufacturer is overall more profitable than the retailer. This is largely due to differences in pricing policies. Whilst the manufacturer's expenses are twice as high as the retailer's, the manufacturer applies a mark-up of 114 per cent, as compared to only 50 per cent for the retailer.

FIGURE 8.8

COMPARISON OF THE PROFITABILITY OF TWO BUSINESSES

Retailer X	£	Manufacturer Y	£
Sales	15 000	Sales	15 000
Cost of Goods	10 000	Cost of Goods	7 000
Gross Profit	5 000	Gross Profit	8 000
Expenses	2 000	Expenses	4 000
Net Profit	3 000	Net Profit	4 000

FIGURE 8.9

COMPARISON OF PROFITABILITY RATIOS

Retailer X

Net margin $= \frac{£3\,000}{£15\,000} * 100 = 20\%$

Gross margin $= \frac{£5\,000}{£15\,000} * 100 = 33.33\%$

Mark-up $= \frac{£5\,000}{£10\,000} * 100 = 50\%$

Manufacturer Y

Net margin $= \frac{£4\,000}{£15\,000} * 100 = 26.67\%$

Gross margin $= \frac{£8\,000}{£15\,000} * 100 = 53.33\%$

Mark-up $= \frac{£8\,000}{£7\,000} * 100 = 114\%$

Exercise 8.5

Figure 8.10 shows extracts from the profit and loss accounts of two businesses operating in the same industry. One is a premium priced operator offering large diversity and quality of assortment, whereas the other is a discounter and the cost leader of the industry.

Calculate the missing figures and work out the net margin, gross margin and mark-up for the two businesses. Interpret the figures in the light of the information provided about the companies.

FIGURE 8.10

SUMMARY PROFIT AND LOSS ACCOUNTS

Business X		**Business Y**	
	£000		£000
Sales	800	Sales	600
Cost of Goods Sold	700	Cost of Goods Sold	400
Gross Profit		Gross Profit	
Expenses	80	Expenses	150
Net Profit		Net Profit	

8.5 Assessing and building performance

Whilst a detailed ratio analysis has an important part to play in monitoring and controlling the management of the key resource areas of the business, at the end of the day, investors require a simple key indicator which encompasses and summarises all the other ratios and gives them a conclusive answer to the key question as to how the business has performed compared to other firms in the industry.

The term *PERFORMANCE* describes how much profit has been generated for each £1 invested in the business.

The key ratio is the *RETURN ON CAPITAL EMPLOYED (ROCE)*. This ratio is calculated using the following formula:

Return on capital employed formula

$$\text{ROCE} = \frac{\text{Net profit}}{\text{Net total assets}} * 100$$

The balance sheet equation states that net total assets equal capital employed – thus we have a measure of profitability in relation to investment. To give an example, an ROCE of 24 per cent means that for every £100 put into the business by the investors, during the financial period in question, £24 net profit has been generated.

As discussed above, business performance, as measured by the ROCE, is influenced by two key elements, namely resource utilisation and profitability and the ratio is indeed composed of those two elements:

Return on capital employed formula

$$\text{ROCE} = \frac{\text{Sales}}{\text{Net total assets}} * \frac{\text{Net profit}}{\text{Sales}}$$

or

$$\text{ROCE} = \text{Asset turnover} * \text{Net margin}$$

Exercise 8.6

Making use of the financial information provided in Figure 8.11, complete the following tasks.

(a) Indicate the correct answer to the following questions.

- Which firm has the higher gross margin?
- Which firm is more profitable overall?
- Which firm has the higher capital investment?
- Which firm generates the higher value of sales in relation to its capital investment?
- Which firm is most liquid?
- Which firm has the higher ROCE?

(b) Critically examine the extent to which the differences in the ratios for the above companies can be explained by the fact that one is a retailer and the other a manufacturer.

FIGURE 8.11

COMPARISON OF KEY RATIOS FOR A RETAILER AND A MANUFACTURER

Retailer A: Extract from Balance Sheet		**Manufacturer B: Extract from Balance Sheet**	
	£		£
Fixed Assets	25 000	Fixed Assets	40 000
Current Assets		Current Assets	
Stock	3 000	Stock	5 000
Debtors	1 000	Debtors	5 000
Cash	1 000	Cash	1 000
Current Liabilities		Current Liabilities	
Creditors	7 000	Creditors	6 000
Extract from Profit and Loss		**Extract from Profit and Loss**	
	£		£
Sales	100 000	Sales	100 000
Cost of Goods Sold	80 000	Cost of Goods Sold	50 000
Expenses	10 000	Expenses	30 000

8.6 Summary

This chapter has provided a detailed guide to the calculation and interpretation of key ratios and demonstrated how ratio analysis can be used to assess and monitor the strengths and weaknesses of a business in managing its resources, over time and compared to other operators. An assessment of overall performance, as measured by the ROCE, was used as the focal point to which other ratios were related. The ROCE is determined by resource utilisation, as measured through asset turnover and through profitability, as reflected in net margin. The management of these two key areas was discussed and further ratios introduced which are useful tools for monitoring and control. Thus the current ratio and acid test are used to monitor liquidity and can be influenced at the operating level through the efficient and effective management of stock, debtor and creditor levels. Likewise profitability can be managed through the company's pricing policy, as reflected in the mark-up and gross margin ratios and through the control of costs.

9

Returns to Investors

9.1 Learning objectives

When you have finished working through this chapter you should be able to

- Distinguish between **SHARE FINANCE** and long-term **LOAN FINANCE** and discuss the advantages and disadvantages of the two forms of finance
- Assess the performance of an investment in shares, using the ratios **EARNINGS PER SHARE (EPS)**, **DIVIDEND PER SHARE (DPS)**, **DIVIDEND COVER**, **DIVIDEND YIELD** and the **PRICE EARNINGS RATIO**
- In the context of a simple example, calculate **GEARING** and show the impact of gearing on returns to shareholders by calculating **RETURN ON SHAREHOLDERS' FUNDS (ROSF)**

9.2 Investment ratios

In Chapter 8 you learned how to calculate and interpret a number of key ratios of interest to the management of a business. An analysis of these ratios is used to assess the comparative performance of the business over time and in light of the results achieved by the competition. Strengths and weaknesses can be identified and targets for future performance laid down.

Whilst the ratios introduced in Chapter 8 are sufficient for line management, top management and potential investors also need to consider a further set of issues to do with the broader financial performance of the business. These are related to the financial structure of the business and the potential financial returns to be gained from an investment in the business.

In the UK most large business organisations, the *PUBLIC LIMITED COMPANIES* (plcs), are financed externally through shares and loans. This means that the managers and the owners of the business are not the same, but management are accountable to the owners.

Shares represent an investment in a business where the investors fully participate in all the risks and gains of the business. There are a number of different types of shares which vary in the extent to which shareholders participate in the risks and gains associated with the company's potential financial fortunes. The most common form of share is the *ORDINARY SHARE*, and all the information in this chapter relates to these. For simplicity, in the examples used, the assumption is made that the business only has ordinary shares.

The ordinary shares of plcs are traded publicly on the Stock Exchange. Once a share has been acquired, the holder of the share is entitled to receive the published annual accounts and report of the company, to attend the annual general meeting and to vote on key decisions concerning the financial management of the business. Shares can be sold to other investors through the Stock Exchange, but there is no automatic right to demand back the original amount invested. The value of the share can fluctuate depending on the business's performance and the confidence the City has in the future of the business.

Investors in shares are interested in two forms of returns: an increase in the market price of their shares, or *CAPITAL GAINS*, and the regular receipt of a part of the business's profits, in the form of *DIVIDENDS*. Both are influenced by the profitability of the business and by the confidence City analysts have in the future prospects of the company.

Earnings and dividends

Investors will be in a position to receive a share of the profits only if the business has succeeded in making a profit in the first place. Furthermore, the amount of profit available for each shareholder will also depend on the number of shares issued.

The *EARNINGS PER SHARE (EPS)* ratio shows the relationship between the financial performance of the business and the number of shares. The ratio is calculated using the following formula:

Earnings per share formula

$$\text{Earnings per share} = \frac{\text{Net profit after tax}}{\text{Number of ordinary shares}}$$

The EPS ratio indicates how much profit for a given financial period is theoretically available to be distributed to the holder of each share, should the annual general meeting decide to pay out all profits. In reality, even after a very profitable year, only a part of the profits will be distributed, as it makes sense to *reinvest* most profit in the business. The part which is paid out is called the total dividend. The *DIVIDEND PER SHARE (DPS)* ratio is calculated as follows:

Dividend per share formula

$$\text{Dividend per share} = \frac{\text{Total dividend}}{\text{Number of ordinary shares}}$$

Whilst the payout of a dividend is a way of letting the investors have their share of profits, it can also be used as a political tool. In times of poor profitability, companies often use the tactics of announcing a disproportionately high dividend to signal to investors that everything is under control and there is no need for concern. In such a situation, the calculation of the *DIVIDEND COVER* ratio allows investors to assess whether all the dividend paid is actually backed up by profits of that financial period. This is calculated using the following formula:

Dividend cover formula

$$\text{Dividend cover} = \frac{\text{Earnings per share}}{\text{Dividend per share}}$$

A dividend cover of more than one indicates that profits of the financial period in question exceeded the dividends paid out, leaving some funds for reinvestment in the business.

Capital gains

In order to be able to assess the relative value of the businesses's profits and dividends paid out to the individual investor, these must also be seen in relation to the money tied up in the shares in the first place. There are two reasons for this. First, the investor could easily put the money elsewhere, for example in a high interest bank account. Therefore it is necessary to monitor the performance of the investment constantly in order to be sure that the money is invested in the best possible way, so as to yield the highest returns. Secondly, the business's performance is likely to have an impact on the constantly fluctuating market price of the shares and it is therefore important to monitor changes in market prices to decide when to buy or sell shares.

The *DIVIDEND YIELD* ratio provides a measure of the returns received from an investment in a given share, as compared to possible alternative investments. It is calculated as follows:

Dividend yield formula

$$\text{Dividend yield} = \frac{\text{Dividend per share}}{\text{Share price}} * 100$$

This means that if a share costs £2.50 on the Stock Exchange and the dividend paid out for the year is £0.10 per share then the yield is 4 per cent. All else being equal, the investor may well be able to get more interest from a building society account. However, the investor is likely to see dividend yield in the light of any increases in the market price of the shares over time and may find a low yield acceptable as long as the market price is rising steadily.

Note that in calculating dividend yield, you are working out the relationship of the most recent historical dividend to the current market price of the share, as quoted in the financial press. This is only a rough and ready indicator, since market prices of shares fluctuate. Also, there is no guarantee that historical dividends will be maintained in the current year.

Market prices of shares are partly related to the earnings capacity of the business, as expressed by its past performance, but they are also determined by the *subjective opinions* of market analysts who guide the large insurance companies and pension funds, the main investors in the UK, towards buying and selling certain types of shares in the light of overall economic and market conditions. Market confidence can be assessed by calculating the *PRICE EARNINGS RATIO (P/E)*, using the following formula:

P/E ratio formula

$$\text{Price Earnings ratio} = \frac{\text{Share price}}{\text{Earnings per share}}$$

A high P/E ratio means that the current market price of a share is quite high in relation to the earnings generated by the business. This implies that the City analysts have confidence in the future performance of the business and have encouraged investors to purchase these shares, which has pushed the price up.

When using investment ratios, ideally you should take care only to compare the performance of companies in the same industry sector. Where a key player is part of a larger conglomerate, an evaluation of the investment ratios can get very difficult, as you are no longer comparing like with like.

Example

Having recently won a substantial amount of money in the National Lottery, a novice investor is trying to decide which companies' shares to invest in. As she has always worked as a sales representative in the building and construction industry, she wishes to make an investment in this sector. Table 9.1 shows information available from the financial pages of leading UK newspapers and the company annual reports, which she is using to guide her thinking.

TABLE 9.1

BUILDING AND CONSTRUCTION PORTFOLIO 16 MAY 1995

	EPS (pence)	DPS (pence)	Price (pence) Current	Hi	Lo
Wimpey	8.26	6.9	128	138	113
Barratt	14.34	8.19	195	195	158
Banner Homes	6.0	2.1	88	108	70
Beazer Homes	12.74	6.7	149	149	122

In order to gain a greater insight into the respective performance of the companies, she decides that she needs to calculate a range of investment ratios. The calculations are shown for Wimpey in Figure 9.1.

FIGURE 9.1

WIMPEY: CALCULATION OF INVESTMENT RATIOS

$$\text{Dividend cover} = \frac{\text{Earnings per share}}{\text{Dividend per share}} = \frac{8.26}{6.9} = 1.2$$

$$\text{Dividend yield} = \frac{\text{Dividend per share}}{\text{Share price}} * 100$$

$$= \frac{6.9}{128} * 100 = 5.4\%$$

$$\text{Price Earnings ratio} = \frac{\text{Share price}}{\text{Earnings per share}} = \frac{128}{8.26} = 15.5$$

Exercise 9.1

Using Wimpey as an example, complete Table 9.2 in the same way.

TABLE 9.2

PORTFOLIO PERFORMANCE

	Dividend Cover	Dividend Yield	P/E Ratio
Wimpey	1.20	5.4%	15.5
Barratt			
Banner Homes			
Beazer Homes			

Interpretation of these figures implies contrasting and comparing the performance of the shares throughout in order to assess their potential as a prospective investment. The following picture emerges.

Barratt had the highest EPS and DPS, closely followed by Beazer Homes. Also, both their current share prices are at the highest point they have been for the financial period. Banner Homes had the lowest EPS, but this has resulted in a very cautious DPS, so that cover is highest for Banner, thus reassuring shareholders that prudent management and reinvestment of the currently low profits may result in better returns in the future. For Wimpey, the picture is different; here EPS are the second lowest of the four, but DPS is the second highest. This tactic serves to reassure shareholders that the currently low profitability is only a 'blip' in an otherwise good track record. This is also reflected in a high dividend yield and the highest P/E ratio of all four. The high P/E ratio shows that the market has confidence in the future performance of the company.

Exercise 9.2

During the late 1980s and early 1990s the large UK grocery chains competed fiercely in a move away from the traditional high street sites towards out-of-town superstore developments. By 1994, the market appeared to be reaching saturation point. At the same time, the property market was depressed, putting downward pressure on site values. As a result, the major grocers decided to modify their accounting treatment of fixed assets in order to reflect this. Table 9.3 offers an insight into some of the key performance statistics for two leading food retailers.

TABLE 9.3

FOOD RETAILING STATISTICS

Sainsbury (Group)

	Total Sales Area (000 sq ft)	EPS (pence)	DPS (pence)
1993	14 186	28.5	10.0
1994	15 297	8.0	10.6

	EPS (pence)	DPS (pence)	Share Price (pence) Current	Hi	Lo
May 1995	30.3	14.93	439	440	403

Kwik Save

	Total Sales Area (000 sq ft)	EPS (pence)	DPS (pence)
1993	5 400	55.5	18.3
1994	6 000	57.3	19.3

	EPS (pence)	DPS (pence)	Share Price (pence) Current	Hi	Lo
May 1995	55.6	24.5	584	611	519

(a) Use the information provided to calculate dividend cover, as well as dividend yield and the P/E ratio for the current, highest and lowest share price for the two organisations for May 1995.

(b) Contrast and compare the performance of Kwik Save with that of Sainsbury, discussing reasons behind the figures where possible. Indicate any further information you might require to make an investment decision, assuming that it is your intention to use your own personal funds to invest in company shares.

9.3 Capital structure

The *CAPITAL STRUCTURE* of a business organisation is defined as the combination of different sources of long-term finance which makes up the overall investment in the company. There are two main sources of long-term finance for any business, the owners' investment in the form of share finance plus any retained profits, and long-term loan finance.

Gearing

In the analysis of capital structure the term *GEARING* is used to describe the proportions to which a business's long-term financial structure is founded on debt on one hand and on share finance on the other. The gearing ratio is calculated using the following formula:

Gearing formula

$$\text{Gearing} = \frac{\text{Share capital} + \text{Long-term loan capital}}{\text{Share capital}}$$

For example if a business has £100 000 worth of share finance and takes out a long-term loan of £50 000, then gearing would be calculated as demonstrated in Figure 9.2.

FIGURE 9.2

CALCULATION OF GEARING

$$\text{Gearing} = \frac{£100\,000 + £50\,000}{£100\,000} = \frac{£150\,000}{£100000} = 1.5$$

This means that overall the amount of money invested in the business is 1.5 times that raised through share finance alone. The level of gearing acceptable at any point in time depends largely on the profitability of the business and management attitudes towards risk.

Impact of gearing on returns to shareholders

As stated above, large business organisations are financed through shares and loans. Whilst the shareholders have no automatic right to repayment and share in all the risks and profits of the business, *LOAN FINANCE* works on the principle that a set interest rate is paid (this is an expense before taxation) and eventually the loan is repaid in full, regardless of whether or not the business has made a profit.

Both forms of finance have their advantages and disadvantages. From the point of view of the top managers of the business, the main advantage of using share finance is that it gives them greater discretion in the distribution of profits due to a lack of legal obligations to pay out part of the profits. The shareholders take all the risks. If the business makes a loss, they have no legal right to a dividend and if the worst comes to the worst and the business goes under they have to accept the loss of their investment. The disadvantage is that the more shares there are the thinner the earnings are spread which will be reflected in a low EPS ratio. This problem can be addressed through the use of loan finance which can be used to boost the returns to shareholders. Clearly any additional finance raised for the business is set to work in order to generate more turnover and more profits. When the business is making a healthy profit, there is still only a set interest rate payable on loan finance. This means that any additional profit over and above the interest payment is available to be shared amongst existing shareholders. However, the drawback is that in times of low profitability the interest still needs to be paid, and this can turn what would have been a modest profit into a loss. As a result, businesses often opt for low gearing in times of recession when there is a greater danger of profits being low, whereas higher gearing is popular in times of economic boom.

Example

Two recently set up competing companies have the same overall capital investment. They differ, however, in their financial structure as set out in Figure 9.3.

FIGURE 9.3

COMPARISON OF TWO COMPANIES: FINANCIAL STRUCTURE

	Company **A**	Company **B**
Ordinary Shares (@ £1 each)	£200 000	£ 60 000
Long-term Loan (10% interest)	0	£140 000
Total Capital Employed	£200 000	£200 000

As the companies are new to the market, forecasting profitability is difficult and market conditions uncertain. It is therefore considered prudent to plan for three different profit scenarios, as set out in Table 9.4.

An evaluation of the expected EPS of the two companies shows that financial structure can make a big difference.If we ignore taxation for simplicity, for the optimistic profit forecast for Company **A**, EPS is calculated as shown in Figure 9.4.

For company **B**, the payment of 10 per cent interest on the £140 000 loan is an additional expense in the

TABLE 9.4

SCENARIOS FOR CONTINGENCY PLANNING

Scenario	**Profit Forecast (ignoring tax)** £
Optimistic	40 000
Indifferent	20 000
Pessimistic	10 000

profit and loss account which must be taken into account in the profit calculation before EPS can be worked out. However, the remaining profit is shared amongst fewer shares. The EPS calculation for Company **B** is also presented in Figure 9.4.

FIGURE 9.4

EPS CALCULATIONS

$$\text{Earnings per share} = \frac{\text{Net profit}}{\text{Number of ordinary shares}}$$

Company A

$$\text{EPS} = \frac{£40\,000}{200\,000} = £0.20$$

Company B

$$\text{EPS} = \frac{£40\,000 - £14\,000}{60\,000} = £0.43 \text{ (rounded)}$$

The impact of the difference in financial structure between the two companies at high profit levels is that the returns to the shareholders of the highly geared Company **B** are enhanced.

This effect can be expressed through the calculation of a further ratio, the *RETURN ON SHAREHOLDERS' FUNDS* ratio. This ratio is calculated using the following formula:

Return on shareholders' funds formula

Return on shareholders' funds

$$= \frac{\text{Net Profit (\textit{minus} loan interest)}}{\text{Share finance}}$$

In this example, for the optimistic profit forecast of £40 000, ROSF for the two companies is shown in Figure 9.5.

FIGURE 9.5

ROSF CALCULATIONS

	Company A	**Company B**
ROSF	$\frac{£40\,000}{£200\,000}$	$\frac{£40\,000 - £14\,000}{£60\,000}$
ROSF	= 0.20	= 0.43

This shows that for Company **A**, the return on shareholders investment was 20 per cent or 20 pence in every £1 invested in shares, whereas for shareholders in Company **B** it was 43 per cent or 43 pence in every £1 invested.

Please note that the ROSF ratio is simply the ROCE multiplied by the gearing figure, as shown Figure 9.6.

FIGURE 9.6

IMPACT OF GEARING ON PERFORMANCE

Equations used:

$$\text{ROCE} = \frac{\text{Net profit (\textit{minus} Loan interest)}}{\text{Net total assets}}$$

(with Net total assets = Total capital employed as follows from the balance sheet equation)

and

ROSF = ROCE * Gearing

	Company A	**Company B**
Profit forecast:	£40 000	
ROCE	$\frac{£40\,000}{£200\,000}$	$\frac{£40\,000 - £14\,000}{£200\,000}$
	= 0.20	= 0.13
*		
Gearing	1	3.3
=		
ROSF	0.20	0.43

Exercise 9.3

(a) For Company **A** and Company **B** in the example above, compare EPS and ROSF for the two remaining projected profit levels
(b) Calculate the gearing ratio for both companies
(c) Discuss your findings

Exercise 9.3 illustrates the fact that the calculation of the gearing and ROSF ratios is important for the financial manager as well as for the potential investor as it reflects the risk involved in the way the business is financed. From the company's point of view, share finance is a fairly risk free source of finance, as the owners are not legally entitled to get their money back and they do not have an automatic right to dividends either. In contrast, long-term loan finance is more risky. It has to be repaid in full at an agreed future point in time, and in the meantime interest must be paid. This can be a heavy financial commitment if the business is going through a bad patch.

From the investors' point of view, much depends on the attitude taken towards risk. Investment in the shares of a highly geared company can offer enhanced returns. However, the higher risk associated with this also implies the potential of greater losses, if profits are depressed.

All this means that top management must weigh up the potential risks and returns very carefully when deciding which level of gearing is right for their company at any given point in time and they must constantly monitor profitability and economic conditions to assess the need for any adjustments to the financial structure of the business.

Exercise 9.4

Use the information presented in Figure 9.7 to evaluate the comparative performance of two companies.

(a) Based on a comprehensive analysis of the ratios you calculate from the figures presented in Figure 9.7, answer the following questions:

- Which company has the higher net margin?
- Which company has the higher capital investment?
- Which company has the higher asset turnover?

FIGURE 9.7

COMPARISON OF COMPANY PERFORMANCE

	Company X	Company Y
	£	£
Fixed Assets	70 000	111 000
Current Assets		
Stock	15 000	5 000
Debtors	10 000	2 000
Cash and Bank	10 000	0
Current Liabilities		
Creditors	5 000	15 000
Bank Overdraft	0	3 000
Sales	160 000	150 000
Cost of Goods Sold	80 000	80 000
Net Profit	12 000	15 000

- Which company has the higher return on capital employed?
- Which one would you invest in? Give reasons for your choice.

(b) The shareholders of Company **X** are convinced that their earnings from their shareholding could be boosted further by taking out loan finance to fund an expansion programme. This would finally give them a competitive edge over Company **Y**. Currently Company **X**'s capital consists of 100 000 £1 shares, in other words, it is pure share finance (we are assuming for simplicity that all shares have a balance sheet value as well as a market value of £1).

Calculate EPS based on the figures given above, ignoring taxation.

It is intended that a further £100 000 will be raised for the expansion of the business. Two alternatives are suggested:

- It could be in the form of further share finance, bringing this to 200 000 £1 shares
- It could be in the form of a 15 per cent debenture loan, repayable in the year 2010 (this means that the loan becomes repayable in full in the year 2010, in the meantime interest has to be paid at a rate of 15 per cent)

For both alternatives, the possible profit levels predicted for the first year are shown in Table 9.5.

TABLE 9.5

PROFIT FORECASTS	
State of the Economy	**Profit before Loan Interest**
	£
Recession	10 000
Indifferent	25 000
Boom	40 000

Compare EPS and ROSF for the two alternatives for each of the three scenarios.

9.4 Summary

In this chapter the use of ratio analysis for investors and financial managers was introduced. Examples were used to show the use of the ratios EPS, DPS, P/E, dividend cover and dividend yield in assessing investment performance. The advantages and disadvantages of share finance and long-term loan finance were discussed and the gearing ratio as a measure of capital structure introduced. The impact of gearing on returns to shareholders was discussed and illustrated with examples, making use of the return on shareholders' funds ratio.

10
Analysis of Profit Pathways

10.1 Learning objectives

When you have finished working through this chapter you should be able to

- Discuss how the ratios covered in previous chapters relate to each other and construct a **PROFIT TREE** to show the profitability pathways adopted by an organisation
- Make use of the information provided in the profit tree to construct a coherent and logical argument identifying the reasons behind an organisation's performance and relating overall performance back to decisions and systems at the operational level
- Use the profit tree model to carry out a detailed comparative analysis and interpretation of two sets of accounts
- Make use of a spreadsheet to construct a **TEMPLATE** for the profit tree model
- Use the profit tree spreadsheet to examine the impact of a range of proposed changes at the operating level on the overall future performance of the business

10.2 Constructing the profit tree

Having worked through Chapters 8 and 9, you have probably noticed that none of the ratios exist in isolation, but they are all linked together and influence each other. When you carry out a detailed ratio analysis, it is therefore important to show these links in your interpretation of the ratios and to demonstrate that you understand how the various measures of an organisation's activities at the operating level translate into wider measures of overall performance, such as ROCE and ROSF. In this, there can be a number of alternative ways of achieving a similar ROCE, as there are often trade-offs between business decisions.

Exercise 10.1

Table 10.1 shows the ratios for two competing retailers. One is a discount operator, trading from a market stall. The other is a premium priced operator, trading from upmarket high street premises.

TABLE 10.1

COMPARISON OF PERFORMANCE RATIOS

	Discounter	Premium Priced
ROCE	14%	14%
Net margin	2%	10%
Asset turnover	7 times	1.4 times

FIGURE 10.1

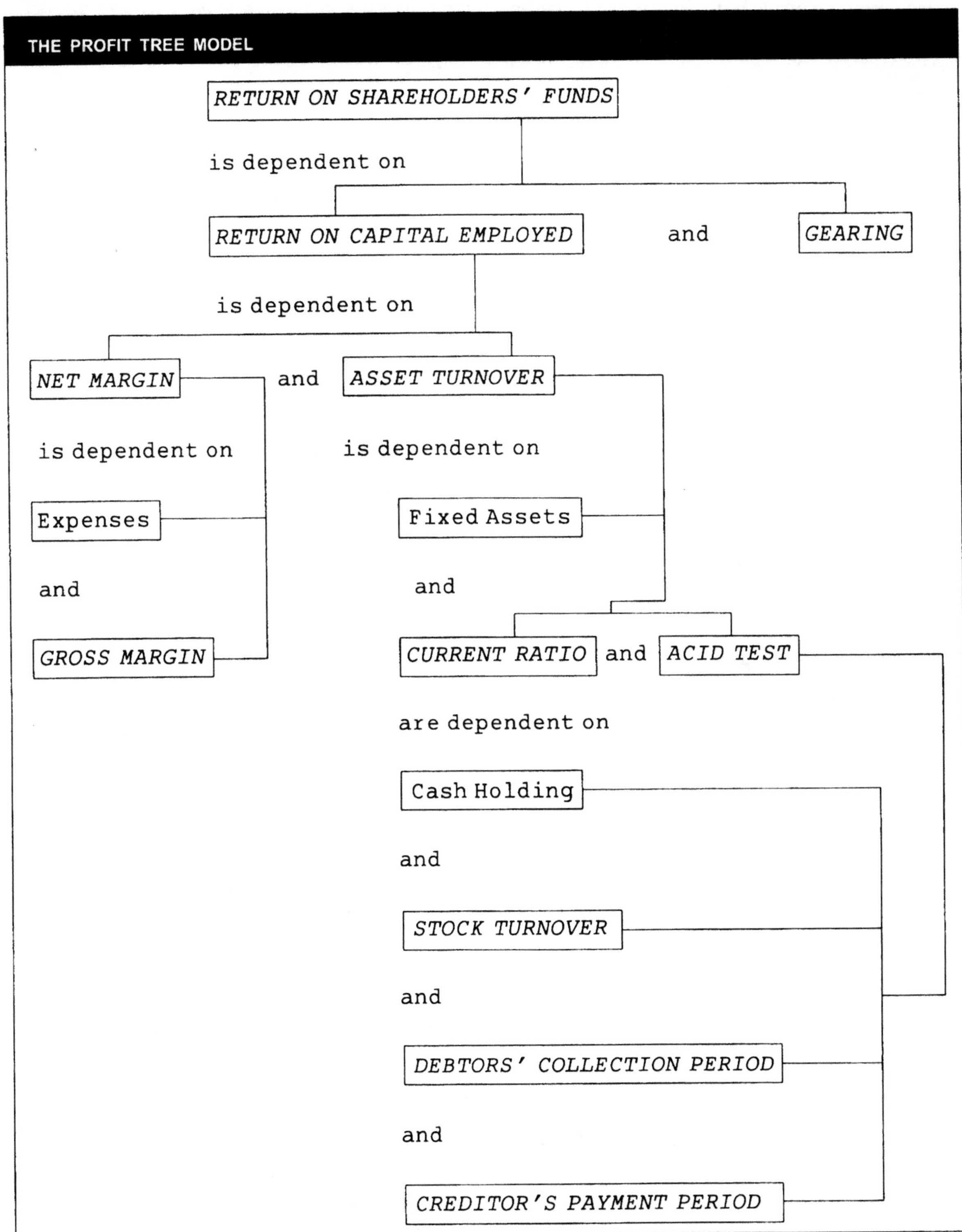
THE PROFIT TREE MODEL
RETURN ON SHAREHOLDERS' FUNDS
is dependent on
RETURN ON CAPITAL EMPLOYED
and
GEARING
is dependent on
NET MARGIN
and
ASSET TURNOVER
is dependent on
Expenses
and
GROSS MARGIN
is dependent on
Fixed Assets
and
CURRENT RATIO
and
ACID TEST
are dependent on
Cash Holding
and
STOCK TURNOVER
and
DEBTORS' COLLECTION PERIOD
and
CREDITOR'S PAYMENT PERIOD

Explain how the ratios show the difference in the strategic path chosen by the two businesses to achieve the same overall performance as measured by the ROCE.

Exercise 10.1 illustrates that the same overall performance, as measured by ROCE, can be achieved through very different strategic approaches. The discounter has only a minimal capital investment in the market stall, charges relatively low prices and therefore achieves very high turnover. In contrast the premium priced operator has invested in more expensive premises to create the kind of image and ambience which encourages customers to put up with much higher prices.

This shows that it would be wrong to try and interpret any one of the ratios on its own and judge it against some 'ideal' standard. Interpretation must take a holistic approach and look at all the ratios together, making links between the different areas. Also, it is always advisable to take a historic perspective and look at developments over a number of financial periods to get the bigger picture. In addition, wherever possible, a comparison with industry standards should be used as a yardstick for the evaluation.

An assessment of the interplay between the different areas the ratios measure is made easier by constructing a *PROFIT TREE* model, as shown in Figure 10.1. The model shows the conceptual links between the ratios and traces the interpretation of what is behind the overall performance of the business all the way back to the activities carried out at the shop floor operating level.

This model can be used as a guide to interpretation. The model takes the form of a tree, branching out from the ROSF ratio. You can take each branch in turn and investigate what went into creating the overall picture.

Exercise 10.2

The profit and loss statements and balance sheets presented in Figures 10.2 to 10.5 are adapted from the annual accounts for J Sainsbury plc, 1993 and 1994. The sales figures presented exclude VAT and sales taxes, the net profit figures refer to profit on ordinary activities before tax and after loan interest.

For both years, calculate the following ratios:

- ROSF
- Gearing
- ROCE
- Net margin
- Asset turnover
- Current ratio
- Acid test
- Stock turnover

Please note that, as an outsider, you cannot calculate debtors' collection period and creditors' payment period, as you do not have access to the information on how much was bought and sold on credit as opposed to cash terms. So when interpreting the figures, refer back to the actual entry for debtors and creditors instead.

Having calculated the ratios in Exercise 10.2 above, we now need to consider how we can interpret the figures, making links between the ratios and seeing the overall performance of the business as a result of strategic and operating decisions taken.

Figure 10.6 shows how the ratios calculated in Exercise 10.2 look if you put them all together into the model. In this case, in 1993 a ROSF of 24.19 per cent was brought about by a ROCE of 19.5 per cent and the multiplier effect of a gearing of 1.24. By 1994, ROSF had fallen to 12.13 per cent. This was mostly due to a drop in ROCE to a level of 9.9 per cent, with gearing relatively stable. You can find an explanation for the drop in ROCE by investigating the branches of the tree. As you probably recall from Chapter 8, ROCE is determined by profitability on one hand and resource utilisation on the other. These are represented by the two branches starting with Net margin and Asset turnover respectively. You can therefore take each in turn and look at the further ratios which net margin and asset turnover depend on.

First, profitability in 1993 is summarised by a net margin of 7.6 per cent. However, by 1994 this had fallen to a mere 3.5 per cent. Looking further along the branches of the model, this drop was due to two key factors. Between 1993 and 1994, expenses increased quite dramatically from £264.1m to £639.9m. If you read through the 1994 company report, you will find that this increase was due to a company decision to respond to a drop in demand for

FIGURE 10.2

J SAINSBURY PLC (GROUP): PROFIT AND LOSS ACCOUNT FOR THE PERIOD MARCH 1992 TO MARCH 1993

		£m
	Sales	9685.5
–	Cost of Goods Sold	8688.9
=	Gross Profit	996.6
–	Expenses	263.8
=	Net Profit (before tax)	732.8

FIGURE 10.3

J SAINSBURY PLC (GROUP): BALANCE SHEET AS AT 12 MARCH 1993

	£m	£m
Fixed Assets		4477.9
Current Assets		
Stock	448.2	
Debtors	95.3	
Cash and Bank	260.5	
Creditors: due within one year		
Trade Creditors	1524.6	
		(–720.6)
Net Total Assets		3757.3
Creditors: due after one year		
Long-term Loan Capital		728.6
		3028.7
Share Capital		3028.7

FIGURE 10.4

J SAINSBURY PLC (GROUP): PROFIT AND LOSS ACCOUNT FOR THE PERIOD MARCH 1993 TO MARCH 1994

		£m
	Sales	10 583.2
–	Cost of Goods Sold	9 574.5
=	Gross Profit	1 008.7
–	Expenses	639.9
=	Net Profit (before tax)	368.8

FIGURE 10.5

J SAINSBURY PLC (GROUP): BALANCE SHEET AS AT 12 MARCH 1994

	£m	£m
Fixed Assets		4659.5
Current Assets		
Stock	460.0	
Debtors	113.0	
Cash and Bank	258.0	
Creditors: due within one year		
Trade Creditors	1782.9	
		(– 951.9)
Net Total Assets		3707.6
Creditors: due after one year		
Long-term Loan Capital		668.1
		3039.5
Share Capital		3039.5

retail sites and depressed property prices by instigating a devaluation of some of its property and by increasing depreciation charges. Also, at the same time gross margin dropped from 10.3 per cent in 1993 to 9.5 per cent in 1994, possibly as a result of increasing pressure on prices from the discounters. The combination of higher expenses and lower gross margin resulted in the large drop in net margin.

Secondly, resource utilisation is summed up by an asset turnover figure of 2.58 in 1993 and remains fairly steady with some improvements in 1994. This is explained by looking at changes in fixed assets and liquidity. The overall investment in fixed assets increased only slightly even though further stores were built. This was due to the revaluation mentioned above.

FIGURE 10.6

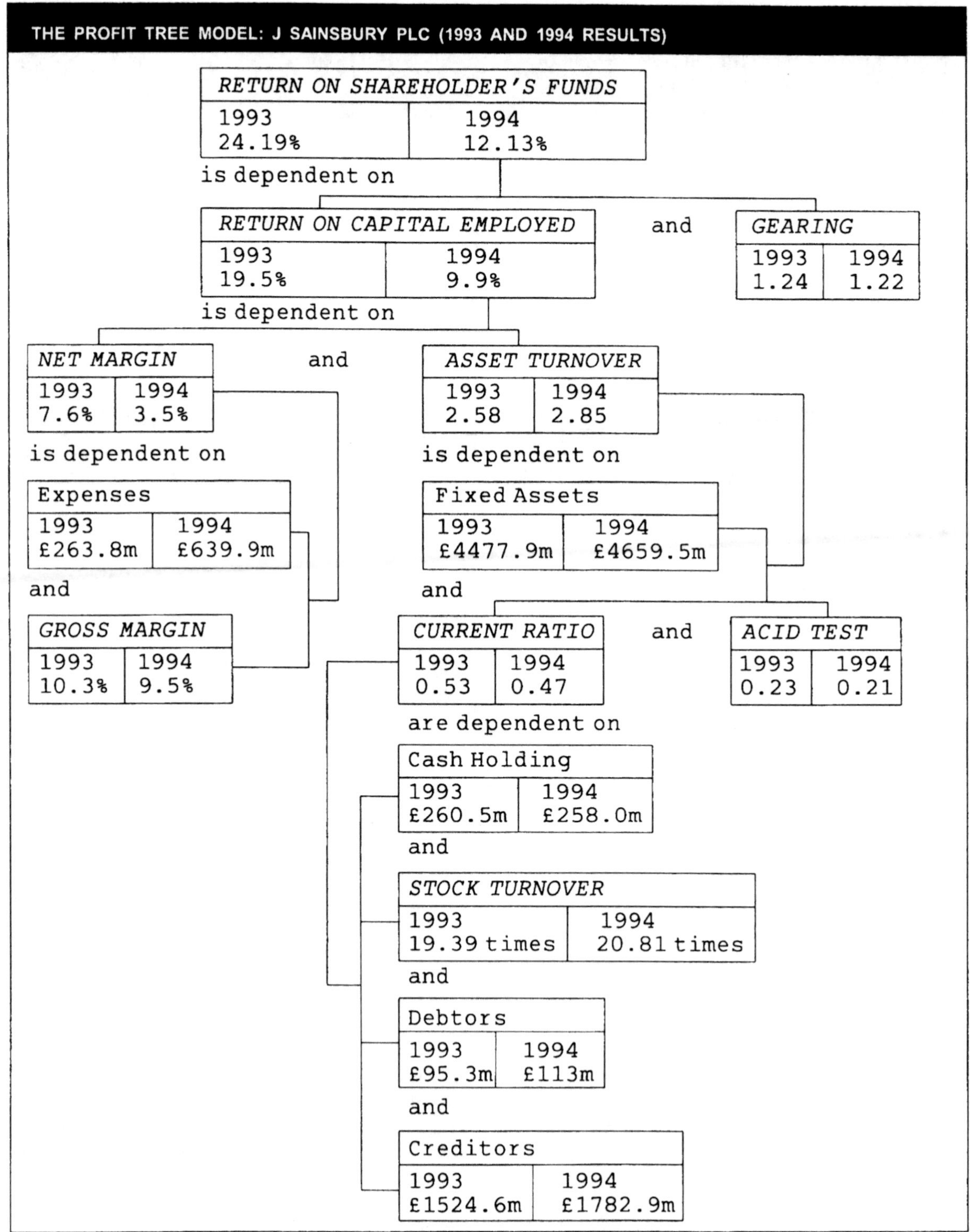
THE PROFIT TREE MODEL: J SAINSBURY PLC (1993 AND 1994 RESULTS)
RETURN ON SHAREHOLDER'S FUNDS
1993
24.19%
1994
12.13%
is dependent on
RETURN ON CAPITAL EMPLOYED
1993
19.5%
1994
9.9%
and
GEARING
1993
1.24
1994
1.22
is dependent on
NET MARGIN
1993
7.6%
1994
3.5%
and
ASSET TURNOVER
1993
2.58
1994
2.85
is dependent on
Expenses
1993
£263.8m
1994
£639.9m
and
GROSS MARGIN
1993
10.3%
1994
9.5%
is dependent on
Fixed Assets
1993
£4477.9m
1994
£4659.5m
and
CURRENT RATIO
1993
0.53
1994
0.47
and
ACID TEST
1993
0.23
1994
0.21
are dependent on
Cash Holding
1993
£260.5m
1994
£258.0m
and
STOCK TURNOVER
1993
19.39 times
1994
20.81 times
and
Debtors
1993
£95.3m
1994
£113m
and
Creditors
1993
£1524.6m
1994
£1782.9m

A slight decrease in liquidity, as measured by the current ratio and the acid test, also shows that management were trying very hard to counterbalance the drop in profitability by making their assets work harder and achieving greater resource utilisation. The difference between the current ratio and the acid test points to the importance of the stock turnover ratio, which in this case increased from 19.39 to 20.81 times. Improvements in stock turnover indicate effective use of information technology, such as sales-based ordering and electronic data interchange (EDI). As noted earlier, outsiders cannot calculate the debtors' collection period and the creditors' payment period, but using the figures for debtors and creditors, we can assess liquidity further. Thus the relatively low liquidity of the business is tentatively explained by the high level of amounts owed to trade creditors, indicating relatively long payment periods and a high degree of buyer power. On the other hand supermarkets have rather a low level of debtors, as people pay cash for their groceries.

Exercise 10.3

The profit and loss statement and balance sheet presented in Figures 10.7 and 10.8 are adapted from the annual accounts for Allied Domecq plc, 1994. In their original format, these accounts do not show the cost of goods sold as such. For the purposes of this exercise, cost of goods sold were taken to include raw materials, customs and excise duty, changes in stock and staff costs. Staff costs were included to reflect the strong manufacturing element of this company.

FIGURE 10.7

ALLIED DOMECQ PLC:
PROFIT AND LOSS ACCOUNT FOR THE PERIOD MARCH 1993 TO MARCH 1994

		£m
	Sales	5526
–	Cost of Goods Sold	3472
=	Gross Profit	2054
–	Expenses	1448
=	Net Profit (before tax)	606

FIGURE 10.8

ALLIED DOMECQ PLC:
BALANCE SHEET AS AT 5 MARCH 1994

	£m	£m
Fixed Assets		4001
Current Assets		
Stock	1069	
Debtors	969	
Cash and Bank	145	
Creditors: due within one year		
Trade Creditors	1655	
		528
Net Total Assets		4529
Creditors: due after one year		
Long-term Loan Capital		1828
		2701
Share Capital		2701

(a) Carry out the same calculations of ratios as in Exercise 10.2.

(b) Make use of the profit tree layout provided in Figure 10.9 and fill in the ratios and figures for Allied Domecq 1994 next to those for J Sainsbury 1994.

(c) Carry out a full interpretation of the figures, contrasting and comparing the results of the two organisations. In doing this, make full use of the logical structure provided by the profit tree to construct a logical argument which shows the links between the ratios.

10.3 Constructing a spreadsheet template for the profit tree

Exercises 10.2 and 10.3 have shown you how you can make use of the profit tree model to evaluate overall performance by looking at all the ratios in a holistic way and by taking into account how they fit together. In addition, we have observed that, depending on the nature of the business and the strategic direction

FIGURE 10.9

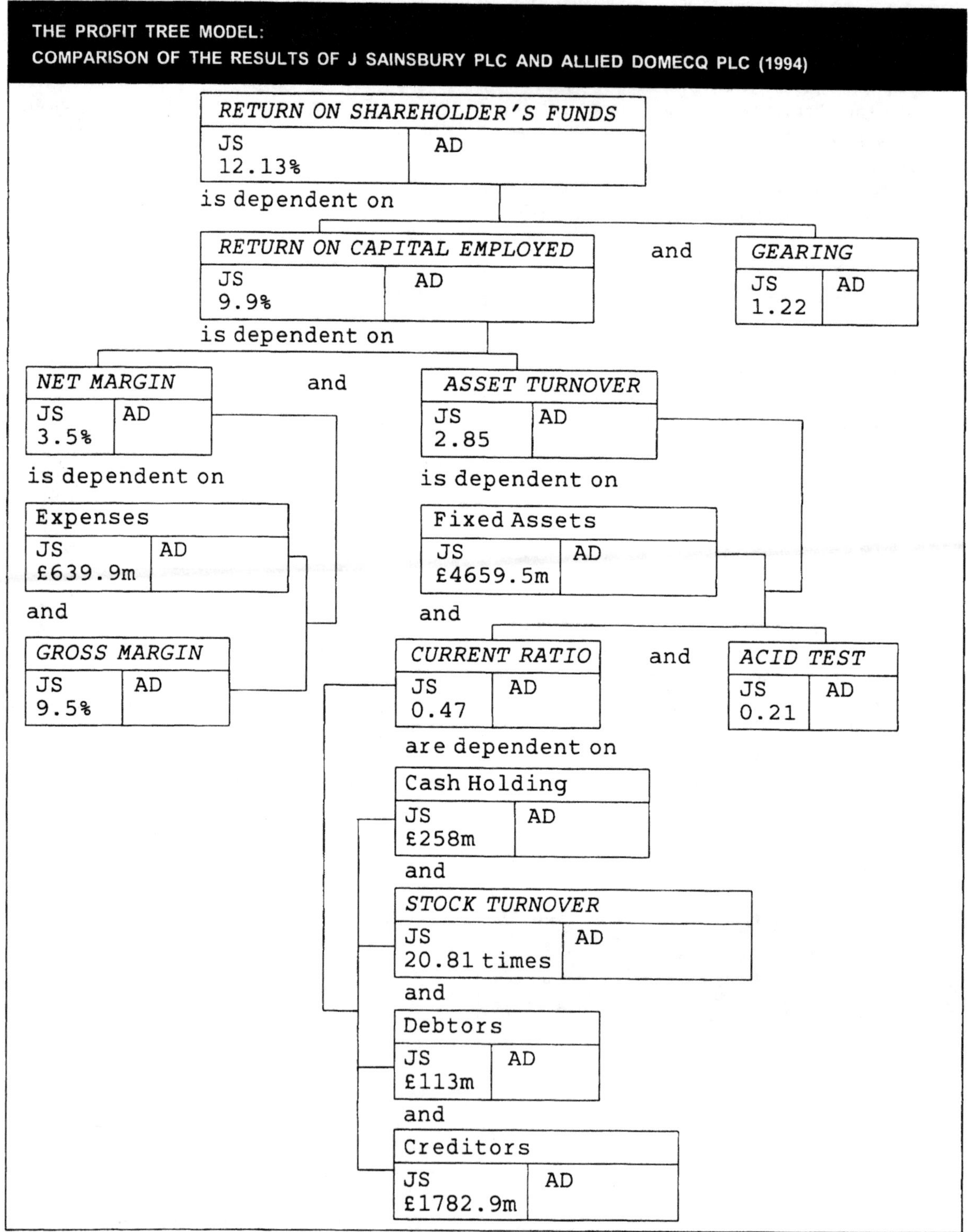
THE PROFIT TREE MODEL:
COMPARISON OF THE RESULTS OF J SAINSBURY PLC AND ALLIED DOMECQ PLC (1994)
RETURN ON SHAREHOLDER'S FUNDS
JS 12.13%
AD
is dependent on
RETURN ON CAPITAL EMPLOYED
JS 9.9%
AD
and
GEARING
JS 1.22
AD
is dependent on
NET MARGIN
JS 3.5%
AD
and
ASSET TURNOVER
JS 2.85
AD
is dependent on
Expenses
JS £639.9m
AD
and
GROSS MARGIN
JS 9.5%
AD
is dependent on
Fixed Assets
JS £4659.5m
AD
and
CURRENT RATIO
JS 0.47
AD
and
ACID TEST
JS 0.21
AD
are dependent on
Cash Holding
JS £258m
AD
and
STOCK TURNOVER
JS 20.81 times
AD
and
Debtors
JS £113m
AD
and
Creditors
JS £1782.9m
AD

chosen, different approaches can result in a similar level of overall performance.

So far, we have only considered ratio analysis as a tool for evaluating historical performance. However, this technique allows us to pinpoint the strengths and weaknesses of a business and relate them to industry averages and the wider business environment. Therefore ratio analysis can also be used to identify objectives for the future and to examine the likely impact of potential future changes in operating practices or trading conditions. Thus it can facilitate the development of a business plan for a range of scenarios and aid the assessment of the organisation's vulnerability to potential future events.

Exercise 10.4

Test your understanding of the profit tree model by assessing the impact of the future scenarios presented in Table 10.2 on the performance of the business. Indicate which ratios are affected along the branches of the model and show whether they are expected to increase or decrease as a result of the event described.

TABLE 10.2

IMPACT OF DIFFERENT SCENARIOS ON KEY RATIOS

Scenario	**Ratio Affected Increase/Decrease**
A key supplier reduces the period for trade credit	
The price of raw materials rises, resulting in higher cost of goods sold	
Stock control is improved, resulting in lower average stock	

Exercise 10.4 illustrates that planning for different scenarios implies changing individual figures in the model and assessing the overall impact of such a change. This is a form of *SENSITIVITY ANALYSIS*, as it allows the business to examine how vulnerable it is to a range of future events.

This type of analysis is greatly aided by the use of a spreadsheet.

Exercise 10.5

Plan a spreadsheet *TEMPLATE* for the profit tree model.

(a) To do this, set aside the top left hand corner of the spreadsheet as a separate data section where you are intending to input the information contained in the original profit and loss account and the balance sheet.

(b) Underneath the data section, set out the headings and formulae of the profit tree model, drawing on the cells in the data section for the actual numbers.

(c) Save the template under the name **TREE**. (An example of one possible solution to this is shown in the answer section.)

(d) Now input the figures from the 1994 Sainsbury accounts, as presented in Exercise 10.2, into the data section of the spreadsheet template. Check the profit tree, which should now show the same figures as the 1994 figures in Figure 10.2. This serves as a check that you have set out the spreadsheet correctly. Save the finished spreadsheet under a different name. You now have two files, your original profit tree template and your Sainsbury 1994 specific profit tree.

Exercise 10.6

Acting as a consultant to Sainsbury management, you have identified a number of different future scenarios and wish to evaluate their impact on the overall performance of the company. For each scenario take the Sainsbury 1994 specific profit tree spreadsheet as a starting point. Input the changes projected and evaluate the impact on performance and returns to shareholders.

Scenario 1

The pressures from discounters are such that selling prices have to be decreased. This results in a drop of the value of sales by 2 per cent, with cost of goods sold remaining at the same level.

Scenario 2
A new government introduces a high level minimum wage and enhanced pension rights for part-time staff. This results in expenses increasing by 2 per cent.

Scenario 3
The company negotiates another week's trade credit. This has the effect that the value of creditors increases by 6 per cent.

Scenario 4
The company introduces more non-food lines. As a result average stock holding increases by 7 per cent. Also the value of sales increases by 8 per cent, due to the higher prices which can be charged on these lines. Cost of goods sold only increases by 4 per cent.

Scenario 5
The company invests in new stores. As a result, the value of fixed assets increases by 15 per cent. However, the resulting sales increases are not likely to happen until two years later.

10.4 Summary

In this chapter you have learned how to make use of the profit tree model to show relationships between the ratios and evaluate company performance in a holistic way, in the light of historical trends and industry averages. To aid the use of ratio analysis in the context of sensitivity analysis and scenario planning, a spreadsheet template of the profit tree was constructed. This was used to evaluate a range of possible scenarios.

The skills of carrying out an integrated ratio analysis in the context of a real business situation can be practised further by working through Case Study 2 which follows on from this chapter and concludes Part II of the book.

Case Study 2

Carla Firenze Trading Ltd: a Benetton Franchise

This case study was compiled by Claudio Vignali, Barry J. Davies and Ruth A. Schmidt

1 Company background

At the end of 1993, Carla Firenze was looking for a business opportunity. Having had a long-standing career in management, Carla had become increasingly dissatisfied with what she perceived as a lack of autonomy with regard to important business decisions. When she was made redundant after 10 years of service and found herself footloose and fancy free, with a sizeable nest egg in the bank, she felt that she was ideally placed to become self-employed and set up her own fashion business.

In the course of researching the different business opportunities in the fashion trade, Carla was impressed with the recent growth of franchising in the UK. It seemed to Carla that this option had a lot of advantages over starting a brand new business from scratch. In franchising, the overall concept of the business is tried and tested by the franchisor. The franchisor then grants authorisation to use the established trade marks, trade name and business systems to the franchisee who has to pay an initial fee in return. This greatly reduces the risk to the franchisee and as a result franchised small businesses have a lower failure rate than other start-ups.

And no wonder, Carla thought. The availability of back-up and help, the proven concept and name must make a big difference. Franchising seemed like the best of both worlds. The individual franchises are legally separate business organisations, thus giving the owners all the advantages of self-employment. However, in the eyes of the public the impression is created that there is only one large and uniform business organisation. This means that considerable economies of scale arise in the areas of buying, marketing and distribution, which would normally be beyond the reach of a small business.

Thinking back on making her decision, Carla says:

> 'It seemed like an ideal opportunity of working for myself, but with an experienced business partner to hold my hand and guide me through the minefield of book-keeping, leasing, VAT, marketing and shop fitting, not to mention the various tax problems I felt I was likely to encounter.'

2 The Benetton system

Carla carefully researched a number of franchising organisations, amongst them Benetton. In the end,

Benetton held a particular appeal because of the Italian connection – the Firenze family had moved to the UK in the 1960s, and whilst Carla had spent all her working life in the UK, she still had strong family contacts in Italy and had some sentimental feelings for 'the old country'. However, the deciding factor was her perception of the strength and creative flair of successive Benetton advertising campaigns and their success in building and maintaining a strong global premium priced brand image.

Initial discussions with Benetton revealed the following picture. Benetton sell the rights for using their trade mark in a given geographical area and then proceed to sell their goods exclusively to the franchisee with favourable payment systems. In order to maintain a uniform company identity, Benetton exert strong control over their franchisees and determine most elements of the retail marketing mix.

The products sold through the shop are supplied exclusively by Benetton and no other products may be sold through the outlet. Ordering of new seasonal product ranges takes place 12 months in advance and this process is aided by a model stock plan supplied by the franchisor. This is semi-fixed in nature. The plan contains compulsory ranges which must be selected by the franchisee, as well as optional ranges. For the optional ranges, choice is severely restricted by the fact that for items voluntarily selected, a standard size and colour mix will automatically be supplied. By controlling the franchisee's product decisions, the franchisor can maintain a standardised store layout and colour blocking regime in all Benetton stores, thus maintaining a uniform image. Six months after the order has been made out, the whole new seasonal range is delivered at once.

The retail prices charged for the goods are determined centrally by the franchisor. Again, this serves to maintain a uniformity in the pricing policy of all Benetton shops. By comparison to other fashion ranges competing for the same market, Benetton goods are sold at premium prices. Twice a year, a 'sales' period of one month's duration takes place to clear dated seasonal stock. These sales consist entirely of the sale of marked down branded Benetton items, with no special sales items being bought in. The structure of mark-downs is dictated by the franchisor and consists of a 10 per cent – 15 per cent mark-down on selected current lines, combined with much deeper mark-downs (up to 50 per cent) on the previous season's merchandise.

Benetton's premium pricing policy is supported by centrally coordinated national and international advertising campaigns which support a quality image and maintain high brand awareness. Whilst in the late 1980s the 'United Colours of Benetton' campaign was most dominant, during the early 1990s public awareness became focused on the new and controversial campaign, which made use of visual images selected to shock. The consensus among franchisees is that the successive campaigns have resulted in a high degree of marketing exposure and that the Benetton brand is a valuable asset.

Furthermore the biannual 'sales' periods are supported by additional promotional material provided by the franchisor, including special price stickers, banners, posters and additional point of sale material. For the duration of the 'sales', the franchisees are also given some discretion to advertise locally and to use further handwritten supplementary material. Also store layout and merchandising decisions related to the sale can be taken at the store level.

3 Carla's Benetton franchise

After initial discussions with Benetton, Carla was convinced of the enormous potential of the franchised brand and decided to go ahead with the acquisition of a Benetton franchise.

With the help of Benetton guidelines for site selection she identified and finally acquired shop premises within a busy shopping centre located in the town centre of a small town in Lancashire. The shopping centre contains a mix of fashion retailers, ranging from market stalls to national operators, such as Richard Shops, River Island, BHS and Burtons. Centre management carry out regular pedestrian flow counts and the figures provided to Carla showed every indication of rising customer throughput figures.

With the aid of a Benetton representative, Carla drew up a sales forecast and business plan for presentation to her bank manager. Carla proposed to set up a private limited company and to invest her own capital of £10 000, which she had saved after her redundancy, in the business. In addition, she proposed to borrow £16 000 from the bank, repayable over a 10 year period. The bank manager was impressed with her thoroughness of preparation and said she would be happy to oblige. She explained to Carla that it was the bank's policy to give preferential treatment to requests for loan finance for the acquisition of a well-known franchise. She pointed out that the reason for this lies in the strength of the franchisor's track record and the established potential of their product, which makes a new franchise much more like an already existing venture, rather than a completely new start-up. For this reason, she not only agreed to the loan but also proposed a generous bank overdraft facility up to a limit of £12 000.

4 Two years later...

During the first two years of trading, the Firenze franchise had somewhat disappointing results, as shown in Figures C2.1 and C2.2 (p. 88). Whilst not many people would expect a new business to make a substantial profit in its first financial year, at the end of the second year Carla is beginning to feel quite concerned about the volatility of the returns, especially in view of the relatively narrow asset base, as compared to commitments to short-term creditors.

This is partly to do with trading conditions, as the population of the town she operates in is affected by high unemployment and a continuing recessionary climate. However, some of it can also be attributed to the way in which the franchisor controls the business. Whilst Carla found her expectations of a strong 'partner' fully met and is full of praise about the training and support she has received from Benetton, she does feel that the stocking policy is not flexible enough and does not allow her to respond fully to local demand. On many occasions she could have sold many more items of the popular ranges in sizes 12–16, but ran out and got stuck with the smaller sizes instead. As long as she has to order the full range included in the model stock plan, this cannot be avoided. Also, she has found that approximately 40 per cent of the annual revenue is derived from the 'sales' periods. Whilst average mark-ups of around 120 per cent are the norm during non-sales periods, these can fall to zero and sometimes result in losses of up to 10 per cent of cost prices during sales periods, as she needs the sales periods to sell off dead stock from previous seasons.

In consequence, actual profits are rather lower than those forecast in the original business plan. Carla has the uneasy feeling that the initially anticipated relationships between price, cost, sales volume and profit, which had formed the basis for her business plan, are drastically altered by this. However, she is not quite sure how to assess the exact impact of the sales period. She comments: 'I feel that essentially the recession is to blame ... There have been many redundancies in the area and people are just not willing to spend the money any more ... My main worry is what will happen if the bank really starts putting pressure on me to start reducing the overdraft. In times like these the small businesses are always hardest hit, especially if interest rates go up again ... It's all very unpredictable and worrying.'

Tasks

Acting as a financial adviser to Carla, you are required to complete the following tasks.

Task 1

Make use of your profit tree spreadsheet template to calculate a number of key ratios for Carla Firenze's Benetton franchise for the two years for which financial statements are provided in Figures C2.1 and C2.2.

Task 2

Carry out an in-depth analysis of the strengths and weaknesses of Carla Firenze's Benetton franchise. A detailed ratio analysis should form an integral part of this and you should use a discussion of the ratios to support your arguments.

Task 3

Select a major national fashion retailer listed as a plc on the Stock Exchange and get access to their latest annual report and accounts. These are available from

FIGURE C2.1

CARLA FIRENZE TRADING LTD: PROFIT AND LOSS ACCOUNT

	1 April 1995 to 31 March 1996	1 April 1994 to 31 March 1995
	£	£
Sales	122 395	110 146
Cost of Goods Sold	68 814	68 164
Gross Profit	53 581	41 982
Expenses:		
Wages	16 013	15 020
Casual labour	697	554
Social security costs	1 112	1 061
Directors' fees	2 000	–
Staff welfare	115	90
Motor expenses	1 288	971
Travelling, accommodation and subsistence	661	1 000
Entertaining	311	608
Rent and rates	11 398	11 398
Heat, light and power	1 157	1 314
Insurance	933	933
Postage	9	20
Printing and stationery	152	213
Advertising and publicity	967	1 045
Sales promotions	431	200
Theft of stock	–	1 293
Telephone	414	500
Security system rental	1 276	1 725
Repairs	536	813
Equipment maintenance	–	28
Trade subscriptions	30	10
Cleaning	207	230
Sundry expenses	408	405
Bank charges	938	23
Credit card commission	1 506	932
Bank overdraft interest	1 538	505
Bank loan interest	2 652	3 105
Auditors' remuneration	680	819
Formation expenses	–	406
Depreciation	4 113	3 918
Total Expenses	51 542	49 139
Net Profit/(Loss)	2 039	(–7 157)

FIGURE C2.2

CARLA FIRENZE TRADING LTD: BALANCE SHEET

as at	31 March 1996	31 March 1995
	£	£
Fixed Assets	41 349	45 037
Current Assets		
Stock	43 129	33 695
Debtors	11	–
Cash and Bank	778	3 236
	43 918	36 931
Creditors: due within one year		
Trade Creditors	53 979	63 682
Bank Overdraft	12 123	–
	66 102	63 682
Net Current Liabilities	(22 184)	(26 751)
Net Total Assets	19 165	18 286
Creditors: due after one year		
Bank Loan	14 283	15 443
	4 882	2 843
Shareholders' Funds:		
Share Capital	10 000	10 000
Retained Profit/(Loss)	(5 118)	(7 157)
	4 882	2 843

university and public business libraries. Alternatively you can get your own copy by writing to the company. For this retailer, carry out a detailed ratio analysis. Contrast and compare your findings to those in Task 2. Use the comparison to illustrate the differences which could be due to the great disparity in size between the two businesses examined.

Part III
Forecasting

11 Time Series Analysis

11.1 Learning objectives

When you have finished working through this chapter you should be able to

- Appreciate the need for **FORECASTING**
- Be aware of the requirements of a forecasting system
- Know that there are various quantitative forecasting methods
- Distinguish between the requirements for **SHORT-TERM** and **LONG-TERM FORECASTING**
- Be aware of the different forecasting techniques appropriate for new and for established outlets
- Understand what is meant by **TIME SERIES ANALYSIS**
- Be able to draw a **HISTORIGRAM**
- Identify the components of a time series: **TREND**, **CYCLICAL VARIATION**, **SEASONAL VARIATION** and **RESIDUAL VARIATION**
- Estimate the trend by the method of **MOVING AVERAGES**
- Estimate seasonal variations and calculate **SEASONAL ADJUSTMENT FACTORS**
- Estimate residual variations
- Be able to produce a forecast
- Be aware of the limitations of the forecasting process

11.2 Introduction to forecasting

In Parts I and II we were looking at the financial records of the business and trying to make sense of what had happened in the past. When drawing up financial statements or carrying out a ratio analysis, essentially you are concerned with the analysis of *historical* data. This can give you useful insights into the past performance of the business and may provide valuable clues as to the best future course of action to build on strengths and overcome weaknesses.

However, in order to plan for the future, just an examination of the past is not enough. Every business also needs to *forecast*. You can probably think of several variables, such as sales, demand, stock, number of employees, for which we require estimates in either the short or long term or both.

Exercise 11.1

Give three reasons why a business needs to forecast demand for its products.

In particular, sales forecasts are needed to initiate the *BUDGET*ing process which we study in detail in Part IV. Buyers in many industries, such as retail fashion, have to place orders many months in advance. Some estimates of future sales are vital as these in turn affect such variables as the staffing level, the costs of selling and the cash flow.

Of course, forecasts do not come 'out of the air'. They are based on historical data, many of which are collected and analysed routinely as normal business practice.

Exercise 11.2

Thinking of a company where you have worked or hope to work, what information is available to management which might be helpful in the forecasting process?

Although it is possible to make forecasts based on hunches or personal judgement, there are several *quantitative techniques* available to the manager to help him or her make more reliable forecasts. It is important that a forecasting technique should be easy to initiate and implement. Sophisticated methods involving much data and computer analysis are not appropriate if the cost outweighs the likely benefits to be achieved from the forecasts. The techniques should be easy to understand and be adaptable if circumstances change. Any assumptions and computations should be able to be scrutinised and understood by others so that models and calculations can be constantly checked and improved.

In this part we shall consider **three** important forecasting techniques in the context of estimating sales:

- Time series analysis
- Exponential smoothing
- Correlation and regression

Each is appropriate in different circumstances. *TIME SERIES ANALYSIS* assumes that sales data are available over several past time periods. The data are examined for long-term movements and for any recurring patterns. Having analysed these components, we can then make future predictions for as far ahead as we believe the underlying assumptions will remain unchanged. It is particularly suitable for established outlets where long data series are available. The rest of this chapter and Chapter 12 are concerned with this technique.

EXPONENTIAL SMOOTHING also uses sales data from past time periods but does not attempt to analyse the movements. Instead it assumes that in the short term, future sales levels are likely to reflect past sales patterns to some degree. It predicts the sales for just one period ahead by using a weighted average of historical sales. Most recent sales are given more importance than earlier sales but the actual weighting can be adjusted using a *SMOOTHING CONSTANT*. This method is very quick to use and is appropriate when large numbers of forecasts have to be made routinely. It is commonly used for forecasting daily demand for different food lines in supermarkets. An introduction to exponential smoothing is provided in Chapter 13.

When new ventures are started, historical data for the exact situation are not available and a different approach is required. *CORRELATION* looks at similar ventures to see whether there is a relationship between sales and some other variable whose value is known. If this found to be the case, then applying a regression technique enables us to construct an equation to describe the relationship. We can then use this equation to make predictions in circumstances where conditions are similar to those on which the equation is based. This is covered in depth in Chapters 14–17.

11.3 Components of a time series

A *TIME SERIES* is a series of observations taken at regular intervals in time. The time interval may be annual, quarterly, monthly, weekly, daily or even minute-by-minute, depending on the variable of interest.

Exercise 11.3

Identify **four** different variables associated with a company and state the time period over which observations of the variable would be made.

Table 11.1 shows the quarterly sales for Supertoys Ltd, a retailer of children's toys and models.

TABLE 11.1

SUPERTOYS LTD: SALES (£000) 19X0 TO 19X3

Year	Quarter 1	Quarter 2	Quarter 3	Quarter 4
19X0	64	75	80	157
19X1	68	80	86	170
19X2	69	83	91	188
19X3	72	86	97	202

FIGURE 11.1

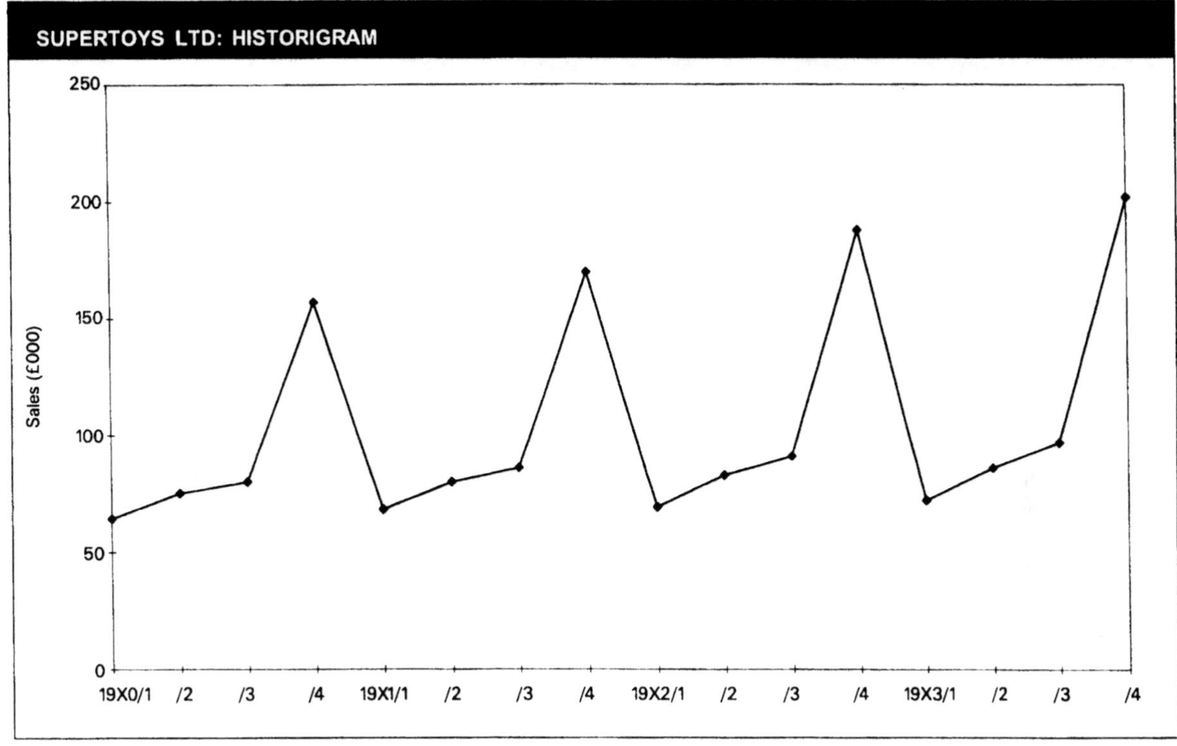

The first stage in a time series analysis is to draw a line chart of the data, as shown in Figure 11.1. This type of graph is called a *HISTORIGRAM* because it shows the history of the series. The graph can be drawn on graph paper or with the help of a spreadsheet or graphics package.

Exercise 11.4

Write down the main features that strike you about the pattern of sales in Figure 11.1.

The regular pattern of sales from year to year is referred to as the *SEASONAL VARIATION*. The overall upward movement in the sales over the years is termed the *TREND*. They are just two of four time series components that we can identify and analyse.

> The *TREND* is the underlying long-term movement of the series.

We can see in our example that sales in the corresponding quarter of each year have been rising steadily from year to year.

> *SEASONAL VARIATION* is a short-term fluctuation about the trend which is repeated regularly.

In our example, the first three quarters of each year exhibit slowly rising sales but at a relatively low level, with the highest sales being achieved every fourth quarter. This pattern is repeated every year. In this example the peaks and troughs do in fact follow the seasons of the year but this type of variation is still called 'seasonal' even when, for example, we have daily data showing higher sales towards the end of every week than at the beginning. It is the regularity and short-term nature of the variation as compared to the length of the series that are the distinguishing features.

If we are analysing a time series over a long period of years, *CYCLICAL VARIATION* will be apparent. The so-called *BUSINESS CYCLE* or *ECONOMIC CYCLE* of boom, recession, depression and expansion is repeated over the years.

This type of variation is long-term and is not regular, although economists try to construct mathematical models in which seven-year cycles are commonly put forward. It is important to realise that every business is affected by what happens in the economy as a whole and to take account of this in long-term forecasting. In short-term forecasting, however, it is safe to ignore the cyclical component. For the remainder of this chapter, we assume that we are interested only in the short to medium term.

The fourth component of a time series consists of the *RESIDUAL VARIATION* that remains when the other components are removed. This may be of two kinds:

- *CATASTROPHIC VARIATION* – abnormal large movement of the time series that affects a single observation. For example, a scare over the contamination of a food product would lead to a temporary reduction in sales. Similarly, a fire at a warehouse might affect the sales of several products. Chance events such as these cannot be predicted and we would be aware of any such occurrences when we analyse our own company data and be able to make adjustments to our forecasts.
- *RANDOM VARIATION* – small variations that cannot be predicted and which are equally likely to push the sales up or to lower them in the long run. We are saying that we do not expect to be able to explain absolutely all of the sales variation each quarter, Some quarters sales just happen to be slightly higher or lower than expected for no apparent reason.

We have identified the types of variation that may be present in a time series. We use a *MULTIPLICATIVE MODEL* to combine the different elements:

Sales = Trend * Seasonal variation * Residual variation

We now need to estimate first the trend and secondly the seasonal components so that we can produce a forecast.

11.4 Estimation of trend

If you look again at Figure 11.1, you may be tempted to think that you could draw freehand a curve through the data to represent the upward trend. There are mathematical techniques that enable us to find the trend in a more objective way. The technique usually used when seasonal variations are present is the method of *MOVING AVERAGES*.

The layout of the calculation is shown in Table 11.2.

The data in Table 11.1 are put in columns **A** and **B**. We move through the data quarter by quarter smoothing out the sales peaks and troughs. For a start, consider the first year of the series and find the average quarterly sales for that year. We then move on one quarter and find the average sales over the next four quarters so that again the highs and lows of the year have been balanced out. The calculations are shown in Figure 11.2.

FIGURE 11.2

SUPERTOYS LTD: WORKINGS FOR FOUR-QUARTERLY MOVING AVERAGES

Average sales (£000s) for first four quarters

$$= \frac{(64 + 75 + 80 + 157)}{4} = 94.0$$

Average sales (£000s) for second four quarters

$$= \frac{(75 + 80 + 157 + 68)}{4} = 95.0$$

We continue in this way through the series until we reach the last four quarters for which we have data: 19X3 quarters 1–4 in Table 11.2. The calculations are displayed in column **C** of Table 11.2. The first average we have calculated gives us the average sales for the first year and is positioned halfway between the second and third quarters of 19X0. The average for the next four quarters is positioned halfway between the third and fourth quarters and so on. The figures in column **C** are a moving average trend.

There is just one problem! In order to continue our time series analysis and estimate seasonal variations, we need to know the trend at exactly the same time as the data so we centre it by adding every pair of moving averages and dividing by two. The *CENTRED AVERAGE* is our estimate of the *TREND*. The calculations are set out in columns **D** and **E** of Table 11.2.

This trend is then plotted on the historigram and in Figure 11.3, you can see how our calculations have achieved their objective in smoothing out the historical data.

TABLE 11.2

SUPERTOYS LTD: TIME SERIES ANALYSIS					
A Period (Yr/Qtr)	**B** Sales £000	**C** 4-Quarterly Moving Average	**D** Add in Pairs	**E** Centred Average (Trend) (£000)	**F** $\frac{\text{Sales}}{\text{Trend}} * 100$
19X0/1	64				
/2	75				
		94.0			
/3	80		189.0	94.5	84.7
		95.0			
/4	157		191.25	95.6	164.2
		96.25			
19X1/1	68		194.0	97.0	70.1
		97.75			
/2	80		198.75	99.4	80.5
		101.0			
/3	86		202.25	101.1	85.1
		101.25			
/4	170		203.25	101.6	167.3
		102.0			
19X2/1	69		205.25	102.6	67.3
		103.25			
/2	83		211.0	105.5	78.7
		107.75			
/3	91		216.25	108.1	84.2
		108.5			
/4	188		217.75	108.9	172.6
		109.25			
19X3/1	72		220.0	110.0	65.5
		110.75			
/2	86		225.0	112.5	76.4
		114.25			
/3	97				
/4	202				

In column **E**, we have rounded off the trend to one decimal place. In general, you should calculate the trend to one more decimal place than the original data series but do not round off until after you have done the centring to avoid the build-up of rounding errors. Your calculator or computer will probably show many more places of decimals but these have no practical relevance since in this example the sales figures provided were accurate only to the nearest thousand.

11.5 Forecasting the trend

To predict the trend of sales during each quarter of 19X4, we need to extend the moving average trend on the graph. This is usually easy to do since the smoothing process has removed the marked fluctuations. The extension of the trend is shown as a dashed line in Figure 11.4. We can then read the estimates for each quarter from the graph as shown in Table 11.3.

FIGURE 11.3

SUPERTOYS LTD: SALES AND TREND
Sales (£000)
250
200
150
100
50
0
19X0/1
/2
/3
/4
19X1/1
/2
/3
/4
19X2/1
/2
/3
/4
19X3/1
/2
/3
/4
SALES
TREND

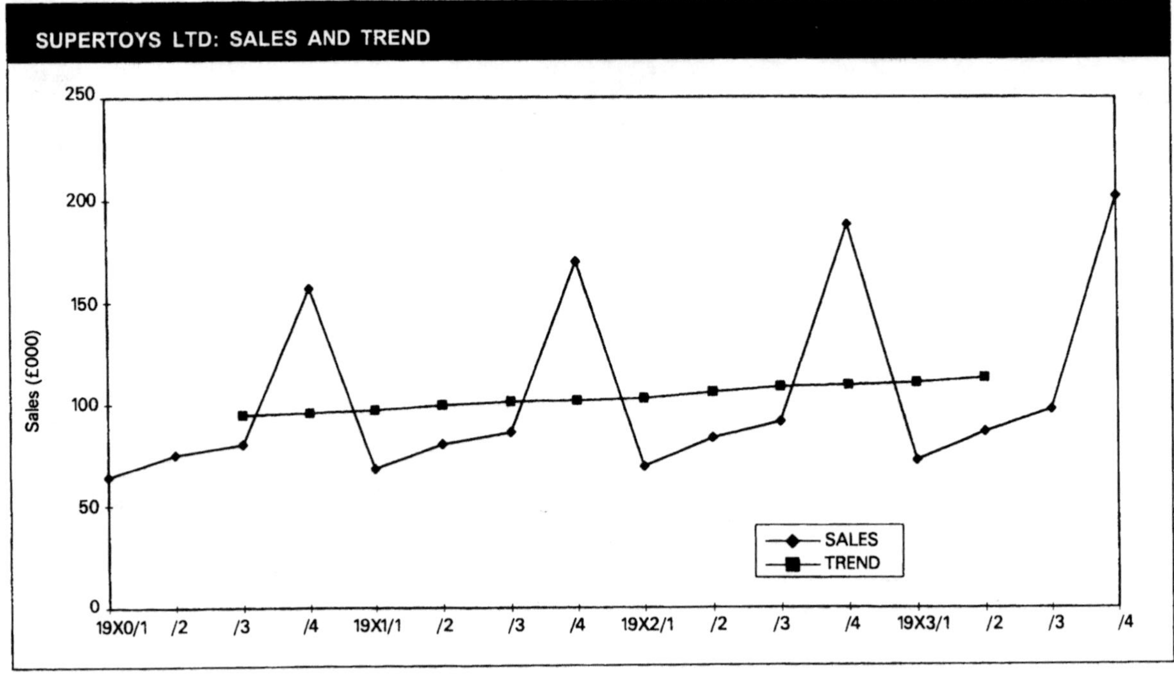

FIGURE 11.4

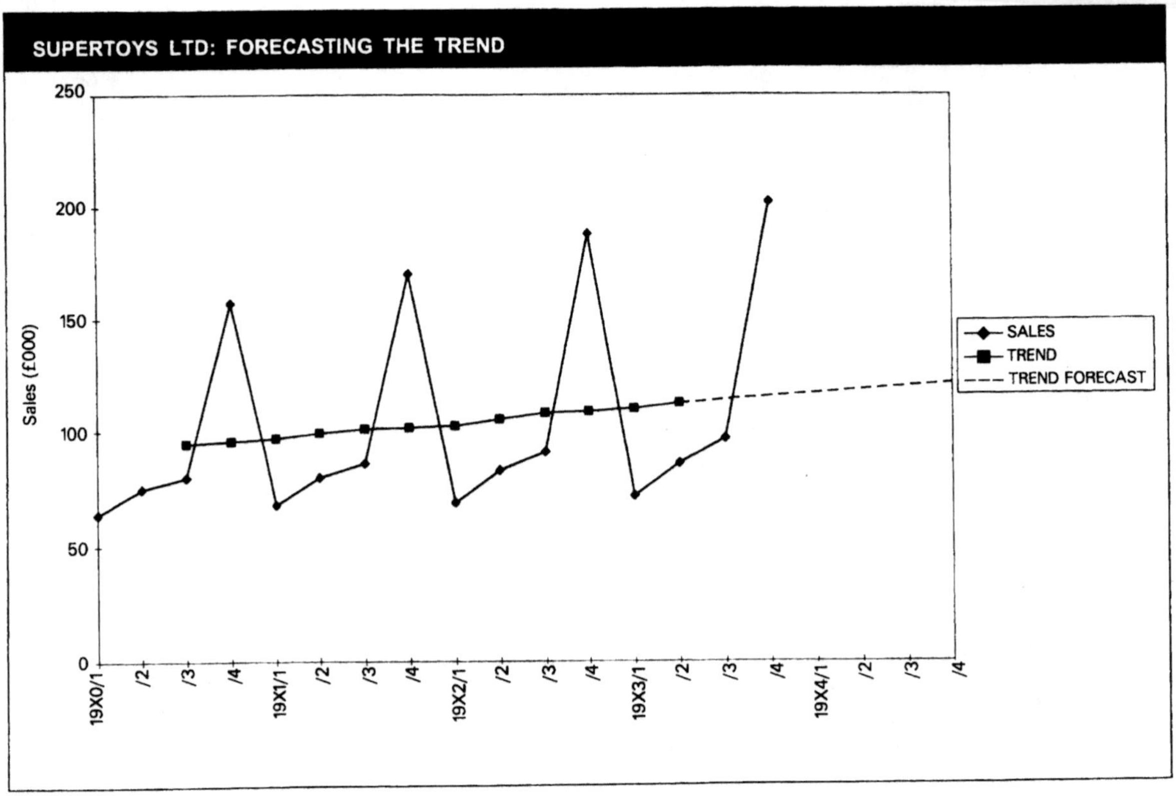

SUPERTOYS LTD: FORECASTING THE TREND
Sales (£000)
250
200
150
100
50
0
19X0/1
/2
/3
/4
19X1/1
/2
/3
/4
19X2/1
/2
/3
/4
19X3/1
/2
/3
/4
19X4/1
/2
/3
/4
SALES
TREND
TREND FORECAST

TABLE 11.3

SUPERTOYS LTD: TREND FORECAST (£000)		
19X4	Quarter 1	117
	Quarter 2	118.5
	Quarter 3	120
	Quarter 4	121.5

Note that we do not have an equation that we can use to predict the trend. This is seen as a disadvantage by some analysts but the advantage of the moving average approach is that it is responsive to *change* and the trend is not fixed into a particular type of mathematical format for evermore.

11.6 Estimating the seasonal variations

To obtain realistic estimates of the sales in each quarter of 19X4 we need to look in detail at the seasonal pattern and to estimate the seasonal variations. We take the historical sales data and remove the trend component so as to see the seasonal pattern more clearly. As we are using a multiplicative model for our time series analysis we need to divide each sales figure by the trend for that quarter, as shown in the following formula:

Multiplicative model

Sales = Trend∗Seasonal variation∗Residual variation

$$\frac{\text{Sales}}{\text{Trend}} = \text{Seasonal variation} * \text{Residual variation}$$

The results of the calculations are shown in Table 11.2, Column **F**. The values have been multiplied by 100 to change them to percentages and then rounded to one decimal place.

We now take each type of quarter in turn and find out on average how much each quarter's sales are above or below the trend. It is easiest to display this calculation as shown in Table 11.4.

The unadjusted averages in Table 11.4 contain both the seasonal and the residual variations. We are interested only in the seasonal component so we have

TABLE 11.4

CALCULATION OF AVERAGE QUARTERLY VARIATION

Year	Quarter 1	Quarter 2	Quarter 3	Quarter 4	
19X0	–	–	84.7	164.2	
19X1	70.1	80.5	85.1	167.3	
19X2	67.3	78.7	84.2	172.6	
19X3	65.5	76.4	–	–	
Total	202.9	235.6	254.0	504.1	TOTAL
Unadjusted average	67.6	78.5	84.7	168.0	398.8

to adjust the averages to remove any residual variation. In the long run the amounts by which the sales in the high quarters are above the trend must be balanced by the amount by which the sales in the low quarters are below the trend so the average seasonal components should add up to exactly 400 per cent. You will notice that the unadjusted averages add up to 398.8 in this example. We must multiply each of the averages by an adjustment factor to ensure that the sum is 400.

This adjustment factor is calculated using the following formula:

Adjustment factor formula

$$\text{Adjustment factor} = \frac{400}{\text{Sum of unadjusted averages}}$$

$$= 1.003$$

The seasonal variations can now be calculated as shown in Table 11.5.

TABLE 11.5

CALCULATION OF SEASONAL VARIATIONS	
Quarter 1	67.6∗1.003 = 67.8
Quarter 2	78.5∗1.003 = 78.7
Quarter 3	84.7∗1.003 = 85.0
Quarter 4	168.0∗1.003 = 168.5
	TOTAL 400.0

These values enable us to predict that, for example, in the first quarter of the year, sales are on average only 67.8 per cent of the trend value whereas in the fourth quarter sales are 168.5 per cent of the trend.

11.7 Sales forecast

We now have all the information we need to forecast the sales in each quarter of 19X4. We estimated the quarterly trend in Table 11.3 and we need to multiply these estimates by the seasonal variation appropriate to each quarter. This is shown in Table 11.6.

The forecasts have been rounded to the nearest thousand pounds which is the same degree of precision as the data in Table 11.1.

TABLE 11.6

MAKING SALES FORECASTS

	£000
Sales forecast for 19X4 Quarter 1	
= 117 * 67.8% =	79
Sales forecast for 19X4 Quarter 2	
= 118.5 * 78.7% =	93
Sales forecast for 19X4 Quarter 3	
= 120 * 85.0% =	102
Sales forecast for 19X4 Quarter 4	
= 121.5 * 168.5% =	205

We are assuming in these forecasts that the trend will continue to change in a similar way to its movement in the recent past, and that the seasonal pattern will remain the same. Of course, if we knew that these assumptions might not be true, then we may need to modify the forecast in the light of our expert judgement. For example, if another major toy retailer moved into the area and undercut our prices, the trend of sales would change and we would need to adjust our forecasts accordingly.

Exercise 11.5

Information on UK consumers' expenditure on clothing other than footwear is given in Table 11.7. Use the techniques demonstrated in this chapter to prepare a forecast of expenditure in this category in each quarter of 1992. Find out what the true figures were in 1992 and compare them with your estimates. Try to explain any discrepancies between your forecast and the actual expenditure.

TABLE 11.7

CONSUMERS' EXPENDITURE (£M) ON CLOTHING OTHER THAN FOOTWEAR 1988 TO 1991

Year	Quarter 1	Quarter 2	Quarter 3	Quarter 4
1988	3034	3284	3486	4831
1989	3077	3327	3458	4768
1990	3068	3358	3507	4657
1991	3043	3274	3452	4699

Source: Economic Trends.

11.8 Modifications for other time intervals

The analyses in this chapter have used quarterly data but the method of moving averages can be used to find the trend for data collected at other time intervals and having a seasonal pattern. Monthly and daily data, for example, are met with quite often.

If the averaging is done over an even number of periods such as the four quarters of the year or the twelve months of the year, then the centring of the trend is necessary as demonstrated in Table 11.2. This is because the four-quarterly average or the twelve-monthly average will fall halfway between two quarters or two months, respectively. If, however, the averaging has to be done over an odd number of periods, such as the seven days of the week, no centring is necessary because the seven-day average will correspond exactly in time to one of the days of the week. An example will make this clearer.

Example

The daily sales at Scrumtello's DIY Superstore over the past four weeks are shown in column **B** of Table 11.8.

TABLE 11.8

SCRUMTELLO'S DIY SUPERSTORE: SALES (£000)

A Period (Week/Day)		B Sales	C 7-Day Moving Average	D $\frac{\text{Sales}}{\text{Trend}} * 100$
1	Monday	26		
	Tuesday	30		
	Wednesday	27		
	Thursday	24	31.6	76.0
	Friday	30	31.7	94.6
	Saturday	44	30.9	142.6
	Sunday	40	30.4	131.5
2	Monday	27	31.1	86.7
	Tuesday	24	31.7	75.7
	Wednesday	24	31.1	77.1
	Thursday	29	31.0	93.5
	Friday	34	30.6	111.2
	Saturday	40	31.3	127.9
	Sunday	39	32.1	121.3
3	Monday	24	31.7	75.7
	Tuesday	29	31.4	92.3
	Wednesday	30	31.4	95.5
	Thursday	26	31.1	83.5
	Friday	32	31.4	101.8
	Saturday	40	30.9	129.6
	Sunday	37	30.4	121.6
4	Monday	26	30.6	85.0
	Tuesday	25	30.3	82.5
	Wednesday	27	29.7	90.9
	Thursday	27	29.3	92.2
	Friday	30		
	Saturday	36		
	Sunday	34		

An inspection of these sales data shows that there is a marked seasonal pattern with higher sales at the weekends and lower sales during the week. To remove this seasonal pattern we need to average sales over seven days:

Workings for seven-daily moving averages

Average sales for first seven days

$$= \frac{(26 + 30 + 27 + 24 + 30 + 44 + 40)}{7}$$

$$= 31.6\ (£000)$$

Average sales for second seven days

$$= \frac{(30 + 27 + 24 + 30 + 44 + 40 + 27)}{7}$$

$$= 31.7\ (£000)$$

The complete set of seven-day moving averages is shown in column **C** of Table 11.8. The first average was for the seven days from Monday to Sunday so the middle of that time period is Thursday so the first average is positioned at Thursday of week 1. Similarly, the middle of the second seven-day period is Friday so the second seven-day average is positioned at Friday of week 1 and so on for the remaining averages. Since these averages correspond exactly to the timings of the original data, no centring is necessary. We can proceed directly to forecasting the trend.

Exercise 11.6

Plot a historigram for the sales of Scrumtello's DIY Superstore using the data from Table 11.8. Plot the seven-day moving average trend on your graph. Comment on the movement in the trend over the four-week period. Estimate the trend for every day in week 5.

The seasonal variations in sales corresponding to the different days of the week can be calculated. In column **D** of Table 11.8, each sales figure has been divided by the corresponding trend value. The resulting figures are shown again in Table 11.9, where they are displayed by day of the week.

We take each day of the week in turn and find out on average how much each day's sales are above or below the trend. The unadjusted averages in Table 11.9 should add up to 700 as there are seven days in the week but their total is 700.8 so we must calculate the adjustment factor:

Calculation of adjustment factor

Adjustment factor

$$= \frac{700}{\text{Sum of unadjusted averages}} = 0.9989$$

The adjusted averages giving the seasonal (daily) variations are shown on the bottom line of Table 11.9.

TABLE 11.9

SCRUMTELLO'S DIY SUPERSTORE: CALCULATION OF AVERAGE DAILY VARIATION

Week	Mon	Tue	Wed	Thu	Fri	Sat	Sun	
1				76.0	94.6	142.6	131.5	
2	86.7	75.7	77.1	93.5	111.2	127.9	121.3	
3	75.7	92.3	95.5	83.5	101.8	129.6	121.6	
4	85.0	82.5	90.9	92.2				TOTAL
Unadjusted average	82.5	83.5	87.8	86.3	102.5	133.4	124.8	700.8
Adjusted average	82.4	83.4	87.7	86.2	102.4	133.2	124.7	700.0

Exercise 11.7

Use the seasonal variations calculated in Table 11.9 and your trend estimates from Exercise 11.6 to predict the sales on every day of week 5 at Scrumtello's DIY Superstore.

11.9 Summary

In this chapter you have learned how to analyse historical data by identifying the trend and the seasonal variations. This knowledge enables you to predict the future movement of a time series, assuming similar conditions obtain. You should never apply the method mechanically, however. You should always try to be aware of any developments and changes that may affect the series so that you can modify your forecasts in the light of experience.

12 Using a Spreadsheet in Time Series Analysis

12.1 Learning objectives

When you have finished working through this chapter you should be able to use a spreadsheet to perform the following tasks

- Draw a historigram
- Calculate the trend of a time series by the method of moving averages
- Superimpose the trend curve on the historigram
- Calculate seasonal variations

12.2 Introduction

All the graphical and arithmetical calculations that we performed in Chapter 11 can be done easily using a spreadsheet package. In fact, for preference, we would always use a spreadsheet since the calculations are repetitive. You can easily set up a *TEMPLATE* for a time series analysis that can be used over and over again. Any spreadsheet package may be used.

12.3 Historigram

A historigram may be drawn using the line chart option available in the spreadsheet, as demonstrated in Chapter 6. To do this enter the times and values in adjacent columns **A** and **B**. Figure 12.1 shows the layout using the data from Table 11.1. Remember to enter the (£000) in **B2** as text.

It is important that the time periods are labelled in such a way that they appear clearly on the horizontal axis of the graph. The labels must fit into just one spreadsheet cell, as shown in Figure 12.1.

FIGURE 12.1

SPREADSHEET LAYOUT

	A	B
1	PERIOD	SALES
2	(Yr/Qtr)	(£000)
3		
4	19X0/1	64
5	/2	75
6	/3	80
7	/4	157
8	19X1/1	68
9	/2	80
10	/3	86
11	/4	170
12	19X2/1	69
13	/2	83
14	/3	91
15	/4	188
16	19X3/1	72
17	/2	86
18	/3	97
19	/4	202

Highlight the two columns, select the chart option and format as a line chart.

Make sure that you give the chart a suitable title and that the **Y**-axis is labelled and any units clearly stated. Check the vertical scaling to ensure that it starts at zero. If the scale has been foreshortened with a suppressed zero, a distorted impression of the data is given as any variations are magnified out of proportion to their size.

The resulting chart should be similar to Figure 11.1.

12.4 Calculation of the trend

Returning to the spreadsheet, we now need to enter formulae to carry out the trend calculations shown in Table 11.2. The layout in the spreadsheet has to be different from that in the table because we do not want to have any empty cells between successive data entries since these would cause trouble when we copy formulae.

We enter the formula for calculating the four-quarterly moving average in cell **C6** as follows

=SUM(**B4**:**B7**)/4

Copy this formula down as far as cell **C18**. Format the column to two decimal places.

To get the trend, which you will recall is the centred average, we first add consecutive pairs in column **C** and then divide them by two. In cell **D6**, enter the formula

=**C6**+**C7**

Copy this formula down as far as cell **D17**.

Next in cell **E6**, enter the formula

=**D6**/2

and copy this down to **E17**. The resulting numbers should be identical to those shown in Table 11.2.

12.5 Graphing the trend

To show the trend on the historigram, highlight column **E** from **E4** to **E17**. Even though there are no numbers in cells **E4** and **E5**, we need to highlight them to get the trend correctly positioned on the graph. Return to the chart you drew previously and add the highlighted trend series as a second set of **Y**-values.

When you view the chart, you will now need to add a legend to distinguish between the data series and the trend.

You may wish to thicken the trend line or format it with/without symbols. Also remember that although lines may appear distinctive on a colour screen, there may be confusion when they are printed out in black and white so reformatting may be necessary.

The resulting graph should be similar to Figure 11.3.

12.6 Calculating the seasonal variations

This calculation is done in two parts.

First, return to the spreadsheet and in column **F** we need to calculate the *detrended series*. To do this, highlight cell **F6** and enter the formula

=**B6**/**E6***100

Copy this formula down to cell **F17**. Format these cells to one decimal place.

Second, to average these seasonal components, move to another part of the spreadsheet such as cell **A30** and set up a new table to perform the calculations shown in Table 11.4. First type in the row labels (the years) and the column labels (the quarters). Rather than typing in all the numbers from column **F**, it is simpler to enter the cell addresses so =**F6** should be typed in cell **D31**, =**F7** in cell **E31**, =**F8** in **B32**, =**F9** in **C32** and so on down to cell **F17**.

Then we need to average each column. In cell **B35**, enter the formula

=AVERAGE(**B32**:**B34**)

Do the same for columns **C**, **D** and **E**, taking care to include the appropriate cells in each average as the positioning is not exactly the same in each column.

In cell **F35** enter the formula

=SUM(**B35**:**E35**)

You will remember from Chapter 11 that we require the total of the seasonal components to equal 400. To adjust the components, move to cell **B36** and enter the formula

=**B35***400/**$F$35**

Copy this formula through to cell **F36** and check that the figure in **F36** does now equal 400.

FIGURE 12.2

SPREADSHEET LAYOUT WITH FORMULAE

	A	B	C	D	E	F
1	PERIOD	SALES	4-QUARTERLY	ADD IN PAIRS	CENTRED AVERAGE	SALES/TREND*100
2	(Yr/Qtr)	(£000)	MOVING AVERAGE		(TREND) (£000)	
3						
4	19X0/1	64				
5	/2	75				
6	/3	80	=SUM(B4:B7)/4	=C6+C7	=D6/2	=B6/E6*100
7	/4	157	=SUM(B5:B8)/4	=C7+C8	=D7/2	=B7/E7*100
8	19X1/1	68	=SUM(B6:B9)/4	=C8+C9	=D8/2	=B8/E8*100
9	/2	80	=SUM(B7:B10)/4	=C9+C10	=D9/2	=B9/E9*100
10	/3	86	=SUM(B8:B11)/4	=C10+C11	=D10/2	=B10/E10*100
11	/4	170	=SUM(B9:B12)/4	=C11+C12	=D11/2	=B11/E11*100
12	19X2/1	69	=SUM(B10:B13)/4	=C12+C13	=D12/2	=B12/E12*100
13	/2	83	=SUM(B11:B14)/4	=C13+C14	=D13/2	=B13/E13*100
14	/3	91	=SUM(B12:B15)/4	=C14+C15	=D14/2	=B14/E14*100
15	/4	188	=SUM(B13:B16)/4	=C15+C16	=D15/2	=B15/E15*100
16	19X3/1	72	=SUM(B14:B17)/4	=C16+C17	=D16/2	=B16/E16*100
17	/2	86	=SUM(B15:B18)/4	=C17+C18	=D17/2	=B17/E17*100
18	/3	97	=SUM(B16:B19)/4			
19	/4	202				
20						
21						
22						
23						
24						
25						
26						
27						
28						
29						
30	YEAR	QTR 1	QTR 2	QTR 3	QTR 4	
31	19X0			=F6	=F7	
32	19X1	=F8	=F9	=F10	=F11	
33	19X2	=F12	=F13	=F14	=F15	
34	19X3	=F16	=F17			TOTAL
35	Unadjusted ave	=AVERAGE(B32:B34)	=AVERAGE(C32:C34)	=AVERAGE(D31:D33)	=AVERAGE(E31:E33)	=SUM(B35:E35)
36	Adjusted ave	=B35*400/$F$35	=C35*400/$F$35	=D35*400/$F$35	=E35*400/$F$35	=F35*400/$F$35

The entries in cells **B36** to **E36** are the seasonal variations and should agree with the values displayed in Table 11.5.

The completed worksheet should appear as in Figure 12.2, which is in View formula mode.

You can keep a copy of this with empty data cells in column **B** as a *TEMPLATE* for other similar calculations. All you need to do is to enter the new data in column **B** and the spreadsheet will automatically perform the necessary calculations. Of course, you will need to make slight adjustments if your time series is longer and has more data points.

Exercise 12.1

Rework Exercise 11.5 using a spreadsheet.

12.7 Summary

In this chapter you have learned how to perform a time series analysis using a spreadsheet. You have set up a template so that you can perform time series calculations routinely in future.

13 Short-term Forecasting

13.1 Learning objectives

When you have finished working through this chapter you should be able to

- Understand the limitations of time series analysis for **SHORT-TERM FORECASTING**
- Explain the term **EXPONENTIAL SMOOTHING**
- Understand how the value of the **SMOOTHING CONSTANT**, α, affects the forecast
- Define the terms **MEAN** and **SMOOTHED MEAN ABSOLUTE DEVIATION**
- Calculate the **FORECAST ERROR**
- Monitor the accuracy of the forecasting procedure using the smoothed mean absolute deviation

13.2 Nature of short-term forecasting

In our discussion of time series analysis in Chapter 11, we needed to have historical data available so that we could estimate the trend and the seasonal components over a period of time. Gradual changes are accommodated by the moving average method and the trend is not fixed into a specific mathematical form, as is the case when regression methods are used, as we shall see in Chapter 14. Adjustments for any sudden changes, however, cannot be made using this method. If there is a food scare, such as salmonella in eggs, or violent storms, how can we predict the immediate demand for eggs or roofing tiles? In situations such as these we are more concerned in predicting one day or one week ahead rather than for one year.

The nature of the business may determine what type of forecast is appropriate. When the product is expensive and time-consuming to produce, such as in the aerospace or pharmaceutical industries, it is important to have detailed and accurate sales forecasts for some years ahead. When the product is cheap or perishable, we need to have a quick and easy method of forecasting that can routinely predict just one period ahead.

When estimating the seasonal components in a quarterly analysis of a time series, we averaged all the data for a first quarter, for example, whether they were recent data or from some time back. When we want to forecast just a short time ahead, it would seem logical to give more emphasis to the most recent data and less weight to historic data.

13.3 Exponential smoothing

The technique used to overcome the specific problems posed by the need for short-term forecasting is *EXPONENTIAL SMOOTHING*. The most recent data are given a greater weight than historic data; the method quickly provides a forecast for one period ahead and automatically adjusts any future forecast in light of the difference between the actual and predicted result. It is the method most commonly used to forecast demand.

The simple exponential smoothing model is represented by the following equation:

Exponential smoothing model

Forecast demand for next period =
Smoothing constant * Actual demand in the current period
+ (1 − Smoothing constant) * Forecast for the current period

In symbols we have

$$\mathbf{F_{t+1}} = \alpha \mathbf{D_t} + (1-\alpha)\mathbf{F_t}$$

where α = smoothing constant
$\mathbf{F_t}$ = forecast for current period (time **t**)
$\mathbf{F_{t+1}}$ = forecast for next period (time **t + 1**)
$\mathbf{D_t}$ = actual demand at time **t**

The forecast for the current period will depend in some way on historic data and we will see later how its value can be determined in a specific example.

The *SMOOTHING CONSTANT* is a number between 0 and 1 that is chosen by the forecaster to satisfy the requirements of a particular application.

If α is chosen to be zero, you can see from the equation that the forecast for next period will be exactly the same as the forecast for the current period so the new forecast relies solely on *historical data* and takes no account of the most recently available actual data.

At the other extreme, if α equals one, no weight is given to historical data and the prediction will rely solely on the actual demand in the *current period*. This might be appropriate just after a new supermarket has opened as there are no historical data available to make a forecast of demand.

In general, values of α between 0.2 and 0.4 are most commonly used in the steady-state situation but higher values of α, in the range 0.7–0.9, might be used at certain times of the year, particularly in the run up to Christmas in supermarkets. It is obviously important to have sufficient stock available to meet the current demand and with the tendency in the 1990s for the Christmas spending rush to start later, it is important to have the stock in place at the time when the customer is going to buy.

Example

A chain of off-licences uses exponential smoothing to estimate its weekly demand. For cigarettes, it uses a smoothing constant of 0.3. The current demand for cigarettes in one of its shops was for 750 packets as against a forecast of 720. The use of the exponential smoothing formula to forecast the demand for cigarettes in the next week can be illustrated as follows:

Application of smoothing formula

$$\begin{aligned}\text{Forecast demand} &= 0.3 * 750 + (1-0.3) * 720\\ &= 225 + 504\\ &= 729 \text{ packets}\end{aligned}$$

Exercise 13.1

The off-licence chain uses a smoothing constant of 0.7 for spirits. The current demand for spirits in the same shop was 12 cases, whereas the forecast was 14 cases. Forecast the demand for spirits next week using the exponential smoothing formula.

For the off-licence chain, it makes sense to have a lower value of the smoothing constant for cigarettes since cigarette sales are fairly steady all the year round. Sales of spirits, however, are very seasonal with most being bought in the fourth quarter of the year. The cost of spirits is high and the off-licence will not want to have too many bottles sitting on the shelves. Using a high value of the smoothing constant means that the shops react to the most recent demand. When demand changes, their forecasts immediately respond.

TABLE 13.1

SOFTLIGHT VERTICAL BLINDS: SALES (£)

Week	Sales
1	9 540
2	10 350
3	9 760
4	9 250
5	10 960
6	10 650
7	10 040
8	9 870
9	9 890
10	9 430
11	9 130
12	9 980

Example

A company manufacturing vertical Venetian blinds for sale direct to the public wants to set up a short-term forecasting system. Sales of its Softlight vertical blinds over a 12-week period were as shown in Table 13.1.

The company is not sure what is the appropriate value of the smoothing constant, α, to apply in this instance. Should it use $\alpha = 0.4$ or $\alpha = 0.8$?

We need to calculate the forecast for each week using the two different values for α and compare them with the actual data. In order to start the forecasting process a forecast for week 1 is required. In the absence of any other information we take the forecast in week 1 to be equal to the actual value in week 1. Each sales forecast

TABLE 13.2

SOFTLIGHT VERTICAL BLINDS:
EXPONENTIALLY SMOOTHED FORECASTS ($\alpha = 0.4$)

Forecast for Week 2
$= 0.4 * 9540 + (1 - 0.4) * 9540 = 9540$
Forecast for Week 3
$= 0.4 * 10350 + (1 - 0.4) * 9540 = 9864$
Forecast for Week 4
$= 0.4 * 9760 + (1 - 0.4) * 9864 = 9822$
Forecast for Week 5
$= 0.4 * 9250 + (1 - 0.4) * 9822 = 9593$
Forecast for Week 6
$= 0.4 * 10960 + (1 - 0.4) * 9593 = 10140$
Forecast for Week 7
$= 0.4 * 10650 + (1 - 0.4) * 10140 = 10344$
Forecast for Week 8
$= 0.4 * 10040 + (1 - 0.4) * 10344 = 10222$
Forecast for Week 9
$= 0.4 * 9870 + (1 - 0.4) * 10222 = 10081$
Forecast for Week 10
$= 0.4 * 9890 + (1 - 0.4) * 10081 = 10005$
Forecast for Week 11
$= 0.4 * 9430 + (1 - 0.4) * 10005 = 9775$
Forecast for Week 12
$= 0.4 * 9130 + (1 - 0.4) * 9775 = 9517$

TABLE 13.3

SPOTLIGHT VERTICAL BLINDS:
EXPONENTIALLY SMOOTHED FORECASTS ($\alpha = 0.8$)

Forecast for Week 2
$= 0.8 * 9540 + (1 - 0.8) * 9540 = 9540$
Forecast for Week 3
$= 0.8 * 10350 + (1 - 0.8) * 9540 = 10188$
Forecast for Week 4
$= 0.8 * 9760 + (1 - 0.8) * 10188 = 9846$
Forecast for Week 5
$= 0.8 * 9250 + (1 - 0.8) * 9846 = 9369$
Forecast for Week 6
$= 0.8 * 10960 + (1 - 0.8) * 9369 = 10642$
Forecast for Week 7
$= 0.8 * 10650 + (1 - 0.8) * 10642 = 10648$
Forecast for Week 8
$= 0.8 * 10040 + (1 - 0.8) * 10648 = 10162$
Forecast for Week 9
$= 0.8 * 9870 + (1 - 0.8) * 10162 = 9928$
Forecast for Week 10
$= 0.8 * 9890 + (1 - 0.8) * 9928 = 9898$
Forecast for Week 11
$= 0.8 * 9430 + (1 - 0.8) * 9898 = 9524$
Forecast for Week 12
$= 0.8 * 9130 + (1 - 0.8) * 9524 = 9209$

FIGURE 13.1

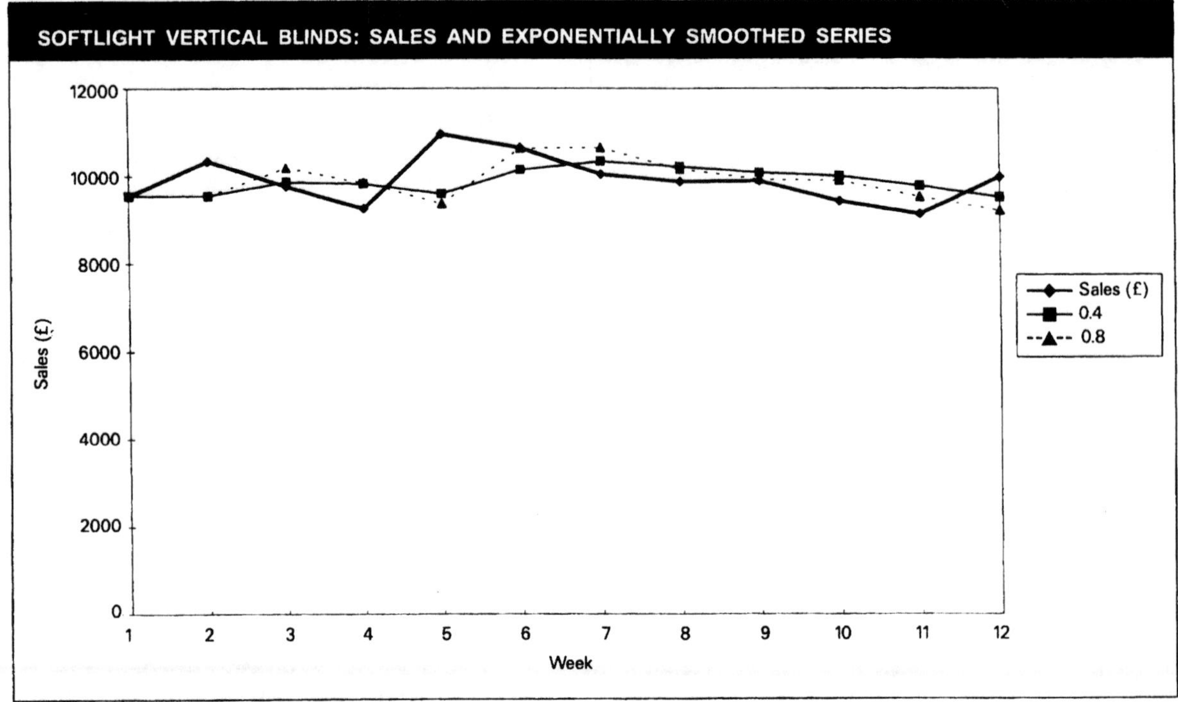

is rounded to the nearest pound and the rounded value used to produce the next forecast. The results are shown in Tables 13.2 and 13.3.

The graphs of the actual sales together with the two exponentially-smoothed series are shown in Figure 13.1.

You can see that the higher value of the smoothing constant gives a series that is much more responsive to the current changes in sales. The lower value of α gives a much smoother series. In this situation where the sales are fluctuating from week to week the higher value of α would probably be preferred.

Exercise 13.2

It has been suggested to the manager of a cycle shop that he should forecast his monthly demand using an exponential smoothing model with a smoothing constant equal to 0.3. He is not convinced and asks you to calculate what predictions the method would have given for his past year's results, which are shown in Table 13.4. On the basis of your calculations, what advice would you give to the manager?

TABLE 13.4

CYCLE SHOP: DEMAND DURING 19X3

Month	Actual Demand	Month	Actual Demand
January	32	July	56
February	20	August	46
March	36	September	65
April	43	October	37
May	47	November	35
June	50	December	75

13.4 Monitoring the forecasting system

In Section 13.3 we selected a suitable value for the smoothing constant by looking at graphs of the series and comparing the fit by eye. It is possible to monitor an exponential smoothing model in a more objective way so that we can assess whether a change to the value of the smoothing constant is necessary. We do this by calculating some statistics.

You may remember that the arithmetic mean, usually referred to simply as the *MEAN*, is the average of a set of values and is evaluated by summing the values and dividing by the number of values.

Exercise 13.3

The demand in number of cases for shampoo in a supermarket last week is shown in Table 13.5.

Calculate the mean daily demand.

TABLE 13.5

CASES OF SHAMPOO: WEEKLY DEMAND

Mon	Tues	Wed	Thur	Fri	Sat	Sun
6	7	7	8	10	10	8

To interpret the mean in this exercise think of it as being the demand per day if the demand every day were the same. In fact, we know that on some days demand is greater than on other days but, by comparison with the mean demand for the period, we get some idea as to whether an individual day has been good or poor.

In forecasting we are concerned as to how close our forecast is to the true value. We define the error in our forecast as

Forecast error = Forecasted value − Actual value

Note that we are using the word 'error' to describe the difference or deviation between two values. We are not using it to imply that there is some mistake in our calculations. We recognise that we do not expect our forecast always to agree exactly with the actual values as there will be random effects that cannot be predicted.

You can see that if our forecast is above the actual value we will have a *positive* error and if the forecast is below the actual value we have a *negative* error. In monitoring the errors the sign of them, whether positive or negative, is not as important as their size, so we choose to work with the *ABSOLUTE DEVIATIONS* which are the positive differences between the forecasted and actual values disregarding any negative signs. Thus an absolute deviation is always positive.

The absolute deviations in our forecasts using the example from Section 13.3 are shown in Table 13.6 when $\alpha = 0.4$.

TABLE 13.6

SOFTLIGHT VERTICAL BLINDS: FORECAST ERRORS (α =0.4)

Week	Demand £	Forecast (α=0.4)	Forecast Error	Absolute Deviation
1	9 540	–	–	–
2	10 350	9 540	−810	810
3	9 760	9 864	+104	104
4	9 250	9 822	+572	572
5	10 960	9 593	−1 367	1 367
6	10 650	10 140	−510	510
7	10 040	10 344	+304	304
8	9 870	10 222	+352	352
9	9 890	10 081	+191	191
10	9 430	10 005	+575	575
11	9 130	9 775	+645	645
12	9 980	9 517	−463	463

The forecast errors tell us that in seven of the weeks we overestimated demand and in four we underestimated. The absolute deviations are relatively small in most weeks although in week 5, the deviation was more than 10 per cent of the actual demand. To evaluate how good on average the forecasts have been we can work out the *mean of the absolute deviations*. In the case of Softlight Vertical Blinds our findings are:

Calculations of mean absolute deviation

($\alpha = 0.4$)

Mean Absolute Deviation

$$= \frac{5893}{11}$$

$= 536$ to the nearest pound

On average, we can say that the forecast with a smoothing constant of 0.4 is in error by £536. Note that an acceptable abbreviation for mean absolute deviation is *MAD*.

There is one reservation, however. In working out the mean absolute deviation we have given equal weight to all the values regardless of when they occurred. It can be argued that we should give more emphasis to the more *recent* values. This argument may sound familiar to you from Section 13.2 and we can overcome the difficulty in a similar fashion by calculating the *SMOOTHED MEAN ABSOLUTE DEVIATION* which incorporates the same value for the smoothing constant as we used in our forecasts. The formula for this is as follows:

Formula for smoothed mean absolute deviation

Smoothed mean absolute deviation at end of current period
$= \alpha *$ Absolute deviation for current period
$+ (1-\alpha) *$ Smoothed mean absolute deviation at end of previous period

To initiate the calculation for the Softlight Vertical Blind example with $\alpha = 0.4$, we put the smoothed mean absolute deviation in week 2 equal to the absolute deviation in week 2 in the absence of other information. The smoothed mean absolute deviations are shown in Table 13.7 where they have been rounded to the nearest pound at every stage.

We can see that after a relatively high value of 874 in Week 5 the smoothed mean absolute deviation fell steadily in later weeks but then increased again in Week 10. This alerts us that a change might have occurred and we may need to consider using a different value for α if the position does not stabilise in the next few weeks.

A statistical test can be set up based on *Trigg's tracking signal* which is the ratio of the smoothed forecast error to the smoothed mean absolute deviation (Stoodley, Lewis and Stainton, 1980). If the numerical value of this ratio approaches the value one, then the forecasting process is becoming out of control and a change in α should be made. In the most common situation of demand forecasting for hundreds of products, this tracking signal is a built-in feature of a computer forecasting and monitoring procedure.

TABLE 13.7

SOFTLIGHT VERTICAL BLINDS: SMOOTHED MEAN ABSOLUTE DEVIATION (£) ($\alpha = 0.4$)

Smoothed MAD Week 2
$= 810$

Smoothed MAD Week 3
$= 0.4 * 104 + (1-0.4) * 810 = 528$

Smoothed MAD Week 4
$= 0.4 * 572 + (1-0.4) * 528 = 546$

Smoothed MAD Week 5
$= 0.4 * 1367 + (1-0.4) * 546 = 874$

Smoothed MAD Week 6
$= 0.4 * 510 + (1-0.4) * 874 = 728$

Smoothed MAD Week 7
$= 0.4 * 304 + (1-0.4) * 728 = 558$

Smoothed MAD Week 8
$= 0.4 * 352 + (1-0.4) * 558 = 476$

Smoothed MAD Week 9
$= 0.4 * 191 + (1-0.4) * 476 = 362$

Smoothed MAD Week 10
$= 0.4 * 575 + (1-0.4) * 362 = 447$

Smoothed MAD Week 11
$= 0.4 * 645 + (1-0.4) * 447 = 526$

Smoothed MAD Week 12
$= 0.4 * 463 + (1-0.4) * 526 = 501$

Exercise 13.4

Refer back to Table 13.1 and Table 13.3. Calculate the forecast errors and the smoothed mean absolute deviation for the Softlight Vertical Blinds data when $\alpha = 0.8$. Comment on your results and advise the company as to the value of smoothing constant to be used in its forecasting.

Exercise 13.5

The monthly demand, in cases, for three brands, **(a)**, **(b)**, and **(c)**, of washing-up liquid is shown in Table 13.8. For each of the data sets, fit exponential smoothing models with values of $\alpha = 0.3$, 0.5 and 0.7. Advise which value of α appears most appropriate in each instance. Using that value of α, forecast the demand for January 19X4.

TABLE 13.8

WASHING-UP LIQUID:
MONTHLY DEMAND 19X3

	(a)	(b)	(c)
Jan	242	186	152
Feb	215	205	145
Mar	215	223	145
Apr	257	189	156
May	232	175	186
Jun	245	208	194
Jul	225	296	160
Aug	242	279	225
Sep	246	260	217
Oct	223	285	196
Nov	232	276	231
Dec	267	270	229

13.5 Summary

In this chapter the method of exponential smoothing was used to provide short-term forecasts by calculating a weighted average of current and historic data. The smoothing constant, α, is chosen so as to best reflect the pattern of changes in historic data. A low value of α is appropriate for a relatively stable series but a high value is preferred if there are large changes.

Once the forecasting system is in place, its accuracy can be monitored by calculating the forecast errors and the smoothed mean absolute deviation.

14 Forecasting Using Relationships Between Variables

14.1 Learning objectives

When you have finished working through this chapter you should be able to

- Draw a **SCATTER DIAGRAM**
- Understand what is meant by a **LINEAR RELATIONSHIP**
- Distinguish between and identify **EXPLANATORY** and **DEPENDENT VARIABLES**
- Define the term **CORRELATION**
- Distinguish between **POSITIVE CORRELATION** and **NEGATIVE CORRELATION**
- Measure the strength of a linear relationship using a **CORRELATION COEFFICIENT**
- Understand that strong correlation does not necessarily imply a causal relationship

14.2 Introduction

The forecasting techniques demonstrated so far have assumed that historical data are available but when we are faced with completely new situations, such as when a new product is launched or when a new outlet is opened, we have to try a different approach to help us with our sales forecasts. It is of crucial importance in assessing the viability of new ventures that we have some indication of future sales. We can then prepare budgets based on our estimated income and expenditure.

The approach we take is to see whether the level of sales in similar situations is related to the values of other variables. For example:

- Sales of a product may be related to the advertising expenditure on the product
- Sales in a superstore may be related to the numbers of people living within a 30-minute travel time to the store
- Daily sales of umbrellas may be related to the amount of rainfall that day

The variables such as advertising expenditure, numbers of people and rainfall are referred to as *EXPLANATORY* or independent variables whereas the variable to be predicted, such as sales in the above examples, is termed the *DEPENDENT* variable.

To set up a forecasting system, we collect data for the variables and analyse them to see whether there is a relationship between the dependent and explanatory variable and if so how strong the relationship is. This is *CORRELATION*. If we find there is a strong relationship between the variables, we can then try to construct a mathematical equation to describe this relationship. This is *regression*. To make our forecast in a new situation we need to know the value of the explanatory variable and then we can calculate the value for the dependent variable.

The techniques of correlation and regression have wide application and can be used to investigate relationships between variables in many different contexts.

14.3 Scatter diagram

The first stage in the correlation analysis is to collect data concerning the variables we think may be related.

Example

Table 14.1 shows data collected concerning average weekly turnover at 10 branches of a multiple chain of fashion retailers. The branches have been selected randomly. Also shown are the numbers of people living within 30 minutes' travel time of each branch. It is thought that there may be a relationship between the turnover achieved in each store and the size of the population living within 30 minutes' travel time.

Exercise 14.1

Study the data in Table 14.1 and say whether you believe there might be a relationship between the turnover in the stores and the population within 30 minutes' travel time. Briefly explain your answer.

TABLE 14.1

FASHION RETAILER:
AVERAGE WEEKLY TURNOVER IN BRANCHES

Store	Turnover £000	Population 000
1	24	287
2	15	161
3	18	75
4	22	191
5	43	450
6	35	323
7	32	256
8	25	312
9	19	142
10	23	210

We are only able to make a tentative assessment about a relationship from looking at a table of the data. To obtain a clearer picture of any possible relationship we draw a *SCATTER DIAGRAM*. This is a special type of *XY CHART* as we saw in Section 6.8, p. 48. Two axes are drawn at right angles, as shown in Figure 14.1. The **X**-axis is the horizontal axis and the **Y**-axis is vertical. Values for the explanatory variable go on the **X**-axis and those for the dependent variable on the **Y**-axis. Using the data in Table 14.1, we are trying to investigate a possible relationship between sales and population size in order to predict sales so sales is the *DEPENDENT* variable and population size is the *EXPLANATORY* variable.

To plot the data on a sheet of graph paper, we take each outlet in turn, identify its population size on the **X**-axis and its sales on the **Y**-axis. Mark a point on the graph at the intersection of these two values. Repeat the procedure until all ten pairs of values are shown, as in Figure 14.1. In general you will obtain points scattered across the graph, hence the name of the diagram. In this example, it confirms our suspicions that higher sales are indeed associated with larger population sizes. We say that sales and population size are *POSITIVELY CORRELATED*. Because the points form a pattern which appears to be close to a straight line we say this is *strong* correlation.

Scatter diagrams may show many different types of pattern and some examples are shown in Figure 14.2.

In **(a)** we see that the points lie exactly on a straight line sloping upwards from left to right. This is *perfect* positive correlation. It is perfect because the plotted points lie exactly on a straight line. Similarly, **(b)** shows perfect *NEGATIVE CORRELATION*. The points lie exactly on a straight line sloping downwards from left to right so higher values of **X** are associated with lower values of **Y**. In **(c)** there is strong negative correlation. In **(d)** there is a great scatter in the points but still a tendency for higher values of **Y** to be associated with higher values of **X**, so we would term this *weak* positive correlation. In **(e)** it is difficult to see any relationship at all between the values of **X** and **Y** since sometimes there are both high and low values of **Y** associated with the same value of **X**. In **(f)** there does appear to be a relationship but it is a *curved* relationship rather than a linear relationship.

FIGURE 14.1

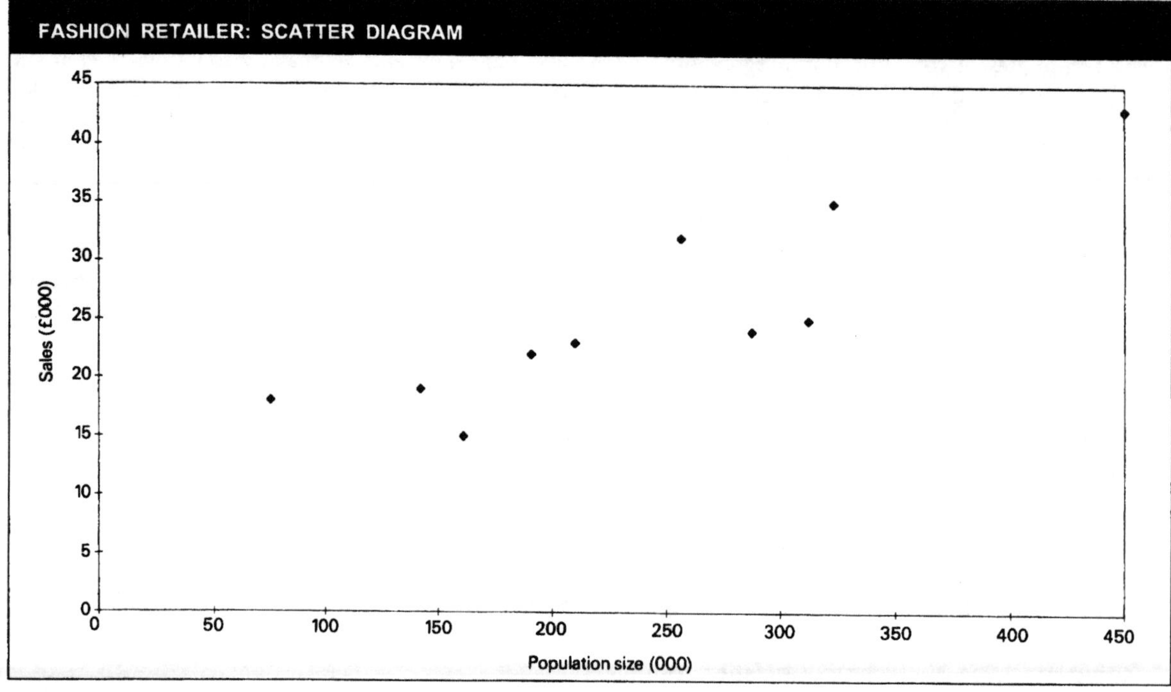

FIGURE 14.2

EXAMPLES OF SCATTER DIAGRAMS

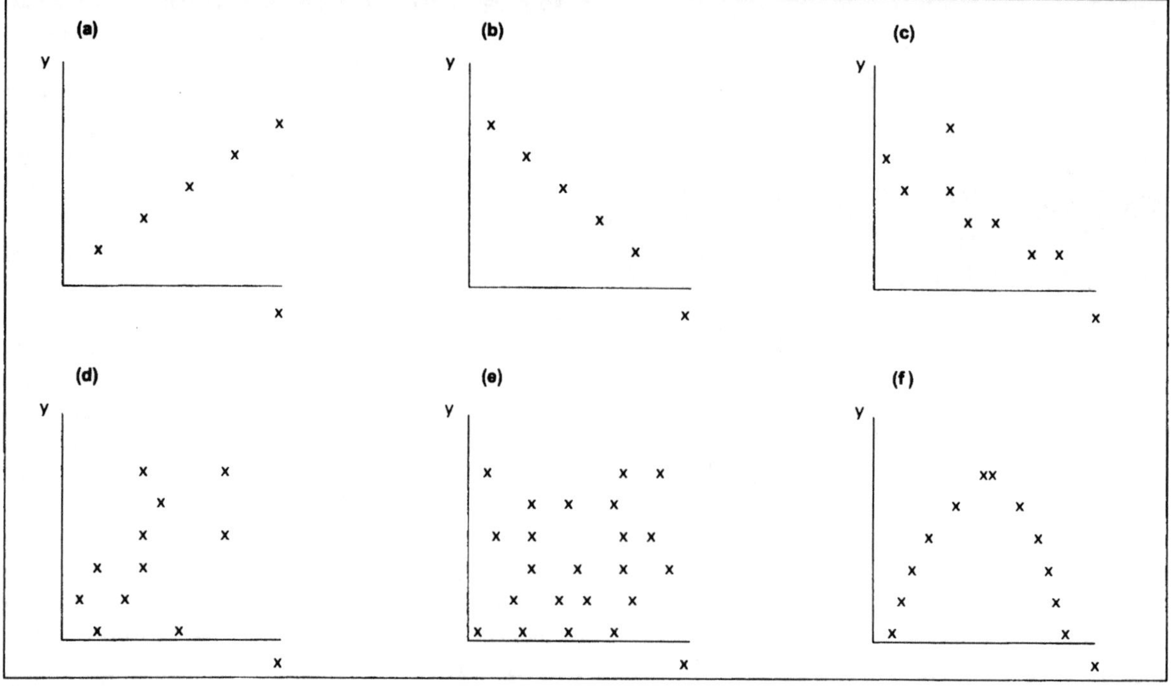

(a) (b) (c)

(d) (e) (f)

We would expect there to be a strong positive correlation, for example, between the petrol consumption of a car and the distance travelled – in other words, the longer the journey, the more petrol used. There is a negative correlation between number of warm scarves sold and the midday temperature – this means that as the temperature decreases, the number of scarves sold increases. The yield of a crop may show a curvilinear correlation with rainfall – this implies that in years where there is extremely high rainfall or extremely low rainfall, poor crops result: the highest yields are obtained in years of moderate rainfall.

Exercise 14.2

Give examples of pairs of variables that you believe may be **(a)** positively correlated, **(b)** negatively correlated, **(c)** perfectly correlated, **(d)** not correlated, **(e)** correlated curvilinearly (this means in a curved relationship).

14.4 The correlation coefficient

If the points on the scatter diagram are perfectly correlated, we can fit a straight line through the points, determine its equation and then use this equation to predict our sales. Although in scientific applications, where this technique originated, linear relationships are common, in business applications it is rare to get perfect linear relationships. If the points show strong correlation, however, it is still worthwhile trying to fit the 'best' straight line through the points as we will be able to use the line to make predictions which we hope on average will give us reliable results.

We need to have some way of deciding whether the correlation is strong enough for us to say that there is an underlying linear relationship. We base our decision on the value of the *CORRELATION COEFFICIENT*. This is a number calculated from the data in such a way that we obtain a value of +1 if there is perfect positive correlation (see Figure 14.2**(a)**), and −1 if there is perfect negative correlation (see Figure 14.2**(b)**). In every other case the correlation coefficient will be between −1 and +1. The closer it is to +1 or to −1, the stronger the correlation. Diagrams such as those in Figure 14.2**(e)** and **(f)** will give values close to zero. It may seem surprising that the correlation coefficient is zero in **(f)** but the correlation coefficient measures the strength of *linear* relationships. This illustrates how important it is to look at the scatter diagram as well as carrying out the calculations, otherwise an obvious relationship, such as the one in Figure 14.2**(f)**, may be overlooked.

The symbol used to denote the correlation coefficient is **r**. The formula used to calculate it from the data values is quite formidable but many calculators now have an **LR** mode which enables the calculation to be done routinely and spreadsheet packages, such as Excel and Lotus 1-2-3 also have a similar facility.

If you do need to calculate **r** manually, the formula to use is as follows:

Formula for the correlation coefficient, r

$$\mathbf{r} = \frac{\mathbf{n}\sum \mathbf{xy} - \sum \mathbf{x} \sum \mathbf{y}}{\sqrt{(\mathbf{n}\sum \mathbf{x}^2 - (\sum \mathbf{x})^2)}\sqrt{(\mathbf{n}\sum \mathbf{y}^2 - (\sum \mathbf{y})^2)}}$$

where **n** is the number of pairs of values and $\sum$ is the summation sign

Example

Using the data from Table 14.1, we can work out the necessary summations as shown in Table 14.2.

Putting the totals into the formula for **r** we obtain the following results:

Calculation of correlation coefficient

$$\mathbf{r} = \frac{10*69\,030 - 2407*256}{\sqrt{(10*684\,369 - (2407)^2)}*\sqrt{(10*7222 - (256)^2)}}$$

$$= \frac{690\,300 - 616\,192}{\sqrt{(6\,843\,690 - 5\,793\,649)}*\sqrt{(72\,220 - 65\,536)}}$$

$$= \frac{74\,108}{\sqrt{1\,050\,041}*\sqrt{6684}}$$

$$= \frac{74\,108}{1024.7*81.756}$$

$= 0.885$ to 3 decimal places

TABLE 14.2

FASHION RETAILER: CALCULATIONS OF SUMS FOR EVALUATION OF r

Store	Turnover £000 y	Population 000 x	y^2	x^2	xy
1	24	287	576	82 369	6 888
2	15	161	225	25 921	2 415
3	18	75	324	5 625	1 350
4	22	191	484	36 481	4 202
5	43	450	1849	202 500	19 350
6	35	323	1225	104 329	11 305
7	32	256	1024	65 536	8 192
8	25	312	625	97 344	7 800
9	19	142	361	20 164	2 698
10	23	210	529	44 100	4 830
	$\sum y = 256$	$\sum x = 2407$	$\sum y^2 = 7222$	$\sum x^2 = 684\,369$	$\sum xy = 69\,030$

The value of **r** we have computed is close to +1 and confirms that we have strong positive correlation between Sales and Population numbers.

Exercise 14.3

Table 14.3 records the weekly demand for wool sweaters at a city centre boutique together with the average midday temperature for the week. Use the formula for **r** to calculate the correlation coefficient between demand and temperature. Draw a scatter diagram and comment on your findings.

TABLE 14.3

DEMAND FOR SWEATERS AND TEMPERATURE

Demand (Number of sweaters)	Temperature (degrees Celsius)
5	20
11	7
4	19
7	22
25	4
9	12
7	10
12	8

We shall see in Chapter 15 how to calculate **r** more easily using a spreadsheet. If your calculator has an **LR** mode, you can evaluate **r** directly once you have entered the pairs of values into the calculator. The calculator manual will detail how this can be done for a particular model. Look for the section labelled linear regression. Check that you obtain the same answer for **r** as we did using the formula.

14.5 Interpretation of the correlation coefficient

When we find that a correlation coefficient is close to +1 or to −1, we have a strong linear relationship between our two variables. In such cases, it will be appropriate to fit a straight line to the data using regression techniques (see Chapter 15), and to use the straight line equation to make predictions. If **r** is close to zero, then a straight line relationship is not appropriate. By studying the scatter diagram, we may feel that some sort of *curved* relationship is indicated and it is possible to extend regression techniques to the curvilinear case (see for example Stoodley, Lewis and Stainton, 1980) but the calculation becomes more complicated and we shall not consider it here.

Even when strong correlation is indicated, you must be careful not to interpret this as indicating a *causal* relationship. Depending on the context, it may well be that a cause-and-effect link does exist. The whole of the advertising industry, for example, is based on the premise that an increase in advertising expenditure causes an increase in sales of the product.

There are instances, however, where two variables show a strong correlation as measured by the correlation coefficient but yet changes in the value of one could not be said to cause changes in the value of the other. For example, if you take a sample of men or a sample of women, you will find that there is a strong positive correlation between the variables Height and Weight. We cannot say that a person's weight causes their height or vice versa. There is a strong correlation because both of the variables are dependent on hereditary, nutritional and environmental factors affecting each individual. If you look back over the years, there is a strong correlation between the number of teachers employed and the number of police employed in a particular year. An increase in the number of teachers does not give rise to an increase in the number of police. Both variables are dependent on public expenditure and increase or decrease in line with the availability of public funds.

If you search around and calculate correlation coefficients between different variables, it may happen by chance that you find a high value of the correlation coefficient but there is no reason to suppose that there is any relationship between the variables. For example, the fashionable length of women's skirts in a particular year was found to be highly correlated with the degree of sunspot activity! Correlations of this type are termed spurious. Do not interpret a value of **r** close to +1 or to −1 as evidence of a causal relationship unless you have other evidence to explain the nature of the relationship.

14.6 Summary

In this chapter we have seen how to investigate the relationship between two variables using a scatter diagram. The correlation coefficient was used to measure the strength and direction of the relationship. If strong correlation exists, then changes in one variable, the *explanatory* variable, can be used to predict changes in the other variable, the *dependent* variable. This method is of particular use in helping to predict sales in new outlets when no historical record exists.

15

Regression

15.1 Learning objectives

When you have finished working through this chapter you should be able to

- Understand the term **LINEAR REGRESSION**
- Recognise the **EQUATION OF A STRAIGHT LINE**
- Draw the graph of a straight line from its equation
- Understand and interpret the **SLOPE** of a straight line
- Understand and interpret the **INTERCEPT** of a straight line
- Be able to obtain and interpret the equation of the **LEAST SQUARES REGRESSION LINE**
- Use the regression line to make a forecast
- Assess the relative reliability of **INTERPOLATION** and **EXTRAPOLATION**

15.2 Introduction

In Chapter 14 we calculated the correlation coefficient **r** to investigate whether a strong linear relationship exists between two variables. If we find that the relationship is strong, then we can fit a straight line to the data and use it to make predictions about the expected behaviour of the dependent variable in new situations. This process is termed *LINEAR REGRESSION*. Before we can look at this in detail we need to know something of the mathematics of a straight line equation.

15.3 Equation of a straight line graph

We used the symbol **x** in Chapter 14 to represent values of the explanatory variable, which is plotted on the horizontal axis of an **XY** graph, and the symbol **y** to represent values of the dependent variable, which is plotted on the vertical axis.

> If the relationship between **x** and **y** is linear, then the equation connecting **x** and **y** always has the same general form:
>
> $$\mathbf{y} = \mathbf{a} + \mathbf{b} * \mathbf{x}$$
>
> Conversely, every equation of this form represents a straight line.

The letters **a** and **b** represent constants, in other words, numbers. The values of these numbers determine the *position* and *direction* of the line. Once these values are specified, the line is fixed.

Example

Plot the graphs of the following lines on graph paper.

(a) $y = 2 + 3x$

(b) $y = 2 - 3x$

(c) $y = -1 + 2x$

A straight line can be drawn once we know two of the points that it passes through because then we can just use a ruler to join up the points. It is usually safer, however, to calculate three of the points the line passes through to make sure we have not made any numerical mistakes when working from the equation.

Let us consider three values of **x** and find the corresponding values of **y** from the equation. Any convenient values of **x** may be chosen and what is convenient will vary depending on the context of the application. The calculations are as follows:

Calculations of coordinates of points to plot

(a) $y = 2 + 3x$

When $x = 0$, $y = 2 + (3 * 0) = 2 + 0 = 2$
When $x = 2$, $y = 2 + (3 * 2) = 2 + 6 = 8$
When $x = 4$, $y = 2 + (3 * 4) = 2 + 12 = 14$

(b) $y = 2 - 3x$

When $x = 0$, $y = 2 - (3 * 0) = 2 - 0 = 2$
When $x = 2$, $y = 2 - (3 * 2) = 2 - 6 = -4$
When $x = 4$, $y = 2 - (3 * 4) = 2 - 12 = -10$

(c) $y = -1 + 2x$

When $x = 0$, $y = -1 + (2*0) = -1 + 0 = -1$
When $x = 2$, $y = -1 + (2*2) = -1 + 4 = 3$
When $x = 4$, $y = -1 + (2*4) = -1 + 8 = 7$

All the lines are shown in Figure 15.1.

From Figure 15.1, you will probably have noticed that when **b** is a positive number +3 or +2, the line slopes upwards form left to right. When **b** is negative, −3, the line slopes downwards from left to right.

The line with **b** equal to +3 is steeper than the line with **b** equal to +2. This demonstrates that **b** measures the *SLOPE* or gradient of the line. The value of **b** tells us how much the value of **y** changes when **x** increases by one. In equation **(a)**, every time **x** increases by one, the value of **y** goes up three. In equation **(b)**, when **x** increases by one, the value of **y** goes down three.

When we have positive correlation, the regression line will have a positive slope and **b** will be positive. In negative correlation, the regression line slopes downwards and **b** will be negative.

In Figure 15.1, look closely to see where each line crosses the **y**-axis. You will see that lines **(a)** and **(b)** both cross where **y** equals 2 and line **(c)** crosses below the origin where **y** equals −1. If you look back at the equations, you will see that these are the same values as the first term, **a**, in each equation. **a** is called the *INTERCEPT* on the **y**-axis and in every case is the value of **y** when **x** equals zero.

Once we have the mathematical equation of a straight line, we can read off the values of the slope and the intercept straightaway.

Exercise 15.1

Write down the slope and the intercept of these straight line equations.

(a) $y = 10 + 3x$

(b) $y = 250 - 10x$

(c) $y = 0.256 - x$

(d) $y = 4x$

Plot separate graphs of these straight lines using a convenient range of values.

In the equation $y = a + b * x$, **a** is sometimes referred to as the *constant* term because its value does not change as **x** changes. By contrast the term $b * x$ is called the *variable* term since every time we consider a new value of **x**, the value of this term will also change. Of course, the value of **b** remains fixed and it is sometimes referred to as the *coefficient* of **x** as it is the constant number that multiplies **x**. It does not matter in which order you write the terms. The equations $y = 2 + 3x$ and $y = 3x + 2$ represent exactly the same line.

FIGURE 15.1

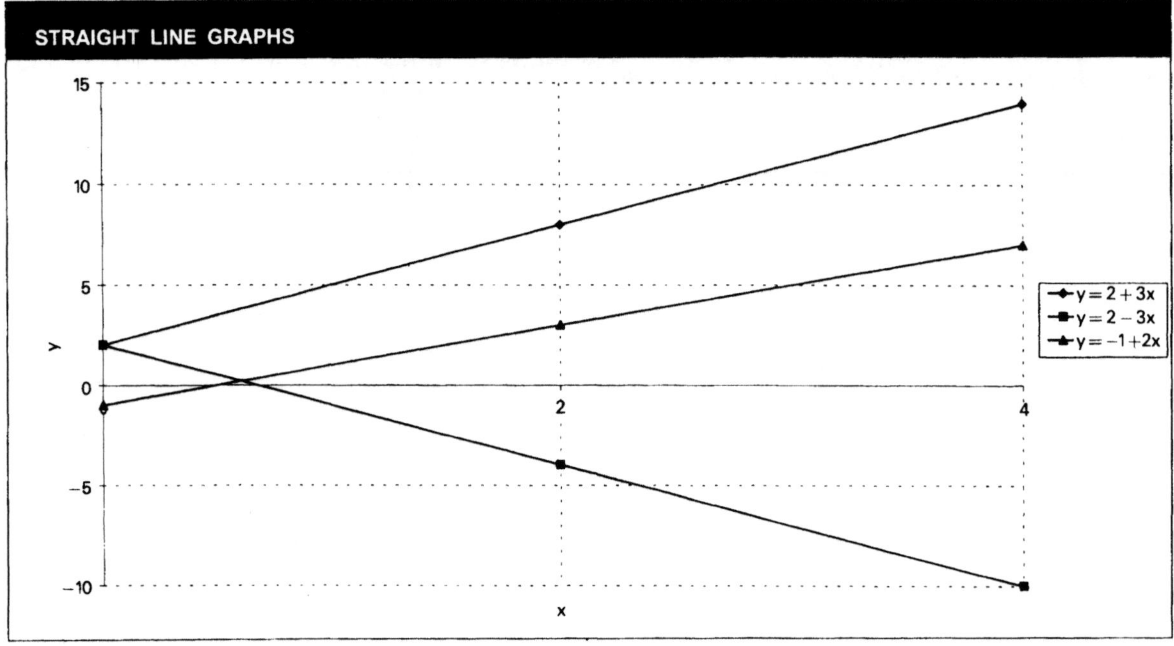

Exercise 15.2

Martin believes that the daily cost **(y)** of production of printed circuit boards (PCBs) at his electronics factory can be represented by the equation

$$\mathbf{y} = 150 + 12\mathbf{x}$$

where **y** is in £ and **x** is the number of PCBs produced per day.

(a) What is the cost of producing 200 PCBs in a day?
(b) Interpret the slope of the line in the context of this question.
(c) What does the value of the intercept tell you about production costs at this factory?

15.4 Least squares regression line

We can now return to the problem of finding the equation of the line that is a 'best' fit to the points in the scatter diagram. You might think that you can do this simply by using a ruler and trying to get all the points as close to the line as possible. This method is subjective, however, and we need to have some criterion for deciding which is the line of 'best' fit.

The criterion that is used is the *least squares criterion,* and this minimises the sum of the squares of the vertical deviations of the points from the line.

Using this criterion, we can work out from the data the values of **a** and **b** for the regression line equation. Usually we would let a calculator or spreadsheet do the arithmetic for us. Calculators with an **LR** mode are pre-programmed to work out the values of **a** and **b** at the same time as **r**, the correlation coefficient. Some spreadsheets also have this facility. Further details will be given in Chapter 16.

The formulae for **a** and **b** in detail if you want to work them out are as follows:

Formulae for a and b

$$\mathbf{b} = \frac{\mathbf{n}\sum\mathbf{xy} - \sum\mathbf{x}\sum\mathbf{y}}{\mathbf{n}\sum\mathbf{x}^2 - (\sum\mathbf{x})^2} \qquad \mathbf{a} = \frac{\sum\mathbf{y} - \mathbf{b}\sum\mathbf{x}}{\mathbf{n}}$$

We worked out all the required sums in Table 14.2 for our fashion retailer example. Substituting in the equations we obtain the following results:

Fashion Retailer: Evaluation of a and b

$$\mathbf{b} = \frac{10 * 69\,030 - 2407 * 256}{10 * 684\,369 - (2407)^2}$$

$$= \frac{690\,300 - 616\,192}{6\,843\,690 - 5\,793\,649}$$

$$= \frac{74\,108}{1\,050\,041}$$

$$= 0.07057629$$

$$\mathbf{a} = \frac{256 - 0.07057629 * 2407}{10}$$

$$= \frac{86.1228657}{10}$$

$$= 8.61228657$$

The equation of the regression line is

$$\mathbf{y} = 8.612 + 0.07058\mathbf{x}$$

where **a** and **b** have been rounded to 4 significant figures. Remember that **y** is the turnover in thousands of pounds and **x** is the population in thousands.

The value of **b** tells us that for every extra thousand people within 30 minutes' travel time, the turnover will increase by 0.07058 thousand pounds, that is by £70 approximately.

We can now add the line to our scatter diagram. The range of **x** values in the data was from 75 to 450 so if we consider **x** equals 100 and 400 we will have convenient values to plot.

When $\mathbf{x} = 100$,

$$\mathbf{y} = 8.612 + 0.07058 * 100$$

$$= 8.612 + 7.058 = 15.670$$

When $\mathbf{x} = 400$,

$$\mathbf{y} = 8.612 + 0.07058 * 400$$

$$= 8.612 + 28.232 = 36.844$$

Figure 15.2 shows the original scatter diagram with the regression line superimposed. We extend the line so that it covers the complete range of data values. You can see that it really does appear to be a line of 'best' fit.

If you are unsure about whether your values of **a** and **b** are correct or whether you have plotted the points accurately, there is a final check you can make. Any regression line must pass through the point whose coordinates are

(Mean of the **x** data values, Mean of the **y** data values)

For this example, the means are calculated as follfows:

Calculation of the means

$$\text{Mean of } \mathbf{x} \text{ data values} = \frac{2407}{10} = 240.7$$

$$\text{Mean of } \mathbf{y} \text{ data values} = \frac{256}{10} = 25.6$$

From the graph in Figure 15.2 it appears that our regression line does indeed go through the point (240.7, 25.6).

Exercise 15.3

Using the data from Exercise 14.3, calculate the equation of the least squares regression line and plot it on your scatter diagram.

15.5 Forecasting using the regression line

Once we have the equation of the regression line we can use it to forecast the value of **y** for a given value of **x**.

Example

Using the equation found in Section 15.4, forecast the branch turnover expected when the population within 30 minutes travel time is 250 000.

FIGURE 15.2

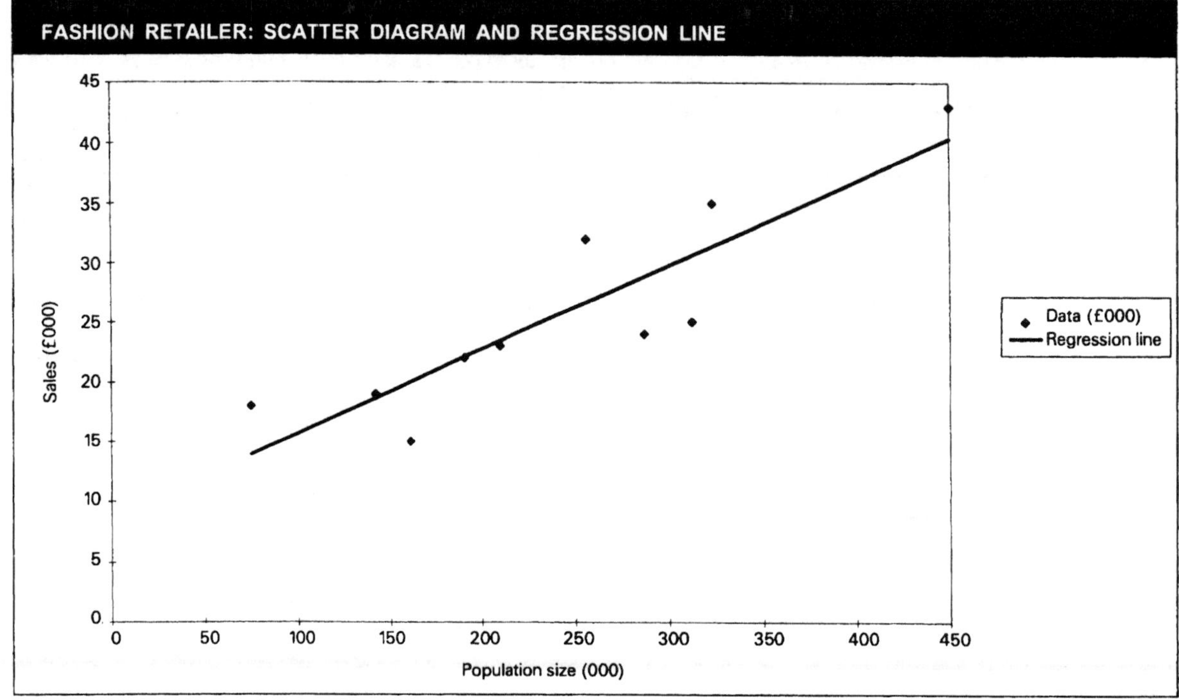

The equation is $\mathbf{y} = 8.612 + 0.07058\mathbf{x}$, where $\mathbf{x}$ is the population in thousands so the given value of $\mathbf{x}$ is 250.

When $\mathbf{x} = 250$,

$$\mathbf{y} = 8.612 + 0.07058 * 250$$

$$= 8.612 + 17.645 = 26.257$$

Expected turnover is 26.257 thousand pounds = £26 257.

We should round this estimate to the nearest thousand pounds since the data were given to that accuracy.

We are not saying that the turnover at the branch will be exactly £26 000 but if we took many branches with a population of 250 000 within 30 minutes' travel time, we would expect that on average their turnover would be £26 000.

Note that, instead of working out the forecast from the equation, we could use the graph. Find $\mathbf{x} = 250$ on the $\mathbf{x}$-axis and draw a line vertically upwards until you reach the line. Then from this point, draw a horizontal line to meet the $\mathbf{y}$-axis and read off the value of $\mathbf{y}$.

The procedure we have demonstrated here is called *INTERPOLATION*. We were making a prediction for an $\mathbf{x}$ value that is within the range of our original data. All things being equal, if the value of $\mathbf{r}$ indicates strong correlation, we would expect that our forecast would be accurate.

Sometimes we try to predict *outside* the range of the data. This is termed *EXTRAPOLATION*.

Example

Using the equation found in Section 15.4, forecast the branch turnover expected when the population within 30 minutes' travel time is 750 000.

When $\mathbf{x} = 750$,

$$\mathbf{y} = 8.612 + 0.07058 * 750$$

$$= 8.612 + 52.935 = 61.547$$

We forecast an expected turnover of £62 000.

You may feel slightly uneasy about this estimate. The population figure is much larger than anything we considered in setting up the equation. If there are more people around, then it is likely there might be more competitors around so the turnover may not be as high as we expected. On the other hand, as there many more people, it could be that the turnover 'takes off' and is much higher than we expected from the lower population figures. The point is that we are in unknown territory as we have no data values as large as this and so this forecast carries less weight than our previous one. Always take great care if you decide to extrapolate the data. You cannot assume that the same relationship will hold under changed conditions.

Exercise 15.4

Using the equation of the regression line calculated in Exercise 15.3, predict the demand for wool sweaters in a week when the average midday temperature is **(a)** 13 degrees Celsius, **(b)** 1 degree Celsius.

State any reservations you have about these forecasts.

15.6 Summary

In this chapter you have learned how to recognise the equation of a straight line. You can use the equation to plot the graph and to determine its slope and intercept. You know what is meant by the least squares regression line and can determine its equation with the help of a calculator. You appreciate that this calculation is tedious and prone to arithmetical slips so the use of a spreadsheet is preferred. You can use the regression line to make forecasts and you appreciate the difference between interpolation and extrapolation.

16 Linear Regression on the Spreadsheet

16.1 Learning objectives

When you have finished working through this chapter you should be able to

- Use a spreadsheet to draw a **SCATTER DIAGRAM**
- Command the spreadsheet to perform a linear regression analysis
- Interpret the spreadsheet output of a linear regression analysis
- Use the spreadsheet to plot the graph of the regression line
- Understand the meaning of the **COEFFICIENT OF DETERMINATION**
- Understand the meaning of the **P-VALUE** of an explanatory variable
- Use the spreadsheet to make forecasts using the regression equation

16.2 Drawing a scatter diagram

All spreadsheet packages have the facility to draw a scatter diagram, although as noted in Section 6.8, p. 48, it is usually referred to in the manual as an *XY CHART*.

Exercise 16.1

Enter the data from Table 14.1 into a spreadsheet as shown in Figure 16.1. Use the spreadsheet to draw a scatter diagram with Population as the **X**-variable and Turnover as the **Y**-variable.

16.3 Linear regression commands

Not every spreadsheet package is equipped to perform linear regression calculations so check your manual to make sure that it is possible with your package. Both Lotus 1-2-3 and Excel, for example, can perform the desired calculations.

Example

We are going to use the regression command in Excel to calculate the regression line of turnover on population for the data in Figure 16.1.

Having entered the data on to the spreadsheet we need to call up the following commands from the Menu Bar: **Tools**, **Add ins**, **Analysis ToolPak**, **Tools**, **Data analysis**, **Regression**. (If you have added in the Analysis ToolPak in your current session at the computer, you need only use the commands **Tools**, **Data Analysis**, **Regression**.) All we have to do is input the **Y**-range **B4:B13** and the **X**-range **C4:C13**, press **OK** and Excel produces the printout shown in Figure 16.2. By default this output is placed on a new sheet in the Excel workbook but you can specify where you want the output to appear. Other packages produce similar output but it is not always so comprehensive.

FIGURE 16.1

DATA LAYOUT FOR REGRESSION CALCULATION

	A	B	C	D
1	Average weekly turnover in branches of fashion retailer			
2	Store	Turnover	Population	
3		(£000s)	(000s)	
4	1	24	287	
5	2	15	161	
6	3	18	75	
7	4	22	191	
8	5	43	450	
9	6	35	323	
10	7	32	256	
11	8	25	312	
12	9	19	142	
13	10	23	210	

FIGURE 16.2

REGRESSION OUTPUT FROM EXCEL

SUMMARY OUTPUT						
Regression Statistics						
Multiple R	0.884593					
R Square	0.782506					
Adjusted R Square	0.755319					
Standard Error	4.262822					
Observations	10					
ANOVA						
	df	*SS*	*MS*	*F*	*Significance F*	
Regression	1	523.0267831	523.0268	28.78256639	0.000673674	
Residual	8	145.3732169	18.17165			
Total	9	668.4				
	Coefficients	*Standard Error*	*t Stat*	*P-value*	*Lower 95%*	*Upper 95%*
Intercept	8.612286568	3.441432398	2.50253	0.036796715	0.676324095	16.548249
X Variable 1	0.070576292	0.013155098	5.364939	0.000673674	0.040240562	0.10091202

16.4 Interpretation of linear regression output

The output shown in Figure 16.2 may appear daunting but the values of some of the numbers may appear familiar to you from the previous chapters. The printout gives more information than we require for our purposes so we need to select those values of use to us.

Regression line equation

First of all, look at the **Intercept** and the **X Variable 1** rows at the foot of Figure 16.2. In the column headed **Coefficients**, we find the values of **a** and **b**, respectively, that we calculated in Chapter 15. These tell us that the equation of our regression line is

$$\mathbf{y} = 8.612 + 0.7058\mathbf{x}$$

where we have rounded the values to four significant figures.

An easy way to get the regression line plotted on the scatter diagram is to add a fourth column to your spreadsheet entitled **Fit** as shown in Figure 16.3. Copy the values of **a** and **b** from the regression output to a convenient location. We have chosen to use cells **C14** and **C15**.

In column **D** we need to work out what the regression equation predicts the turnover will be at each of the population levels listed in column **C**.

Starting in cell **D4**, we need to type the regression formula to calculate the turnover when the population is 287 000.

The spreadsheet formula to enter in **D4** is

=$C$14 + $C$15 * C4

We have put the **$** signs to make these cell references absolute because the values of **a** and **b** are fixed for all our fit calculations.

We now copy this formula down column **D** to obtain the values shown in Figure 16.3.

If we move back to the scatter diagram that we drew for the data originally, we need to add a second **Y**-series, namely the **Fit** that we have calculated in column **D**. Format this series so that it appears as a line on the **XY** chart with no symbols showing. This is

FIGURE 16.3

CALCULATION OF FIT USING REGRESSION EQUATION

	A	B	C	D
1	Average weekly turnover in branches of fashion retailer			
2	Store	Turnover	Population	Fit
3		(£000s)	(000s)	(£000s)
4	1	24	287	28.87
5	2	15	161	19.98
6	3	18	75	13.91
7	4	22	191	22.09
8	5	43	450	40.37
9	6	35	323	31.41
10	7	32	256	26.68
11	8	25	312	30.63
12	9	19	142	18.63
13	10	23	210	23.43
14	Intercept (a) =		8.6122866	
15	X Variable 1 coefficient (b) =		0.0705763	

the appropriate format because the regression equation holds for any value of **x** within the range of the sample data. Add a legend to the chart to distinguish between the data points and the regression line.

The finished chart should be similar to Figure 15.2.

Coefficient of determination

Continuing our interpretation of Figure 16.2, look next at the top line, labelled **Multiple R**, in the **Regression Statistics** section. This is the value of the correlation coefficient, **r**, which we calculated in Chapter 14. It is given a different name in the Excel table because the regression command in Excel can be used when we have multiple **X**-variables as we will explain in Chapter 17.

On the next line of Figure 16.2, we find **R** square and this is the correlation coefficient squared. **R** square is termed the *COEFFICIENT OF DETERMINATION.*

You may think that it is slightly odd that the spreadsheet package prints out the value of **R** Square, the coefficient of determination. In fact, the coefficient of determination is a very useful value to know when we are assessing whether the regression equation is a *good* fit to the data.

The coefficient of determination tells us how much of the variation in the dependent variable, the **Y**-variable, is explained by the regression equation. As the value of the **X**-variable, the explanatory variable, changes then the regression equation gives a value for **y**. If we go through all the **x** values in the data set, we can calculate all the corresponding values for **y**. (This is what we did in Figure 16.3 when we were calculating the fit.) If this set of **y** values agreed exactly with the data values, we would have a perfect, 100 per cent, fit. In practice, of course, we cannot expect to get a 100 per cent fit but the coefficient of determination tells how good the fit actually is.

In our example, the value of **R** Square is 0.782506 or 0.783 to three significant figures. We can say, therefore, that 78.3 per cent of the variation in turnover is explained by changes in population numbers through our regression equation. In other words, 21.7 per cent of the variation in turnover remains unexplained by our equation.

In some applications we may not be sure what is an appropriate explanatory variable to use. We may try various different regression equations. The coefficient of determination enables us to determine which of the equations, if any, is giving us a good fit to the data. In general, we would select the equation with the *highest* value for the coefficient of determination.

We will use the coefficient of determination in connection with multiple regression in Chapter 17.

Exercise 16.2

A group of clothing manufacturers has commissioned some research. They want to know whether the annual amount spent on clothing by a household is more closely related to household income or to the number of persons in the household. After surveying 50 families the researcher has reported that his calculations show that the coefficient of determination between amount spent on clothing and household income is 0.744 and the coefficient of determination between amount spent on clothing and household size is 0.545. Interpret these values for the manufacturers.

P-value

There is just one other value that we need to consider in Figure 16.2. If we return to the **X Variable 1** line and look in the column headed **P-value**, we find 0.000673674. If you want to know whether you can have confidence in the regression equation containing this **X**-variable, you should check that the **P**-value in this cell is less than 0.05. In our example, 0.000673674 is very much less than 0.05 so we can have every confidence in our regression equation.

Exercise 16.3

Using the printout in Figure 16.4, write down the regression equation, the correlation coefficient, the coefficient of determination and the **P**-value corresponding to **X Variable 1**. Use the equation to predict the value of the monthly sales for an electrical store with a floor area of 2500 sq ft. State with reasons whether you have confidence in this prediction.

FIGURE 16.4

EXERCISE 16.3: REGRESSION OUTPUT

Electrical goods stores						
Store	Monthly sales	Floor area				
	(£000s) (y)	(sq. ft.) (x)				
1	50	3050				
2	37	1130				
3	42	1890				
4	23	1750				
5	40	1010				
6	68	2690				
7	88	4210				
8	55	2820				
9	58	2030				
SUMMARY OUTPUT						
Regression Statistics						
Multiple R	0.818663489					
R Square	0.670209908					
Adjusted R Square	0.623097037					
Standard Error	11.69995992					
Observations	9					
ANOVA						
	df	*SS*	*MS*	*F*	*Significance F*	
Regression	1	1947.33212	1947.332	14.22562	0.006967548	
Residual	7	958.2234351	136.8891			
Total	8	2905.555556				
	Coefficients	*Standard Error*	*t Stat*	*P-value*	*Lower 95%*	*Upper 95%*
Intercept	16.00101798	10.11998219	1.581131	0.157861	-7.928920222	39.93096
X Variable 1	0.015402859	0.004083812	3.771687	0.006968	0.005746186	0.02506

16.5 Making predictions using the regression equation

Having obtained our regression equation, we can make predictions in the same way as we did in Chapter 15. Of course, we can get the spreadsheet to do the calculations for us.

Example

Using the regression equation, forecast the branch turnover expected by the fashion retailer when the population within 30 minutes' travel time is

(a) 250 000

(b) 750 000.

FIGURE 16.5

CALCULATION OF PREDICTIONS FROM REGRESSION EQUATION

	A	B	C	D	E	F
1	Average weekly turnover in branches of fashion retailer					
2	Store	Turnover	Population	Fit	Population	Predictions
3		(£000s)	(000s)	(£000s)	(000s)	(£000s)
4	1	24	287	28.87	250	26.26
5	2	15	161	19.98	750	61.54
6	3	18	75	13.91		
7	4	22	191	22.09		
8	5	43	450	40.37		
9	6	35	323	31.41		
10	7	32	256	26.68		
11	8	25	312	30.63		
12	9	19	142	18.63		
13	10	23	210	23.43		
14	Intercept (a) =		8.6122866			
15	X Variable 1 coefficient (b) =		0.0705763			

Move to column **F** on the worksheet and head it **Predictions**. Put the two population figures in column **E**, as shown in Figure 16.5. Then move to the adjacent column **F** and type in the formula to calculate the predicted turnover in exactly the same way as in Section 16.4 when we calculated the fit. In cell **F4**, enter the formula

=$C$14+$C$15*E4

Copy the formula to cell **F5** to obtain the values shown.

The turnover forecasts agree with those found in Section 15.5. The same comments about their reliability apply as discussed in Chapter 15. We have simply used the spreadsheet as an aid to calculation but we have not changed the underlying forecasting method.

Exercise 16.4

Perform a regression analysis on a spreadsheet for the data of Exercise 14.3. Extract the following from the regression output:

(a) The equation of the regression line of sales on temperature
(b) The correlation coefficient
(c) The coefficient of determination
(d) The **P**-value corresponding to **X variable 1**

State with reasons whether you believe the regression equation you have calculated is a good fit to the data. Use the spreadsheet to estimate the number of sweaters sold when the temperature is 12 degrees.

Draw a scatter diagram on the spreadsheet and add the regression line to it.

16.6 Summary

In this chapter you have learned how to use the spreadsheet to draw a scatter diagram and to calculate the regression line. You are able to interpret the output and can use the coefficient of determination and the **P**-value to assess how well a regression equation fits the data. You can use the spreadsheet to draw the regression line on the scatter diagram and to make forecasts.

17 Multiple Regression

17.1 Learning objectives

When you have finished working through this chapter you should be able to

- Define **MULTIPLE REGRESSION**
- Use a spreadsheet to carry out a multiple regression analysis
- Interpret spreadsheet output relating to multiple regression
- Select the most appropriate regression model from an inspection of the spreadsheet output relating to various possible models on the basis of **P**-values and **R** square values

17.2 Introduction

Although linear regression can provide an adequate model for forecasting in many situations, it does not always do so. It is unreasonable to expect that all the variations in sales figures, for example, can be explained by changes in just one other variable. It is likely that sales will be influenced by many factors, such as selling area, number of employees, number of checkouts, number of competing stores in the vicinity, prices charged, number of products stocked and so on.

The linear regression model we have used can be extended to situations where we believe that sales may be related to several other variables and this is referred to as *MULTIPLE REGRESSION.*

As before, we label the dependent (sales) variable $\mathbf{y}$ but we now have several explanatory variables so we label them $\mathbf{x}_1$, $\mathbf{x}_2$, $\mathbf{x}_3$ etc. The multiple regression model is

$$\mathbf{y} = \mathbf{a} + \mathbf{b}_1\mathbf{x}_1 + \mathbf{b}_2\mathbf{x}_2 + \mathbf{b}_3\mathbf{x}_3 + \cdots$$

17.3 Setting up a multiple regression model

Example

The marketing department of the Pandora Fashions retailing organisation wants to be able to estimate the level of sales when new outlets are opened. Two factors that may influence sales are thought to be the floorspace available and the number of employees. Data from a sample of existing stores are given in Table 17.1. The sales are for the month of May. The number of employees is the average number of full-time or full-time equivalent sales assistants in each store per day.

TABLE 17.1

PANDORA FASHION: SALES

Store	Sales £000	Floorspace 000 sq ft	Number of Employees
1	90	10	10
2	272	15	14
3	130	20	11
4	228	20	12
5	192	27	11
6	280	33	11
7	240	37	11
8	296	49	10
9	280	52	11
10	320	32	14

Investigation of a possible linear relationship

First let us see whether a linear regression model can be used to fit the data. We have two choices, we can work out the linear regression equation of Sales on Floorspace or the linear regression equation of Sales on Number of employees.

Using a spreadsheet, we first perform a linear regression analysis of Sales on Floorspace in exactly the same way as in Section 16.3. The print-out from the Excel spreadsheet is shown in Figure 17.1.

The Sales on Floorspace analysis is shown in the top part of the output. Interpreting this output, we see the linear regression model is

$$\mathbf{y} = 129.8 + 3.493\mathbf{x}$$

where $\mathbf{y}$ = Sales (£000) and $\mathbf{x}$ = Floorspace (000 sq ft).

Alternatively, we can write the model as

$$\text{Sales (£000)} = 129.8 + 3.493 * \text{Floorspace (000 sq ft)}$$

The other values of interest to us from the output are

- the correlation coefficient (**Multiple R**) 0.649
- the coefficient of determination (**R square**) 0.422
- the **X Variable 1** (Floorspace) **P-value** 0.0422

We conclude that we have fairly strong positive correlation and that 42.2 per cent of the variation in Sales can be explained by this linear relationship with floorspace. The **P**-value for the Floorspace variable is less than 0.05, so we can be confident that there is a linear relationship with floorspace.

Exercise 17.1

Draw a scatter diagram showing the relationship between Sales and Floorspace. Draw in the regression line. Comment on the graph.

Exercise 17.2

In the middle part of Figure 17.1, a regression analysis of Sales on Number of employees has been performed. Interpret this output and assess whether this regression equation provides an explanation of the variation in the observed data. Draw the scatter diagram and the regression line and comment on the graph.

Investigation of a possible multiple regression model

From our two linear analyses of the data, we have found that the first one, Sales on Floorspace, does provide some explanation of the variation in sales but the second one, Sales on Number of employees is not of much use. The values of **R** square in each case show that a relatively small percentage of the total variation has been explained. We must now attempt to fit a multiple regression model to the data to see whether the two variables together give more explanation.

Although the calculations for this are tedious to do manually, they can be done easily in the spreadsheet. Get into the **Regression** menu on your spreadsheet as before and specify the Sales data as the **Y**-series. Make sure that your Floorspace data and Number of Employees data are in adjacent columns. Select the block containing both these columns of data and enter the block as the **X**-series. This is the only difference between entering the data for linear regression and for multiple regression. The rest of the analysis proceeds as before but when the output appears, two **X**-coefficients are displayed, as shown in the lowest third of Figure 17.1.

FIGURE 17.1

PANDORA FASHIONS: REGRESSION OUTPUT

SUMMARY REGRESSION OUTPUT

SALES on FLOORSPACE

Regression Statistics	
Multiple R	0.6494
R Square	0.4217
Adjusted R Square	0.3494
Standard Error	60.2932
Observations	10

ANOVA

	df	SS	MS	F	Significance F
Regression	1	21207.47	21207.47	5.83381	0.04216
Residual	8	29082.13	3635.27		
Total	9	50289.60			

	Coefficients	Standard Error	t Stat	P-value	Lower 95%	Upper 95%
Intercept	129.7664	46.7253	2.7772	0.0240	22.0176	237.5151
X Variable 1	3.4927	1.4460	2.4153	0.0422	0.1581	6.8272

SALES on NUMBER OF EMPLOYEES

Regression Statistics	
Multiple R	0.4707
R Square	0.2215
Adjusted R Square	0.1242
Standard Error	69.9537
Observations	10

ANOVA

	df	SS	MS	F	Significance F
Regression	1	11141.4	11141.41	2.2768	0.1698
Residual	8	39148.2	4893.524		
Total	9	50289.6			

	Coefficients	Standard Error	t Stat	P-value	Lower 95%	Upper 95%
Intercept	-49.4162	188.3386	-0.2624	0.7997	-483.7262	384.8937
X Variable 1	24.5405	16.2639	1.5089	0.1698	-12.9641	62.0452

SALES on FLOORSPACE and NUMBER OF EMPLOYEES

Regression Statistics	
Multiple R	0.9237
R Square	0.8533
Adjusted R Square	0.8114
Standard Error	32.4672
Observations	10

ANOVA

	df	SS	MS	F	Significance F
Regression	2	42910.78	21455.39	20.354	0.00121
Residual	7	7378.82	1054.117		
Total	9	50289.6			

	Coefficients	Standard Error	t Stat	P-value	Lower 95%	Upper 95%
Intercept	-304.7867	99.0189	-3.0781	0.0179	-538.9290	-70.6443
X Variable 1	4.4194	0.8050	5.4898	0.0009	2.5159	6.3230
X Variable 2	35.4099	7.8038	4.5375	0.0027	16.9569	53.8630

Interpreting this output gives a multiple regression model:

$$\mathbf{y} = -304.8 + 4.419 * \mathbf{x}_1 + 35.41 * \mathbf{x}_2$$

where $\mathbf{y}$ = Sales (£000), $\mathbf{x}_1$ = Floorspace (000 sq ft) and $\mathbf{x}_2$ = Number of employees.

Alternatively, we can write the model as

Sales (£000) =

−304.8 + 4.419 ∗ Floorspace (000 sq ft)

+ 35.41 ∗ Number of employees

We do not attempt to represent this model graphically as we would need three dimensions and in a situation where we are considering more than two explanatory variables it is impossible to get any graphical representation.

Assessment of fit of multiple regression model

To assess the fit, we first look at the value of the coefficient of determination, **R** square which, as in the linear case, tells us how much of the variation in sales is explained by this model. Here, **R** square is 0.853 so 85.3 per cent of the variation is now explained so we have a much better fit.

In the case of multiple regression, the next value to consider is in the ANOVA section of the Figure 17.1 print-out on the **Regression** row in the column headed **Significance F**. Its value here is 0.0012. If this value is less than 0.05, we can be confident that overall our model is a good fit to the data. (We did not need to look at this value in the linear regression case because then it is always equal to the **P**-value of X Variable 1, as you can confirm by glancing at the first two sections of Figure 17.1.)

The **P**-value for X Variable 1 (Floorspace) is 0.0009 and the **P**-value for **X** Variable 2 (Employees) is 0.0027. Both of these values are well below 0.05 so we can be confident that each of these **X**-variables should be included in the regression model.

All these figures are unanimous in telling us that we have improved our fit to the data and that we now have a very good fit. We would therefore recommend that the multiple regression model be used to describe the data rather than the linear models.

Interpretation of the coefficients in the multiple regression equation

We know that

Sales (£000) =

−304.8 + 4.419 ∗ Floorspace (000 sq ft)

+ 35.41 ∗ Number of employees

In Section 15.4, we interpreted the value of **b** in the linear regression equation. In a similar way, we can interpret the values of the multiple regression coefficients. Every additional thousand square feet of floorspace can be expected to be associated with an increase in sales of 4.419 in (£000), in other words, £4420. Similarly, every additional employee is associated with an expected increase in sales of £35 410. This information is invaluable in assessing the costs of new development or store expansions.

Making predictions using the multiple regression equation

To make predictions of sales, we need to know both the floorspace and the number of employees. Suppose a new store is planned with 14 employees and 35 000 sq ft of floorspace. The sales estimate using the multiple regression model is

$$\text{Sales (£000)} = -304.8 + 4.419 * 35 + 35.41 * 14$$
$$= 345.6$$

We predict sales of £346 000 to three significant figures.

Remember that our regression analysis is based only on our sample of data so any predictions we make should be based on staffing and floorspace values that are within the range of our data.

Exercise 17.3

Estimate the sales expected for a store with 14 employees and 35 000 sq ft of floorspace, using the linear regression models displayed in Figure 17.1. Comment on your answers.

17.4 Warning

Do not expect that a multiple regression model should always be used in preference to a linear regression equation. More time and effort is involved in collecting and processing the data for multiple regression analysis and this might involve unacceptable delays or costs.

The multiple regression process can be extended to include more **X**-variables. To perform the analysis on the spreadsheet we must put all the **X**-variables in neighbouring columns and highlight them as a block as the **X**-series in the regression analysis. You may think that the more variables that are included the better but that is not the case. In fact, it is usually best to use the fewest number of variables that are needed to obtain an acceptable fit. You should always have some logical reason for investigating a relationship. You should never just see whether you get a low **P**-value when you include a particular variable and then try to find an explanation afterwards! You must have some idea that there is a relationship and use the regression analysis to support or refute this conjecture.

You may find that including an extra variable leads to very little more explanation of the variation. This could be because that variable has no relationship with sales or it could be that the variable is highly correlated with one of the other **X**-variables so no new explanation is forthcoming.

Exercise 17.4

The Lively Oldies Travel Company specialises in luxury overseas holidays for those aged over 50. The company wants to know whether the annual amount spent on holidays by its customers is related to the age of the traveller or the traveller's income or both. The data in Table 17.2 was collected in a recent survey of their customers.

TABLE 17.2

LIVELY OLDIES TRAVEL COMPANY: SURVEY RESULTS

Customer	Annual Expenditure on Travel £000	Age	After-tax Income per annum £000
1	38	59	19
2	50	72	34
3	50	64	45
4	35	59	12
5	43	60	38
6	34	61	20
7	30	60	10
8	47	73	29
9	20	59	23
10	32	72	32
11	45	75	30
12	41	82	21

Use a spreadsheet to perform linear and multiple regression analyses of the data and advise the company as to the most appropriate regression equation to use.

Use your chosen equation to predict the annual amount spent on travel by a 65-year-old with an after-tax income of £25 000.

Explain to the company any reservations you may have about your estimate.

17.5 Summary

In this chapter you learned how to extend regression analysis to a situation where there is more than one possible explanatory variable. You are able to estimate the coefficients in a multiple regression model by interpreting the spreadsheet output. You are able to assess whether a linear regression model or a multiple regression model provides the best explanation of the variation in a data set.

Case Study 3

Collett Brothers plc: Forecasting to Improve Efficiency

1 History of the company

Collett Brothers plc started life one hundred years ago in Manchester as a high-class grocer's shop in the Deansgate area. It was renowned for the quality of its cheese and butter which were supplied daily from farms in Cheshire. The brothers offered a wide range of tea, coffee and spices that were imported through Liverpool and sent by train to Manchester. As the city expanded and the gentry moved their residences to the surrounding villages, the brothers opened up other shops around Manchester.

The company was keen to take advantage of new technology as it was introduced. Its Manchester shop was one of the first in the area to have electric lighting. After the Second World War refrigeration was introduced in all its stores and it then proved possible to stock fresh meat. Descendants of the Collett brothers still ran the company in the early 1970s. They were quick to recognise the advantages of the supermarket layout that was being introduced from the United States. This involved much greater selling space so new centrally located premises were bought in Manchester and proved a great success.

In the late 1970s the decision was made to close down the 'village' shops in the city's outskirts and to open up supermarkets in the major cities of Lancashire and Yorkshire. In order to do this, the company was floated on the Stock Exchange and there was no shortage of eager investors. The Head Office has remained in Manchester but today the company's network of stores stretches to Glasgow and Edinburgh in the north and to Northampton, Oxford and Bristol in the south. Expansion was particularly brisk in the late 1980s, with an average of eight new stores opening each year.

2 Current issues

Collett Brothers, in common with other food retailers, is keen to improve its efficiency. The directors have identified customer loyalty and staffing costs as the two main areas to be targeted in its efficiency drive but any consumables, such as carryout bags, are also being examined to see whether purchase costs can be reduced. Because of the urgency of the situation arising from fierce competition in the market place, the directors have decided to employ a forecasting consultant to advise them.

Customer loyalty

The company relies heavily on computer technology to run its business and all stores are currently being

TABLE C3.1

LEEDS STORE: TAKINGS (£000) DURING TRIAL OF LOYALTY CARD			
Week	**Takings £000**	**Week**	**Takings £000**
1	53.2	9	61.1
2	52.1	10	63.2
3	56.1	11	58.6
4	57.2	12	91.5
5	55.2	13	61.9
6	88.0	14	61.5
7	66.0	15	66.3
8	60.8	16	67.5

upgraded with new EPOS terminals that will allow for the introduction of a customer loyalty card. This card entitles customers to a £3 voucher for every £100 spent in the company's stores. This scheme was trialled in its Leeds store for 16 weeks with the results shown in Table C3.1. Every six weeks a special promotional day was held where customers with a loyalty card were entitled to a 10 per cent discount on all goods bought on the Thursday of that week. The company is undecided as to whether or not to have the promotional day as well as the discount scheme in the rollout to all its stores. There are added costs of staffing, advertising and stocking up for these days and these, combined with the discount, mean that in the promotional week the usual margin of 12 per cent is reduced to 9½ per cent. If the 10 per cent promotional day is abandoned, the sales in Weeks 5 and 6 of each cycle are expected to be similar to those in the previous and following weeks, respectively.

Staffing costs

In its efforts to keep costs under control, the company is looking closely at staffing levels. In common with other superstores it moved to seven-day trading but is increasingly employing part-time rather than full-time staff. The part-timers are multi-skilled, that is, they can perform either checkout or shelf-filling duties and this provides greater flexibility in staff scheduling.

In order to help them with staff planning it is essential that the company has accurate forecasts of the likely daily sales. Customers expect to have a choice of greengrocery, meat and bakery products, for example, at whatever time of day they shop and they do not like to be in long queues at the checkouts. On the other hand, the company cannot afford to have excessive stock wastage nor to have checkout operators sitting waiting to serve customers. At the Stockport store, the total daily sales have been monitored over the past four weeks as shown in Table C3.2. The company intends to base its daily staffing plans on these figures. Each item scanned has an average value of 98 pence. Each checkout operator can process fifteen items per minute on average allowing for payment time as well as scanning. Each part-time employee can work for four hours per day without a break and currently the stores are open twelve hours per day except on Sundays when, because of legal restrictions, only six hours trading is allowed. On Sundays, the checkout operators each work for three hours on the tills and one hour on other duties round the store.

TABLE C3.2

STOCKPORT STORE: DAILY SALES (£000)					
Week 1	Sun	8.1	**Week 3**	Sun	7.2
	Mon	10.3		Mon	9.8
	Tue	8.9		Tue	10.2
	Wed	7.2		Wed	8.7
	Thu	10.4		Thu	11.1
	Fri	17.3		Fri	15.2
	Sat	15.6		Sat	13.7
Week 2	Sun	8.7	**Week 4**	Sun	8.2
	Mon	7.2		Mon	7.4
	Tue	7.1		Tue	8.6
	Wed	9.6		Wed	8.5
	Thu	12.3		Thu	10.3
	Fri	15.2		Fri	13.0
	Sat	14.6		Sat	12.1

Carryout bags

In another cost-cutting exercise, the company has been assessing the cost of providing carryout bags. Records at its Edinburgh store over the past three

TABLE C3.3

EDINBURGH STORE: QUARTERLY COSTS (£) OF CARRYOUT BAGS

	Quarter	Costs (£)
Year 1	1	13 668
	2	13 842
	3	16 253
	4	13 428
Year 2	1	13 602
	2	13 442
	3	16 942
	4	13 543
Year 3	1	13 858
	2	13 907
	3	16 948
	4	13 420

years revealed the quarterly costs of bags used and these are shown in Table C3.3. The company has been approached by different bag suppliers and needs to assess which offer is going to be most economical to use in future.

The Taiwan Carry Bag Company quoted a price of £35 per box of 1000 bags with a minimum order quantity of ten boxes. The HK Hold All Company charged £33 per box of 1000 bags but will deliver only a van load of 1000 boxes at a time. This means that the company would have to provide storage space at an approximate cost of £200 per quarter. Alternatively Collett Brothers can continue with its existing supplier.

The company is not sure whether the number of bags used is related more closely to number of items scanned or to the value of items scanned so they observed several customers and the results are shown in Table C3.4.

The predicted quarterly takings and number of items for each quarter of next year are shown in Table C3.5.

Tasks

Collett Brothers has commissioned your services as a forecasting consultant to advise on their uncertainties.

TABLE C3.4

EDINBURGH STORE: CUSTOMER USAGE OF CARRYOUT BAGS

Customer	Bags Used	Number of Items	Total Value of Sale £
1	4	37	34.57
2	6	46	54.23
3	1	6	8.34
4	8	64	78.56
5	6	42	36.78
6	4	32	28.96
7	5	49	46.32
8	7	68	61.38
9	10	85	102.65
10	6	52	73.46

TABLE C3.5

EDINBURGH STORE: PREDICTED QUARTERLY TAKINGS AND NUMBER OF ITEMS SCANNED

	Quarter	Takings £000	Number of Items 000
Year 4	1	33 826	34 300
	2	33 148	33 817
	3	39 778	40 727
	4	32 892	32 062

Task 1

Using Table C3.1, forecast the takings in the Leeds store for the next six weeks assuming the 10 per cent promotional day continues. Forecast the takings for the next six weeks assuming the promotional day does not take place and advise the store whether or not it should continue with the 10 per cent promotional day.

Task 2

Using Table C3.2, forecast the sales for every day of week 5 and hence estimate the number of checkout operators needed every day.

Task 3

Using Table C3.3, forecast the quarterly costs of continuing with the same bag supplier next year.

Task 4

Using Table C3.4, investigate whether the number of bags used by customers is related more closely to number of items scanned or to the value of items scanned and establish the regression equation to predict the number of bags used by a customer based on your chosen variable.

Task 5

Using Table C3.5 and your results from Task 4, what recommendation would you make about a bag supplier?

Part IV
Costing and Budgeting

18

Introduction to Costing Systems

18.1 Learning objectives

When you have finished working through this chapter you should be able to

- Appreciate the need for and uses of a **COSTING SYSTEM**
- Define the term **COST**
- Appreciate the difference between **ACTUAL** and **STANDARD COSTS**
- Define the terms **COST CENTRE** and **PROFIT CENTRE**
- Give an example of a cost centre which is not a profit centre
- Define and contrast the terms cost **ALLOCATION** and cost **APPORTIONMENT**
- Identify a suitable base for the apportionment of a cost item
- Discuss the different ways in which costs are related to products in manufacturing and retail organisations
- Define the term **DIRECT PRODUCT COST** and give three examples of direct product costs
- Discuss the limitations of the **GROSS MARGIN** as a measure of profitability
- Explain what is meant by **DIRECT PRODUCT PROFITABILITY**
- Use a DPP decision tree in the context of product mix and space allocation decisions

18.2 Introduction

In Part II you learnt how to analyse and interpret financial statements. This skill is needed to evaluate company performance over time and by comparison with the competition. Ratio analysis enables management to learn from the past and set targets for the future which can then serve as yardsticks against which actual performance can be measured.

Part III focused on future performance and we discussed the use of a number of forecasting techniques which make use of historical data to anticipate and predict what is likely to occur next. A good forecasting system helps reduce uncertainty and acts as a map to the future. Actual performance is constantly monitored against the forecast to evaluate progress.

Part IV is concerned with the detailed capture of sales and costs information and the use of such information in drawing up budgets. This chapter focuses on different approaches towards the gathering of historical cost data and explains how cost data can be related to business activities. Chapters

18 and 19 introduce the use of a budgetary control system as a management tool for planning future performance.

18.3 The need for a costing system

At any given point in time the resources available to a business organisation are limited. This means that a plan is required as to how these resources can be used in the most effective manner to achieve the objectives of the business. Such a plan includes detailed forecasts of both future sales revenues and key cost items, such as the cost of goods for resale and labour costs.

Large organisations need a great number of people to work effectively as a team towards a common goal. This implies that the analysis and interpretation of financial data must be taken farther than the stage where you are just calculating ratios and making forecasts which are related to the results of the whole organisation. To provide adequate information for planning and decision-making purposes, the data must be broken down to show the results for *individual parts* of the organisation, from regions and stores down to individual managers' areas of responsibility.

Management accounting is about the use of techniques and technology designed to enable managers at all levels in the organisation to monitor and influence performance in their own spheres of responsibility. The monitoring and control aspect of a manager's work is carried out most effectively where costs and revenues can be related to activities, branches, departments or even products within the business organisation, in relation to which sales were achieved and costs incurred. The aim is to control costs and maximise profits. As you can appreciate, it is very important for management to know as accurately as possible how much it actually costs to carry out the activities of the business. Without such knowledge no rational decisions about the future courses of action available to the business can be made, and the company will soon lose out to its better informed competitors. A good *COSTING SYSTEM* is therefore needed to provide such information at the appropriate level of detail required to meet management information needs.

18.4 Relating overhead costs to activities

So far, the term cost has been used synonymously with the term expense.

> For management control purposes, a *COST* is defined as the amount of expenditure which is incurred on, or can be related to, a specified product, person or process.

In order to ensure that the business survives and prospers, management must ensure that in the long run all costs are covered. Some costs are easily identified with the individual product lines. However, many costs are less specific. These are known as *OVERHEADS*. In order to be able to understand and control overhead costs, management link them to *COST CENTRES*.

It is essential to know how costs are related to activities if a rational basis for decision-making is considered important. The reasons are as follows:

- Facilities are shared between parts of the organisation, examples are the staff canteen and the EPOS system, so the cost should also be shared
- Where there is internal competition between branches and departments it is important to be able to gauge and compare profitability
- Where managers are held responsible for the financial performance of their departments, it must be clear on what basis performance will be evaluated
- Where management salaries are partly linked to profitability there must be an accurate and reliable basis for calculations of bonuses

> A *COST CENTRE* is defined as a location, a function or items of equipment in respect of which costs may be ascertained and related to cost units for control purposes.

This definition is necessarily very general. Cost centres can be branches, departments, counters, or even product lines (a special case of the identification of costs with products is direct product profitability, which is discussed in Section 18.5).

Imagine the organisation as a *hierarchy* of cost centres, with each larger cost centre, such as a branch, made up of smaller cost centres, such as departments. This is

FIGURE 18.1

ORGANISATIONAL STRUCTURE AND COST CENTRES

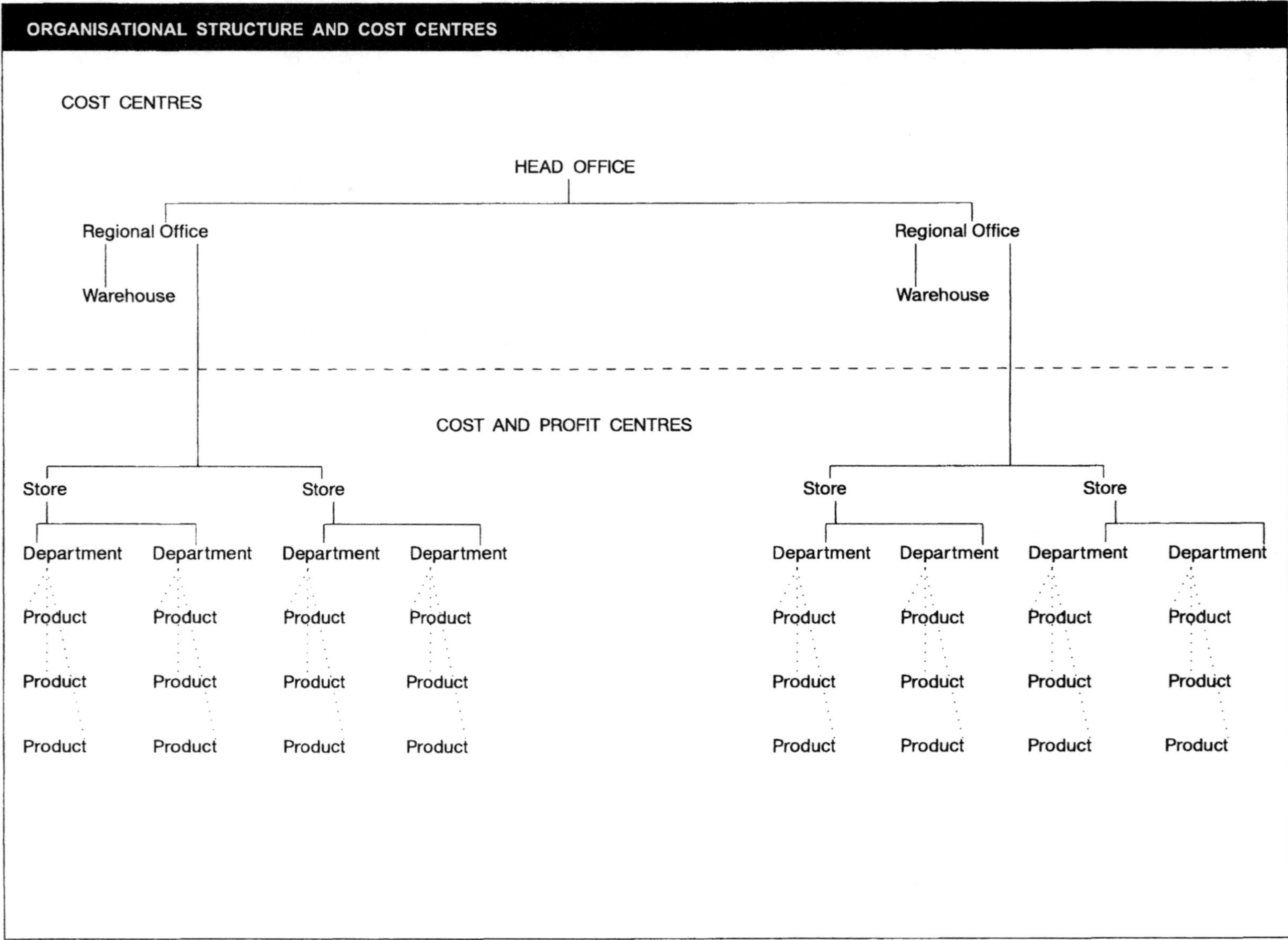

shown in Figure 18.1, where a retail organisation is used to illustrate the general principle.

The manager of each of the larger cost centres has a distinct set of responsibilities and a clearly identified superior who is in charge of monitoring the performance of the cost centre and to interfere if things are not going according to plan. Responsibilities vary depending on the nature of the cost centre. For example, a decision to cease trading in Scotland is based on the results of several regions, whereas a decision to mark down what is left behind the bread counter at five o'clock in the afternoon may be left to the discretion of the departmental manager.

Exercise 18.1

(a) Explain in your own words, what is meant by the term 'cost centre'.

(b) How do you think common costs can be spread fairly across cost centres?

Some costs can be directly identified with a cost centre and are *allocated* to it. For example, the cost of purchasing one item for resale to customers can clearly be identified with that item. However, some costs cannot be allocated without being split over several cost centres. An example of this is the cost of running a large car park next to one of the stores. Clearly this cannot be allocated to just one department, as customers for all the departments make use of it. Costs must therefore be shared by the departments. Where this is the case we say they are *apportioned*.

> Cost *APPORTIONMENT* is defined as the division of costs among two or more cost centres in proportion to the benefits received, using an appropriate base, for instance, sales volume, square footage occupied or number of employees.

Exercise 18.2

Indicate which of the following costs can be directly allocated to the delicatessen department (a cost centre within a small supermarket in Sheffield) and which have to be apportioned on an equitable basis.

- Rent
- Counter staff wages
- £20 worth of perishable items which have passed their sell-by date, and must be destroyed
- Electronic scales
- Store manager's salary
- Cleaner's wage
- Plastic bags
- Set of knives

The basis on which they are apportioned varies, depending on the cost – cause relationship, fairness and judgement. The following examples illustrate this.

- The rent of a supermarket's premises must be apportioned fairly between departments, using square footage occupied (for example) as a logical base
- The cost of running an EPOS system can be apportioned to the departments on the basis of turnover (for example)

Exercise 18.3

The cost items listed in Figure 18.2 are to be apportioned between the departments of the head office of Purely Travel Ltd, a large tour operator based in London, which is split into six departments, each focusing on a

FIGURE 18.2

PURELY TRAVEL LTD:
COST ALLOCATION AND APPORTIONMENT

Cost item	Base for Apportionment
Heat and Light	
Rates	
Clerical Expenses	
Computer System, Depreciation and Maintenance	
Canteen	

particular holiday destination. For each cost item suggest which base would be most appropriate:

- Floor space
- Turnover
- Number of employees
- Labour hours

Within a large business organisation only certain parts of the organisation are involved in generating revenue. These are known as *PROFIT CENTRES*. Profit centres are also cost centres, but not all cost centres are profit centres, as not all cost centres are involved in selling products; many are there to provide services to the profit centres.

Exercise 18.4

The following is the structure of a supermarket split into cost centres:

Grocery, Provisions, Bakery, Wines and Spirits, Kiosk, Produce, Hard Goods, Soft Goods, Checkouts, Warehouse, Service, Canteen.

(a) Identify those cost centres which are also profit centres

(b) Show how costs can be more closely identified with activities by breaking each department down into further cost centres

(c) Explain how the concept of a cost centre can be used to help management control costs

Ultimately all costs must be met by the profit centres. This means apportioning the costs incurred by those cost centres that only exist to service the profit centres between the profit centres. For example, head office running costs are not directly related to the individual stores, but may be apportioned on the basis of profitability. Also, the cost of running a staff canteen can be shared between departments, for instance by using number of employees as a base.

Example

For a typical week the profit and loss statement for 'The Hound and Horse', a popular pub and restaurant, is shown in Figure 18.3.

FIGURE 18.3

'THE HOUND AND HORSE': PROFIT AND LOSS ACCOUNT FOR WEEK ENDING 23 APRIL 199X

	£
Sales	8 000
Cost of Goods Sold	6 800
Gross Profit	1 200
Expenses:	
Rent and Rates	275
Salary Cook	110
Salary Manager	200
Wages Other Staff	320
Depreciation of Fixtures	30
Heat and Light	50
Administration	30
Total Expenses	1 015
Net Profit	185

The manager wishes to introduce a new costing system. This will highlight the respective profitability of the two parts of the business, which will be treated as separate cost and profit centres. The additional information available to you is shown in Table 18.1.

TABLE 18.1

'THE HOUND AND HORSE': ADDITIONAL DATA

	Restaurant	Bar	Total
Floor Area	400 sq ft	600 sq ft	1000 sq ft
Percentage Split	40%	60%	100%
Sales	£5000	£3000	£8000
Percentage Split	62.5%	37.5%	100%
Gross Profit	£900	£300	£1200
Percentage Split	75%	25%	100%

In order to be able to draw up separate income statements for each of the restaurant and the bar, you need to take the following steps:

Step 1
Decide which cost items can be *allocated* directly to the cost centres and which should be *apportioned*.

Step 2
For each item to be apportioned, decide on an appropriate *base.*

Step 3
Split the costs and draw up the two income statements.

In doing your answer, note that in this type of situation, decisions are often based on the manager's best judgement. It is therefore possible to come up with several different 'right' answers to a problem of this nature. The following is how we answered it, you may approach it slightly differently, for example choose different bases, as long as you have thought it through and can justify your answer.

Step 1
In this case the only cost which is directly allocated is the cook's salary. This is based on the assumption that the cook just works in the restaurant and has nothing to do with the bar. All other cost items are shared and must be apportioned.

Step 2
The choice of base is determined by potential cause–effect relationships.

We decided to use floor area as the base for apportioning

- Rent and rates
- Depreciation fixtures
- Heat and light

using the logic that there is a logical link between the space taken up by the cost centres and the above items. This means that 40 per cent of these costs is apportioned to the restaurant and 60 per cent to the bar.

Wages were apportioned on the basis of sales with the idea in mind that staff may work towards sales targets and may have to work harder to achieve higher sales. This means that 62.5 per cent of these costs is apportioned to the restaurant and 37.5 per cent to the bar.

The manager's salary was apportioned on the basis of gross profit making the assumption that the manager's performance would be judged by the profitability of the outlet. This means that 75 per cent of these costs is apportioned to the restaurant and 25 per cent to the bar.

Finally, administration costs were apportioned on the basis of gross profit. This means that 75 per cent of these costs is apportioned to the restaurant and 25 per cent to the bar. However, there is no strong case for this and another base would probably do just as well.

Step 3
The profit and loss statement can now be restated showing the results of the two profit centres clearly, as shown in Figure 18.4.

As you can see, this has been a useful exercise as it has highlighted the fact that at present the restaurant is subsidising the bar, which is in fact making a loss. This can be the trigger for plans to refurbish the bar, have a weekly quiz night to attract new customers or have a regular happy hour! In this sense it is very useful information. However, it could also easily lead to the wrong conclusions: obviously it would be foolish not to have a bar at all.

FIGURE 18.4

'THE HOUND AND HORSE': PROFIT AND LOSS ACCOUNT FOR WEEK ENDING 23 APRIL 199X, SHOWING PROFIT AND COST CENTRES

	Restaurant	Bar	Base
	£	£	
Sales	5000	3000	
Cost of Goods Sold	4100	2700	
Gross Profit	900	300	
Expenses			
Rent and Rates	110	165	**sq ft**
Salary Cook	110		**allocated**
Salary Manager	150	50	**gross profit**
Wages Other Staff	200	120	**sales**
Depreciation			
Fixtures	12	18	**sq ft**
Heat and Light	20	30	**sq ft**
Administration	22.5	7.5	**gross profit**
Total Expenses	624.5	390.5	
Net Profit	275.5	(–90.5)	

Exercise 18.5

Lorraine runs a combined bread shop and coffee shop from premises in the Sheaf market in Sheffield. Her business's profit and loss statement for a typical week is shown in Figure 18.5.

There is an opportunity to rent additional space adjacent to the present premises. Lorraine is trying to decide whether it would be more profitable to expand the coffee shop or the bread shop. She has asked you to advise her as to how a more sophisticated costing system could help with this decision. The additional information available is summarised in Table 18.2.

(a) Allocate all costs which can be directly identified with one of the cost centres. Apportion the remaining costs between cost centres, using an appropriate choice of base. In each case, briefly explain your choice of base.

(b) Draw up separate profit and loss statements for the bread shop and the cafe.

(c) Comment on the financial performance of the two sides of the business and advise Lorraine with regard to the proposed expansion of the business. Which other factors should be taken into account when making the decision which side to expand?

FIGURE 18.5

LORRAINE'S BREAD SHOP AND COFFEE SHOP: PROFIT AND LOSS ACCOUNT 9 OCTOBER TO 15 OCTOBER 199X

	£	£
Sales		10 000
Cost of Goods Sold		6 500
Gross Profit		3 500
Expenses		
Staff Wages	800	
Salary Cook	150	
Depreciation		
Fixtures and Fittings	88	
Rent and Rates	510	
Heat and Light	40	
Bags	35	
Salary Manager	285	
		1 908
Net Profit		1 592

TABLE 18.2

LORRAINE'S BREAD SHOP AND COFFEE SHOP: ADDITIONAL INFORMATION

	Total	Bread Shop	Coffee Shop
	£	£	£
Sales	10 000	6000	4000
Cost of Goods Sold	6 500	4500	2000
Gross Profit	3 500	1500	2000
	sq ft	sq ft	sq ft
Sales Area	1 300	800	500

18.5 Costing a product's journey through the value chain

Much business activity is about producing goods which are ultimately sold to the consumer. In this, they start as raw materials and pass through various stages from manufacturing through retailing and ultimately to the end consumer. At each stage, *costs* are incurred in transforming the product and something of *value* is added in return. For each of the organisations in this chain of exchange relationships, it is important to know precisely what the costs are in order to be able to charge the right prices to enable the businesses to survive and operate profitably. The costing systems of a business link costs to cost centres in order to ensure that they are ultimately absorbed by the products the business makes or sells. The reason for this is that in the end all the cost of running a business operation must be met by the revenues generated through selling the business's goods or services. It follows that, in principle, it is useful to have a system which links as many costs as possible directly to products, as this enables management to evaluate which products are most profitable and should therefore be given greater priority and marketing effort.

Traditionally, costing systems in manufacturing have been devised with this objective in mind and have succeeded in costing jobs or processes as the basis for determining how much to charge for goods produced. This is normally done by carrying out time and motion studies to ascertain all the materials, work processes and use of machinery involved in producing each item. This then serves as the basis for specifying the cost of making the item and is used as an aid to pricing decisions.

Whilst a study of *ACTUAL COST* patterns is the starting point for determining the cost of making each item, once this has been established, it is then applied as a *STANDARD COST* for future decision-making. The reason for this is that prices must be quoted to customers long before the actual process of making the goods has been carried out. It is therefore not possible to use the true actual cost as the basis for the price. It would also be very time-consuming and expensive if time and motion studies had to be performed repeatedly. Clearly it is much easier to work with standard costs. As a result cost items such as direct raw materials, direct labour and machine time can be charged on the basis of the average amount used or time taken for a product of this kind. A comparison can then be made once the actual cost data are known to see whether they continue to match the standards.

Where goods are then sold to a retailer, the price charged by the manufacturer becomes the retailer's cost of goods. The retailer's gross profit is the difference between the price the retailer charges to the customer and the price the retailer paid to the manufacturer.

Exercise 18.6

As you know, gross margin is only one of many factors influencing the profits generated by a retailer through selling a product line. State three other factors which have an influence.

As you can see, cost of goods sold is only one of the costs associated with getting the goods to the end consumer. Further examples are stock turnover, space allocation, handling and storage requirement, and wastage, as all these factors contribute to the cost associated with retailing the goods. There is certainly an argument that, much as in manufacturing, the above cost items should also be directly related to products, as they are all to do with the processing of products for sale to the customers and ultimately each unit sold benefits from this process.

Despite this, until the 1990s gross margin dominated product mix and pricing decisions in the majority of retailing businesses. The reason is that it was simply too difficult and costly to find ways of relating the other costs directly back to the goods sold. With the increasing use of fully integrated computer systems in retailing, it became possible to capture and process large amounts of data on sales and costs, as well as timing, space usage and deliveries.

As a result a new costing system, known as *DIRECT PRODUCT PROFITABILITY* was developed, specifically with retailing organisations in mind. Here, instead of using gross margin as the deciding factor in decision making, *DIRECT PRODUCT COST* (*DPC*) is determined, by relating all the elements of cost which can be directly identified with individual products to them, such as the cost of handling the product, occupation of warehouse space, shelf space and delivery.

> *DIRECT PRODUCT PROFIT* (*DPP*) is defined as the individual contribution made by a product to general overhead costs and profit, after all the costs attributable to the product have been accounted for.

This information can then be used to guide tactical marketing decisions aimed at maximising the profitability of each product line. This is done by looking at both sales volume and direct product profitability, as shown in the decision tree depicted in Figure 18.6. Each category can stimulate a number of responses to improve product performance.

The decision tree for analysing results highlights how DPP is best used – as the diagnostic tool with which management are pointed to look at areas of the products supply chain and can choose the best response for each individual product. In this way pricing decisions can be taken in the context of larger strategic concerns, costs are controlled much more effectively, the best possible sales mix and space allocation can be chosen and overall profits maximised.

Direct product costing systems can be quite detailed in their approach and often group direct product costs according to the various stages of the distribution process. For example, as the goods are delivered into the retailer's centralised warehouse, costs are incurred in the processes of receiving, checking, moving, storing, pricing and picking goods for the stores. Following this, transportation costs are incurred, depending on distance and mode of transport selected. Finally, in

FIGURE 18.6

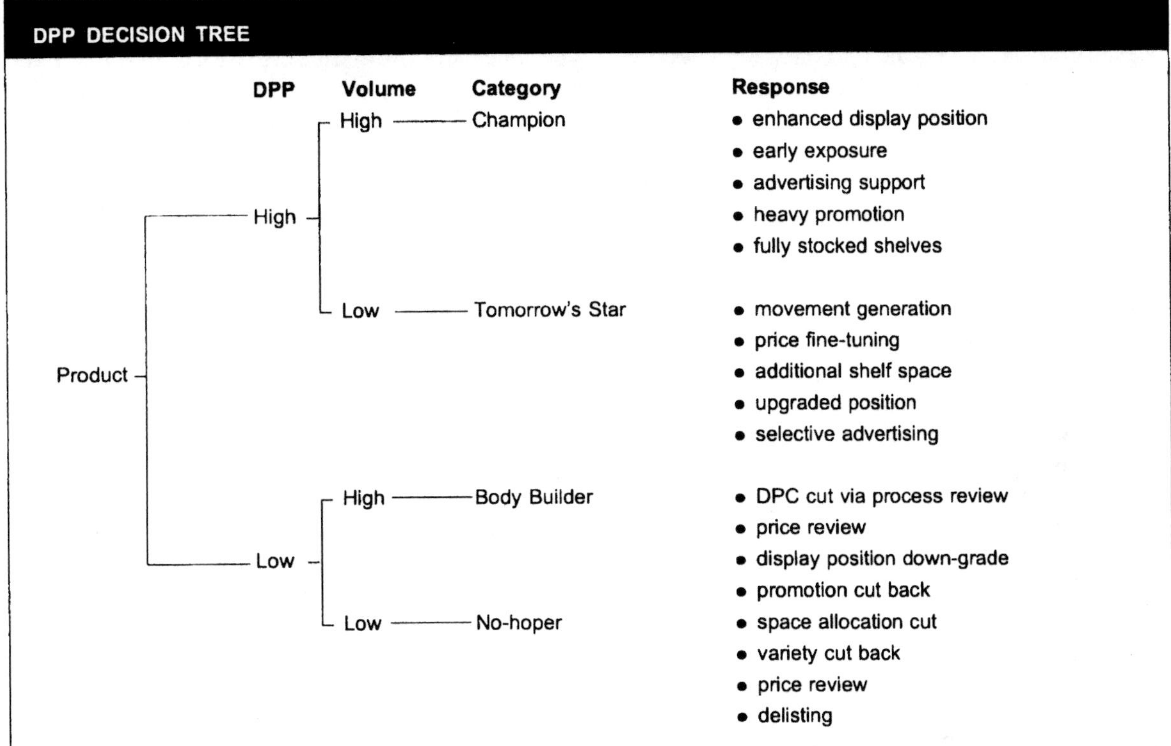

the actual retail store, there are costs to do with receiving, checking, moving and storing goods, both in the backroom and related to actual shelf space.

It follows that extensive studies of the movement of each product through the retail organisation must be carried out to determine the average or standard costs associated with each item before it reaches the consumer. These standard costs feed into the calculation of the direct product profitability of the product line.

As you can see, costing systems in both manufacturing and retailing are guided by roughly the same principles – where possible, costs are related to products, using standards determined by a detailed study of work processes. Clearly, each organisation wishes to keep cost as low as possible whilst at the same time maximising sales volume. This is done by making the processes involved more efficient, as this has a positive impact on profitability. The relationship between the place of organisations in the value chain and their costing systems is shown in Figure 18.7.

The introduction of direct product costing systems for retailers means that there is a unique opportunity to integrate the approaches taken by the different organisations in the supply chain. Retailers give feedback to manufacturers and advise them on the basis of the information gathered. For example, it may make little difference to the manufacturer's costs which pack sizes and shapes are selected, but this may have

FIGURE 18.7

COSTING SYSTEMS AND THE VALUE CHAIN

Place in value chain	**Manufacturer ⟶**	**Retailer**
Examples of direct product costs	Raw materials Labour costs Machine usage Packing	Cost of goods Storage Handling Distribution
Costing systems	Job costing ⟶ Process costing	Direct product costing

a considerable impact on retailer DPP. This is exactly the reasoning which went into the design of small packs of concentrated washing powder and liquids. Naturally, care must be taken that there is no negative impact on consumer perceptions, so the new design must always be test-marketed.

To set up a DPP system which will provide the most use for both suppliers as well as retailers, the definitions of the processes and items to be costed must be clearly standardised for the industry. Cost data should be collected for the industry as a whole and standards worked out, which can be related to an individual store's situation. For many large retailers and manufacturers close cooperation already exists and often Electronic Data Interchange (EDI) links are already established. Many large manufacturers are global operators and have strong relationships with a number of retailers in the same industry. Considering the complexity and detail of the information required it is much less time-consuming and expensive for retailers and manufacturers to cooperate in the collection of cost data which can be used as industry standards.

Collating cost data in this systematic way ensures comparability between different types of stores and alternative systems, so new ways of packaging or processing goods can easily be evaluated on the merits of the cost savings they entail. Once standards have been calculated, a computerised model can be developed which will calculate the DPP for individual product lines, as the data relating to the product line and the individual store are put into the system. The software used in developing this type of model is based on a spreadsheet package.

18.6 Summary

In this chapter the need for a costing system as a basis to guide decision-making was introduced. The term cost was defined and a distinction was made between costs which can be directly related to the production and processing of goods ultimately destined for the end consumer and overhead costs which are of a more general nature. All costing systems are based on the use of standard costs, based on an average figure derived from the study of the processes involved, as well as historical data.

For the treatment of overhead costs, an *ABSORPTION COSTING* system was introduced. For this, the organisation is subdivided into cost centres and profit centres and management responsibility for these centres is identified. Following the principle that all costs must be covered in the long run, cost items that are not easily related to particular products or activities are split, or apportioned, between cost centres, using another variable, such as number of employees or space occupied, as the basis.

This is a useful aid to decision-making, as subdividing an organisational profit and loss statement by profit centres can provide useful additional insights into their respective contribution to the overall profitability of an organisation. This can aid decisions as to which areas of activity to expand or downsize.

Approaches to the costing of products throughout the supply chain were discussed. Direct product profitability is a computerised system for the direct allocation of direct product costs (DPCs) to products. Direct product profit (DPP) is calculated by deducting all direct product costs from the gross profit generated by the product.

This system enables retailers, wholesalers and manufacturers to work together with the common aim of minimising costs and maximising the profitability of each product line. A knowledge of the DPP and sales volume achieved for individual product lines can be evaluated using the DPP decision tree, which was specifically developed to help retailers in making product mix and space allocation decisions.

19
Budgeting

19.1 Learning objectives

When you have finished working through this chapter you should be able to

- Define the term **BUDGET** and explain what is meant by budgetary control
- State at least four objectives of a budget
- Explain what is meant by responsibility accounting
- Define the terms **MANAGEMENT BY OBJECTIVES (MBO)** and **MANAGEMENT BY EXCEPTION (MBE)**
- Contrast and compare the **BOTTOM UP** and **TOP DOWN** approaches to budgeting
- Contrast and compare **ZERO-BASE BUDGETING** with an **INCREMENTAL** approach to budgeting
- Explain what is meant by a **MASTER BUDGET** and name the three main components of the master budget
- In the context of a simple example, compile operating budgets for stock, debtor and creditor control, a **CASH BUDGET**, a **BUDGETED PROFIT AND LOSS STATEMENT** and a **BUDGETED BALANCE SHEET**; in other words, construct a master budget

19.2 Business objectives and the budgetary control process

Once the organisation has been subdivided into cost and profit centres, as shown in Chapter 18, this enables management to analyse the performance of each part of the organisation, to identify strengths and weaknesses and to set targets for future performance which are based on the standards derived from an analysis of the past. This facilitates the budgeting process.

> A *BUDGET* is defined as a detailed plan concerning the allocation of physical resources, expressed in money terms.

- **Plan**
  It is concerned with the future
- **Allocation**
  It recognises the fact that resources are limited, therefore a choice must be made, as to how they should be used

- **Physical resources expressed in money terms**
  Only those aspects of the business which can be quantified and assigned a money value can be planned in this way.

In constructing a plan for the future activities and performance of the business, a budget makes use of the information derived by making a sales forecast (as discussed in Chapters 11–17) and matches this with the information provided by the organisation's costing systems (as discussed in Chapter 18).

The aims of a budget are:

- To serve as a yardstick against which actual performance can be compared
- To motivate staff by setting challenging targets
- To control costs
- To devolve responsibility to line management
- To communicate top to bottom, and vice versa

Drawing up a budget forces management to define the common goal very clearly and to translate it into individual financial goals for each member of the organisation. This means that it is possible to identify the member of staff who is responsible for each aspect of the plan and to give them the training and authority required to carry out their task. It also serves to translate the long-term goals of the business into short-term goals.

A budget is drawn up for a specific *time period.* The appropriate time frame depends on the level within the organisation and the magnitude and timing of the expenditure planned. Many organisations have a five-year strategic plan within which one-year plans are contained. This facilitates the planning of capital expenditure and organisational expansion. The one-year plan serves as a yardstick for the next financial year. However, within this, regular reviews are necessary, as the future is uncertain and many unforeseen things can happen which throw the original plan off course. For instance, inflation may result in an increase in the cost prices of merchandise, the cost of wages may increase more than expected, a downturn in the economy may result in reduced sales volumes. In all these instances it is necessary to make an adjustment to the plan to take these changes into account. As a result, a breakdown into *monthly* or even *weekly* budgets for the operational cost centres can be a useful aid to management.

19.3 Implications of budgeting for line management

In the above it has become apparent that the budgetary planning process follows the structure of the organisation. Budgets are drawn up for all the cost and profit centres. It is therefore necessary to define each cost and profit centre in terms of the authority and responsibility held by its manager. This involves identifying *staff responsibility* for each cost item. Also there is a need to identify which costs can be directly influenced by this manager and staff, in other words, which costs are *controllable* at that level.

Exercise 19.1

Match the following costs with the organisational level at which they can be controlled.

Costs

(1) Stock wastage and shrinkage **(2)** Capital expenditure on building new premises **(3)** Cost of sales staff making cold calls to potential new customers

Organisational levels

(A) Board of Directors **(B)** Regional Manager **(C)** Departmental manager on shop floor

RESPONSIBILITY ACCOUNTING means that for each cost target the appropriate level of control and the specific manager responsible can be identified. To get maximum commitment to the budgetary targets it is therefore important to take the views of the managers responsible into consideration when drawing up the budget, rather than just imposing targets which could then be seen as unrealistic by line management.

There are two extreme approaches to the human side of budgeting, bottom up and top down. The *BOTTOM UP* approach is based on the assumption that sales staff and line management are the best judges of what can be achieved in terms of generating sales and controlling costs. They should therefore draw up budgets for their individual sections which are brought together to formulate the master plan. In contrast, the *TOP DOWN* approach is based on the perspective that the top management of the company have a coherent view of the company as a whole, as well as the state of the market, competition, sources of finance available, new products and trends in society. In addition, a large organisation has the advantage of certain economies of scale. Top management can afford to buy expensive market reports and have designated staff whose job it is to carry out detailed analyses of market conditions. Because of this, they are in the best position to formulate the organisation's strategy and translate it into action plans for each branch and ultimately each manager.

To achieve the best results, the two approaches should come together. Line management should be involved in drawing up the budget – otherwise they will not be motivated to work to it. Top management must ensure that the company's strategic goals are clearly defined and that the goals of individual cost centres are aligned to the overall goal and everybody is working towards this in a congruent manner. Top management can also take on a coordinating role to ensure that individual targets, whilst realistic, remain challenging.

Drawing up a master plan which breaks down into detailed action plans for every part of the organisation and each manager is an approach known as *MANAGEMENT BY OBJECTIVES* (*MBO*). MBO translates the objectives of the whole organisation into objectives for regions, areas, branches, departments, and eventually – all the way down the line – into individualised objectives for each member of staff. These individual objectives are agreed in an appraisal and serve as a yardstick against which subsequent performance is measured.

There is evidence that a realistic, yet challenging, budget which is accepted by the managers throughout the organisation can enhance motivation to achieve the targets set. This means that each manager's superior only needs to interfere when the evaluation process shows that actual cost figures have been significantly in excess of the targets. This is known as *MANAGEMENT BY EXCEPTION* – if things are going according to plan, they are left alone. Only where things go wrong, action is taken. This saves a great deal of management time.

19.4 Master budgets

The starting point of the budgeting process must be a detailed sales forecast as the level of activity expected affects the cost of operating and is related to the level of investment required. The sales forecast directly determines the purchases and average stock levels required. Cash inflows and the level of debtors will be directly related to sales; cash outflows and creditor balances will be determined by the purchases. In the short run the operating expenses vary with the level of activity, in the long run, investment levels will be linked to anticipated sales. In this sense costs also can only be predicted accurately if sales levels can be anticipated.

An accurate *sales forecast* is therefore the cornerstone of the budgeting process.

Once the sales forecast has been translated into a detailed sales budget, purchases and stock budget, these can be used together with historical figures to plan debtor and creditor levels for the months ahead, as well as the expenses associated with the budgeted level of activity. All these are brought together in a set of *MASTER BUDGETS*. The master budgets integrate and summarise the individual budgets drawn up for the different cost and profit centres and unite them into one coherent master plan for the whole organisation. They consist of a *CASH BUDGET*, a *BUDGETED PROFIT AND LOSS STATEMENT* and a *BUDGETED BALANCE SHEET*.

The cash budget

The first of these master budgets is the *CASH BUDGET*, which expresses all the future activities of the business in terms of cash inflows and outflows. Drawing on the information from the other resource budgets, the cash budget acts as a crystal ball, showing the expected future cash flows of the business and its component parts.

The resource requirements of the different parts of the business are expressed in cash terms. In business start-ups such a cash budget provides a detailed business plan for the owner and the bank manager. In established businesses it allows management to raise extra cash where shortfalls are expected.

Depending on the nature of the budgeting process, the cash budget can also be used to facilitate the allocation of resources to the areas where they will be employed most profitably.

Where a top down approach to budgeting is used, cash budgets for the branches and departments will be set centrally and passed down to the line managers responsible for working to those budgets. This is often based on historical cost and sales data with a certain percentage added to allow for inflation and growth. This is known as an *INCREMENTAL* approach to budgeting. One drawback of this approach is that it often fails to detect where improvements in efficiency are possible. A different approach which introduces fierce grass roots competition for resources is known as *ZERO-BASE BUDGETING*. Here line managers are required to submit detailed requests for resources, justifying their future expenditure plans. Cash resources are allocated on the basis of the relative merits of the proposals. The advantage of this is that it provides a better safeguard against inefficiency, as nobody can take their cash allocation for granted. However, a lot of management time can be wasted in drawing up proposals.

The technicalities of drawing up a cash budget are very similar to those involved in drawing up a cash flow statement. The difference lies in the fact that when drawing up a cash flow statement you are using actual historical data, whereas a cash budget is based on a forecast of the future activities of the business. Based on *STANDARDS* derived from past average figures, or from comparable businesses, you are forecasting future receipts and payments, as well as monthly opening and closing balances.

Example

On 1 January 199X Jeremy Weed starts in business, marketing and supplying a book with the title '10 000 Fabulous Ideas How To Become A Millionaire Within A Year!'

- In December Jeremy had a meeting with his bank manager. As a result the bank agreed to lend him £10 000 to put into the business. The following are the projected figures which Jeremy presented to his bank manager as the foundation of his business plan:
- Jeremy himself will invest £15 000 capital in the business. This is money he has been paid on account of being made redundant in his previous job in the printing industry.
- On 1 January, Jeremy will open a business bank account, and will put his own £15 000 as well as the £10 000 borrowed from the bank into it.
- In January, Jeremy will have to pay out £20 000 to acquire premises, £3000 for fixtures and fittings, and £1000 for office equipment, stationery and sundries. These will be depreciated over 10 years with zero scrap value at the end, using the straight line method.
- In January, Jeremy plans to employ two part-time members of staff, a receptionist and a clerical assistant, and he will pay them £415 per month. Wages will be paid in the month when the work is done.
- The book will be advertised in the press, at an estimated cost of £125 per month.
- It is estimated that the following sales can be generated:

	Jan	**Feb**	**Mar**	**Apr**	**May**	**Jun**
Sales (units)	200	220	280	350	400	330

- Selling price per book is £10. In any month it is likely that half the customers will pay cash, the rest will take two months' credit.
- The printing of the books will be sub-contracted to a small printing firm.
- The following supply schedule is envisaged:

Units received from printer	**Jan**	**Feb**	**Mar**	**Apr**	**May**	**Jun**
	250	200	250	380	500	450

- Printing costs are £6 per book, payable one month after the books have been received from the printing firm.

Jeremy Weed does not intend to take any money out of the business for his own use until March when he will need to take out £1000. The question is, if everything goes according to plan, can he afford to do this without jeopardising his business's cash flow position?

Figure 19.1 shows the cash budget for Jeremy Weed's business for each month from January until June. You can see from this that Jeremy can afford to take out £1000 in March without needing to go overdrawn, however, he still needs to be fairly careful with cash in the next few months after that.

To complete the planning aspect of the budgeting cycle, two further Master Budgets need to be drawn

FIGURE 19.1

JEREMY WEED'S BUSINESS: CASH BUDGET JANUARY TO JUNE 199X						
	Jan	Feb	Mar	Apr	May	Jun
	£	£	£	£	£	£
Opening Balance	0	1460	520	180	990	1570
Cash Receipts						
Cash Sales	1000	1100	1400	1750	2000	1650
Receipts from Debtors	0	0	1000	1100	1400	1750
Capital Investment	25000					
Cash Payments						
Payments to Creditors	0	1500	1200	1500	2280	3000
Wages	415	415	415	415	415	415
Advertising	125	125	125	125	125	125
Drawings			1000			
Premises	20000					
Fixtures and Fittings	3000					
Office Sundries	1000					
Closing Balance	1460	520	180	990	1570	1430

up – a *budgeted* profit and loss statement for the budgetary period, showing the anticipated changes in the financial position of the business over the period in question, and a *budgeted* balance sheet, depicting the financial state the business will be in at the end of the budgetary period if all goes according to plan.

The skills required to do this are identical to the skills acquired in drawing up profit and loss accounts and balance sheets based on historical data, which you learned to do in Chapters 2 and 3. The only difference is that here we are dealing with a forecast of future costs and sales revenues, based on standards.

Operating budgets

In order to be able to draw up the budgeted profit and loss statement and the budgeted balance sheet, you first need to draw up a number of operating budgets in order to plan the management of stock, debtors and creditors over the time period. As with the cash budget, you can draw up a detailed plan, covering each month. Alternatively you can simply draw up a summary for the whole period, as in Figures 19.2–19.4.

FIGURE 19.2

JEREMY WEED'S BUSINESS: STOCK BUDGET SUMMARY JANUARY TO JUNE 199X	
	£
Opening Stock	0
Purchases	12180
Sales (at cost)	10680
Closing Stock	1500

FIGURE 19.3

JEREMY WEED'S BUSINESS: DEBTORS' BUDGET SUMMARY JANUARY TO JUNE 199X	
	£
Opening Balance Debtors	0
Credit Sales	8900
Receipts from Debtors	5250
Closing Balance Debtors	3650

FIGURE 19.4

JEREMY WEED'S BUSINESS: CREDITORS' BUDGET SUMMARY JANUARY TO JUNE 199X

	£
Opening Balance Creditors	0
Credit Purchases	12 180
Payments to Creditors	9 480
Closing Balance Creditors	2 700

The budgeted profit and loss statement

Having drawn up the operating budgets for stock, debtors and creditors, we are now in a position to put all the information together in the form of a budgeted profit and loss statement and a budgeted balance sheet. These are shown in Figures 19.5 and 19.6.

Note that for the budgeted profit and loss statement, the cost of goods sold figure was drawn from the stock budget. Also, in addition to the figures contained in the cash budget, this statement contains a charge for depreciation for the six month period.

FIGURE 19.5

JEREMY WEED'S BUSINESS: BUDGETED PROFIT AND LOSS ACCOUNT SUMMARY JANUARY TO JUNE 199X

	£	£
Sales		17 800
Cost of Goods Sold		10 680
Gross Profit		7 120
Expenses		
Wages	2 490	
Advertising	750	
Depreciation	1 200	
		4 440
Net Profit		2 680
Drawings		1 000
Retained Profit		1 680

FIGURE 19.6

JEREMY WEED'S BUSINESS: BUDGETED BALANCE SHEET FOR END OF JUNE 199X

	Cost	Depreciation	Net Book Value
	£	£	£
Fixed Assets			
Premises	20 000	1 000	19 000
Fixtures and Fittings	3 000	150	2 850
Office Equipment	1 000	50	950
			22 800
Current Assets			
Stock	1 500		
Debtors	3 650		
Cash and Bank	1 430		
		6 580	
Creditors: due within one year			
Trade Creditors	2 700		
		2 700	
Net Current Assets			3 880
Net Total Assets			26 680
Creditors: due after one year			
Long-term Loan Capital			10 000
			16 680
Owner's Capital		15 000	
Retained Profit		1 680	
			16 680

The budgeted balance sheet

The budgeted balance sheet shows the financial position the business will be in at the end of June if all goes according to plan. The budgeted balance sheet summarises the other budgets, drawing on information from each:

- The stock figure is the closing balance of the stock budget

- The debtors' figure is the closing balance of the debtors' budget
- The cash figure is the closing balance of the cash budget
- The creditors' figure is the closing balance of the creditors' budget
- The retained profit figure is drawn from the profit and loss statement.

Exercise 19.2

John Bloggs has been made redundant and decides to become self-employed. In his previous job he was the manager of a busy toy and games department in a town centre store, and he is keen to use his expertise. The opportunity arises to acquire the lease on a small shop in a busy part of town for £50 000. The shop sells war games and fantasy games and has been established in this part of town for the last 10 years. John forms a private limited company and raises the share finance needed to pay for the lease. However, the premises are badly in need of refurbishment, which will cost another £10 000. John decides to approach his bank manager to enquire about a business loan of £10 000. He is confident of getting the loan. However, he is keen to impress the bank manager and to build a good relationship for the future. He therefore decides to carry out extensive market research, and to use his personal computer to draw up a financial business plan for the first three months.

The previous owner of the games shop lets him have access to last sales year's figures. The following picture emerges:

- For the three months from October to December, which is the time period when John will be starting in business, the monthly share of total annual sales was:

  October 5 per cent, November 9 per cent, December 17 per cent.

- John is confident that promotions and refurbishment, as well as a good knowledge of fashions and trends in the market for war and fantasy games will enable him to achieve sales to the value of £250 000 in the first year.

When drawing up the plan, John is making the following assumptions:

- He will acquire the shop as a going concern, paying the previous owner £20 000 for his opening stock.
- All sales will be on a cash basis – no credit will be given. The shop will be operating on a gross margin of 60 per cent. (For the purposes of your calculations assume that goods are purchased in the month when they are sold and the closing stock at the end of December will be valued at £20 000.)
- John's trade suppliers will let him have one month's credit straight away, since he is already well known in the trade. For the purposes of his forecast John assumes that the months October to December will carry the same percentage of total sales as they did in the previous year. The lease for the shop has 10 years to run, and the new fixtures and fittings will also be useful for 10 years, with no scrap value at the end of the period. Both are to be depreciated using the straight line method.
- Rent, rates and water charges will be paid quarterly (in advance) in January, April, July and October, the respective annual charges are rent £16 000, rates £7000 and water £800.
- John plans to promote his business and he intends to spend 10 per cent of the value of sales in any given month on promotions.
- John is going to draw a salary of £14 000 per annum in the form of monthly payments.
- All staff are going to be employed on a part-time basis and their wages will come to 18 per cent of sales. They are paid in the month when the work is carried out.

Using the above information and a sales forecast of £250 000 per annum, you are required to draw up

(a) a cash budget for the months October to December
(b) a budgeted profit and loss statement for the same period
(c) a budgeted balance sheet as it will be at the end of December if all goes according to plan

19.5 Summary

In this chapter the principles of the budgetary planning and control process were introduced. A budget was defined as a detailed plan dealing with the allocation of financial resources for a future accounting period. It is used to set monetary sales, cost and profit targets for all parts of the organisation and each member of staff. The division of the organisation into cost and profit centres makes it possible to draw up mini-budgets for each centre, thereby fixing responsibility for each cost item. This is known as management by objectives. Budgets can be drawn up on the basis of historical cost and sales data, using an incremental approach. An alternative approach is zero-base budgeting, where managers submit detailed proposals, competing for funds. In some organisations budgets are imposed by head office, this is known as the top down approach. In others, line management actively contributes to drawing up the budget. This is known as the bottom up approach.

This chapter has introduced the concept of the master budget. This is an integrated budget, drawing together the mini-budgets for the different parts of the organisation. The sales forecast forms the starting point for the budgeting process, this is followed by a detailed plan of purchasing requirements, stock, debtors and creditors. The full master budget consists of three parts: the cash budget, the budgeted profit and loss account and the budgeted balance sheet. It provides a resource plan for the whole organisation, which is based on the detailed forecasts and budgets of all the cost and profit centres within the organisation.

20
Budgetary Control

20.1 Learning objectives

When you have finished working through this chapter you should be able to

- Differentiate between **IDEAL STANDARDS** and **ATTAINABLE STANDARDS**
- Differentiate between **CONTROLLABLE COSTS** and **UNCONTROLLABLE COSTS**, and illustrate this distinction with examples from different levels of the business organisation
- Define the term **VARIANCE**
- Distinguish between **FAVOURABLE** and **ADVERSE** variances and identify appropriate courses of action to be taken in response to such variances arising
- In the context of an example, carry out a detailed **VARIANCE ANALYSIS**, including the calculation and interpretation of variances
- Calculate and make use of a **FLEXIBLE BUDGET**
- Design a spreadsheet **TEMPLATE** for drawing up a flexible budgeted income statement

20.2 Variance analysis and budgetary control

In Chapter 19 you learnt how to devise a budgetary plan incorporating the different levels of a business organisation. You also gained an insight into the respective roles played by head office and line management and the interplay between the two in constructing the budget.

The budgeting process is an ongoing one. It starts with an analysis of the historical performance of the company, treated in Chapters 7–10, which dealt with ratio analysis. This historical analysis in conjunction with the company's mission statement informs the formulation of company objectives for the next budgetary cycle, set to match organisational strengths with opportunities identified, and to minimise the impact of possible weaknesses and threats in the environment. Company objectives have to be expressed in concrete terms for all levels of the organisation and responsibility for the achievement of these objectives clearly identified with individual line managers. This process is known as *MANAGEMENT BY OBJECTIVES* (*MBO*) and was explained in Chapter 19. That chapter also showed how the objectives are translated into a detailed plan, expressed in money terms, in the form of the *MASTER BUDGET*. The final step of the budgetary cycle is to do with using the master budget as a yardstick for comparison, as the actual costs of running the business become known. At this stage the budget is used as a tool to aid the control of the costs of running the business and therefore the achievement of the objectives. Working through the exercises set in Chapters 18 and 19, you may have wondered how the use of standard costs can enable a business organisation to make an accurate forecast of expenses. Reason and experience tell you that in real life expenses can vary a great deal from month to month, and it would be quite difficult to make an accurate prediction of a company's overheads for even a month, not to mention a whole year or five-year period. Budgets are not usually based on the most recent exact historical actual costs, but on *STANDARDS*, which are derived from a knowledge of what the average sales and costs are likely to be. The budget provides a useful yardstick, to which the actual costs of the current financial period can be compared.

Budgets which make use of standard costs are often based on an assumption that there is a link between sales revenues and certain cost items. For instance, you would expect there to be a link between sales and the cost of goods sold. Likewise you might expect to find a relationship between sales and wages. In manufacturing organisations the link between production volumes and the labour input for each item produced is easily established. The same principle can also be applied in retail and service organisations, especially in those which have a lot of part-time labour, which can be scheduled to match demand patterns, as is the case in supermarkets. Such assumptions form the basis for drawing up the budget in Exercise 20.1.

Exercise 20.1

Figure 20.1 gives the profit and loss account of a small toy manufacturer for the 19X4 financial year.

A budget is to be drawn up using the historical statement provided in Figure 20.1 as the basis and making the following assumptions:

A sales forecast indicates that sales can be increased to the level of 330 000, if advertising expenditure is increased to the level of 10 per cent of sales. It is expected that the cost of goods sold, as well as the wages costs would increase in line with sales, in other words, they would remain the same percentage of sales as they were in the original profit and loss statement. Rent and rates should remain the same regardless of the level of sales.

FIGURE 20.1

TOY MANUFACTURER: PROFIT AND LOSS STATEMENT FOR THE PERIOD 1 JANUARY 19X4 TO 31 DECEMBER 19X4

		£	£
	Sales		225 000
–	Cost of Goods Sold		150 000
=	Gross Profit		75 000
–	Expenses		
	Wages	22 500	
	Advertising	11 250	
	Rent and Rates	26 250	
			60 000
=	Net Profit		15 000

Using these assumptions, draw up the budgeted profit and loss statement for the period 1 January 19X5 to 31 December 19X5, using the layout given in Figure 20.2.

FIGURE 20.2

TOY MANUFACTURER: BUDGETED PROFIT AND LOSS STATEMENT FOR THE PERIOD 1 JANUARY 19X5 TO 31 DECEMBER 19X5

		£	£
	Sales		330 000
–	Cost of Goods Sold		
=	Gross Profit		
–	Expenses		
	Wages		
	Advertising		
	Rent and Rates		
=	Net Profit		

Whilst it may be relatively straightforward to make use of time and motion studies to work out the standard costs of manufacturing goods, it can be a little more difficult to apply the same approach to general overhead costs.

Exercise 20.2

For each of the following retail and service organisations, name **two** necessary work processes for which it would be difficult to work out standard times and costs:

(a) Grocer
(b) Public house
(c) University

As you can see from Exercise 20.2, management should bear in mind that the greater the 'people' element involved in the organisation's overall product offering, the harder it is to standardise and the more flexibility is needed. In addition, it is also useful to consider staff motivation when setting budgetary standards. To do this, management should set *ATTAINABLE STANDARDS* rather than *IDEAL STANDARDS*. Ideal standards are those that would be achieved if the organisation could always work at maximum efficiency, sales volumes could be predicted perfectly and no member of staff ever missed a day's work. Clearly this is not likely to happen and staff could get very frustrated if they felt they had to work to such standards. They would then feel that they had no say concerning the budget set for them and they might respond by trying to 'fiddle the budget', rather than use it as a working tool. In contrast, attainable standards are based on a realistic assessment of historical figures and current working practices, resulting in an achievable yet challenging plan.

Motivation theory indicates that people work best when they feel that they have to stretch themselves to achieve a desired outcome, but that it is under their control to do so and that they will be rewarded if they are successful. In terms of budgetary control this means that the budget should be hard but not impossible to achieve, budgetary targets should focus on those costs which can be controlled by the manager in question and there should be a reward, for instance in the form of extra pay or enhanced promotion prospects if targets are met or exceeded. The implication is that in setting objectives, it is important to distinguish for each level of line management between *CONTROLLABLE COSTS* and *UNCONTROLLABLE COSTS*. Nobody should be held responsible for costs they can do nothing about, as this only leads to resentment and frustration.

In the course of the financial year, as actual sales revenues and costs become known, they are compared to the budget.

The difference between the two is known as the *VARIANCE*. Variances can be *ADVERSE* (this means that actual performance is below the budgetary plan), or *FAVOURABLE* (in this case actual performance exceeds budgetary targets). When calculating variances, adverse variances are normally shown with a negative sign and favourable variances with a positive sign.

Exercise 20.3

Using the budget and actual results of Jinx Ltd shown in Figure 20.3, calculate the variances, indicating whether they are adverse or favourable. Use this exercise to derive a general rule for calculating variances.

FIGURE 20.3

JINX LTD: VARIANCE ANALYSIS

	Budget	Actual	Variance	Adverse/Favourable
	£	£	£	
Sales	10 000	9 000		
Cost of Goods Sold	6 000	5 800		
Gross Profit	4 000	3 200		
Expenses	3 000	2 800		
Net Profit	1 000	400		

As you can see from the answer to Exercise 20.3, the rule for calculating variances has to be split into two parts.

For sales and profits, a variance is favourable if the actual figure is *higher* than the budgeted figure. This should be shown by a positive sign. Therefore the variance is calculated by taking the budgeted figure away from the actual figure. For costs it is the other way round. Here a favourable variance means that the actual cost is *lower* than the figure budgeted for. Therefore the variance is calculated by taking the actual figure away from the budgeted figure.

Variance analysis is used as a control and motivational tool, as shown in Figure 20.4, which sets out management responses to the results of a variance analysis.

As you can see, budgetary control is a classical example of *MANAGEMENT BY EXCEPTION* (*MBE*) (see Chapter 19). By far the greatest amount of response is required where an adverse variance of a controllable cost arises. This means that variance analysis helps direct management attention and activity towards those areas where things are going wrong and intervention is necessary. This preserves valuable resources and saves management time. However, as pointed out above, it is also necessary to provide rewards where things are going well, otherwise staff will lose motivation. In retail organisations, motivation is often boosted through internal competition via the use of league tables to compare the performance of different branches of the same company. In service organisations, schemes such as 'employee of the month' perform a similar function.

Figure 20.5 illustrates that variance analysis should be used frequently throughout the budgetary cycle to facilitate control. The budget should then be adjusted in the light of what is actually happening, otherwise the next set of comparisons might become quite unrealistic.

Exercise 20.4

In Exercise 20.1 you drew up a budgeted profit and loss account. Figure 20.6 shows a comparison of the budget with the actual results for the period.

Discuss the variances, commenting on possible reasons behind them.

FIGURE 20.4

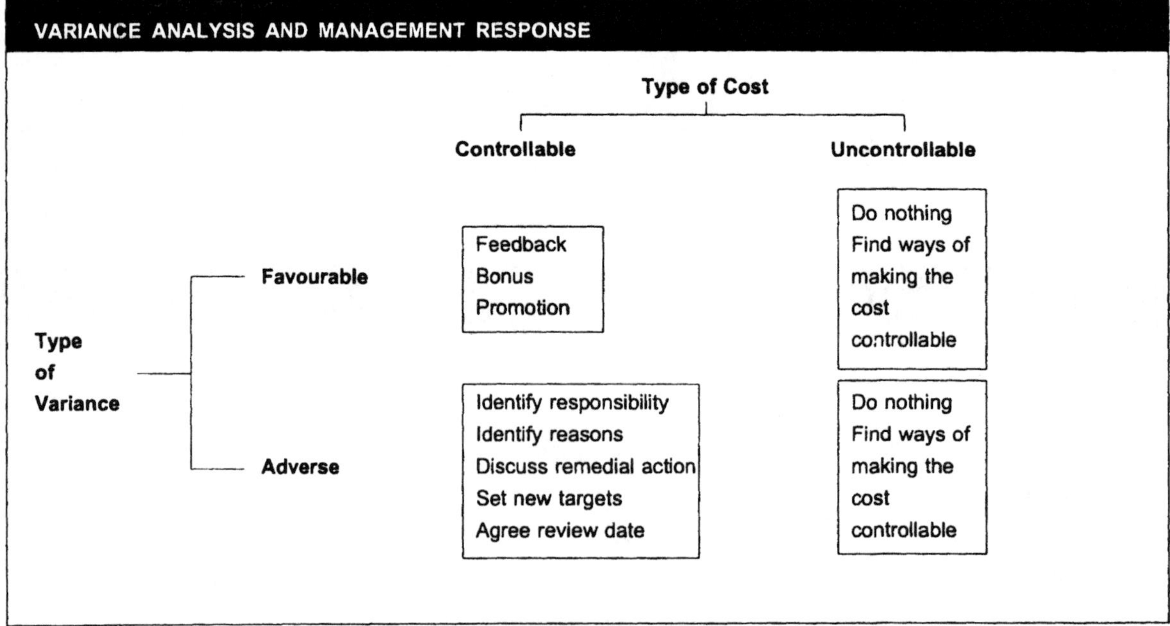

FIGURE 20.5

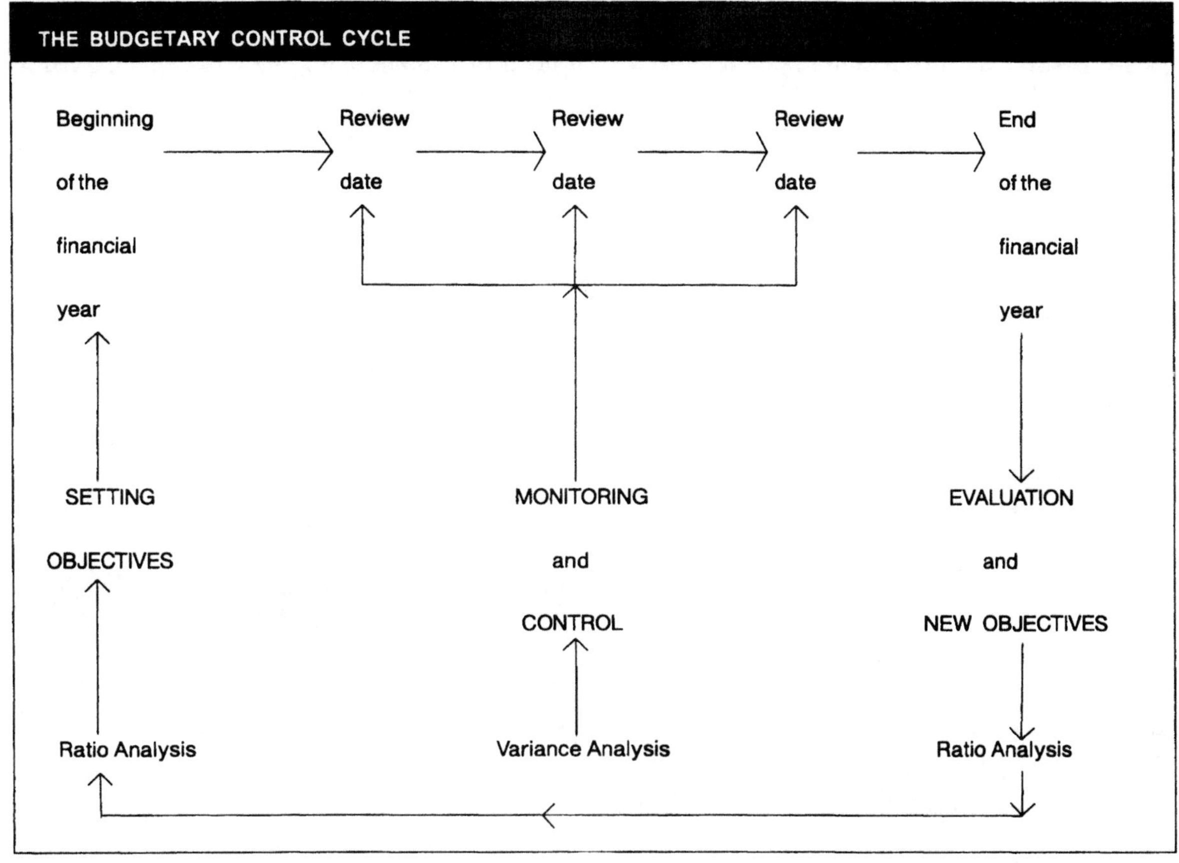

FIGURE 20.6

TOY MANUFACTURER: VARIANCE ANALYSIS FOR THE PERIOD 1 JANUARY 19X5 TO 31 DECEMBER 19X5

		Budgeted	Actual	Variance
		£	£	£
	Sales	330 000	270 000	(60 000)
–	Cost of Goods Sold	220 000	200 000	20 000
=	Gross Profit	110 000	70 000	(40 000)
–	Expenses			
	Wages	33 000	30 000	3 000
	Advertising	33 000	25 000	8 000
	Rent and Rates	26 250	30 000	(3 750)
=	Net Profit	17 750	(15 000)	(32 750)

It is likely that you did not find it easy to interpret the variances in this example in a meaningful way that would enable you to take appropriate action. The reason is that the whole plan was thrown by the large variance in sales volume. As you know from Chapter 19 and from the assumptions stated in Exercise 20.1, many of the mini-budgets for the different areas and cost items in the business are directly linked to the sales forecast. This means that if the sales forecast proves to be wrong, the whole plan will be unrealistic. A budget which is based on one sales level only is called a *FIXED BUDGET*. Unfortunately it is very hard indeed to come up with a completely accurate sales forecast, so you are likely to encounter the same problems as in Exercise 20.4, whenever you attempt to work with a fixed budget. If the actual sales level is different from the forecast, then all the cost variances will be distorted as a result and interpretation becomes difficult, as it is impossible to see at a glance which variances were due to factors other than the difference in sales levels. The answer to this problem is to use a *FLEXIBLE BUDGET*. This means you make contingency plans and draw up the budget in such a way that it can easily be adjusted for different possible sales levels.

Example

In Exercise 20.4 you carried out a variance analysis. The problem with interpreting the variances was to do with the great difference in sales levels. Clearly if you plan for a much higher sales level than the one actually achieved, then many of your cost forecasts will also be too high. To *flex* the budget means to adjust the whole budget to the sales level actually achieved, so a meaningful comparison is possible. In this case that means that once it becomes known that the actual sales level achieved is £270 000, not £330 000 as originally assumed, you can rework the whole budget with that in mind, using the assumptions given in Exercise 20.1. This is shown in Figure 20.7.

FIGURE 20.7

TOY MANUFACTURER: FLEXED BUDGETED PROFIT AND LOSS STATEMENT FOR THE PERIOD 1 JANUARY 19X5 TO 31 DECEMBER 19X5 (BASIS: SALES £270 000)

		£	
	Sales	270 000	
–	Cost of Goods Sold	180 000	(1)
=	Gross Profit	90 000	
–	Expenses		
	Wages	27 000	(2)
	Advertising	27 000	(3)
	Rent and Rates	26 250	(4)
=	Net Profit	9 750	

Notes:

(1) As in Exercise 20.1, cost of goods sold is two-thirds of sales, or £270 000 * 2/3 = £180 000.

(2) As in Exercise 20.1, wages are assumed to be 10 per cent of sales.

(3) As in Exercise 20.1, advertising costs are assumed to be 10 per cent of sales.

(4) This remains as originally forecast, as there is no relationship between this cost and sales.

Using the information in Figure 20.7 you can carry out a variance analysis, comparing the flexed budget and the actual figures. The outcome is presented in Figure 20.8. The results in this form are much more meaningful, as you are now comparing like with like. You can now see at a glance that the company actually overspent on cost of goods sold and wages, both of which had appeared to carry favourable variances when using the fixed budget as a base. In this way, flexing the budget helps draw management attention to those areas which need immediate attention.

FIGURE 20.8

TOY MANUFACTURER: VARIANCE ANALYSIS FOR THE PERIOD 1 JANUARY 19X5 TO 31 DECEMBER 19X5 (BASIS: FLEXED BUDGET FOR SALES £270 000)

		Budgeted	Actual	Variance
		£	£	£
	Sales	270 000	270 000	
–	Cost of Goods Sold	180 000	200 000	(20 000)
=	Gross Profit	90 000	70 000	(20 000)
–	Expenses			
	Wages	27 000	30 000	(3 000)
	Advertising	27 000	25 000	2 000
	Rent and Rates	26 250	30 000	(3 750)
=	Net Profit	9 750	(15 000)	(24 750)

Exercise 20.5

A market trader sells various items of crockery. On average, each customer spends £5.60 and on average a gross margin of 40 per cent is achieved.

On top of purchase costs, other costs are staffing, which comes to 14 per cent of sales; wrapping material, at 2 per cent of sales; storage and handling costs, which are estimated to be 7 per cent of sales.

In addition, the trader incurs a number of costs which are independent of the sales level. These are rent at £5000 per annum and depreciation, £1000 per annum.

For the year 199X, sales are expected to be linked to the overall state of the economy. If there are boom conditions, it is expected that there will be 20 000 customers spending on average £5.60 each but, if there is a recession, only 10 000 such customers can be expected.

(a) Draw up a flexible budgeted profit and loss statement for the market trader for the year 199X, providing budgets for both possible states of the economy

(b) At the end of 199X, the actual results for the period were as follows:

The economy went into recession and a sales volume of 10 000 units was achieved. However, the value of each average sale was slightly lower than expected at £5.55. Unexpectedly competition moved into the main market of the trader. A mini-price war resulted and on average a gross margin of only 24 per cent was achieved. However, because of increased efficiency, staff costs came to 10 per cent of sales and wrapping material to 1.5 per cent of sales. Storage and handling costs increased to 7.5 per cent of sales. Rent unexpectedly was increased to £5200 per annum, whereas the depreciation charge remained unchanged.

Draw up the actual profit and loss statement for 199X and carry out a variance analysis, comparing actual figures to the flexed budget.

Another way of constructing a flexible budget, popular with many business organisations, is to show the relationship between sales and the various cost items by expressing costs and profits as a *percentage* of sales.

Example

In Figure 20.9 you will find an extract of the branch budget of a DIY retailer.

Notice how the comparison of the percentage columns adds to our knowledge. For example, whilst the variance for cost of goods sold appears to be favourable, a comparison of the percentage columns shows at a glance that it was actually higher than budgeted for, resulting in a gross margin of 1.4 per cent less than planned.

20.3 Drawing up a flexible budget on a spreadsheet

The invention of spreadsheets has made it very easy for management to use flexible budgets in practice. Spreadsheets are ideal for the construction of budgets and the calculation of variances, as the task is fairly straightforward but entails a lot of repetitive calculations, which need to be carried out every time the budget has to be revised in the light of new information. This would be tedious and prone to human error if it had to be done by hand. The spreadsheet allows management to set up the basic format needed for the calculations in the form of a *TEMPLATE* (see Section 6.7), which can then be used to carry out the required calculations automatically as budgeted and actual figures are put in.

Exercise 20.6

Reproduce the extract from the DIY retailer's branch budget, shown in Figure 20.9, on the spreadsheet, putting in appropriate formulae. Pay attention to efficient spreadsheet design – the idea is to get the spreadsheet to carry out the calculations for you.

FIGURE 20.9

DIY RETAILER: BRANCH BUDGET

	Current Period				
	£	%	£	%	£
	Actual	Sales	Budget	Sales	Variance
Sales	401 693	100%	410 500	100%	(8 807)
Cost of Sales	251 179	62.5%	262 200	63.9%	11 021
Gross Profit	150 514	37.5%	148 300	36.1%	2 214
Selling Expenses					
Wages	52 389	13.0%	53 740	13.1%	1 351
Heat and Light	2 970	0.7%	3 100	0.8%	130
Maintenance	3 030	0.8%	3 060	0.7%	30
Telephone	1 144	0.3%	1 190	0.3%	46
Credit Charges	1 967	0.5%	2 300	0.6%	333
Cleaning	4 109	1.0%	3 430	0.8%	(679)
Till Discrepancies	310	0.1%	0	0	(310)
Travel	475	0.1%	360	0.1%	(115)
Printing and Postage	1 899	0.5%	1 730	0.4%	(169)
Other	10 723	2.7%	6 700	1.6%	(4 023)
Total Selling Expenses	79 016	19.7%	75 610	18.4%	(3 406)
Other Branch Expenses	53 180	13.2%	53 150	12.9%	(30)
Concession Income	587	0.1%	490	0.1%	97
Store Contribution	18 905	4.7%	20 030	4.9%	(1 125)

20.4 Summary

Working through this chapter, you were introduced to the use of variance analysis as a tool for budgetary control. Budgets are based on historical averages of the costs of producing and selling goods and services. These standards go into the formulation of a detailed plan. This serves as a yardstick against which actual figures can be compared, once they become known. The difference between actual and budgeted figures is the *variance*. Variances can be either favourable or adverse. Management responses will depend on whether or not the item concerned is controllable at the level in question. In order to make the best use of the budget as a motivating device, it is important to make sure that responsibilities are clearly identified at the outset and that managers feel that the achievement of budgetary targets is under their control. It is also recommended to link the achievement of budgetary targets to rewards, whilst aiming to identify and rectify adverse variances swiftly.

Case Study 4

'The Sycamore' Public House: Introducing a Budgetary Control System

1 Introduction

'The Sycamore' is a popular public house located on the outskirts of Bradford. The property is owned by Joshua Tetley and Son Ltd and has been run on a tenancy basis by Deborah and Gary Wardle for the last eight years.

2 A business opportunity

In 1991 the couple were offered the opportunity of acquiring a 10-year lease on the business, at a cost of £10 000. They saw this as an excellent opportunity to build their equity stake in this small business, which after all under their management had already established a very good track record of turnover growth and high profitability. In addition, they were reassured by the promise of the brewery's business development manager that a comprehensive back-up and advice service would be provided. The business development manager was involved at all stages of the negotiation of the lease and was particularly helpful in advising the Wardles to draw up a detailed business plan. Having no financial background, this was an area they both felt very uncertain about. As a result, they decided to approach an accountant who was happy to draw up a cash flow and profit forecast for them. The cost of the lease was met partly through existing savings. In addition, however, it was necessary to take out a £5000 bank loan.

3 A profile of current trade

'The Sycamore' pub is classified as a 'Quality Food Suburban' outlet. A definition of this category is provided in Table C4.1. The pub currently opens all day and is particularly busy at lunch time, attracting trade from the nearby suburban shopping centre. In the evening, the food trade is rather busy until around 8.30pm, after that the majority of turnover is on the wet side.

On the wet side, lager has recently been rather dominant for an outlet of this type. Lager sales overtook ale sales for the first time in 1992. Despite the greater freedom of choice on the supply side which followed the 1989 Monopolies and Merger Commission report, the Wardles are content to obtain most of their supplies from the brewery. They feel that the business development manager looking after them has got a great deal of experience in running pubs and they are happy to rely on his/her judgement.

TABLE C4.1

DEFINITION OF 'QUALITY FOOD SUBURBAN'	
Location:	• Main road • Suburb • Near to industry
Facilities:	• High food sales (day and evening) • No games • One room • Car park • Garden
Product mix:	• High bitter • High premium lager • High wines

In recent years the team has been concentrating its efforts on developing the food side of the business, which consists of typical British pub fare, including a range of sandwiches and toasties, plus a number of main courses with a choice of baked potato, jacket potato or chips, as well as either salad or mixed vegetables. A recent development has been a move towards the increased provision of vegetarian meals. To this purpose, both Deborah and Gary have attended several catering courses provided by the brewery. Approximately 10 per cent of the menu now caters to vegetarian tastes.

4 Problems, problems...

An examination of the profit and loss accounts of the business over the 1988 to 1992 period (see Figure C4.1), shows a growing business. However, there is some cause for concern, as profitability seems to have declined quite sharply in recent periods. The Wardles are baffled by this. They feel that considering the current period of recession, sales have been growing at an acceptable rate. This seems to be borne out by a comparison of 1992 sales with the 1992 budget (see Figure C4.2), which had been set in cooperation with the business development manager, using a brewery managed standard reference house as the basis.

At the end of 1992, the Wardles are convinced that they have a cash flow problem on their hands and they are looking for ways of exerting greater control over the revenues and costs of the business. To this end they have approached the business development manager, who recommends that they should carry out a trend analysis for the 1988 to 1992 period, as well as a detailed variance analysis for 1992. This should serve as a useful starting point in identifying the strengths and weaknesses of the pub and help pinpoint areas where greater control is needed. This information could be used to feed into the budget for the next year.

The Wardles now see that it is important to become more knowledgable and independent in the area of financial management. They hope that the business development manager will help them to get a better understanding of the financial side of the business and enable them to make better use of financial analysis and budgetary control as tools for building their business.

Independent advice is particularly important in the area of budgetary control, where the Wardles have a disagreement. Gary feels that it should be the firm objective of the next financial period to cut down on all unnecessary costs and to make the business as efficient as possible. Deborah partly agrees, as she shares his worries over the poor cash flow position. On the other hand she feels quite strongly that a high level of expenditure in such areas as staff training, entertainment and maintaining a broad menu is justified. Her argument is that such expenses are an investment in quality and therefore in the future of the business. Since they cannot agree on this point, they have agreed to ask the advice of the business development manager.

Tasks

Imagine that you are acting as the business development manager in charge of 'The Sycamore'. You are required to carry out the following tasks.

Task 1

Drawing on prior research into the industry as well as on a detailed analysis of financial trends, ratios and

FIGURE C4.1

'THE SYCAMORE': ACTUAL SALES AND COSTS 1988 TO 1992

	1988 £	1990 £	1992 £
Sales (VAT ex):			
Ale	50113	48986	47013
Lager	46009	48997	50643
Cider	1342	1125	1571
Minerals	12908	17689	20748
Wine	5677	4998	6110
Spirits	17965	15467	18613
Crisps/Tobacco	1679	3325	2098
Total Wet Sales	135693	140587	146796
Catering Sales	86570	97980	104699
Machine Income	0	0	4583
Total Sales	222263	238567	256078
Cost of Sales:			
Wet	63775	63263	72376
Dry (= catering)	47614	54870	43817
Other (= machine)	0	0	1405
Total Cost of Sales	111389	118133	117598
Gross Profit:			
Wet	71918	77324	74420
Dry (= catering)	38956	43110	60882
Other (= machine)	0	0	3178
Total Gross Profit	110874	120434	138480
Expenses:			
Labour:			
Wages	45673	49786	46729
Relief	556	776	374
Energy			
Electricity:	8769	12094	11678
Gas	3456	4008	4263
Controllables:			
Entertainment	4003	3897	4866
Glasses/utensils	1008	876	1218
Cleaning materials	1987	2089	2965
Telephone	510	645	710
Repairs of fittings	876	667	1492
Sundries	5564	4356	7115
Total Controllables	72402	79194	81410
Controllable Profit	38472	41240	57070
Establishment Costs:			
Business rate	8000	10000	11422
Licence duty	56	76	86
Depreciation	400	500	1000
Rent	15434	17896	33153
Accountant and Insurance	1500	1500	1500
Stocktaker	350	350	250
Total Establishment Costs	25740	30322	47411
Net Profit before Tax	12732	10918	9659
Additional Information:			
Tenant's Net Total Assets	20000	20000	30000

FIGURE C4.2

'THE SYCAMORE': BUDGET 1992 (BASIS: STANDARD MANAGED REFERENCE HOUSE)

	£
Sales (VAT ex):	
Ale	
Lager	
Cider	
Minerals	
Wine	
Spirits	
Crisps/Tobacco	
Total Wet Sales	167567
Catering Sales	91380
Machine Income	4573
Total Sales	263520
Cost of Sales:	
Wet	77081
Dry (= catering)	40207
Other (= machine)	845
Total Cost of Sales	118133
Gross Profit:	
Wet	90486
Dry (= catering)	51173
Other (= machine)	3728
Total Gross Profit	145387
Expenses:	
Labour:	
Wages	53998
Relief	228
Energy	
Electricity:	4897
Gas	3027
Controllables:	
Entertainment	2765
Glasses/utensils	1583
Cleaning materials	2292
Telephone	315
Repairs of fittings	825
Sundries	4958
Total Controllables	74888
Controllable Profit	70499
Establishment Costs:	
Business rate	10682
Licence duty	80
Depreciation	1000
Rent	38163
Accountant and Insurance	1500
Stocktaker	250
Total Establishment Costs	51675
Net Profit before Tax	18824
Additional Information:	
Tenant's Net Total Assets	30000

variances for 'The Sycamore' during the 1988–1992 period, carry out a SWOT (Strengths, Weaknesses, Opportunities, Threats) analysis for the business.

Use this information as a basis for advising the publican on a suitable strategy (broken down into a range of complementary action points), which could be used to enhance the performance of the business.

To be able to do this, you will need to take the following steps in preparation:

(a) Use the profit and loss accounts and other information provided to carry out a detailed SWOT analysis for 'The Sycamore' pub, incorporating trends and key ratios as appropriate

(b) Set up a spreadsheet to carry out a detailed variance analysis for 1992, flexing the budget as appropriate

(c) Through the use of secondary sources, gain an in-depth insight into the issues facing the pub retailing industry, to enable you to recommend an appropriate strategy for an outlet such as 'The Sycamore' to maximise performance over the next five years

Task 2

Critically examine the role of budgetary control systems in services retailing, as applied to the situation of 'The Sycamore' public house. In view of the likely trade-offs between marketing effectiveness and operating efficiency, flexibility and standardisation, discuss how the Wardles can make the best use of their budget.

Task 3

Demonstrate your spreadsheet skills by providing a printout of the formulae.

Part V
Decision-making

21 Introduction to Decision-making

21.1 Learning objectives

When you have finish working through this chapter you should be able to

- Define the term **FACTOR**
- Distinguish between a **VARIABLE FACTOR** and a **FIXED FACTOR**
- Define the terms **FIXED COST**, **VARIABLE COST** and **SEMI-VARIABLE COST**
- Classify costs as fixed, variable or semi-variable
- Define the terms **TOTAL COST** and **AVERAGE COST**
- Understand what is meant by **ECONOMIES OF SCALE**

21.2 Introduction

In Parts I and II we learned how financial information is collated, presented and analysed. This enabled management and shareholders alike to monitor and assess business performance on the basis of historical data.

In Parts III and IV we turned to the future and learned how to make forecasts and translate them into budgetary plans. This aided resource allocation and provided a yardstick against which actual business performance could be monitored.

Part V is concerned with the wider management uses of financial information for decision-making purposes. This chapter lays the conceptual foundation for decision-making by classifying costs in relation to time-frames. Types of decision-making techniques are then taken in turn. Chapters 22 and 23 introduce break-even analysis as an approach which makes use of the relationship between cost, volume and profit to evaluate alternative approaches of carrying out business projects. Chapter 24 introduces the idea of marginal costing in the context of short-term decision-making. Chapter 25 develops this and contrasts it with a full cost approach in relation to pricing decisions. The remainder of Part V is concerned with techniques for making long-term capital investment decisions.

21.3 The factors of production

In Chapter 20, you practised drawing up both fixed and flexible budgets. We found that it was often difficult to analyse the variances between a fixed budget and actual results when the actual sales level was very different from the budget. Some of the inputs varied with sales volume whereas others did not. The use of a flexible budget, which adjusts to the actual sales level achieved, removes these difficulties of comparison.

It is crucial for the managers of a business to be aware of the relationships between the costs of running the business and the sales volume and profit achieved. Should a car manufacturer completely automate its paint spraying process or should it continue with semi-automatic methods that require manual finishing? It will depend to some extent on the relative costs of the paint spraying machine and the wages of the paint sprayers and also on the quality of the finished product. Should a retailer install Electronic Point of Sale (EPOS) systems to record all its sales and the time and place they occurred? It will depend to some extent on the cost of the EPOS systems and the extra benefits to be gained in knowing stock levels, sales patterns and the productivity of workforce.

Any input that is used by a firm to produce output is termed a *FACTOR* of production.

Exercise 21.1

List **five** factors of production of a manufacturing company or a retail organisation.

In your answer you may have named such items as land, labour, machinery and buildings, to give a few examples. If you look at the resources you listed, you will find that you can divide them into two broad categories:

- The *FIXED FACTORS* are those which can be changed only over a relatively long period of time. For example, the actual building that houses a factory or store ties up capital for several years. Once the building is in use, it is difficult to alter it quickly. Furthermore, the extension of premises would take at least a year, given all the stages involved from obtaining planning permission and raising the capital through to the actual construction and fitting-out of the building. Thus, the business has to plan to operate within the limits of these fixed resources which can be changed only in the long run.
- *VARIABLE FACTORS*, on the other hand, can be changed quickly in response to demand. For example, the hours worked by part-time staff can be adjusted on a daily basis to reflect a factory's orders or the number of supermarket checkouts needed. These resources can be changed easily in the short run.

Exercise 21.2

Identify **one** fixed factor and **one** variable factor that are elements of the following businesses.

(a) An airline
(b) A restaurant chain
(c) A shoe retailer with a single outlet
(d) A fruit-canning factory

21.4 Classification of costs

Looking at your answer to Exercise 21.2, you will note that the key difference between a fixed factor and a variable factor is in the length of time it takes to *change the use* of an input. Every input has costs associated with it. Those costs associated with a fixed factor will change only in the long run whereas costs associated with a variable factor change in the short run in line with sales volume.

The cost of using a fixed factor is incurred whether or not any sales are made. The airline has to dispatch its planes whether they are fully laden or have plenty of empty seats. The restaurant has to open its premises and provide tables and chairs regardless of the number of customers.

These types of costs which do not change with the volume of trade are termed *FIXED COSTS*.

The cost of using a variable factor, however, does depend on the volume of sales. The airline will need less fuel and fewer in-flight meals if it has fewer passengers. The restaurant will need more staff and will use more power for cooking and washing up at busy times than at quiet times.

These type of costs which vary in direct proportion to sales volume are termed *VARIABLE COSTS*.

Of course, there are some costs that do not fall into either the fixed or the variable category but contain elements of both. For example, almost every business requires a telephone. The most common charging method is a quarterly or monthly standing charge plus a charge based on the number of units used.

Assuming the number of calls made increases in line with sales volume, which is a reasonable supposition, the call charges are a variable cost but the standing charge is a fixed cost because it is payable regardless of whether any calls are made or not. This type of cost is termed *SEMI-VARIABLE*.

Exercise 21.3

Give examples of fixed costs, variable costs and semi-variable costs incurred by the following business organisations:

(a) A shoe retailer with a single outlet
(b) A fruit-canning factory

21.5 Determining the optimal resource mix

The *TOTAL COST* of running a business is the sum of the fixed costs and the variable costs for the sales volume achieved. The decision-maker usually has to make choices about how to accomplish the various tasks involved in running the business, bearing in mind its mission statement. Generally, management is working to maximise the long-term wealth of the company and minimise total costs. It is seeking to determine the optimal resource mix to achieve this end.

Example

A US leisurewear retailer is considering setting up operations in the UK. It could operate from traditional High Street outlets. To get nationwide coverage would need a minimum of 50 shops. Alternatively, based on its experience in the USA, it could set up a mail order operation although it would expect most of its sales to be telephoned in using a freephone number with payment by credit card. It would use contractors to deliver the goods and would hope to achieve delivery anywhere within the UK within a week of ordering and in most cases within 48 hours.

The High Street operation would use a large amount of fixed factor, such as the provision of premises and shop managers employed on permanent contracts.

The mail order operation would use a relatively small amount of fixed factor in setting up a head office and an efficient telephone system. However, there would be a large amount of variable factor involved, in the form of telephone calls, home delivery, telesales workers and the cost of holding a great deal of stock.

The cost implications of the High Street operation are relatively high fixed costs but low variable costs. The mail order operation incurs relatively low fixed costs but high variable costs.

In Chapter 22 we will see how we can compare such situations graphically so as to determine which of the two approaches would be preferred, given the likely sales volume. In general, the use of variable factors makes a business flexible and able to respond to changing economic conditions.

There are other considerations to be borne in mind. Once a resource mix has been chosen for a business, in the short run the amount of the fixed factors available to the business is constrained. The company can only continue manufacturing and/or selling within these limits. Once the business has expanded to these limits, further growth can be achieved only by additional investment in fixed factors. For example, if the US leisurewear company is successful in the High Street and its shops become overcrowded, it will need to expand its existing stores or open new outlets. If it were successful in the mail order operation so that the telesales staff could not cope, more telephone lines would be needed.

The *AVERAGE COST* of selling an item is the total cost divided by the number of items sold.

In general, when a new business opens, its sales volume is low, and the average cost is relatively high. As the business becomes established, the sales volume increases. The total cost, being the sum of the fixed and variable costs, also increases but initially the fixed cost is the more important element since for example, premises, equipment, a manager are needed and these costs remain the same. This means that the average cost of selling an item falls, giving *ECONOMIES OF SCALE*.

A second reason for economies of scale is specialisation. A sole trader has to carry out all the tasks of a business whereas in a larger business workers can be assigned their own specialist tasks which they learn to perform efficiently so that the whole business is run more effectively than if everyone is trying to do all the jobs. Of course, another economy in large-scale operations is that it becomes worthwhile to bring in better machinery and equipment such as automatic handling and computer systems.

Above a certain sales volume, *diseconomies of scale* may set in as the management of the company becomes more difficult. Increased bureaucracy is needed to control and organise a larger number of workers, for example. In this situation, the average cost begins to rise and the resource mix must then be re-examined.

Exercise 21.4

A supermarket chain has operated in-store bakeries in its larger stores for a number of years. Each bakery is run by a master baker who is responsible for all decisions from staffing and ordering to amount of bread and cakes to be made. The supermarket has control of range of offering, recipes and display material.

Because of the shortage of master bakers, the company is considering a change to its operations. Bakery goods will be prepared centrally, part-baked, chilled and distributed to the stores. The goods will be finished as needed in the stores. This can be done by semi-skilled labour as, for instance, colour charts will be provided to guide operatives on the required extra baking time for loaves.

(a) Identify the fixed and variable factors in each of the two methods of operation.
(b) Analyse the resource mix in each case.
(c) Which method gives the greater opportunity for economies of scale? Give reasons for your answer.

Exercise 21.5

In Case Study 2 at the end of Part II, you were asked to examine the financial situation of a Benetton franchisee. Discuss how a franchise operation such as this makes use of potential economies of scale.

Exercise 21.6

To what extent have the large supermarket retailers realised economies of scale through the introduction of information technology?

21.6 Summary

In this chapter you have been introduced to terminology relating to the classification of costs for decision-making purposes.

A business organisation employs two main types of resources or factors. Variable factors can be changed in the short run in response to the demand for products and services. Fixed factors are inputs to the business that can be changed only in the long run.

As a consequence of this, the cost of using a variable factor varies in proportion to the volume of sales and is termed a variable cost. The cost of using a fixed factor, however, is the same regardless of the sales level and is termed a fixed cost. In practice, many costs have both a fixed and a variable component and are termed semi-variable costs.

The decision-maker has to determine the optimum resource mix for the business. The use of variable factors allows flexibility. The use of fixed factors gives economies of scale up to a certain sales volume. Eventually diseconomies of scale set in and to achieve further growth more fixed factors must be employed.

22
Introduction to Break-even Analysis

22.1 Learning objectives

When you have finished working through this chapter you should be able to

- Understand what is meant by **BREAK-EVEN ANALYSIS**
- Define the term **BREAK-EVEN POINT**
- Define the term **UNIT CONTRIBUTION**
- Calculate the break-even point
- Draw a **BREAK-EVEN CHART** and show the break-even point
- Use a break-even chart to compare alternative strategies
- Appreciate the limitations of break-even analysis

22.2 Introduction

In Chapter 21, we identified the different types of costs incurred in running a business and classified them as fixed, variable or semi-variable. In determining the optimum resource mix, the decision-maker needs to analyse the relationship between these costs and the company's sales volume and profit. This can be done using *BREAK-EVEN ANALYSIS.*

This technique compares total costs to sales revenues for a range of sales volumes. It examines the relationship between the fixed cost and variable cost mix, sales volume or revenue, and profit.

We can determine the *BREAK-EVEN POINT* which is the sales volume or the sales revenue when the total cost equals the total revenue, in other words, it is the sales level at which neither a profit nor a loss is made.

22.3 Calculating the break-even point

Example

Maria is planning to open a dance studio with multi-gym, sauna and aerobics facilities in the centre of Norwich. Initial costs incurred are

	£
Refurbishment	30 000
Weight training equipment	10 000
Sauna equipment	5 000

Refurbishment and equipment costs are to be depreciated over a six-year period, using the straight line method and assuming zero scrap value at the end of the period.

Recurring annual costs will be

	£
Maintenance	3 000
Insurance	4 000

Staff costs will vary according to the level of demand. It is expected that they will average out at £100 per customer per year. An annual membership fee of £150 per head will be charged.

Maria wants to know how many members need to enrol every year before the business breaks even.

First we must identify which of Maria's costs are *fixed* and which are *variable*. She has to cover her fixed costs each year whether she gets 50 members or 500 members.

The initial capital investment comes to a total of £45 000 and depreciating this over six years with zero scrap value gives an annual depreciation charge of £7500.

Maria's annual fixed costs therefore are as set out in Table 22.1.

TABLE 22.1

MARIA'S STUDIO: FIXED COSTS

	£
Depreciation	7 500
Maintenance	3 000
Insurance	4 000
TOTAL	14 500

The only variable costs are the staff costs of £100 per member per year.

The sales revenue is £150 per member per year. For every extra member Maria enrols the revenue exceeds the variable costs by £150 − £100, or £50. This is called the *UNIT CONTRIBUTION*. In general, the definition of unit contribution is:

Unit contribution =
Selling price per unit − Variable cost per unit

Maria will first of all have to use this contribution to defray her fixed costs but once all the fixed costs have been paid the additional contribution will be her profit. In order to determine the break-even point where she makes neither a profit nor a loss, we need to find out exactly how many members' contributions are needed to cover the fixed costs.

This is done using the following formula:

Break-even point formulae

$$\text{Break-even point (units)} = \frac{\text{Total fixed costs}}{\text{Unit contribution}}$$

Break-even point (£) =
Break-even point (units) * Selling price

For Maria's studio, these calculations are:

Break-even point calculations

$$\text{Break-even point (units)} = \frac{£14\,500}{£50}$$

$$= 290 \text{ members}$$

Break-even point (£) = 290 * £150 = £43 500

In conclusion, we can inform Maria that her business will break even if it gets 290 members in a year and that is equivalent to a sales revenue of £43 500.

Exercise 22.1

Bracken Ltd manufactures garden gnomes which the company sells at £4 each. The following costs are incurred

	£
Cost of materials	2 per unit
Rent of premises	3000 per year
Rates	2000 per year
Handling and storage costs	0.50 per unit

How many gnomes does Bracken Ltd need to sell each year to break even? What level of sales revenue does this represent?

22.4 Break-even chart

Although we have answered the initial question of how many units need to be sold to break even, there are still other questions to consider, such as the profit or loss made at a given sales volume or the effect on the break-even point if an element of the fixed or the variable costs changes.

Example

In the first year of operation, Maria believes that she will succeed in getting annual subscriptions for her dance studio from between 250 and 500 members, with 400 members seeming the most likely number.

The following shows how to calculate the profit or loss made for a membership levels of 500.

Remember that Maria's break-even point was 290 members. If she recruits 500 members she will have 500 − 290 or 210 additional contributions that will be profit. Each contribution was £50, so her profit will be 210 * £50 or £10 500.

From this example, we can now work out a general formula to work out the profit for different membership levels. This formula is:

> **Profit formula**
>
> Profit/Loss = ›
> (Actual number of units − Break-even number of units)
> * Unit contribution

Exercise 22.2

Apply the general profit formula to calculate the profit or loss Maria's dance studio will make if the annual membership levels are:

(a) 250 members
(b) 400 members

When we want to consider different sales volumes and to get an overall view of the relationship between the costs, revenue and profit or loss, it is convenient to draw a *BREAK-EVEN CHART.*

This chart is an **XY** graph with sales volume shown on the **X**-axis and costs and revenue shown on the **Y**-axis. On the chart we draw lines to represent the behaviour of the following costs and revenue as the sales volume changes:

> Total revenue
> Fixed costs
> Variable costs
> Total costs (= Fixed costs + Variable costs)

Example

Let us construct a break-even chart for Maria's studio.

You will find it useful to draw this chart out on graph paper. Each cost and revenue line can be drawn if we know the co-ordinates of two points on it. From the information we have been given, the maximum sales volume, (number of members) is expected to be 500 so that tells us that our **X**-axis scale should go from 0 to 500.

Before we can draw the **Y**-axis scale, we need to do some calculations.

From Section 22.3, we have

> Revenue = £150 per member per year
> Fixed costs = £14 500 per year
> Variable costs = £100 per member per year

To plot the total revenue line

> When sales volume = 0, sales revenue = 0
> When sales volume = 500,
> sales revenue = 500 * £150 = £75 000

This tells us that our **Y**-axis scale should go from 0 to £75 000.

We can now draw the axes, scale them, plot the two revenue points and join them with a straight line as shown in Figure 22.1.

To plot the fixed costs line, we note that the fixed costs are always £14 500 whatever the sales volume so we draw a horizontal line across the chart starting at £14 500 on the **Y**-axis.

FIGURE 22.1

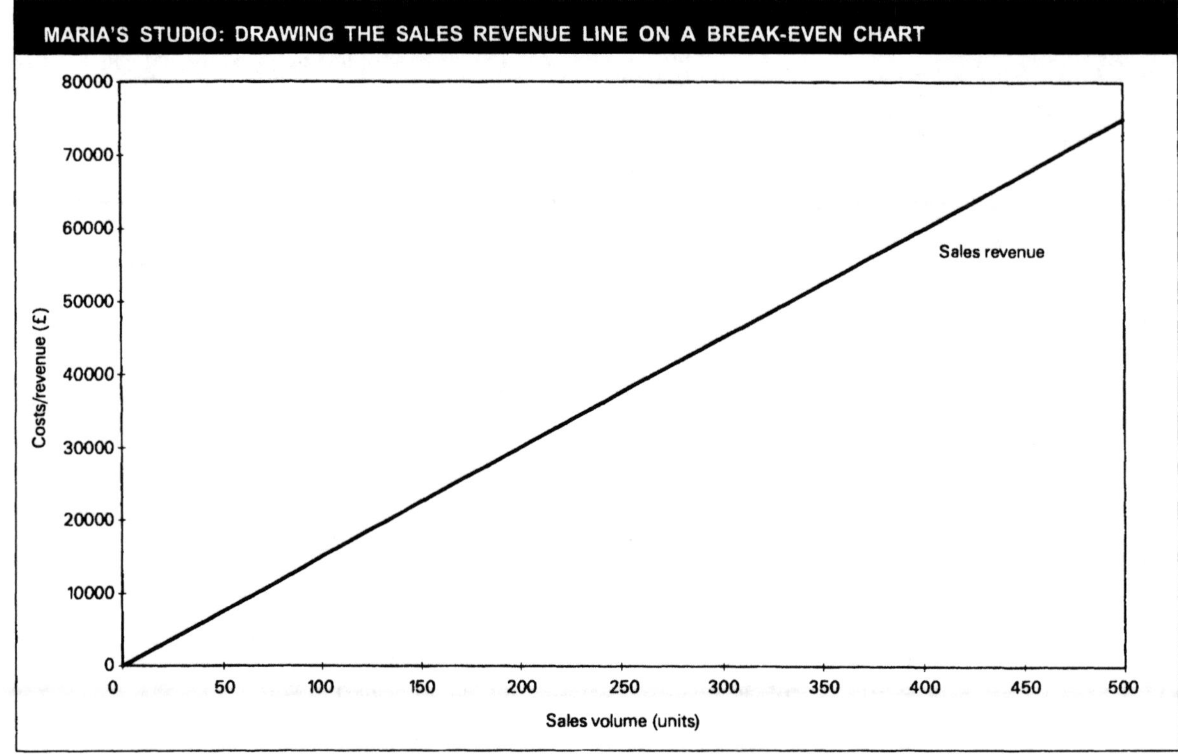

To plot the variable cost line

When sales volume = 0, total variable cost = 0
When sales volume = 500,
total variable cost = 500 * £100 = £50 000

We plot these two points on the chart and join them with a straight line.

To plot the total cost line, we need to add together the fixed costs and the variable costs at a given sales volume:

Maria's Studio: Calculating points for the total cost line

When sales volume = 0,	
fixed cost	= £14 500
variable cost	= £0
total cost	= £14 500

When sales volume = 500,	
fixed cost	= £14 500
variable cost	= £50 000
total cost	= £64 500

The completed chart with all four lines drawn in and labelled is shown in Figure 22.2.

You can clearly see where the total revenue line meets the total cost line. This is the *break-even point.* Reading from the **X**-axis scale, the break-even point corresponds to 290 members. Reading from the **Y**-axis scale, the break-even point corresponds to a sales revenue of £43 500.

For sales volumes above the break-even figure, which means if the membership is above 290, Maria will make a profit as shown by the shaded region in Figure 22.2. For example, if Maria enrols 400 members, the amount of the profit is given by the difference between the total revenue and the total cost when **X** equals 400 so reading from the graph we obtain

Profit from 400 members = £60 000 – £54 500

= £5 500

For sales volumes below the break-even figure, in other words if the membership is below 290, Maria will make a loss as shown in Figure 22.2. For example,

FIGURE 22.2

MARIA'S STUDIO: BREAK-EVEN CHART

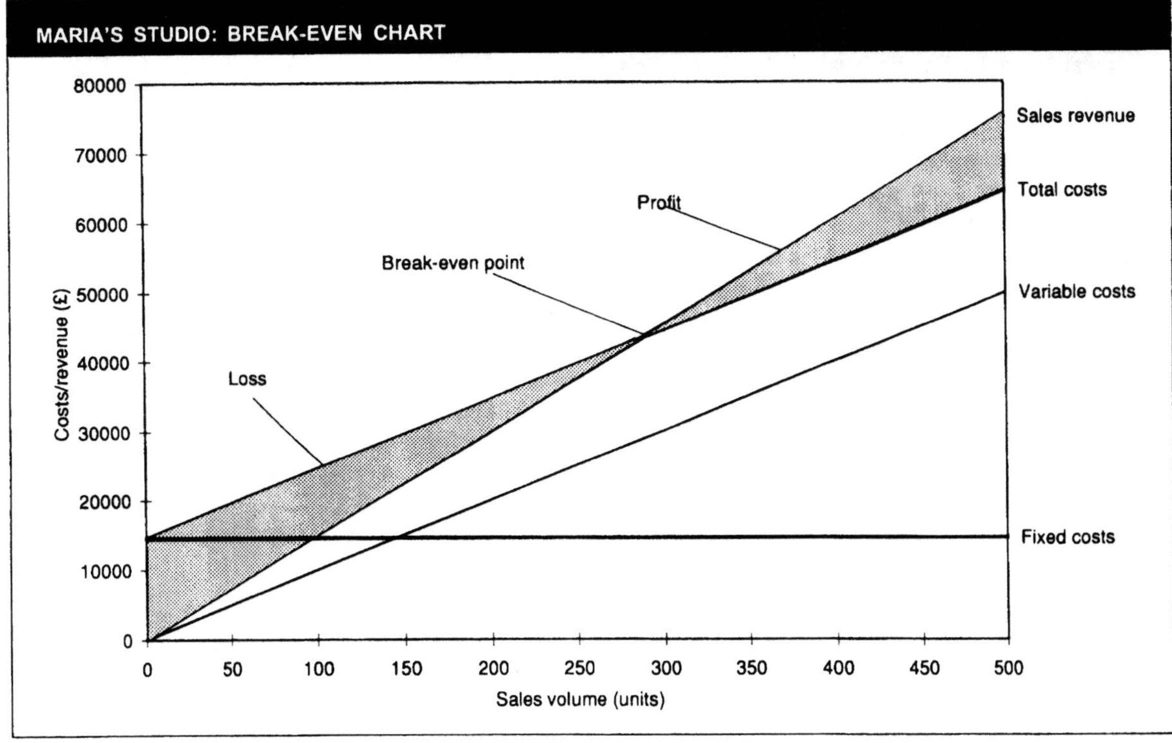

if Maria enrols only 250 members, the amount of the loss is given by the difference between the total cost and the total revenue when **X** equals 200 so reading from the graph we obtain

$$\text{Loss from 250 member} = £39\,500 - £37\,500$$
$$= £2\,000$$

Note that this agrees with the answer obtained in the previous section.

Exercise 22.3

Draw a break-even chart for Bracken Ltd, using the cost and revenue information given in Exercise 22.1. The maximum production level is 6000 gnomes. Work out the profit or loss, if the sales level is

(a) 5000 gnomes
(b) 3000 gnomes

Exercise 22.4

Maria has commissioned some market research and has been told that she could increase her membership to 750 from its current level of 400 if she dropped her membership fee to £120. What is her new break-even point? Show it on a diagram. Is it worth doing from a profit point of view?

22.5 Using break-even analysis to compare alternative strategies

We can use the break-even chart to assess the impact of any changes in the cost structure. In Exercise 22.4, we simply investigated a change in the unit selling price but we can easily compare completely different strategies.

Exercise 22.5

Maria's dance studio has been open for a year and membership has held at 400. The idea is getting fashionable, however, and another gym, with a similar offering was opened by Kevin two blocks down the road from Maria's studio one month ago.

As we have seen from the previous sections, Maria's cost structure has a relatively low fixed cost element since the equipment is sturdy but basic. Maria's policy has been to attract hard core body builders and aerobics fanatics, mainly through excellent, caring staff who are providing individualised service.

Kevin is pursuing a different strategy. His gym consists of state-of-the-art electronic equipment with electronic monitoring of physical responses. In consequence, minimal supervision is required. The initial cost of the equipment was high at £150 000 (to be depreciated over six years, using the straight line method, assuming no scrap value at the end) and maintenance costs come to £4000 per year. Insurance costs are the same as Maria's. Variable costs are kept quite low and work out at £56 per customer per year. Kevin has priced his membership fee at the same level as Maria, which is £150.

Use break-even analysis to calculate the break-even point for Kevin's gym. Show the break-even point on a break-even chart. Compare and contrast the strategies of Maria and Kevin.

From your answer to Exercise 22.5, you will have realised, as we emphasised in Chapter 21, that there is often a trade-off between the use of fixed and variable factors. A high initial investment in capital equipment leads to high fixed costs which must be met regardless of the sales volume achieved. This can lead to high losses if the sales volume is much lower than forecast. It also makes the business less flexible than that of a competitor who relies more strongly on variable factors.

On the other hand, a high commitment to fixed factors can mean lower variable costs per unit and bring about economies of scale. This in turn leads to high unit contributions. At high sales volumes, profits will exceed those of a competitor who relies on variable factors.

There is no one correct way of running a business. When you are evaluating alternatives or comparing competing businesses, you should consider the two elements: fixed cost and unit contribution.

- With a high fixed cost, there is a high risk of making a loss if the predicted sales volume cannot be achieved
- With a high unit contribution, there is the opportunity to make high profits once fixed costs have been paid

The best combination may be to pile your goods high and sell them cheap – this implies low fixed costs, low unit contribution and high sales volumes. Alternatively, you may operate in a niche market selling exclusive high quality goods at a premium price. In this case you incur high fixed costs, high unit contribution and low sales volumes. In between these two extremes, there are many different combinations of factors but using break-even analysis enables you to assess which is the best combination taking all factors into account.

22.6 Limitations of break-even analysis

Break-even analysis is a very useful tool in the early stages of the decision-making process when it is important to get a general overview of the issues involved. You must be aware, however, of the assumptions underlying the analysis as they may not hold true in every application. These are:

- All costs can be identified and labelled as fixed or variable.

  This is not always possible as there may be unforeseen costs. Some costs are not easily classified.

- All variable costs change in direct proportion to sales volume.

  Costs may take a quantum leap, for example, when another employee is taken on or if raw materials have to be purchased in some minimum quantity.

- The sales mix is constant. There is no allowance for loss or damage to goods. Everything produced or provided is sold.

  Products do not remain the same indefinitely. Every operation is likely to suffer shrinkage of some kind.

- The system is in a steady state.

  Break-even analysis cannot accommodate economies of scales. Initially, when a new product or service is launched, there is a learning process as staff become more efficient at their tasks. This is referred to as the *LEARNING CURVE*. In this situation the variable cost per unit is changing until the operation has reached its full capability and a steady state has been reached.

- It is based on forecasts of costs and revenues.

  As we saw in Part III, however we refine our forecasting methods, the unexpected can happen and our forecasts may be inaccurate.

We will see in Chapter 23 how we can allow for changes in costs and revenues by performing a sensitivity analysis using a spreadsheet. In Chapter 27 we explore more generally how we can allow for uncertainty in the future.

Exercise 22.6

Maria's dance studio has started to feel the impact of the competition from Kevin's gym. Membership currently is 20 per cent down compared to the same month last year, when the total membership for the year came to 400.

One suggestion is to make better use of a room that is being used as a store room.

This room could be sublet to a slendertone consultant, generating a concession income of £150 per week.

Alternatively, this part of the premises could be converted into a massage parlour. This would mean hiring further qualified staff at a cost of £9000 per year and spending £1800 on additional equipment. It is expected that customers could be charged at £10 per half-hour session with a half-hour relaxation period at the end. Variable costs would come to £1.50 per session.

A third alternative is to dedicate part of the premises to a float tank. The experiences of prominent London gyms indicate that this may quickly become popular. An initial investment of £30 000 in equipment (tank, steel reinforcement of floor and redecorating) would be necessary. Customers could be charged £20 per one hour session. The charge for additional staffing and cleaning would come to £100 per week. Variable costs would be £2.50 per customer.

Using break-even analysis, evaluate all these proposals and decide on the best course of action. Assume that the new facilities are open 60 hours per week and 50 weeks per year. All depreciation of equipment is by the straight line method over a six year lifetime, after which it will have zero scrap value.

22.7 Summary

In this chapter we have seen how break-even analysis can be used to analyse the relationship between costs, sales volume and profit.

At the break-even point, the total costs equal the total revenue and neither a profit nor a loss is made. This point can be shown on a break-even chart.

The difference between the selling price per unit and the variable cost per unit is termed the unit contribution. Before a profit can be made, all fixed costs must be paid. To calculate the break-even point we use the formulae shown on p. 178. Break-even analysis can be used to assess the impact of alternative strategies on break-even point and profit.

The technique is easy to apply and understand but it is based on assumptions that may not be fully justified in practice. Nevertheless, it is a worthwhile starting point for assessing the viability of business projects.

23

Sensitivity Analysis for Break-even Analysis

23.1 Learning objectives

When you have finished working through this chapter you should be able to

- Understand what is meant by **SENSITIVITY ANALYSIS**
- Appreciate why it is advisable to carry out a sensitivity analysis in addition to the basic break-even analysis
- Set up a spreadsheet template to perform a sensitivity analysis and apply it to different examples
- Interpret the results of a sensitivity analysis

23.2 Sensitivity analysis

In Chapter 22, we introduced break-even analysis to investigate the relationships between the cost, revenue, sales volume and profit mix. You also learned how to use the technique to compare alternative strategies.

As there are so many ways in which we might want to assess the effect of changes to our initial plans, it is convenient to set up a spreadsheet template so that any alternatives can be quickly evaluated without the need for repetitive calculations on our part. The spreadsheet does the calculations, leaving us to concentrate on interpreting the output.

A break-even analysis is performed using what we believe is the most likely scenario of costs, revenue and sales volume. We then conduct a *SENSITIVITY ANALYSIS*, which involves consideration of all the factors that we believe may impact on this analysis. We consider one change at time from the original scenario and work out the effect of this on the break-even point and the profit. In this way we can build up an overview of how vulnerable a project is to pricing decisions or to a downturn in the market, for example. In this way, we are better able to identify the financial risks associated with a new project.

Sensitivity analysis is often referred to as a *What If?* analysis because it evaluates the implications of different projected future conditions and their impact on the output derived from applying different decision-making techniques.

In the context of break-even analysis this means that a sensitivity analysis can be carried out to assess what happens if there is a change in

- Selling price
- Fixed costs
- Variable costs
- Sales volume

23.3 Setting up a template

You will remember from Chapter 6 that when we needed to repeat the same calculations with different input values, it was convenient to set up a template, defined as a worksheet with general formulae, and then to use it repeatedly with the different sets of data.

A template for break-even analysis is shown in Figure 23.1 in the **View formula** option.

The template consists of three sections.

Input section

This section is where the standard values of costs, selling price, sales volume are entered for the initial scenario. You will notice that all the inputs needed for the calculation of a break-even point and the subsequent evaluation of profit levels are listed as follows:

- **Inputs**:
  Fixed costs
  Variable cost per unit

FIGURE 23.1

TEMPLATE FOR SENSITIVITY ANALYSIS

	A	B
1	INPUT	
2	Fixed costs	
3	Variable cost per unit	
4	Selling price per unit	
5	Minimum sales volume(units)	
6	Maximum sales volume(units)	
7	Most likely sales volume(units)	
8		
9	SENSITIVITY ANALYSIS	SCENARIO 0
10	Description of change	No change
11	Adjusted input	
12	Fixed costs	
13	Variable cost per unit	
14	Selling price per unit	
15	Minimum sales volume(units)	
16	Maximum sales volume(units)	
17	Most likely sales volume(units)	
18		
19	OUTPUT	
20	Unit contribution	=B14-B13
21	Break-even point (units)	=B12/B20
22	Break-even point (£)	=B21*B14
23	Profit/loss at minimum sales volume	=(B15-B21)*B20
24	Profit/loss at maximum sales volume	=(B16-B21)*B20
25	Profit/loss at most likely sales volume	=(B17-B21)*B20

Selling price per unit
Minimum sales volume (units)
Maximum sales volume (units)
Most likely sales volume (units)

Sensitivity analysis section

This section allows for changes to the initial scenario. The input in the first section is adjusted to correspond to any changes:

- **Adjusted input**:
  Fixed costs
  Variable cost per unit
  Selling price per unit
  Minimum sales volume (units)
  Maximum sales volume (units)
  Most likely sales volume (units)

Output section

This section contains the formulae to perform the break-even analysis.

- **Formulae**:
  Unit contribution = Selling price per unit − Variable cost per unit
  Break-even point (units) = Fixed costs/Unit contribution
  Break-even point (£) = Break-even point (units) * Selling price per unit
  Profit/Loss at minimum sales volume = (Minimum sales volume − BEP(units)) * Unit contribution
  Profit/Loss at maximum sales volume = (Maximum sales volume − BEP(units)) * Unit contribution
  Profit/Loss at most likely sales volume = (Most likely sales volume − BEP(units)) * Unit contribution

If you study Figure 23.1 carefully, you will see that the correct cell addresses have been entered in the formulae to perform all these calculations.

Make a copy of this template using your spreadsheet package. As with all templates you should save a copy of the general version and then when you use it for a specific application save it under a different filename.

Within one application, we can copy the formulae in column **B** to as many columns as we need to consider all possible changes.

23.4 Using the template

Let us now use the template to compare Maria's studio and Kevin's gym, the examples introduced in Chapter 22. You may find it useful to refer back to the examples in Sections 22.3 and 22.4, and to Exercise 22.5. We will assume that the membership forecast for Kevin's gym is the same as that for Maria's studio, which is somewhere between 250 and 500 members with 400 appearing most likely.

Figure 23.2 shows the print-out for Maria and Figure 23.3 for Kevin.

Note that the values in the sensitivity analysis section are the same as in the input section because this is the initial scenario, referred to as Scenario 0. The results agree with the manual calculations of Chapter 22.

We can now consider the sensitivity of Maria's studio and Kevin's gym to various different scenarios.

Scenario 1

Because of the lack of a 'feel-good' factor, fewer people become members and there is a 10 per cent drop in membership for both firms.

Scenario 2

In order to maintain membership both firms have to reduce their prices by 10 per cent.

Scenario 3

The gym and dance workers' union is successful in negotiating a 10 per cent pay rise for its members, resulting in a 10 per cent increase in variable costs for both firms.

Scenario 4

Both firms have under-estimated the costs of equipment maintenance and breakdown. As a result fixed costs are 10 per cent higher than expected.

The sensitivity analyses are given in Figures 23.4 and 23.5.

FIGURE 23.2

MARIA'S STUDIO: BREAK-EVEN ANALYSIS

	A	B
1	**INPUT**	
2	Fixed costs	14500
3	Variable cost per unit	100
4	Selling price per unit	150
5	Minimum sales volume(units)	250
6	Maximum sales volume(units)	500
7	Most likely sales volume(units)	400
8		
9	**SENSITIVITY ANALYSIS**	SCENARIO 0
10	**Description of change**	No change
11	Adjusted input	
12	Fixed costs	14500
13	Variable cost per unit	100
14	Selling price per unit	150
15	Minimum sales volume(units)	250
16	Maximum sales volume(units)	500
17	Most likely sales volume(units)	400
18		
19	**OUTPUT**	
20	Unit contribution	50
21	Break-even point (units)	290
22	Break-even point (£)	43500
23	Profit/loss at minimum sales volume	-2000
24	Profit/loss at maximum sales volume	10500
25	Profit/loss at most likely sales volume	5500

FIGURE 23.3

KEVIN'S GYM: BREAK-EVEN ANALYSIS

	A	B
1	**INPUT**	
2	Fixed costs	33000
3	Variable cost per unit	56
4	Selling price per unit	150
5	Minimum sales volume(units)	250
6	Maximum sales volume(units)	500
7	Most likely sales volume(units)	400
8		
9	**SENSITIVITY ANALYSIS**	SCENARIO 0
10	**Description of change**	No change
11	Adjusted input	
12	Fixed costs	33000
13	Variable cost per unit	56
14	Selling price per unit	150
15	Minimum sales volume(units)	250
16	Maximum sales volume(units)	500
17	Most likely sales volume(units)	400
18		
19	**OUTPUT**	
20	Unit contribution	94
21	Break-even point (units)	351.06
22	Break-even point (£)	52659.57
23	Profit/loss at minimum sales volume	-9500
24	Profit/loss at maximum sales volume	14000
25	Profit/loss at most likely sales volume	4600

Exercise 23.1

Study Figures 23.4 and 23.5 carefully. Use the results to compare and contrast the two competing operations.

Probably, you found it quite difficult to make the comparisons in Exercise 23.1.

The first thing you may have noticed is that both operations make losses if the membership is at the low end of the forecast range with Kevin making greater losses than Maria in every scenario. Kevin's operation is particularly vulnerable to low demand because of his high fixed costs. On the other hand, if the membership is at the top end of the forecast range, Kevin makes far more profit than Maria because of the high unit contribution.

Concentrating now on the profits or losses generated at the most likely membership level, other differences become apparent.

If there is a fall off in membership, as in Scenario 1, we can see that the profits from both operations are reduced with Kevin's gym being more affected because of his higher unit contribution.

It is disastrous to reduce the selling price, as highlighted in Scenario 2, as both operations then suffer a loss. In both cases the unit contribution is reduced to a level that makes it impossible to cover the fixed costs at the anticipated membership levels.

If there is an increase in variable costs, as projected in Scenario 3, Maria's studio is affected more strongly than Kevin's gym as Maria relies more on variable factors to provide individualised service.

If there is an increase in fixed costs, however, as in Scenario 4, Kevin's profits take more of a tumble than do Maria's since Kevin relies more on fixed factors with his state-of-the-art electronic equipment.

Exercise 23.2

The Kumfee Bed Company wishes to introduce a new product to its range. The choice of product has been narrowed down to four and projections are shown in Table 23.1.

The company has heard that you have a break-even analysis template. It is keen to select the product that is most likely to give good profits. However, the costs

FIGURE 23.4

MARIA'S STUDIO: SENSITIVITY ANALYSIS

	A	B	C	D	E	F
1	**INPUT**					
2	Fixed costs	14500				
3	Variable cost per unit	100				
4	Selling price per unit	150				
5	Minimum sales volume(units)	250				
6	Maximum sales volume(units)	500				
7	Most likely sales volume(units)	400				
8						
9	**SENSITIVITY ANALYSIS**	SCENARIO 0	SCENARIO 1	SCENARIO 2	SCENARIO 3	SCENARIO 4
10	**Description of change**	No change	10% decrease	10% decrease	10% increase	10% increase
11	Adjusted input		in units	in price	in variable costs	in fixed costs
12	Fixed costs	14500	14500	14500	14500	15950
13	Variable cost per unit	100	100	100	110	100
14	Selling price per unit	150	150	135	150	150
15	Minimum sales volume(units)	250	225	250	250	250
16	Maximum sales volume(units)	500	450	500	500	500
17	Most likely sales volume(units)	400	360	400	400	400
18						
19	**OUTPUT**					
20	Unit contribution	50	50	35	40	50
21	Break-even point (units)	290.00	290.00	414.29	362.50	319.00
22	Break-even point (£)	43500.00	43500.00	55928.57	54375.00	47850.00
23	Profit/loss at minimum sales volume	-2000	-3250	-5750	-4500	-3450
24	Profit/loss at maximum sales volume	10500	8000	3000	5500	9050
25	Profit/loss at most likely sales volume	5500	3500	-500	1500	4050

FIGURE 23.5

KEVIN'S GYM: SENSITIVITY ANALYSIS

	A	B	C	D	E	F
1	**INPUT**					
2	Fixed costs	33000				
3	Variable cost per unit	56				
4	Selling price per unit	150				
5	Minimum sales volume(units)	250				
6	Maximum sales volume(units)	500				
7	Most likely sales volume(units)	400				
8						
9	**SENSITIVITY ANALYSIS**	SCENARIO 0	SCENARIO 1	SCENARIO 2	SCENARIO 3	SCENARIO 4
10	**Description of change**	No change	10% decrease	10% decrease	10% increase	10% increase
11	Adjusted input		in units	in price	in variable costs	in fixed costs
12	Fixed costs	33000	33000	33000	33000	36300
13	Variable cost per unit	56	56	56	61.6	56
14	Selling price per unit	150	150	135	150	150
15	Minimum sales volume(units)	250	225	250	250	250
16	Maximum sales volume(units)	500	450	500	500	500
17	Most likely sales volume(units)	400	360	400	400	400
18						
19	**OUTPUT**					
20	Unit contribution	94	94	79	88.4	94
21	Break-even point (units)	351.06	351.06	417.72	373.30	386.17
22	Break-even point (£)	52659.57	52659.57	56392.41	55995.48	57925.53
23	Profit/loss at minimum sales volume	-9500	-11850	-13250	-10900	-12800
24	Profit/loss at maximum sales volume	14000	9300	6500	11200	10700
25	Profit/loss at most likely sales volume	4600	840	-1400	2360	1300

TABLE 23.1

KUMFEE BED COMPANY: CHOICE OF PRODUCT PROJECTIONS

(For first year)	Bunkee	Luxuree	Sofee	Foldee
Fixed costs (£)	23 000	75 000	45 000	15 000
Variable cost (£) per unit	54	120	62	40
Selling price (£) per unit	350	1 650	750	120
Sales volume range (units)	100–400	50–250	200–400	300–800
Forecasted sales volume	300	150	350	600

and sales figures are estimates and may be influenced by external factors. It is possible that the following scenarios may become reality:

(a) Demand may be down by 15 per cent
(b) Timber prices might rise resulting in a 20 per cent increase in variable costs
(c) Customers are making bed purchases only at sales times when the company reduces its prices to retailers by 5 per cent
(d) Higher maintenance charges for machinery may push up fixed costs by 5 per cent

Use the spreadsheet template to carry out an analysis of the possible effects of these different scenarios and advise the company as to which bed to produce.

Exercise 23.3

A city centre department store is faced with a quandary. It lets space to various concession operations and one of them, an electrical retailer, has decided to cease trading. This leaves the store with a large area of space to use in its basement.

Two suggestions have been put forward, a video counter or a telephone equipment and accessories department.

(a) Video counter
As the store is in the city centre, it attracts a wide range of city workers, students and shoppers. There would be space to allow the installation of the latest technology which enables customers to search electronically for any video, whether current or not, and this is then downloaded electronically so that the customer could purchase the video there and then without having to place an order and wait for a week to obtain the video. This option involves leasing the computer equipment on an annual basis. There is a standard maintenance charge which guarantees that a technician will be on site within 30 minutes in case of a breakdown but the store has space for four of the computers so management feel confident that the operation can be kept running at an acceptable level of service. Very little input is needed from sales staff as the computers are user-friendly. The only other major cost is the provision and storage of the blank video tapes.

(b) Telephone equipment and accessories department
Because of the increasing demand for telephones of all types whether it be mobile phones, answering machines or modems, the store's management believe they are well situated to cater for this market and the space allows all products to be well displayed. This option will require fully-qualified staff to advise customers but they can be hired on an hourly basis to reflect the changing demand patterns during the week. There would be investment needed in display fixtures and fittings. As new products develop, there will be sufficient flexibility to adjust the range of products stocked.

The store has used the template for break-even analysis to evaluate the two options under various different scenarios.

Scenario 0
This is based on its original forecasts of costs and sales, taking an average figure for the unit selling price.

Scenario 1
Unit selling prices have been reduced by 5 per cent.

Scenario 2
Here variable costs per unit have been increased by 5 per cent.

FIGURE 23.6

EXERCISE 23.3: SENSITIVITY ANALYSIS

INPUT	Video	Telephone
Fixed costs	120000	20000
Variable cost per unit	7.50	47.50
Selling price per unit	12.50	55.00
Minimum sales volume(units)	50000	15000
Maximum sales volume(units)	200000	45000
Most likely sales volume(units)	100000	25000

SENSITIVITY ANALYSIS	SCENARIO 0	
Description of change	No change	
Adjusted input	Video	Telephone
Fixed costs	120000	20000
Variable cost per unit	7.50	47.50
Selling price per unit	12.50	55.00
Minimum sales volume(units)	50000	15000
Maximum sales volume(units)	200000	45000
Most likely sales volume(units)	100000	25000
OUTPUT		
Unit contribution	5	7.5
Break-even point (units)	24000.00	2666.67
Break-even point (£)	300000.0	146666.67
Profit/loss at minimum sales volume	130000	92500
Profit/loss at maximum sales volume	880000	317500
Profit/loss at most likely sales volume	380000	167500

SENSITIVITY ANALYSIS	SCENARIO 1	
Description of change	Selling price down by 5%	
Adjusted input	Video	Telephone
Fixed costs	120000	20000
Variable cost per unit	7.50	47.50
Selling price per unit	11.875	52.25
Minimum sales volume(units)	50000	15000
Maximum sales volume(units)	200000	45000
Most likely sales volume(units)	100000	25000
OUTPUT		
Unit contribution	4.375	4.75
Break-even point (units)	27428.57	4210.53
Break-even point (£)	325714.29	220000.00
Profit/loss at minimum sales volume	98750	51250
Profit/loss at maximum sales volume	755000	193750
Profit/loss at most likely sales volume	317500	98750

SENSITIVITY ANALYSIS	SCENARIO 2	
Description of change	Variable costs up by 5%	
Adjusted input	Video	Telephone
Fixed costs	120000	20000
Variable cost per unit	7.875	49.875
Selling price per unit	12.50	55.00
Minimum sales volume(units)	50000	15000
Maximum sales volume(units)	200000	45000
Most likely sales volume(units)	100000	25000
OUTPUT		
Unit contribution	4.625	5.125
Break-even point (units)	25945.95	3902.44
Break-even point (£)	324324.32	214634.15
Profit/loss at minimum sales volume	111250	56875
Profit/loss at maximum sales volume	805000	210625
Profit/loss at most likely sales volume	342500	108125

SENSITIVITY ANALYSIS	SCENARIO 3	
Description of change	Demand down by 5%	
Adjusted input	Video	Telephone
Fixed costs	120000	20000
Variable cost per unit	7.50	47.50
Selling price per unit	12.50	55.00
Minimum sales volume(units)	47500	14250
Maximum sales volume(units)	190000	42750
Most likely sales volume(units)	95000	23750
OUTPUT		
Unit contribution	5	7.5
Break-even point (units)	24000.00	2666.67
Break-even point (£)	300000.00	146666.67
Profit/loss at minimum sales volume	117500	86875
Profit/loss at maximum sales volume	830000	300625
Profit/loss at most likely sales volume	355000	158125

SENSITIVITY ANALYSIS	SCENARIO 4	
Description of change	Fixed costs up by 5%	
Adjusted input	Video	Telephone
Fixed costs	126000	21000
Variable cost per unit	7.50	47.50
Selling price per unit	12.50	55.00
Minimum sales volume(units)	50000	15000
Maximum sales volume(units)	200000	45000
Most likely sales volume(units)	100000	25000
OUTPUT		
Unit contribution	5	7.5
Break-even point (units)	25200.00	2800.00
Break-even point (£)	315000.00	154000.00
Profit/loss at minimum sales volume	124000	91500
Profit/loss at maximum sales volume	874000	316500
Profit/loss at most likely sales volume	374000	166500

Scenario 3
For this scenario, sales volumes are 5 per cent less than forecast.

Scenario 4
Fixed costs have been increased by 5 per cent.

The company chose 5 per cent in each case as it wanted to assess the effect of changing each input in turn by a comparable amount.

The printout from the sensitivity analysis is shown in Figure 23.6.

Use it to advise the store on which option is likely to be the more profitable choice.

23.5 Summary

In this chapter you have learned how to perform a sensitivity analysis. This allows the effects of changes in costs, selling prices and sales volumes on break-even point and profit to be compared. In this way, we can assess the viability of different options and identify possible areas of vulnerability. It provides us with a wider perspective on the consequences of our decision-making.

Sensitivity analysis is most readily accomplished using a spreadsheet. A general template for break-even analysis has been displayed.

24
Short-term Decision-making

24.1 Learning objectives

When you have worked through this chapter you should be able to

- Explain and illustrate by giving an example the difference between the long-term and short-term aspects of decision-making
- Give three examples of typical short-term decisions
- Define the term **MARGINAL COST**
- Explain what is meant by the **RELEVANT RANGE**
- Explain what is meant by an **INCREMENTAL** volume
- Define the term **DIFFERENTIAL COST**
- Define the term **SUNK COST**
- Define the term **COMMON COST**
- Define the term **OPPORTUNITY COST**
- In the context of an example, identify the costs which are **RELEVANT** in making a short-term decision

24.2 Long-term and short-term decisions

One of the important objectives of most business organisations is to make a profit. The shareholders will not be willing to leave their money invested in a company that is not showing returns better than or in line with competitors' figures.

However, you have seen in Chapters 21–23 that it is not always easy to decide which course of action will lead to the highest profits. This is partly to do with the complex nature of business decisions, but it is also caused by the fact that what is in the long-term interest of the business organisation does not necessarily lead to quick returns, and vice versa.

In other words, the business is concerned with short-term profits on one hand and long-term wealth on the other. The two must be weighed up carefully.

Example

To illustrate this point, let us consider one main difference between two grocers, J Sainsbury plc and the German discounter ALDI who entered the UK market in the early 1990s.

Since J Sainsbury plc is owned by shareholders, they are likely to expect some short-term returns. As you know, shareholders are looking for a dividend as well as a capital gain on the value of their shares. Should Sainsbury's fail to deliver and make a loss for a few years, the shareholders would be free to shop around for a better investment. The large institutional shareholders, which are the insurance companies and pension funds, would indeed consider it their duty to do so, there would be very little loyalty should Sainsbury's fall on hard times.

In contrast ALDI is privately owned by a trust fund which was set up with the stated objective to maximise the long-term wealth of the business. This trust fund is answerable to no-one and does not have to pay out monies and produce instant results. If the managers of this trust fund feel that it is in the best long-term interest of the business to build up market share in a new market, for example the UK or East Germany, then they are free to do so, even if that means making a loss in that particular market for quite a few years. In the meantime all the remaining profit is ploughed back into the business instead of going out to shareholders.

As you can see the two organisations are bound to have a very different outlook on the long-term strategy.

However, in terms of day-to-day decision-making in the branches the picture may be much more similar, both have to plan staffing rotas, decide on mark-downs of perishable items. Naturally the way in which these decisions are taken ultimately also affects the profitability of the company.

From a cost accounting point of view it is useful to differentiate between short-term and long-term decisions. (For a definition of the short and long run see Chapter 21.)

In the short term, *CONTRIBUTION* is most important and *MARGINAL* and *DIFFERENTIAL* costing techniques should be used for decision-making purposes. This is covered in detail in this chapter.

In the long run, all costs must be recovered. In terms of operational decisions, such as pricing policy and space utilisation, amongst others, this means that *ABSORPTION COSTING* and *DIRECT PRODUCT COSTING* are more appropriate. These techniques are covered in Chapters 18 and 25.

Last not least, capital investment decisions are covered in Chapters 26–28.

24.3 Short-term decision-making: incremental analysis

Short-term decision-making deals with decisions concerning the allocation of scarce resources as part of a short-term future course of action, within an existing framework of capital investment and cost structure.

- **Short-term**

This is the time it takes to change the variable factors.

- **Scarce resources**

Since resources are not unlimited, the implications of forgoing the potential benefits from alternative choices must be considered.

- **Future**

The past is irrelevant, we are not concerned with what has happened before, but are only concerned with the likely results of a proposed action.

- **Course of action**

There is usually a comparison of alternatives.

- **Existing framework of capital investment**

There is a 'going concern' assumption. The impact on fixed costs is typically fairly limited; short-term decision-making is a technique for fine-tuning the running of the business rather than deciding on its basic investment and fixed cost structure.

Exercise 24.1

Give **three** examples of typical short-term decisions.

Further examples of short-term decisions are:

- Introduction of a new product line
- Dropping a product line
- Making use of spare capacity
- Make or buy decisions
- Special pricing decisions, such as mark-downs
- Special promotion
- Adjusting part-time staffing requirements
- Pub afternoon opening

This chapter shows you how to use financial criteria to take this type of decision. Naturally, you should bear in mind that no sound business decision can be taken on the grounds of a likely short-term financial gain alone. Doing that might greatly harm the reputation of the company and therefore endanger the long-term wealth of the shareholders. So nothing would be gained. All the same it is useful to know how to evaluate the financial side of a short-term decision. You can then use this, together with other information, to come to a final conclusion.

The principle of short-term decision-making is to consider only those revenues which are a direct result of the decision and to weigh them against those costs which are incurred as a direct consequence of this decision.

In this context, the cost of selling one extra unit is called the *MARGINAL COST*. This is an economist's term which is used to describe the variable costs associated with making a decision. From the above definition of short-term decision-making you would expect this to be adequate to describe the costs incurred as a result of a short-term decision. However, what happens quite frequently is that a short-term decision would require a small amount of an additional fixed factor to be put into the business. In the context of break-even analysis fixed costs were assumed to remain constant. However, from Chapter 21 you know that this is only true for a certain range of possible sales volumes; once this is exceeded, the law of diminishing returns applies and there are diseconomies of scale unless more of the fixed factor is acquired. This range of volumes which can be achieved for a certain mix of resources is called the *RELEVANT RANGE*.

In a short-term decision at the margins of the relevant range, a small fixed cost element must also be considered relevant for the decision. This is not included in the concept of the marginal cost. In such cases, cost accountants use the concept of a *DIFFERENTIAL COST*.

> The cost of selling the *INCREMENTAL* volume (in other words, the additional units) for a specific decision is known as the *DIFFERENTIAL COST*, which can include a variable as well as a fixed cost element.

This offers a much more accurate assessment of the costs involved.

> To pinpoint the costs which must be taken into account when making a decision the important question which must be answered is: Is this cost *RELEVANT* to this decision?

Example

You are at the annual Student Christmas Ball. To get there you have had to spend £30 on the ticket, another £100 on a dress or suit and you have already spent £5 on drinks. Unfortunately you are not enjoying yourself very much, you have got a splitting headache and have fallen out with your friend who accompanied you there. You are trying to decide whether to stay a bit longer or to go home. If you stay, you can get a lift home at the end of the evening. This will cost you nothing. In this event you would be likely to spend another £5 on drinks. Alternatively you could go home immediately – this would cost you around £10 for a taxi. You are feeling a bit mean and are trying to decide using financial criteria only. Which are the *relevant* costs?

The only relevant costs are the costs you might incur in the future as a result of the decision. This is the cost of future drinks as compared to the cost of a future taxi. The difference between these two cost items is the differential cost of the decision. All the other costs – the cost of buying clothes, ticket and past drinks – should not influence the decision. They are called *SUNK COSTS* as they cannot be recovered. Making a decision which takes sunk costs into consideration could be throwing good money after bad!

Exercise 24.2

Jimmy has recently opened a health food shop. He spent £1500 on refurbishment (it used to be a hairdresser's) and £500 on a leaflet campaign. However, the venture was not very successful and after six months of relatively low turnover and some losses, Jimmy is getting concerned. He has to pay £1000 rent a month. He also has to pay for rates, telephone, heat and light and the shop is barely profitable enough.

He is now trying to decide what to do. His son, who is a marketing student, has carried out some market research for him free of charge. The results indicate that there would be demand for a wholefood pizza take-away in the area. Conversion of part of the shop to accommodate a second hand hot pizza counter would cost another £500.

Jimmy originally gave up a job as a lecturer at the local college to start the business, but he is now also considering going back to part-time teaching in the evenings – this could bring in £300 per month but would not leave him enough time for the new pizza counter.

Which are the relevant costs for this decision? Which are sunk costs? Are there any other costs and revenues not so easily classified?

In the short run, the decision is between three alternatives

- Do nothing
- Go back to part-time teaching to supplement the income
- Put in a pizza counter

Note that the decision to close the shop is not under consideration here, as it would have a substantial impact on the fixed factors and could not be carried out in the short-term.

The cost of the leaflet campaign is of course a *sunk* cost. It cannot be recovered, no matter which course of action Jimmy takes. The same applies to the cost of refurbishing the premises.

The cost of rent, rates, heat, light, telephone also do not come into this decision, as they are not really influenced by the decision. These are known as *COMMON COSTS* and you should ignore them for short-term decision-making purposes.

That leaves the additional £500 required for the conversion to accommodate the hot pizza counter. This cost is a *differential cost* and therefore relevant to the decision.

But what about the money Jimmy could earn teaching evening classes part-time? If the pizza counter was put in, he would not have time to do this. Therefore this additional income would be forgone. This type of cost is known as an *OPPORTUNITY COST* and is also relevant to the decision. In other words to take this short-term decision, the cost of the pizza counter plus the teaching salary forgone must be carefully compared to the forecast sales revenue which will result from selling pizzas.

You should note that naturally, all this has long-term implications, too, but they are not considered here.

To summarise, in short-term decision-making you need to ask the following questions.

- Is the cost relevant to the decision?
- If the answer is No, it is a sunk cost or a common cost and you can ignore it.
- If the answer is Yes, it is a differential cost or an opportunity cost and you should base the decision on it.

Exercise 24.3

The 'Spread Eagle', a public house, has the pattern of weekly average costs and revenues illustrated by the figures shown in Figure 24.1.

In 1988, when the change in the licensing law took effect, the 'Spread Eagle' started opening in the afternoon. The brewery with which the pub is associated organised a nation-wide campaign promoting afternoon opening. Each pub was required to make a financial contribution of £1000 to cover the costs of this campaign. For the 'Spread Eagle', afternoon opening also meant employing additional part-time bar staff at a cost of £80 per week.

After the first two months of afternoon opening, an evaluation took place. So far very little additional revenue had been generated – on average around £400 a week. This seemed hardly worth it, especially since the clientele frequenting the pub in the afternoons appeared to be generally of a lower standard than the pub's typical customers. On one occasion a fight broke out and the damage caused cost £150, which could not be recovered. As a result the landlord and landlady were now seriously considering closing again in the afternoons.

FIGURE 24.1

'SPREAD EAGLE': COSTS AND REVENUES

	£
Sales	4500
Costs of Goods Sold	2600
Gross Profit	1900
Expenses	
Salary Landlord	290
Wages Bar Staff	300
Wages Cleaner	50
Lease on Amusement Machines	7
Rent	250
Rates	150
Phone	30
Depreciation	
Electronic Cash Register	15
Net Profit	808

(a) Acting as an advisor to the landlord and landlady of the 'Spread Eagle', evaluate the decision whether or not to stay open during the afternoon

(b) Briefly outline any marketing considerations which should be taken into account in conjunction with the financial considerations, when making this decision

Exercise 24.4

A car manufacturer has to make a decision whether to make or buy a component part. If the part is made then the following costs will be incurred internally:

	£
• Raw materials	20
• Direct labour	15
• Additional overhead	5

Also, two machine hours are required to make each one of this component. This means that during this time the machine can no longer be put to its current use, which is in the production of another component. For every hour, six units of this alternative component are currently manufactured and they yield a contribution of £5 each. A supplier has offered to provide the component at a charge of £110 each.

Use the techniques of short-term decision-making to evaluate whether the company should make or buy the component.

Exercise 24.5

Johnsons, a high class jewellery business which is family-owned, currently trades in the city centre, paying rent and rates on their premises of £300 per week.

Johnsons are always looking to update their range. Currently, consideration is being given to stocking silver charms which they believe might prove popular with parents of young girls. Once a charm bracelet has been purchased, there is a degree of 'pester power' exerted by the child and sales of additional charms are made throughout the year. This would involve a small extra fixed cost element, as a special display stand would have to be purchased from the manufacturer at a cost of £100. It is expected that the sale of the bracelets and charms would generate additional revenue of £200 per week. Of this £80 is required to cover the cost of purchasing and storing the additional stock.

To make space for their new product line, Johnsons would have to reduce the space currently devoted to their range of designer cufflinks in 22 carat gold. This line used to be fashionable with young professional men who work in the locality, but has recently shown declining sales. Even a recent advertisement in the local papers at a cost of £100 has done nothing to revitalise sales. As a result of reducing the space allocation for the cufflinks, revenues are likely to decline by £90 a week and the cost of stock will fall by £40 per week.

Draw up a statement summarising the relevant costs and revenues which are to be considered when deciding whether or not to introduce the new product line.

24.4 Summary

In this chapter the difference between the long-term and short-term aspects of decision-making has been explained and the terminology of short-term decision-making introduced.

In short-term decision-making, costs are considered to be relevant to the decision only if they are different as a direct result of the decision.

Relevant costs include marginal or differential costs – these are the costs which differ between alternatives. They also include opportunity costs – these are the costs of potential benefits forgone by not undertaking an alternative course of action.

Common costs, defined as those that stay the same regardless of which course of action is chosen, and sunk costs, which are those that have already been paid for and cannot be retrieved under any circumstances, are ignored when making a short-term decision.

25

Pricing Decisions

25.1 Learning objectives

When you have finished working through this chapter you should be able to

- Discuss the short-term and long-term aspects of **PRICING** decisions
- Appreciate the importance of corporate strategy for pricing decisions
- Contrast and compare the implications of a **MARKET PENETRATION** and a **SKIMMING** approach for pricing of new products
- Understand the relationship between costing and pricing
- Define the term **FULL COST** (or **COST-PLUS**) **PRICING**
- Identify the main strengths and limitations of cost-plus pricing
- Define the term **MARGINAL COSTING**
- Define the term **MARGINAL COST PRICING**
- Differentiate between situations in which a cost-plus approach to pricing is appropriate and those in which a marginal cost approach is needed

25.2 Introduction

Chapter 24 differentiated between short-term decisions, which had little or no impact on the fixed cost structure of the business and were used for fine-tuning, and long-term capital investment decisions, which have a major impact on the fixed assets of the company and must be evaluated in the light of the opportunity cost of the capital required. This aspect is treated in detail in Chapters 26 and 27.

However, there are many areas of decision-making in business, where both long-term and short-term factors are involved. One such area is *PRICING*.

Naturally, decisions on the prices to charge for different products cannot be made from a financial point of view alone. The non-financial aspects of pricing are covered thoroughly in various key marketing texts, such as Doyle (1994). For this reason, this chapter offers only a very brief overview of strategic marketing aspects of pricing decisions in order to place the financial aspects in the correct context. It will aim to show you how businesses can make the best use of cost information as an important contributory factor in making pricing decisions. It should be borne in mind throughout that cost information must be used together with other information, for instance on customer preferences, competitors' prices and product mix, demand, trends and fashions, to obtain the best possible results. In this sense costs often are one major constraint to decision-making rather than the driving force behind it.

25.3 Strategic aspects of pricing decisions

The decisions as to *what prices to charge* for its products are a key determinant of the financial success and competitive standing of a business organisation. If the prices charged are perceived as too high, customers will switch to alternative suppliers and the business will lose out. If the prices charged are too low, the business will not be able to cover its costs and therefore will be unable to survive.

In a situation where a number of indistinguishable competitors are all offering an identical product it is accepted wisdom that customers would prefer to buy from the firm charging the lowest prices. However, firms are constrained by their costs in how low they can go and still operate profitably. The actual market price is quickly established through the forces of supply and demand and an equilibrium results. In reality, this is quite an unusual situation, which only applies to very few examples, such as the international commodity markets for raw materials. Generally speaking, for most businesses the presence of market forces dictates that there is some relationship between prices charged and sales volume obtained. In the short term, sales volumes can be increased by dropping the price. This can take the form of promotional special offers or end-of-day mark downs. Furthermore, in the long term and in the absence of other factors, such as differences in the level of service or the types of financial packages offered, manufacturers of similar products compete for the same customers on the basis of price. Thus, higher sales volumes can be achieved by undercutting the competition's prices. Likewise in retailing, the discount operator will aim to generate a high sales volume at low prices. At the other end of the market there may be a premium-priced luxury offer which only appeals to few customers, but where the profit on each item is quite high.

The above examples make it clear that for most business organisations there is ample opportunity to apply marketing principles to distinguish their offering from that of the competition, and price serves as an important signalling device, which adds to the overall message to the customer. Each competing firm aims to add superior value to its product and this value to the customer is reflected in the price. The customer's perception of the overall benefit or value received is informed by the combination of different aspects of the marketing mix. Price is evaluated in the light of the relative quality of the goods, the choice offered, the convenience of reaching the place where the goods are sold and the payment terms, to name but a few. In this sense, pricing decisions are related to the overall strategic objectives of the business. It is important that the tactical choices relating to the marketing mix elements work well together to reflect the overall strategic direction and to give out a consistent and persuasive message to prospective customers of the firm.

For a newly introduced product, the two main approaches adopted are known as *MARKET PENETRATION* and *SKIMMING*. A penetration approach is appropriate where a business introduces a new product with the objective of rapidly building up market share. To achieve this it will charge relatively low prices and in this way encourage purchases. Alternatively, the business's objective may be to reap the maximum profits from the new product whilst there are few competitors, an approach known as skimming. If this is the objective, then high prices should be charged to maintain exclusivity and maximise the high profits obtainable from those customers willing to pay the price for the sake of being trend setters.

Likewise, the business's directors have to make decisions concerning its overall strategic positioning. Where the business wishes to position its offering depends on its particular strengths and on the customer group it wishes to target.

Example

Figure 25.1 illustrates the respective positioning of three hairdressers, in terms of the prices charged and the subjective value perceived by their customers.

Clearly there is space for all three firms to succeed in the hairdressing market. The traditional barber

FIGURE 25.1

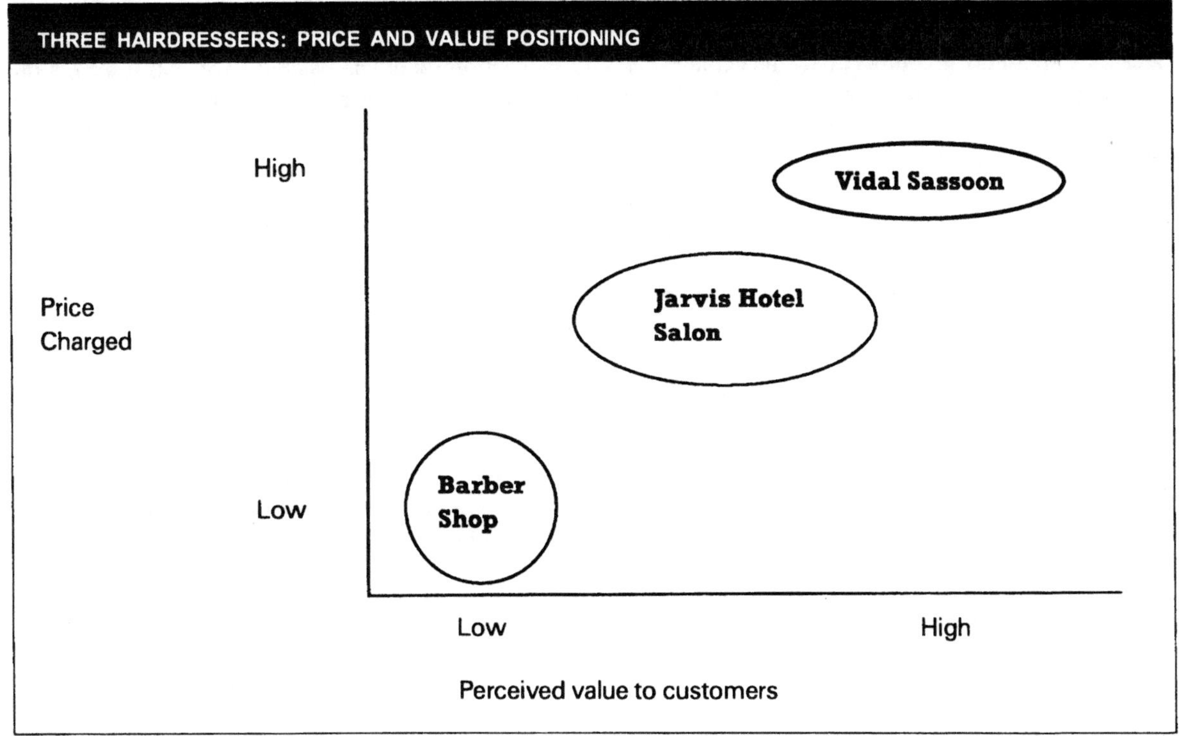

shop has many long-term satisfied customers who just want the basics at a reasonable price and who do not place any great value on sophisticated hair styles. At the other end of the spectrum, there will always be highly fashion-conscious consumers who value the latest styles greatly and are prepared to pay for this. Last not least, the hotel salon will continue to be busy with middle-of-the-road business clients who need a quick and reliable service at medium price levels.

This example from the service industries also illustrates that there is often a relationship between the degree of customisation of a product and the prices charged. The barber probably only has a repertoire of approximately three basic hair styles, whereas the stylists at Vidal Sassoon are very highly trained and need to update their skills regularly to stay in touch with the very latest trends and techniques. This is then reflected in the prices charged. The same principle applies to other product types. For example, you would expect a great deal more if you hired an architect and a builder and got them to design and build a house from scratch and to your specifications than if you purchased a ready-built ex-show home.

TABLE 25.1

OWN BRAND PRODUCT LINES: PRICE COMPARISON

	Sainsbury (£)	ALDI (£)
Cat food (325 g)	0.33	0.29
Baked beans	0.27	0.19
Tinned spaghetti	0.26	0.19
Tinned plum tomatoes	0.19	0.17
Processed peas	0.23	0.19
80 Tea bags	0.78	0.69
Bananas (1 kg)	0.99	0.79
Milk (4 pints)	1.05	0.89
Concentrated washing-up liquid (1 ltr)	0.75	0.79
Apple juice (1 ltr)	0.66	0.39
Orange Juice (1 ltr)	0.49	0.49

Exercise 25.1

Table 25.1 presents the comparative prices charged for 10 own brand product lines by J Sainsbury plc and ALDI(UK) Ltd at the same date, two years after ALDI entered the UK market.

(a) From your general knowledge of the two companies' strategies in the UK, identify what you consider to be the three most important reasons for their respective pricing strategies in terms of their overall competitive positioning.

(b) What do you consider to be the most important constraint on their respective pricing decisions?

Clearly, the above provides only a very brief overview of the strategic factors affecting pricing decisions. However, these factors are very important and must not be ignored. There are surprisingly many businesses where prices are determined simply by carrying out comparisions with the prices charged by near competitors, without any real evaluation of the strategic objectives pursued and the characteristics and needs of the customers targeted.

25.4 The impact of costs on pricing decisions

Exercise 25.1 identified the cost of running the business as the major long-term constraint on the choice of an overall pricing policy. Eventually, all costs must be recovered.

Chapter 18 showed how a business organisations can be subdivided into a hierarchy of cost and profit centres for purposes of cost determination, budgeting and responsibility accounting, in an approach known as *ABSORPTION COSTING*. This is a very useful approach, as it allows the business to base the price of the products directly on the costs of making the product. Often this is done by applying a predetermined mark-up percentage to the cost of the goods. This ensures that all costs are recovered and a bit of profit is made on top. This pricing technique is called *FULL COST PRICING* or *COST-PLUS PRICING*.

Exercise 25.2

List the main strengths of the cost-plus approach to pricing. Can you identify any potential weaknesses?

Whilst the cost-plus approach ensures that all costs are recovered, this approach also has certain weaknesses. It does not automatically take into account the positioning of the business, and this is an important additional consideration to make sure that the mark-up percentage applied is at the right level to achieve the business's objectives. But, most important, if cost-plus is used exclusively, in the short run a number of potentially profitable opportunities may be left unexplored, leaving the business worse off.

Exercise 25.3

Refer back to the short-term decision-making techniques introduced in Chapter 24. Can you think of any situations requiring short-term decisions in which a full-cost approach to pricing would be inappropriate, yet some profits could be made?

Examples are:

- The use of spare capacity in a manufacturing organisation for the completion of a low price order
- The sale of highly perishable goods at mark-down prices
- The sale of low price fashion goods which have been bought in especially for the sale
- The sale of special promotion items which will attract additional customers
- The use of 'loss leaders' to attract extra customers who also then spend on the profitable lines

This list is by no means exhaustive and you have probably listed a number of other situations which were similar in character. All these situations have one thing in common: the gross margin on each item sold may be quite low, in fact probably lower than required under a cost-plus approach. However, this does not matter under the circumstances, which are much like those in short-term decision-making. The fixed cost structure, image, customer base and long-term pricing strategy of the business are already given; all that remains to be done is to fine-tune the pricing decisions on a limited number of special product lines in order to respond to short-term circumstances. Under these conditions the *CONTRIBUTION* made by each sale is the important factor. The relevant question is: What does it cost at the margin to sell the additional products? The *MARGINAL COST* is defined

TABLE 25.2

COMPARISON OF PRICING TECHNIQUES		
	Cost-plus Pricing	**Marginal Cost Pricing**
Rationale	In the long run all costs must be met	In the short run fixed costs must be met in any case
	Prices must be based on the *FULL COST* of running the business	The *CONTRIBUTION* is key factor Prices must be based on the *MARGINAL COST* of selling the extra item

as the additional cost incurred as a result of selling one additional item (this is often equal to the variable cost). As long as the prices charged recover more than the marginal cost of achieving the sale, the business is better off as a result. This approach is known as *MARGINAL COST PRICING*. A summary of the two approaches is given in Table 25.2.

25.5 Implications for pricing strategy

The implication of the above is that in the long run, and together with broader marketing considerations, the full cost of business operations must be one of the key determinants of pricing decisions. In other words, the pricing strategy of the business is founded on a cost-plus approach. However, if this is the only approach used then, in the short run, potentially profitable opportunities may be overlooked and lost. Thus marginal cost pricing is a must for the short run. Marginal cost pricing serves as a technique applied in order to fine-tune the pricing and profitability of the business.

Exercise 25.4

In March 199X Delaney's Department Stores' Leeds branch introduces a range of chilled pre-packed wholefood meals. The costs incurred can be broken down as follows:

Additional cold storage in the warehouse	£650
Purchase of new refrigerated display cabinet	£1800

(Both the cold storage unit for the warehouse and the display cabinet are expected to have a lifespan of at least three years, with no scrap value at the end. They will be depreciated using the straight line method)

Regional advertising campaign	£500
Pilot market survey	£400
In-store promotion	£500

The products are manufactured especially for Delaney's at a cost of £1.20 per unit, including delivery.

The company usually applies a cost-plus approach to pricing decisions, aiming for a mark-up in the region of 25 per cent.

On the basis of the market survey, the sales forecast presented in Table 25.3 has been made.

TABLE 25.3

DELANEY'S: SALES FORECAST						
Month	**1**	**2**	**3**	**4**	**5**	**6**
Sales (units)	300	400	600	850	1000	1100

If these figures are achieved, fixed costs will be covered almost from the beginning and all other initial costs will be recovered very rapidly during the growth stage of the product life cycle. A mark-up of 25 per cent would also mean that the product is introduced at a price which is lower than that of comparable products. This should lead to rapid market penetration. In September the project has to be reviewed. Sales figures for the first six months, as shown in Table 25.4, were disappointing.

This compares unfavourably to the rest of the department. For all other product lines in the food department the target of 25 per cent on cost has been achieved or superseded. Discussions with the departmental manager have shown that the problem is largely caused by much lower than anticipated stock turnover, which has resulted in a substantial incidence of mark-downs as individual items reach their sell-by date.

The launch of an almost identical product range by a well-known national chain of department stores at

TABLE 25.4

DELANEY'S: ACTUAL RESULTS						
Month	**1**	**2**	**3**	**4**	**5**	**6**
	£	**£**	**£**	**£**	**£**	**£**
Sales	150	235	198	273	350	296
Cost of Goods Sold	120	188	158	218	280	237
Markdowns and Wastage	10	27	12	32	39	15
Gross Profit	20	20	28	23	31	44

the same time may have contributed to the problem. However, comparisons show that the competing company have introduced their range at much higher prices. Delaney's management therefore feel that there should be scope to differentiate their product and capture the price-sensitive part of the market. However, there is some concern as to whether this would be compatible with a high quality image.

You are a member of a working party whose brief it is

(a) To make recommendations as to whether or not to continue the product range. Look at this problem in two complementary ways:

- From a financial viewpoint, using break-even analysis, marginal costing and the criteria of short-term decision-making
- From a marketing viewpoint, looking at competition, positioning, and the product life cycle (If you cannot reach a decision on the information given, list what further information you require in order to be able to make a decision).

(b) Suggest criteria for successful product pricing decisions, (other than mark-up)

25.6 Summary

Pricing decisions are very complex, as both long-term and short-term factors must be taken into account.

In the long term, all costs of running the business must be recovered, it is therefore advisable to use an absorption costing system, by which all costs are eventually apportioned to the products sold. Prices are then set at such a level that all costs are covered and a profit is made; this is known as cost-plus pricing.

Where cost-plus pricing is the only technique used, this can mean that the business misses out on potentially profitable opportunities. For example, in a sale, a large amount of additional revenue can be generated. However, the profit margin on individual items could be very small, so this might be rejected as not viable.

This leads to the argument that in the short run the business is committed to a given fixed cost structure, this means that any additional contribution is important. Therefore, marginal cost pricing should be used to make short-term pricing decisions.

Ideally, the two approaches should be combined; using cost-plus pricing as the long-term basis and marginal cost pricing for fine-tuning purposes.

Pricing decisions cannot be seen in isolation, they are part of the business's overall strategy. Whilst this chapter concentrates on the financial aspects of pricing, it is recognised that this is only one aspect.

26 Making Long-term Investment Decisions

26.1 Learning objectives

When you have finished working through this chapter you should be able to

- Understand what is meant by the **FUTURE VALUE** of an investment made now
- Calculate the future value of an amount invested at **COMPOUND INTEREST**
- Understand what is meant by the **PRESENT VALUE** of a sum of money to be paid or received at some future date
- Calculate the present value of a future sum by **DISCOUNTING** at an appropriate interest rate
- Use **DISCOUNTED CASH FLOW (DCF) TECHNIQUES** to appraise the return from long-term projects
- Understand what is meant by the **TIME VALUE** of money
- Understand what is meant by the **NET PRESENT VALUE (NPV)** of an investment
- Calculate the NPV of a project and be able to use **PRESENT VALUE TABLES**
- Understand what is meant by the **INTERNAL RATE OF RETURN (IRR)** of an investment

26.2 Compound interest

When making long-term decisions, both companies and individuals want to know what return they will receive on an investment and to compare the returns from different possible investments.

Of course, investors can just leave their money in the bank where it will attract interest at a rate related to the overall level of interest rates in the money market. When the bank base rate is high, investors can obtain higher rates than when the base rate is low.

In the Western world, interest on an amount placed with a bank or other financial institution is usually calculated at a *COMPOUND INTEREST* rate. By this we mean that after a stated length of time the interest earned on the original investment is added to the investment and the next amount of interest is calculated as a percentage of this new amount. This is then added to the investment before the next interest calculation. In this way, the amount of interest earned in each succeeding period increases. The original investment is termed the *PRINCIPAL*.

Example

Joan and Simon are twins and each inherits £10 000 on their eighteenth birthday. They are obliged to invest the money in a building society until their twenty-first birthday. Joan chooses an account that pays interest compounded annually at 4 per cent per annum. Simon puts his money in an account that compounds interest half-yearly at 4 per cent per annum. How much does each have in their accounts on their twenty-first birthday?

Consider Joan's investment:
During Year 1, the interest earned is 4 per cent * £10 000 = £400 so at the end of the year her total investment is worth £10 000 + £400 = £10 400. The next year, the interest earned is 4 per cent * £10 400 = £416 and at the end of the year her investment is worth £10 400 + £416 = £10 816. The final year, the interest earned is 4 per cent * £10 816 = £432.64 and on her twenty-first birthday she will have £10 816 + £432.64 = £11 248.64 in her account. This amount is termed the *FUTURE VALUE* of £10 000 invested for three years at a compound interest rate of 4 per cent per annum.

Consider Simon's investment:
During the first six months, the interest earned is 2 per cent * £10 000 = £200. Note that as the money has been invested for only half a year, the interest rate used is half the annual rate. At the end of this six month period, the interest is added to the principal and his total investment is now worth £10 200. During the second half-year, the interest earned is 2 per cent * £10 200 = £204 so at the end of the first year, his total investment is worth £10 404. In the third half-year, the interest earned is 2 per cent * £10 404 = £208.08 and his total investment becomes £10 612.08. In the fourth half-year, the interest is 2 per cent * £10 612.08 = £212.24 and the total investment is £10 824.32. In the fifth half-year the interest is 2 per cent * £10 824.32 = £216.49 and the total investment is £11 040.81. In the final half-year the interest is 2 per cent * £11 040.81 = £220.82 and so on his twenty-first birthday, Simon will have £11 261.63 in his account.

Comparing the two future values, you can see that Simon's investment has grown more than Joan's simply because the interest was added more frequently. If you are a lender, the more often the interest is added the better as your sum invested will grow more quickly. If you are a borrower, however, you would prefer to have the interest compounded less frequently!

The calculations we have just performed were a bit long-winded and if you had an investment continuing over many time periods you would need to have a quicker way of performing the calculation. We can do this by using the following formula:

Future value formula

$$\text{Future Value} = \text{Principal} * (1 + \mathbf{i})^{\mathbf{n}}$$

where **i** = the interest rate per period
n = the number of periods for which the investment is made, the interest being added at the end of this period.

Figure 26.1 shows the application of the formula to Joan's and Simon's respective investments.

The application of the general formula gives the same answer as before, apart from a rounding error in the final pence figure.

FIGURE 26.1

JOAN AND SIMON: CALCULATING FUTURE VALUES

Application of the formula to Joan's investment
Principal = £10 000
Period after which interest is added = 1 year
Interest Rate per year = 4% = 0.04
Number of Years = 3
Future Value = £10 000$(1 + 0.04)^3$ = £10 000 * $(1.04)^3$
= £10 000 * 1.124864
(using the power key [x^y] on a calculator, giving £11 248.64 as the final answer, as before)

Application of the formula to Simon's investment
Principal = £10 000
Period after which interest is added = half a year
Interest Rate per half year = one half of 4% = 2% = 0.02
Number of Half Years = 6
Future Value = £10 000 * $(1 + 0.02)^6$
= £10 000 * 1.126162 = £11 261.62

If you are performing many compound interest calculations, it is easiest to use a spreadsheet and we will demonstrate how to do this in Chapter 28.

Exercise 26.1

Calculate to what sum £5000 will accumulate if invested for two years at the following terms:

(a) 5 per cent per annum compounded annually
(b) 5 per cent per annum compounded every six months
(c) 5 per cent per annum compounded quarterly

26.3 Present value

On occasions we may know we have to pay a certain sum of money at some future date. For example, a company usually knows some time in advance if it has to make a major purchase of machinery either for a new process or to replace the existing equipment. The company has to decide how to finance the purchase. One way of doing this is to invest a sum of money now to cover the cost of the purchase. Suppose the company knows that the equipment is likely to cost £200 000 in two years' time. The company does not need to put aside £200 000 now. It needs to invest an amount that will grow to £200 000 in two years' time. Thus, the exact amount to be invested will depend on the current interest rate that the banks are offering. Let us suppose that this is 6 per cent per annum and interest is compounded annually.

What we want to know is what principal to invest now at 6 per cent per annum to provide us with £200 000 in two years time.
Using the compound interest formula, we have

$$\pounds 200\,000 = \text{Principal} * (1 + 0.06)^2$$

or, re-arranging

$$\text{Principal} = \frac{\pounds 200\,000}{(1.06)^2}$$

$$= \frac{\pounds 200\,000}{1.1236}$$

$$= \pounds 177\,999.29$$

If we invest £177 999.29 now at 6 per cent, we will have the £200 000 we need to pay for the machine in two years' time. Of course, in practice, the company would probably round this amount off to £178 000.

We can express this result in another way. We can say that £177 999.29 is the *PRESENT VALUE* of £200 000 in two years' time at 6 per cent per annum compound interest. In other words, £200 000 in two years' time has the same worth to us as £177 999.29 now, given that if we have the money now we can be earning interest at 6 per cent per annum. Thus, when we are comparing earnings or payments, we need to know both the amount of the inflow or outflow and the time at which the earnings are received or the payment is made. This is very important to any investment appraisal because as we have seen £200 000 in two years' time is worth less than £200 000 now. Thus we see that money has a *TIME VALUE*: the earlier we receive it, the more it is worth because we can invest it and get it to earn more for us. When we are comparing projects where the financial returns come in at different times, we must fix a definite point in time as the base when we are going to make financial comparisons. Since, in general, projects will be of differing lengths, the most logical time to choose, that is common to all projects, is the *starting time* which is *now*. In other words, we compare the present values of all the different projects.

Thus the compound interest formula can be rewritten for the calculation of present values.

Present value formula

$$\text{Present value} = \frac{\text{Future value}}{(1 + \mathbf{i})^{\mathbf{n}}}$$

where $\mathbf{i}$ = the interest rate per period
$\mathbf{n}$ = the number of periods

The factor $1/(1 + \mathbf{i})^{\mathbf{n}}$ is called the discount factor and in this context the interest rate, $\mathbf{i}$, is usually termed the *DISCOUNT RATE*. The word 'discount' is appropriate because the present value is always *less* than the future value.

Example

George's Scrap Metal Company has a crushing machine to dispose of and has invited offers from three companies. The offers are

- **Alpha Recyclers**:
  £31 000 payable in a lump sum in three years' time
- **Bravo Disposals**:
  £10 000 now, then £6000 at the end of every year for three years
- **Charlie's Car Dump**:
  £25 000 now

Which offer should George accept if the current discount rate is 5 per cent per annum and interest is compounded annually?

We need to compare the present values of the three different payment methods by *DISCOUNTING* the future sums.

Alpha Recyclers:
The application of the formula to work out the present value is as follows:

Alpha Recyclers:
Present value calculations

$$\text{Present value} = \frac{£31\,000}{(1 + 0.05)^3}$$

$$= £26\,779 \text{ to the nearest £}$$

Bravo Disposals:
As several payments are involved, it is easier to set out the payment schedule as in Table 26.1.

TABLE 26.1

BRAVO DISPOSALS: PAYMENT SCHEDULE

Time	Payment	Present Value
	£	£
Now	10 000	10 000
End Year 1	6 000	5 714
End Year 2	6 000	5 442
End Year 3	6 000	5 183
	Total	26 339

Note that the present values have been worked out using the formula, as follows.

- Present value of £6000 after 1 year
  $= £6000/(1+0.05)$
- Present value of £6000 after 2 years
  $= £6000/(1+0.05)^2$
- Present value of £6000 after 3 years
  $= £6000/(1+0.05)^3$

In total the present value is £26 339.

Charlie's Car Dump:
Present value = £25 000

Comparing these present values, we see that the offer from Alpha Recyclers has the highest present value and on this basis would be accepted by George. There are some qualifications, though. George does not receive any payment from Alpha until the end of three years. What happens if Alpha goes out of business in the meantime? George may be in desperate need of funds now and may need to accept one of the offers giving earlier payment. The calculation has not taken inflation into account. If we estimate the likely rate of inflation, we can do a similar calculation to adjust for the falling value of the pound. The present value calculation should be taken as a starting point in the decision-making process, allowing us to compare sums of money received at different points in time but it is vital that other business considerations are included in the overall decision-making process.

Exercise 26.2

The Bright Office Company has a long-term plan to refurbish its offices in three years' time. The directors have been given three options by the property company for financing the project.

(a) **Option 1**:
Pay £200 000 now

(b) **Option 2**:
Pay £50 000 now, £60 000 at the end of Year 1, £70 000 at the end of Year 2, £80 000 at the end of Year 3

(c) **Option 3**:
Pay £290 000 at the end of three years when the project starts

Which option should Bright Office choose if the discount rate is currently 7 per cent per annum?

26.4 Use of present value tables

Instead of using the formula to calculate the present value of a future sum, we can use present value tables. These tables give the pre-calculated values of the discount factor $1/(1+i)^n$, which is the present value of £1, for various different rates and periods as shown in Table 26.2. They are not usually as accurate as using a calculator as they are only correct to four decimal places but they are quick to use and an approximate value may be all that is required.

Using the tables to find the present value of £200 000 payable in two years' time when the

TABLE 26.2

PRESENT VALUE OF £1

	Discount rate									
Period	1%	2%	3%	4%	5%	6%	7%	8%	9%	10%
1	0.9901	0.9804	0.9709	0.9615	0.9524	0.9434	0.9346	0.9259	0.9174	0.9091
2	0.9803	0.9612	0.9426	0.9246	0.9070	0.8900	0.8734	0.8573	0.8417	0.8264
3	0.9706	0.9423	0.9151	0.8890	0.8638	0.8396	0.8163	0.7938	0.7722	0.7513
4	0.9610	0.9238	0.8885	0.8548	0.8227	0.7921	0.7629	0.7350	0.7084	0.6830
5	0.9515	0.9057	0.8626	0.8219	0.7835	0.7473	0.7130	0.6806	0.6499	0.6209
6	0.9420	0.8880	0.8375	0.7903	0.7462	0.7050	0.6663	0.6302	0.5963	0.5645
7	0.9327	0.8706	0.8131	0.7599	0.7107	0.6651	0.6227	0.5835	0.5470	0.5132
8	0.9235	0.8535	0.7894	0.7307	0.6768	0.6274	0.5820	0.5403	0.5019	0.4665
9	0.9143	0.8368	0.7664	0.7026	0.6446	0.5919	0.5439	0.5002	0.4604	0.4241
10	0.9053	0.8203	0.7441	0.6756	0.6139	0.5584	0.5083	0.4632	0.4224	0.3855
11	0.8963	0.8043	0.7224	0.6496	0.5847	0.5268	0.4751	0.4289	0.3875	0.3505
12	0.8874	0.7885	0.7014	0.6246	0.5568	0.4970	0.4440	0.3971	0.3555	0.3186
13	0.8787	0.7730	0.6810	0.6006	0.5303	0.4688	0.4150	0.3677	0.3262	0.2897
14	0.8700	0.7579	0.6611	0.5775	0.5051	0.4423	0.3878	0.3405	0.2992	0.2633
15	0.8613	0.7430	0.6419	0.5553	0.4810	0.4173	0.3624	0.3152	0.2745	0.2394
16	0.8528	0.7284	0.6232	0.5339	0.4581	0.3936	0.3387	0.2919	0.2519	0.2176
17	0.8444	0.7142	0.6050	0.5134	0.4363	0.3714	0.3166	0.2703	0.2311	0.1978
18	0.8360	0.7002	0.5874	0.4936	0.4155	0.3503	0.2959	0.2502	0.2120	0.1799
19	0.8277	0.6864	0.5703	0.4746	0.3957	0.3305	0.2765	0.2317	0.1945	0.1635
20	0.8195	0.6730	0.5537	0.4564	0.3769	0.3118	0.2584	0.2145	0.1784	0.1486

	Discount rate									
Period	11%	12%	13%	14%	15%	16%	17%	18%	19%	20%
1	0.9009	0.8929	0.8850	0.8772	0.8696	0.8621	0.8547	0.8475	0.8403	0.8333
2	0.8116	0.7972	0.7831	0.7695	0.7561	0.7432	0.7305	0.7182	0.7062	0.6944
3	0.7312	0.7118	0.6931	0.6750	0.6575	0.6407	0.6244	0.6086	0.5934	0.5787
4	0.6587	0.6355	0.6133	0.5921	0.5718	0.5523	0.5337	0.5158	0.4987	0.4823
5	0.5935	0.5674	0.5428	0.5194	0.4972	0.4761	0.4561	0.4371	0.4190	0.4019
6	0.5346	0.5066	0.4803	0.4556	0.4323	0.4104	0.3898	0.3704	0.3521	0.3349
7	0.4817	0.4523	0.4251	0.3996	0.3759	0.3538	0.3332	0.3139	0.2959	0.2791
8	0.4339	0.4039	0.3762	0.3506	0.3269	0.3050	0.2848	0.2660	0.2487	0.2326
9	0.3909	0.3606	0.3329	0.3075	0.2843	0.2630	0.2434	0.2255	0.2090	0.1938
10	0.3522	0.3220	0.2946	0.2697	0.2472	0.2267	0.2080	0.1911	0.1756	0.1615
11	0.3173	0.2875	0.2607	0.2366	0.2149	0.1954	0.1778	0.1619	0.1476	0.1346
12	0.2858	0.2567	0.2307	0.2076	0.1869	0.1685	0.1520	0.1372	0.1240	0.1122
13	0.2575	0.2292	0.2042	0.1821	0.1625	0.1452	0.1299	0.1163	0.1042	0.0935
14	0.2320	0.2046	0.1807	0.1597	0.1413	0.1252	0.1110	0.0985	0.0876	0.0779
15	0.2090	0.1827	0.1599	0.1401	0.1229	0.1079	0.0949	0.0835	0.0736	0.0649
16	0.1883	0.1631	0.1415	0.1229	0.1069	0.0930	0.0811	0.0708	0.0618	0.0541
17	0.1696	0.1456	0.1252	0.1078	0.0929	0.0802	0.0693	0.0600	0.0520	0.0451
18	0.1528	0.1300	0.1108	0.0946	0.0808	0.0691	0.0592	0.0508	0.0437	0.0376
19	0.1377	0.1161	0.0981	0.0829	0.0703	0.0596	0.0506	0.0431	0.0367	0.0313
20	0.1240	0.1037	0.0868	0.0728	0.0611	0.0514	0.0433	0.0365	0.0308	0.0261

discount rate is 6 per cent, we first find the column headed 6 per cent and then move to the row labelled period 2. We find the factor 0.8900. The present value of £200 000 is therefore £200 000 * 0.8900 = £178 000, which, is in close agreement with the result obtained by calculation in Section 26.3.

Exercise 26.3

Repeat Exercise 26.2 using present value tables.

In Chapter 28, we will see how we can use a spreadsheet to perform these calculations.

26.5 Discounted cash flow calculations

We can use the concept of present value to help us with our investment decisions. Usually, an initial capital investment has to be made, perhaps with further outflows of capital in the early stages of a project. The returns on the investment will not occur at once. The inflows will be spread over the lifetime of the project. In some instances, they may have an even spread but in others there may be relatively low returns in the early periods with the major inflows coming towards the end. For example, when opening a superstore, the land has to be acquired, the store built and fitted out, the staff recruited and trained, all before a single customer passes through the doors. Once the store opens, typically there will be a slow build-up of sales and it will be two or three years before the sizeable inflows become established. Of course, there will be a need for store refurbishment after a number of years which will again lead to a cash outflow.

We have two major considerations: first, whether an investment is going to be more profitable than just leaving the money in a bank at the going rate of interest and secondly, when faced with a choice of profitable investments which should be chosen.

Provided we have estimates of the size of the cash flows and their timing, we can discount the cash flows to their present values, assuming an appropriate discount rate. We then total these present values to find the *NET PRESENT VALUE (NPV)* of the investment. If the NPV is positive, the investment will have made more for us than simply leaving the money in the bank at that discount rate. If the NPV is negative, the investment will make less than keeping the money in the bank. If the NPV is zero, our rate of return is exactly the same as the discount rate. This whole process is referred to as a *DISCOUNTED CASH FLOW (DCF)* calculation.

In this context, the term 'cash flow' is being used differently from the way we used it in Parts I, II and IV. Here, over a specific time period, usually one year, we sum the amounts that we will receive, the cash inflows, and sum all the amounts that will have to be paid out, the cash outflows. The difference between these sums is the *net cash flow* for the period.

Example

Molly is considering what to do with £25 000 of redundancy money from her last employment. She intends to travel abroad for three years and wants to invest this lump sum before she departs so as to provide a financial cushion when she returns from her travels. She could leave it in the bank where it would attract interest at 5 per cent per annum, compounded annually. Alternatively, a friend, Jenny, has suggested that Molly invest the money in her curtain-making business. This is well established but needs some larger sewing machines in order to compete for commercial rather than solely domestic orders. Jenny estimates that she would be able to pay Molly £8000 at the end of the first year, £10 000 after two years and £12 000 at the end of three years.

Should Molly leave the money in the bank or should she invest in Jenny's business?

We need to work out the NPV of Molly's investment in Jenny's business assuming a discount rate of 5 per cent. It is easiest to set out the calculation as in Table 26.3. We are looking at the cash flows from Molly's viewpoint so her outgoings are treated as a negative cash flow and her income as a positive cash flow.

The NPV is positive so this tells us that Molly will get a better rate of return on this investment than leaving her money in the bank at 5 per cent per annum. Of course, Molly should not base her decision on this calculation alone. There is more risk attached to Jenny's business than to the bank. The cash flows are only estimates and of course interest rates may change. We shall see in Chapter 27 how we can allow for risk and uncertainty in the decision-making process and in

TABLE 26.3

MOLLY'S INVESTMENT: DCF CALCULATION			
Time	**Cash Flow** £	**Discount Factor**	**Present Value** £
Now	−25 000	1	−25 000
End Year 1	8 000	0.9524	7 619
End Year 2	10 000	0.9070	9 070
End Year 3	12 000	0.8638	10 366
	Net Present Value (NPV) =		2 055

Chapter 28 we will use a spreadsheet to perform sensitivity analyses to assess different scenarios.

Exercise 26.4

Danny has been offered the chance of being the sole UK distributor of a domestic garden cultivator manufactured in the US. He has to pay £100 000 for the distributorship and the net income in the first two years has been estimated at £15 000 per annum rising to £30 000 per annum after that. The current discount rate is 7 per cent. Danny believes that there is a five-year lifespan for this cultivator. Use the DCF technique to advise Danny whether he should invest in this project.

Many companies have a standard rate of return against which any investments are appraised. It may be that a project has to show a rate of return of at least 15 per cent, for example, before it has a chance of being sanctioned. In such a situation we perform a discounted flow calculation using this standard rate. If the NPV turns out positive, the project will be returning better than the standard and can go forward. If the NPV is negative, the project would not be considered further.

Exercise 26.5

Ahmad runs a chain of clothing shops. He is currently seeking a site in Preston. From the build-up of sales in his previous outlets, he estimates that his likely sales are £35 000 in Year 1, £50 000 in Year 2 and £60 000 in Year 3. He forecasts his costs to be £20 000 in Year 1, £15 000 in Years 2 and 3. He has found a shop in Preston at an asking price of £70 000. Should he buy the shop at this price, given that he requires a minimum rate of return of 12 per cent per annum over the first three years of opening a new outlet?

26.6 Comparison of investment proposals

The discounted cash flow method is particularly useful when we have to choose between investment proposals. We may be faced with an array of glossy proposals, each with different timescales and differing cash flows. Once again, in order to allow for the timing of these flows, we calculate the NPV of each proposal at the current discount rate. First, we check that the NPV is positive so that the investment is profitable. We then look to see which of the proposals has the highest NPV since that indicates the most profitable choice, all other things being equal.

Example

The Elite Property Company has the choice of two investments this year. It can go ahead with only one of them because of limited management resources. The current discount rate is 5 per cent. Which investment should it select?

Investment A: Building of 5 luxury homes
This requires an initial outlay of £500 000 to buy the land and £100 000 to install basic facilities to the site. At the end of the first year, building will commence and it is estimated that there will be an outlay of £200 000 at this time and at the end of Years 2 and 3. Buyers of the homes will have to pay £50 000 as work commences and a further £300 000 on completion. It is thought that the first two houses will be started at the end of Year 1 and finished a year later. A further two houses will then be started for completion at the end of Year 3. The fifth house will be started then and all work will be completed at the end of the fourth year.

Investment B: Conversion of a mansion into 10 luxury flats for rent

This requires an outlay of £600 000 immediately, to buy the mansion, and all conversion work will be completed during the first year, involving a total outlay of £1.5 million which will be due for payment at the end of the year. It is expected that five flats will be rented immediately the conversion work is complete, at the end of Year 1, at a rate of £25 000 per flat per year, payable in advance. The remaining five flats are expected to have tenants from the end of year 2, paying rent at the same rate. Elite intend to sell the converted mansion and the tenancies at the end of Year 5 and it is hoped that this will bring in £1.8 million.

See Tables 26.4 and 26.5 for the NPV calculations.

The NPV for Investment **A** is £584 260.
The NPV for Investment **B** is £149 125.

Investment **A** has the higher NPV so this is the preferred investment.

The calculations depend on accurate forecasts of future cash flows and will be sensitive to changes in these forecasts. In Chapter 28, we will see how we can use a spreadsheet to perform a sensitivity analysis to investigate the effects of such changes on our decisions.

26.7 Internal rate of return

From the calculations you have done so far, you will probably have realised that the discount rate is a crucial element of the calculation.

TABLE 26.4

INVESTMENT A: NPV CALCULATION

Time	Outflow £	Inflow £	Net Cash Flow £	Discount Factor	Present Value £
Now	600 000		−600 000	1	−600 000
End Year 1	200 000	100 000	100 000	0.9524	95 240
End Year 2	200 000	700 000	500 000	0.9070	453 500
End Year 3	200 000	650 000	450 000	0.8638	388 710
End Year 4		300 000	300 000	0.8227	246 810
				Net Present Value =	584 260

TABLE 26.5

INVESTMENT B: NPV CALCULATION

Time	Outflow £	Inflow £	Net Cash Flow £	Discount Factor	Present Value £
Now	600 000		−600 000	1	−600 000
End Year 1	1 500 000	125 000	−1 375 000	0.9524	−1 309 550
End Year 2		250 000	250 000	0.9070	226 750
End Year 3		250 000	250 000	0.8638	215 950
End Year 4		250 000	250 000	0.8227	205 675
End Year 5		1 800 000	1 800 000	0.7835	1 410 300
				Net Present Value =	149 125

Example

An initial investment of £450 000 is expected to result in positive cash flows of £115 000, £135 000, £145 000 and £160 000 at the end of the next four years, respectively. How can we work out is the investment profitable if the rate of return required is

(a) 8 per cent
(b) 12 per cent?

The DCF calculations are shown in Table 26.6.

In **(a)** the NPV is positive so the project is profitable if an 8 per cent rate of return is required. In **(b)** the NPV is negative so the project is not profitable if a 12 per cent rate of return is required.

TABLE 26.6

EXAMPLE IN SECTION 26.7: NPV CALCULATIONS

(a) Rate = 8%

Time	Net Cash Flow £	Discount Factor	Present Value £
Now	−450 000	1	−450 000
End Year 1	115 000	0.9259	106 479
End Year 2	135 000	0.8573	115 736
End Year 3	145 000	0.7938	115 101
End Year 4	160 000	0.7350	117 600
	Net Present Value (NPV) =		4 916

(b) Rate = 12%

Time	Net Cash Flow £	Discount Factor	Present Value £
Now	−450 000	1	−450 000
End Year 1	115 000	0.8929	102 684
End Year 2	135 000	0.7972	107 622
End Year 3	145 000	0.7118	103 211
End Year 4	160 000	0.6355	101 680
	Net Present Value (NPV) =		−34 803

The question we can then ask is: At what rate of return would the NPV be zero? This rate of return is called the *INTERNAL RATE OF RETURN (IRR)* of the project. From our calculations in Table 26.6, we can deduce that the IRR of this project is somewhere between 8 per cent and 12 per cent. In order to estimate its value more closely, we need to do further calculations.

Exercise 26.6

For the cash flows in Table 26.6, work out the NPV at a discount rate of 10 per cent. What is your estimate of the IRR of this project? (You may need to do a further calculation.)

From the calculations in Exercise 26.6, we conclude that the IRR in our example was 8.5 per cent. The trial and error method that we had to use is tedious and time-consuming so, in practice, the calculation of an IRR is usually performed on a spreadsheet and this will be demonstrated in Chapter 28.

26.8 Summary

In this chapter you have learned how to make long-term capital investment decisions based on discounted cash flow calculations. The basis for these calculations is the net present value (NPV) of the projected cash flows. This allows for the fact that money has a time value so that a sum received earlier is worth more than the same amount received at a later date. The sum received earlier can be invested at the current rate of interest and consequently will be worth more by the later date.

The internal rate of return (IRR) of a project can be evaluated and compared either with the current discount rate or with a standard rate of return required for a project to proceed.

The calculations have been done using a calculator with a power key or with reference to present value tables.

27

Decision-making Under Risk

27.1 Learning objectives

When you have finished working through this chapter you should be able to

- Recognise that decisions may be affected by chance happenings
- Understand how probabilities may be assigned to different possible outcomes
- Understand the meaning of **EXPECTED MONETARY VALUE** and how to calculate it
- Appreciate the difference between a **STATE OF NATURE** and an option
- Construct a **PAYOFF MATRIX**
- Make a decision by maximising the expected monetary value
- Understand the meaning of the **EXPECTED VALUE OF PERFECT INFORMATION** and how to calculate it

27.2 Games of chance

The UK National Lottery which began in 1994 has caught the imagination of many and millions of pounds are gambled on the lottery each week. Everyone knows that they have a very small chance of winning the jackpot but the lure of a vast amount of wealth tempts them to part with their money. They have made a decision to gamble on the lottery rather than gambling on football pools or horse racing. It may also be that they have decided to play the lottery rather than spend the money on other leisure activities or personal purchases.

Similarly, in business decision-making, companies are faced with making decisions under conditions of risk. Should they go to the expense of putting in a tender to supply goods knowing that if they succeed they will secure a large profit but also knowing that there are several other competitors each of whom might win the contract instead? Is it worth launching a new product that will make a fortune if the economy is booming but will be a loss if there is a recession?

In all of the situations there is a set of different possible monetary outcomes. There is also a stage at which we are able to make a decision as to whether or not to invest. If we are able to assign *probabilities* to each of the different outcomes, then we can set up a *decision rule* to help us make the 'best' decision in the circumstances. It does not guarantee that in practice we will maximise our return but in the long run if we followed this strategy it would prove better than other strategies.

The techniques used in this chapter originally developed out of a study of games of chance.

Example

Jim has been invited to take part in a gambling game. He has to pay 10p each time to take part. A fair six-sided die is rolled. If a six comes up, he receives 20p back; if a four or five comes up, he is given 10p back but if a one, two or three shows, he gets nothing back. Should Jim join the game?

We are told that the die is fair so each side has a one-sixth chance of appearing in the long run. He can expect to receive 20p one-sixth of the time, 10p two-sixths (one third) of the time and nothing three-sixths (one half) of the time.

His expected receipts per throw are

$$(20 * 1/6) + (10 * 1/3) + (0 * 1/2)\ \text{p} = 6.67\text{p}$$

This is less than the 10p he has to pay each time so it would not be worth his while financially to play this game. Of course, he might not mind risking a loss, if he enjoys the excitement of playing the game and he may just strike lucky and get a succession of fours, fives and sixes. What our calculation tells us is that in the long run, if he continued to play this game, he would make a loss.

Exercise 27.1

Jim expressed doubts about the fairness of the game so the rules were modified so that if a six comes up he will get 40p back. Otherwise the rules remain unchanged. Should Jim play?

27.3 Expected monetary value

In a decision-making situation, when we are faced with a *STATE OF NATURE*, which is defined as a happening over which we have no influence, we need to assess all the different possible outcomes that could occur and express these outcomes in monetary terms called *PAYOFFS*. We then need to assign probabilities to these outcomes as it may be that some are more likely than others. If we then multiply each payoff by its probability and add them up, we have the expected payoff or *EXPECTED MONETARY VALUE (EMV)* for this state of nature. This is exactly analogous to Jim's expected winnings in the die-rolling game.

Example

It is January and the managing director of The Beau Garden Seat Company has to decide whether or not to exhibit at the county horticultural show at the start of June. It costs the company £2000 for a stand. If the weather is fine, many people tour the stands and it is estimated that the company will receive orders worth £8000. If the weather is wet, it is known from past experience that orders in the region of £1000 can be expected. If there is a heatwave, people cannot be bothered to tour the stands and only £1500 in new orders is likely.

Going to the local library and looking back over the past 10 years' records for the weather at the beginning of June, the director found that in five years the weather was fine but in four the weather was wet and in one year there was a heatwave.

Analysing all this information, we work out the expected monetary value of exhibiting

$$\begin{aligned}\text{EMV} &= (£8000 * 5/10) + (£1000 * 4/10)\\ &\quad + (£1500 * 1/10)\\ &= £4550\end{aligned}$$

This is considerably higher than the £2000 the company has to pay to exhibit. We can advise the company to take a stand and that its expected income will be £2550.

Note that the company will receive orders of £8000, £1000 or £1500, depending on the weather but, in the long run, if it keeps exhibiting at the show, the company will take orders averaging £4550 per year. The company might consider insuring against wet or very hot weather to offset the losses that will occur if the weather is unkind.

Exercise 27.2

The Outdoor Concert Society runs a series of concerts every summer in the local park. On a fine evening an audience of 750 is likely but if it is wet only 50 keen concertgoers turn up although the concert still goes ahead as the performers are under cover. A flat rate of £5 per seat is charged payable on the night.

Many of the performers are amateurs but star guests are invited and although some with local connections give their services free, the overall cost to the society averages out at £500 per concert. Up to now the Parks Department has allowed the Society free use of the facilities because the various refreshment booths are council owned and do good business on fine concert evenings. A new council leader has decreed that a charge must be made to the Society and has proposed a sum of £200 per concert.

Can the society afford to continue with the concerts, given that on past experience the weather is fine on 70 per cent of concert evenings and wet on the remaining 30 per cent?

27.4 Maximising expected monetary value

When a decision has to be made amongst several different alternative courses of action where the decision-maker knows the probabilities of the various possible monetary outcomes following as a result of this choice, the decision criterion that is most commonly used is to select the option that *maximises the expected monetary value.*

Example

The Arcade Fashion Company has a range of shops in arcades throughout the company. The merchandise is tailored to fit the area so, for example, in spa towns, upmarket dresses and suits are stocked, but in seaside towns, cheap and cheerful leisurewear is the norm. The company has the funds to purchase one new outlet this year. It could buy a shop in a spa town and this is estimated to give an average net profit over the next five years of £25 000 per year if the economy is depressed but £65 000 if the economy expands. The alternative is to buy a shop at the seaside which should provide a net annual profit of £30 000 on average, if the economy is depressed, rising to £35 000 if the economy expands. The company's economic advisers believe that the chance of the economy expanding is 0.6 and the chance of a depressed economy is 0.4.

From the above figures, we can see that both options are profitable but the company should select the alternative that maximises their expected profit. The calculations necessary to assess this are shown in Figure 27.1.

FIGURE 27.1

EXPECTED PROFIT COMPARISON

Spa Town

Expected Profit = (£65 000 * 0.6) + (£25 000 * 0.4)

= £49 000

Seaside Town

Expected Profit = (£35 000 * 0.6) + (£30 000 * 0.4)

= £33 000

We conclude that they should buy the outlet in the spa town. We cannot guarantee that they will make a higher profit here than at the seaside but on the balance of probabilities they will make a higher profit in the spa town.

Exercise 27.3

A burger chain plans to open a new branch in one of two locations. In the first location, the chain estimates that the chance of success is 0.7 and in this case it will make an annual net profit of £80 000. If the branch is unsuccessful, there will be a net loss of £5000. In the second location, the chance of success is estimated at 0.6. If successful, there will be a net profit of £120 000 but, if unsuccessful, the net loss will be £10 000. Advise the company on its decision using the expected monetary value criterion. Comment on your decision.

27.5 Payoff matrix

In more complex situations where there are several states of nature and various options to choose from, it is helpful to set out the different possible monetary outcomes in a special table called a *PAYOFF MATRIX*.

The different possible states of nature are shown by the rows and the alternative decisions that can be made are shown by the columns.

Example

Susan has a market stall where she sells her homemade biscuits. Up to now she has stocked 240 dozen biscuits

TABLE 27.1

SUSAN'S BISCUIT STALL: DISTRIBUTION OF DAILY DEMAND				
Demand per day (dozens)	160	180	200	220
Relative Frequency	0.2	0.2	0.4	0.2

each day. She has found it difficult to predict the demand so she has monitored her sales over the past few months and the results are shown in Table 27.1.

Susan has decided to stock either 180, 200 or 220 dozen biscuits each day but is not sure which of these stock levels will be best for her profits in the long run. Each pack costs 40p on average to produce and she sells them for 70p. Any biscuits left at the end of the day have to be discarded as worthless because they have gone soft.

We can work out how much profit she makes under each possible scenario.

Suppose she decides to stock 180 dozen biscuits:
If the demand is for 160 dozen, she will have the results shown in Figure 27.2.

FIGURE 27.2

SUSAN'S BISCUIT STALL: GROSS PROFIT CALCULATIONS	
Stock 180 dozen	**Demand 160 dozen**
Sales	160 @ £0.70 = £112
Cost of Goods Sold	160 @ £0.40 = £ 64
Waste	20 @ £0.40 = £ 8
Gross Profit	= £ 40

If the demand is for 180 dozen, the gross profit will be

$$180 * £0.70 - 180 * £0.40 = £54$$

If the demand is for 200 or 220 dozen, she will not be able to supply them and she will have to turn away unsatisfied customers. Her gross profit will be £54, as before.

Exercise 27.4

Work out the different gross profits that Susan might make depending on the demand if she stocks the following quantities:

(a) 200 dozen biscuits
(b) 220 dozen biscuits

We can now put the results of the calculations of this section and Exercise 27.4 into a payoff matrix as shown in Table 27.2.

TABLE 27.2

SUSAN'S BISCUIT STALL: PAYOFF MATRIX (STOCK IN DOZENS, PAYOFFS IN £)			
	Decision Options		
State of Nature	**Stock 180**	**Stock 200**	**Stock 220**
Level of Demand			
160	40	32	24
180	54	46	38
200	54	60	52
220	54	60	66

We use the distribution of daily demand to provide the probabilities we need to calculate the expected monetary value for each decision option:

Expected monetary value calculations

Stock 180 dozen

$$\text{EMV} = £40 * 0.2 + £54 * 0.2 + £54 * 0.4 + £54 * 0.2 = £51.20$$

Stock 200 dozen

$$\text{EMV} = £32 * 0.2 + £46 * 0.2 + £60 * 0.4 + £60 * 0.2 = £51.60$$

Stock 220 dozen

$$\text{EMV} = £24 * 0.2 + £38 * 0.2 + £52 * 0.4 + £66 * 0.2 = £46.40$$

The largest expected monetary value is associated with the decision to stock 200 dozen biscuits, so this is the stock level we would recommend to Susan.

In this example we assumed that there was no financial penalty to Susan if she was unable to supply customers on a particular day because she had run out of stock. She would hope that they would come back next day to buy. In practice, she might eventually find she has fewer customers if they cannot buy biscuits when they want them. For some retailers such as newsagents, if they fail to carry enough stock on a given day, they will never recoup a lost sale since there is no market for yesterday's newspaper.

Exercise 27.5

The Fine Furniture Company is to build a new factory to accommodate the most up-to-date machinery. The choice is between a large factory and a small factory. Estimates of the demand for furniture in the long-term suggest that there is a 50 per cent chance of high demand, 30 per cent chance of medium demand and 20 per cent chance of low demand.

Table 27.3 shows the payoffs in thousand of pounds associated with each scenario. The payoffs represent the annual average net profits envisaged once the factory is built.

Calculate the expected monetary value associated with each decision and advise the company as to the size of factory it should build.

TABLE 27.3

FINE FURNITURE COMPANY:
PAYOFF MATRIX (PAYOFFS IN £000)

	Decision Options	
State of Nature Demand	**Build Small Factory**	**Build Large Factory**
High	200	350
Medium	200	175
Low	150	100

Exercise 27.6

The landlord of the 'Brown Bear' Pub sells sandwiches on weekday lunchtimes. The demand is variable and he is never quite sure how many to stock. He estimates that on a quarter of days he sells 30 rounds, on half the days he sells 40 rounds and on the remaining quarter of days he sells 50 rounds. He charges £1.20 per round, regardless of the filling and the cost to him per round is 50p. Any sandwiches left unsold at 3pm are thrown away. If he runs out of sandwiches, he sends out one of the bar staff to the sandwich bar down the road. The sandwiches cost £1.00 but he still sells them at £1.20. His customers know that they can always rely on getting a drink and a sandwich in their lunch hour.

Construct a payoff matrix showing his profits for the differing levels of demand, when he stocks 30, 40 or 50 rounds of sandwiches. Advise him on the optimal number of sandwiches to stock each day.

27.6 Expected value of perfect information

In practice, what every supplier would like to do is to match supply and demand exactly. In this way there is no waste and the customers are satisfied. This ideal scenario can be made more likely by knowing exactly what the demand is going to be. If Susan knew exactly how many biscuits to bake beforehand, she could run her market stall more efficiently. One way of doing this is to ask customers to place orders in advance such as happens with newspapers delivered to homes. Alternatively, she might commission some market research to try to discover more about the buying characteristics of her potential customers. Attempts such as this will inevitably add to her costs. The question is: How much can she afford to pay to obtain better information about the level of demand?

We can answer this by working out how much her profit would be if she knew beforehand exactly which days were going to have demands of 160, 180, 200 or 220 dozen. Referring back to the payoff matrix Table 27.2, we can see that if she knows the demand is going to be only 160, her best option is to stock 180 rather than 200 or 220 as her profit will be £40. Similarly, if the demand is known to be 180, her best option is to stock 180 at a profit of £54. If the demand is 200, she should stock 200 giving a profit of £60 and if the demand is 220, she should stock 220 resulting in a profit of £66.

We know the probabilities of the different levels of demand so we are able to work out her expected profit under conditions of perfect information, which would imply knowing exactly what the demand is going to be.

Expected profit under perfect information

$$= £40 * 0.2 + £54 * 0.2 + £60 * 0.4 + £66 * 0.2$$

$$= £56$$

The best Susan could do without perfect information was to stock 200 dozen leading to an expected profit of £51.60.

She has the possibility of increasing her daily profit by £4.40 to £56. This gives her some indication as to whether there is any benefit in setting up an ordering system or commissioning market research. If it is going to cost her the equivalent of £4.40 per day or more, it is not worth doing.

This difference between the expected monetary values under conditions of risk and conditions of certainty is termed the *EXPECTED VALUE OF PERFECT INFORMATION* (*EVPI*). It is the maximum amount we would be prepared to pay to obtain perfect knowledge of the market.

Exercise 27.7

What is the expected value of perfect information for the landlord of the 'Brown Bear' pub in Exercise 27.6?

Suggest how the landlord might improve his knowledge of customer demand.

27.7 Summary

In this chapter we have tackled the difficulties of decision-making when we cannot be sure which out of several possible outcomes will occur. We have calculated the expected monetary value of different choices and selected the option that maximises this value. We have calculated the expected value of perfect information to give us the maximum amount that we would be prepared to pay to lessen our uncertainty about future events.

28

Long-term Decision-making on the Spreadsheet and Sensitivity Analysis

28.1 Learning objectives

When you have finished working through this chapter you should be able to

- Set up a spreadsheet to perform calculations of net present values and internal rates of return
- Use the spreadsheet functions to perform a sensitivity analysis for long-term decision-making

28.2 Financial functions on the spreadsheet

The main reason why computer spreadsheets were devised was to replicate the financial recording and financial calculations that are necessary to the efficient running of a company, such as DCF calculations. Originally, these calculations were performed manually on a large sheet, hence the name spreadsheet. Every change in interest rates or costs, for example, necessitated alterations to the spreadsheet. Computers can perform these changes much more efficiently. Because of this, every spreadsheet package has built-in financial functions to enable DCF calculations to be carried out speedily.

The names of these functions are the same on all the most popular packages but there are minor differences in the way that some of the inputs have to be made. In this chapter, we will perform the calculations using the Excel spreadsheet. If you are using a different package, you should consult your manual or the **Help** function to check on the appropriate input for your spreadsheet.

Example

A company wishes to find the net present value and internal rate of return of an investment where £30 000 has to be paid now with returns of £5000 after Year 1, £10 000 after Year 2, £15 000 after Year 3 and £10 000 after Year 4 with no further returns. The discount rate is 10 per cent.

Net present value

To perform this calculation using a spreadsheet, we need to enter the cash flows in consecutive cells in either a column or a row of the spreadsheet as shown in Figure 28.1.

FIGURE 28.1

CALCULATION OF NPV: INPUT OF CASH FLOWS

	A	B
1	Rate = 10%	
2	Time	Cash flow (£)
3	Now	-30000
4	End Year 1	5000
5	End Year 2	10000
6	End Year 3	15000
7	End Year 4	10000

The net present value function is

NPV(Interest rate, Cash flow range)

In most spreadsheets, this function evaluates the present values of the cash flows on the assumption that the flows occur at the end of the period. In particular, it is assumed that the first entry in the cash flow range corresponds to the end of the first period. If there is an initial cash flow at the start of the first period, this must not be included in the NPV function but simply added on unchanged as it is already in present value terms.

Referring to Figure 28.2, where the worksheet is in View formula mode, we type

=**B3**+NPV(0.1,**B4**:**B7**)

in cell **B8**. Switching out of View formula mode, the result is shown in cell **B8** of Figure 28.3 as £910, formatted correct to the nearest pound.

FIGURE 28.2

CALCULATION OF NPV: VIEW FORMULA MODE

	A	B
1	Rate = 10%	
2	Time	Cash flow (£)
3	Now	-30000
4	End Year 1	5000
5	End Year 2	10000
6	End Year 3	15000
7	End Year 4	10000
8	NPV	=B3+NPV(0.1,B4:B7)

FIGURE 28.3

CALCULATION OF NPV

	A	B
1	Rate = 10%	
2	Time	Cash flow (£)
3	Now	-30000
4	End Year 1	5000
5	End Year 2	10000
6	End Year 3	15000
7	End Year 4	10000
8	NPV	£910

Internal rate of return

The function we need for calculating the internal rate of return is

IRR(Cash flow range)

Referring to Figure 28.4, we type =IRR(**B3**:**B7**)

FIGURE 28.4

CALCULATION OF IRR: VIEW FORMULA MODE

	A	B
1		
2	Time	Cash flow (£)
3	Now	-30000
4	End Year 1	5000
5	End Year 2	10000
6	End Year 3	15000
7	End Year 4	10000
8	IRR	=IRR(B3:B7)

Note that this time any initial outlay is included in the cash flow range and the spreadsheet requires that this initial outlay is entered as a negative number.

The result is 11.25 per cent, formatted as a percentage correct to two decimal places. This is shown in Figure 28.5.

Note that using some spreadsheet packages you will be asked to input a guess for the rate, as the spreadsheet estimates the internal rate of return in a similar fashion to our trial and error method in Chapter 26 and so needs to be told where to start. A value of 0.1, or 10 per cent, usually works but, if it does not, then simply choose another start until the spreadsheet produces a result.

FIGURE 28.5

CALCULATION OF IRR

	A	B
1		
2	Time	Cash flow (£)
3	Now	-30000
4	End Year 1	5000
5	End Year 2	10000
6	End Year 3	15000
7	End Year 4	10000
8	IRR	11.25%

Exercise 28.1

Repeat Exercises 26.4, 26.5 and 26.6 using a spreadsheet.

28.3 Sensitivity analysis

In the complexities of the modern world, we cannot assume that there will be no unexpected changes. Particularly when we are making long-term decisions, we need to examine our forecasts and assumptions carefully to see what the effects of changes might be. Such sensitivity analysis is easily performed using a spreadsheet.

To carry out an investment appraisal we first work out the net present value and the internal rate of return for a project under what we consider are the most likely conditions. We then consider changes to this scenario and see what individual effect each will have. We may find the project is more vulnerable to some changes than to others and so we can make a better judgement as to whether it is wise to proceed with an investment. Similarly, we can assess the merits of several competing projects under changing conditions and identify their strengths and weaknesses before coming to a decision.

Example

Anna has successfully completed a course in Furniture Making and is in the process of drawing up a business plan in order to set up her own company. It is her intention to make and sell furniture to order, promoting her services through exhibitions and by word of mouth. She already has a number of substantial orders on her books and her sales forecast states that she will be able to generate sales of £18 000 in the first year, increasing by 20 per cent in the second year and by another 30 per cent in the third year, as her business gets to be better known and established.

Provided she can put £1500 of her own money into the business initially, Anna qualifies for a government grant of £50 per week for the first three years with an additional benefit of £30 per week during the first year to assist with the renting of a workshop in council sponsored premises.

Anna has made estimates of the costs of the new business. She will need various items of equipment as listed in Table 28.1.

The rent of the workshop is £32 per week. Insurance will be £150 per annum and the cost of utilities £450. Rates will be £500 each year. She requires a telephone connection at a cost of £99 and expects the telephone bills to be £400 per annum.

The cost of production will be 30 per cent of the sales revenue.

Anna intends to draw £12 000 each year from the business. She considers this a fair reward, given that she could probably earn this amount if she found alternative employment instead.

Anna has £1500 invested in the bank at 6 per cent per annum compound interest. Should she put her

TABLE 28.1

ANNA'S BUSINESS: INITIAL PURCHASES

Item	Estimated Cost £
Router	150
Planes	30
Chisels	40
Work Bench	85
Shelving	35
First Aid Box	25
Facemask and Goggles	25
Sawdust Fence	350
Dust Extraction Equipment	90

money into the business or would she be better off leaving it in the bank? She intends to consider the relative merits over a three-year time period.

To help Anna make her decision, we need to set up a worksheet, as shown in Figure 28.6.

The first part of the worksheet should list her initial outgoings and use the SUM function to find their total.

Following this, we enter details of Anna's income each year for the first three years. We use a formula to calculate the sales in Years 2 and 3 based on Year 1. The SUM function is used to find the total for Year 1. We can use the **Copy** facility where appropriate to enter values for later years when they are identical or when they are calculated by the same formula. The incomes are shown in Figure 28.6.

The next part of the worksheet lists Anna's outgoings each year. We enter the production costs as a formula as they are always 30 per cent of sales revenue.

Finally, we can set up the discounted cash flow analysis. For each year we list the inflows and outflows as previously calculated. We enter the cell addresses of these amounts rather than the actual

FIGURE 28.6

ANNA'S BUSINESS: DISCOUNTED CASH FLOW ANALYSIS ON THE SPREADSHEET

(a) Initial outgoings Year 0	£		
Router	150		
Planes	30		
Chisels	40		
Work bench	85		
Shelving	35		
First aid box	25		
Facemask, goggles	25		
Sawdust fence	350		
Dust extraction equipment	90		
Telephone connection	99		
TOTAL	929		
(b) Annual income (£)	**Year 1**	**Year 2**	**Year 3**
Sales	18000	21600	28080
Government grant	2600	2600	2600
Additional benefit	1560		
TOTAL	22160	24200	30680
(c) Annual outgoings (£)	**Year 1**	**Year 2**	**Year 3**
Rent	1664	1664	1664
Insurance	150	150	150
Utilities	450	450	450
Rates	500	500	500
Telephone bills	400	400	400
Production cost	5400	6480	8424
Drawings	12000	12000	12000
TOTAL	20564	21644	23588
(d) DCF analysis			
Year	Inflow (£)	Outflow (£)	Net cash flow (£)
0		929	-929
1	22160	20564	1596
2	24200	21644	2556
3	30680	23588	7092
Net Present Value			8806

values. We write a formula to calculate the net cash flow in Year 0 and this is copied to the later years. We then apply the NPV function at a rate of 6 per cent.

The resulting net present value is £8806. This is much higher than the £1500 which is the present value of Anna's investment if she just left it in the bank at 6 per cent. It appears that Anna should go ahead with the workshop.

The analysis in Figure 28.6, however, considers just one scenario. Before we give Anna the go-ahead we ought to assess the effects of changes in the estimates. Anna has asked us to consider four possibilities:

Scenario 1
Sales in Year 1 are £10 000, then increasing at the same rates as before.

Scenario 2
Sales in Year 1 are £18 000 but increase by only 10 per cent in Year 2 and a further 20 per cent in Year 3.

Scenario 3
The council charges for rent and business rates may increase by 4 per cent per year without any corresponding increase in the grants and benefit Anna receives.

FIGURE 28.7

ANNA'S BUSINESS: SCENARIO 1

(a) Initial outgoings Year 0	£		
Router	150		
Planes	30		
Chisels	40		
Work bench	85		
Shelving	35		
First aid box	25		
Facemask, goggles	25		
Sawdust fence	350		
Dust extraction equipment	90		
Telephone connection	99		
TOTAL	929		
(b) Annual income (£)	**Year 1**	**Year 2**	**Year 3**
Sales	18000	21600	28080
Government grant	2600	2600	2600
Additional benefit	1560		
TOTAL	22160	24200	30680
(c) Annual outgoings (£)	**Year 1**	**Year 2**	**Year 3**
Rent	1664	1664	1664
Insurance	150	150	150
Utilities	450	450	450
Rates	500	500	500
Telephone bills	400	400	400
Production cost	5400	6480	8424
Drawings	12000	12000	12000
TOTAL	20564	21644	23588
(d) DCF analysis			
Year	Inflow (£)	Outflow (£)	Net cash flow (£)
0		929	-929
1	22160	20564	1596
2	24200	21644	2556
3	30680	23588	7092
Net Present Value			8806

Scenario 4

Anna's production costs might rise and she would not feel able to pass on the full amount to her customers. This could mean that the production costs rise to 35 per cent of sales revenue.

Figures 28.7 to 28.10 show the effects of these changes as compared to the original scenario. In each case we simply take the original spreadsheet and make the appropriate change. The spreadsheet automatically recalculates all the totals and the net present value.

Studying the figures, we see that although Anna's returns are less in every case, it is only in the scenario of low sales in Year 1 that she has a major worry. In the other scenarios, the net present values are all comfortably above £1500 so she need not be too concerned if sales have a slower growth rate or the council charges rise or if production costs rise. What will affect her is poor initial sales. If there is any likelihood of sales in the first year being as low as £10 000, she should not consider the project. We are told she has substantial orders so presumably she is reasonably confident that sales will reach £18 000 but she would be wise to make certain that these orders are confirmed in writing before she goes ahead.

FIGURE 28.8

ANNA'S BUSINESS: SCENARIO 2

Initial outgoings Year 0	£		
Router	150		
Planes	30		
Chisels	40		
Work bench	85		
Shelving	35		
First aid box	25		
Facemask, goggles	25		
Sawdust fence	350		
Dust extraction equipment	90		
Telephone connection	99		
TOTAL	929		
Annual income (£)	**Year 1**	**Year 2**	**Year 3**
Sales	10000	12000	15600
Government grant	2600	2600	2600
Additional benefit	1560		
TOTAL	14160	14600	18200
Annual outgoings (£)	**Year 1**	**Year 2**	**Year 3**
Rent	1664	1664	1664
Insurance	150	150	150
Utilities	450	450	450
Rates	500	500	500
Telephone bills	400	400	400
Production cost	3000	3600	4680
Drawings	12000	12000	12000
TOTAL	18164	18764	19844
DCF analysis			
Year	Inflow (£)	Outflow (£)	Net cash flow (£)
0		929	-929
1	14160	18164	-4004
2	14600	18764	-4164
3	18200	19844	-1644
Net Present Value			-9793

FIGURE 28.9

ANNA'S BUSINESS: SCENARIO 3

Initial outgoings Year 0	£		
Router	150		
Planes	30		
Chisels	40		
Work bench	85		
Shelving	35		
First aid box	25		
Facemask, goggles	25		
Sawdust fence	350		
Dust extraction equipment	90		
Telephone connection	99		
TOTAL	929		
Annual income (£)	**Year 1**	**Year 2**	**Year 3**
Sales	18000	19800	23760
Government grant	2600	2600	2600
Additional benefit	1560		
TOTAL	22160	22400	26360
Annual outgoings (£)	**Year 1**	**Year 2**	**Year 3**
Rent	1664	1664	1664
Insurance	150	150	150
Utilities	450	450	450
Rates	500	500	500
Telephone bills	400	400	400
Production cost	5400	5940	7128
Drawings	12000	12000	12000
TOTAL	20564	21104	22292
DCF analysis			
Year	Inflow (£)	Outflow (£)	Net cash flow (£)
0		929	-929
1	22160	20564	1596
2	22400	21104	1296
3	26360	22292	4068
Net Present Value			5146

Exercise 28.2

The Premier Pub Company has located a city centre site suitable for its new 'Pie and Pint' concept. It is a listed building currently owned by the City Development Corporation. Premier Pub Company has the choice of buying or renting the premises.

If the company rents the premises, under the terms of the lease, the rent will be £35 000 per year payable in advance and subject to review every five years. The company believes that the rent will rise by 20 per cent at the first review.

To buy the building outright will cost £455 000 but the company will then be liable for repairs to the building which are expected to amount to a further £100 000.

However the company chooses to acquire the site, refurbishment of the interior of the building is needed and this is estimated to cost £45 000. Construction of the bar and provision of bar furniture will incur costs of £14 000. Additional start-up capital of £25 000 is needed to purchase stock, for promotion and sundries.

FIGURE 28.10

ANNA'S BUSINESS: SCENARIO 4

Initial outgoings Year 0	£		
Router	150		
Planes	30		
Chisels	40		
Work bench	85		
Shelving	35		
First aid box	25		
Facemask, goggles	25		
Sawdust fence	350		
Dust extraction equipment	90		
Telephone connection	99		
TOTAL	929		
Annual income (£)	**Year 1**	**Year 2**	**Year 3**
Sales	18000	21600	28080
Government grant	2600	2600	2600
Additional benefit	1560		
TOTAL	22160	24200	30680
Annual outgoings (£)	**Year 1**	**Year 2**	**Year 3**
Rent	1664	1731	1800
Insurance	150	150	150
Utilities	450	450	450
Rates	500	500	500
Telephone bills	400	400	400
Production cost	5400	6480	8424
Drawings	12000	12000	12000
TOTAL	20564	21711	23724
DCF analysis			
Year	Inflow (£)	Outflow (£)	Net cash flow (£)
0		929	-929
1	22160	20564	1596
2	24200	21711	2489
3	30680	23724	6956
Net Present Value			8633

There will be additional annual fixed costs as shown in Table 28.2.

When the pub is up and running, part-time staff will be employed to serve on and to do the washing up and cleaning. There will be a manager and a cook on the full-time staff. Fixed labour costs will be £30 000 per year. Variable labour costs are budgeted at 15 per cent of sales.

The forecast for sales is £280 000 in the first year, rising by 15 per cent in the second year and 4 per cent per year subsequently. From its experience in running similar ventures, the company expects that the cost of goods sold will average out at 40 per cent of sales.

TABLE 28.2

PREMIER PUB COMPANY: FIXED COSTS OF SITE

	£
Utilities	14 000
Repairs	6 000
Crockery and Glassware	1 500
Cleaning Materials	900
Rates	13 500
Insurance	2 500
Accountancy	1 000
Sundries	11 000

(a) Use a spreadsheet to calculate the net present value of the expected cash flows associated with the setting up and running of the pub

- If the company buys the building
- If the company rents the building

Consider the project over an eight-year time span, starting with Year 1 and ending with Year 8. Assume a discount rate of 7 per cent. In addition, work out the internal rate of return in each case. Treat the year in which all capital investment costs are incurred as Year 0.

(b) On the spreadsheet, carry out a sensitivity analysis assessing the impact on the net present value and the internal rate of return under each of the following scenarios:

Scenario 1
Sales in the first year are £60 000 above forecast

Scenario 2
Sales in the first year are £40 000 below forecast

Scenario 3
Sales build-up by only 10 per cent in Year 2 and 3 per cent subsequently

Scenario 4
Cost of goods sold rises to 45 per cent of sales

Scenario 5
Cost of goods sold falls to 35 per cent of sales.

(c) Recommend to Premier Pub Company whether it should buy or rent the premises.

28.4 Summary

In this chapter we have seen how we can set up a discounted cash flow (DCF) analysis on a spreadsheet. This enabled us to conduct a sensitivity analysis quickly and efficiently.

Case Study 5

The Bloomsbury Supermarkets plc Coffee Shop Experience: Making Long-term Capital Investment Decisions

1 Introduction

Please note that when working on this case study you are required to imagine that you are reading it in June 1996.

Bloomsbury Supermarkets plc is a large chain operating in the North of England. Their nearest competitors are ASDA and Morrisons. The company opened its first coffee shop in 1995 at Sheffield. By the end of the 1995/96 financial year four coffee shops were in operation and it is planned that by the end of the 1996/97 financial year a further seven will be opened.

2 Size and location

When planning the original coffee shops, the ideal size was taken to be 100 seats in an area of approximately 2500 sq ft and it is intended to plan future coffee shops within these limits. For suitable locations, such as the Derby and Macclesfield branches, there are also plans to site tables and chairs outside the coffee shops during the summer months.

Originally coffee shops were seen as only suitable for out-of-town sites. However, the success of the York coffee shop shows that very good sales can be achieved in an edge-of-town store, despite High Street competition. Bloomsbury Supermarkets plc prices and ambience make the coffee shop attractive to the point where people enter the store specifically to use the coffee shop. York is unique in that the lobby and coffee shop are located in a renovated church, which greatly enhances the attractiveness of the site. Also, the York experience illustrated the need to monitor the extent to which the construction of coffee shops on such sites results in congestion within the store and in the car park, generating a negative overall impression. In 1996 a decision was taken that coffee shops should not be included where parking spaces were limited since on such sites prolonged customer visits should not be encouraged.

In locating a coffee shop within the store, visibility from the main store entrance is a key determinant of success. This is most easily achieved by locating the coffee shop unit inside the main body of the store with access via the main foyer, a strategy followed by all the main competitors. Of the four coffee shops Bloomsbury Supermarkets plc had at the end of the 1995/96 financial year, two were located in lobbies, one in an extension and one within a sub-let unit away from the main store. The latter was not very successful and is likely to close. Consequently, all new coffee shops will be located in clear sight of the main entrance.

3 Control systems

When the first coffee shops were established it was determined that there would be no change to the existing administrative and accounting systems to accommodate them. For control purposes the coffee shop is treated as a profit centre within the branch of which it is part. The coffee shop manager reports directly to the branch manager. A profit and loss account is produced for each coffee shop, applying the standard format used by the branches. Following the successful development of a special keyboard layout and associated software, which was completed during 1995, the coffee shops are fully integrated into the branch Electronic Point Of Sale system.

Coffee shop opening hours match branch trading hours, including Sundays and Bank Holidays. Although there is limited trade immediately after opening and just before closing, the company's image might suffer if coffee shop opening hours differed from those of the branch.

4 Menus

The Bloomsbury Supermarkets plc coffee shop menu is standardised for all branches and features hot and cold beverages and snack food. Main meals are not provided. During 1995, sales were carefully monitored and the menu was refined in the light of experience. Underperforming lines were deleted. To maintain interest amongst regulars and to attract new customers into the coffee shop, a 'special' (such as doughnut and coffee at a discount price) is promoted on a weekly basis through posters located at the store entrance. Store managers have a certain amount of discretion to select the weekly special and to adjust the range of sandwiches in the light of demand patterns.

5 Promotions

Bloomsbury Supermarkets plc coffee shops attract custom through their immediate visibility. The only direct promotional activity so far has been the use of posters featuring the weekly special. Additional promotional initiatives are being designed to boost trading potential. The company is piloting the distribution of 'money off' tokens via the checkouts. Two types of tokens are on trial, featuring price reductions for specific product lines and discounts off the total bill. In addition, coffee shop vouchers are featured in local 'cheque book' promotions for new store openings, which are used to assist with the build up of trade.

6 Pricing

Pricing policy is based on the following criteria.

- Prices in Bloomsbury Supermarkets plc coffee shops should be no higher than those charged by their nearest competitors
- There should not be too many price variations for similar items on the menu
- The catering industry standard of charging three times cost should be used
- The price of directly comparable products sold in the store itself should be considered

A survey of the main competitors' coffee shop prices is conducted every six months in order to ensure that prices are reviewed regularly. In addition, individual branches are encouraged to carry out local price comparisons. Since the establishment of the first coffee shop competitors' prices have increased nationwide and Bloomsbury Supermarkets plc prices were revised in May 1996.

7 Investment appraisal assumptions

The following assumptions form the basis for the preliminary assessment of the projected financial performance of the proposed additional coffee shops. The historical data from which the projected operational and capital costs and margins were derived are very tentative and, hence, a large number of estimates have been made. These assumptions should therefore be treated as indicative only.

Sales forecast

For the case of a standard coffee shop, ultimate average weekly sales of £5500, at 1996 prices, are forecast. The proposed build-up curve of coffee shop sales to their ultimate level is shown in Table C5.1.

TABLE C5.1

BLOOMSBURY SUPERMARKETS PLC: PROPOSED SALES BUILD-UP CURVE

Year	Percentage of Ultimate Annual Sales
1	90
2	100

Obviously, build-up assumptions are highly conjectural at this stage.

Gross margin on sales

Actual gross margins for goods sold in the coffee shops range from over 75 per cent on staples such as tea and coffee to around 50 per cent on cakes and biscuits. On the basis of current profitability, an average gross margin of 65 per cent of sales can be predicted. Margins are generally constrained by a requirement to be competitive with other supermarkets such as Morrisons and ASDA and a wish to avoid adverse comparisons between prices in the store and prices charged in the coffee shop for bakery items.

Stock losses

Actual stock losses are currently running at approximately 7.1 per cent of sales at retail prices. Most of this is stock left at the end of the day which cannot be carried forward.

Labour

The actual labour requirement ranges from 7 full time equivalents (FTEs) at Chesterfield to 12.5 FTEs at York. The requirement is closely related to sales. To appraise the profitability of the coffee shops the average labour requirement at takings of £5500 per week is considered to be 9 FTEs, implying an average variable labour requirement of 5 FTEs. Based on 1996/97 wage and salary rates the estimated labour costs are as follows:

- Fixed (£ per week) £850
- Variable (per cent of takings) 12.8 per cent

Cleaning, utilities and maintenance

An estimate of these costs is summarised in Table C5.2.

TABLE C5.2

BLOOMSBURY SUPERMARKETS PLC: COST PROJECTIONS

	£ per annum (at 1996/97 prices)
Cleaning	6 500
Utilities	7 500
Maintenance	3 000
Wrapping Materials	1 100
Consumables	950

Head office costs

It is estimated that in the region of 90 per cent of the Head Office based Innovations Unit's time is allocated to coffee shops. The 1996/97 staffing level is assumed to be adequate to cover 12 coffee shops. Based on the Unit's budget for 1996/97 this implies a cost of approximately £7000 per store.

Initial capital costs

Since the inclusion of a coffee shop does not trigger an additional land requirement, no site costs will be included in the investment appraisal calculations. An estimate of standard building and fitting-out costs, based on a coffee shop area of 2500 square feet included within the shell of the store is shown in Table C5.3.

TABLE C5.3

BLOOMSBURY SUPERMARKETS PLC: PROJECTION OF INITIAL CAPITAL COSTS AT 1996/97 PRICES	
	£000
Incremental Works to Shell and Site	150
Fitting-out	290
Total	440

On-going capital expenditure

Table C5.4 provides a projection of on-going capital expenditure over the life of the coffee shop.

TABLE C5.4

BLOOMSBURY SUPERMARKETS PLC: ON-GOING CAPITAL EXPENDITURE AT 1996/97 PRICES	
Major Refurbishment	£7 000 every five-years
Minor Expenditure	£1 400 annually

Rates

As per the standard store assumption, a rate of £3 per square foot per annum (at 1996/97 prices) is to be employed in the financial appraisal.

8 Project life and target returns

It is to be assumed that the average life of a coffee shop is 15 years and that the company is aiming for a minimum return on investment of 6 per cent.

Tasks

Imagine that you are to report to senior management in the company, assessing the profitability of the existing coffee shops and evaluating the potential benefits from a substantial capital investment in a further eleven coffee shops.

In addition you will be required to provide a critical evaluation of the current pricing policy applied in the coffee shops, from the viewpoint of the company as well as that of the consumer.

In order to accomplish this you are required to carry out the following tasks.

Task 1

Use a spreadsheet to set up a worksheet to calculate the net present value of the expected cash flows associated with one new coffee shop at a discount rate of 6 per cent, treating the 1996/97 financial year as Year 0, in which the initial capital investment takes place.

Task 2

On the worksheet, carry out a sensitivity analysis, assessing the impact of the scenarios presented in Table C5.5 on the NPV.

TABLE C5.5

BLOOMSBURY SUPERMARKETS PLC: SCENARIOS FOR COFFEE SHOPS	
Scenario 1	Gross margin +/– 1.0 percentage point
Scenario 2	Takings +/– £200 per week
Scenario 3	Slower build-up of sales (85 per cent/ 90 per cent/95 per cent/100 per cent over four years)
Scenario 4	Coffee shop life increased to 20 years
Scenario 5	Initial capital cost increased/decreased by 10 per cent

On the basis of your findings, critically evaluate the strengths and weaknesses of the proposed capital investment project.

Task 3

Consult a range of secondary sources in order to gain a thorough understanding of the objectives, techniques and issues associated with pricing, with particular attention to the interests of the consumer. Based on your reading, provide a critical discussion of the company's pricing policy as applied in the coffee shops.

Answers to Exercises

Chapter 2

Exercise 2.1

The types of assets held are shown in Table A2.1.

TABLE A2.1

BUSINESS ASSETS		
Ice cream manufacturer	**Building society**	**Fairground ride operator**
Stock of ice cream	Building	Caravan
Machinery	Computer	Ride
Refrigerator	Photocopier	Stock of tickets

Exercise 2.2

Table A2.2 lists the assets found in the KoolKurls hairdressing salon, sorted into fixed and current.

TABLE A2.2

KOOLKURLS HAIRDRESSING SALON: FIXED AND CURRENT ASSETS	
Set of professional styling scissors	Fixed
Shampoo	Current
Electric hairdryers	Fixed
Electronic till	Fixed
£10 owed by a customer	Current
£15 in the till	Current

Exercise 2.3

The following is an assessment of the liabilities of Paws&Claws Petshop:

- £50 wages of Lenny, the part-time shop assistant, for work he did during the previous week

This is listed as a prepayment under the heading Current Liabilities. It is for work that has already been completed, that means the business has had the benefit of that work. Now the business owes this to Lenny and must pay him in the short run.

- £300 owed to the wholesaler for cages and petfood purchased and delivered last month

This is listed as a trade creditor under Current Liabilities. The business has already received the goods and therefore potentially had the benefits, but still owes the £300 to the supplier, which must be paid in the short run.

- £15 for stationery ordered but not yet delivered

This is not a Current Liability as the business has not yet received any benefit, neither have the goods been delivered nor has an invoice been received.

- £300 overdraft facility agreed with the bank manager but not yet used.

This is not a Current Liability, as none of the potential benefit agreed has been made use of. An overdraft only becomes a liability when it is actually used and only to the extent to which it is used.

Exercise 2.4

Explanation

The capital of £82 000 represents the value of the owner's original investment in the business. This has long been spent on computer equipment, vans, stock of goods for resale and other things and at the balance sheet date only £2000 of the net worth of the business is actually represented by cash. However, that does not mean that the rest of the money has been wasted. It is not really gone. It has just taken on a different form, that of the various assets.

Exercise 2.5

Figure A2.1 shows the balance sheet as at 5 March 199X.

FIGURE A2.1

ALLIED DOMECQ PLC: BALANCE SHEET AS AT 5 MARCH 199X			
	£m	**£m**	
Fixed Assets			
Buildings		2400	
Plant and Machinery		1300	
Furniture and Fittings		300	
		4000	
Current Assets			
Stock	1000		
Debtors	1000		
Cash	150		
	2150		
Creditors: due within one year			
Trade Creditors	1700		
Net Current Assets		450	(1)
Total Assets *less* Current Liabilities		4450	(2)
Creditors: due after one year			
Long-term Bank Loan		2700	
		1750	(3)
Capital			
Share Capital		1500	
Retained Profit		250	
		1750	

Explanation

(1) Net current assets = Current assets − Creditors (due within one year)
(2) Total assets *less* Current liabilities = Fixed assets + Current assets − Creditors (due within one year)
(3) This is the **Net assets** figure.

Net assets = Fixed assets + Current assets − Creditors (due within one year) − Creditors (due after one year)

Exercise 2.6

(a) The correct answer is **(B)**.

Explanation

There is a new entry 'Creditors: due after one year £1000' on the balance sheet. This is matched by a £1000 increase in the 'Bank and cash' entry.

(b) The correct answer is **(D)**.

Explanation

The entry for 'Stock' has increased by £1000. This is matched by a corresponding increase of £1000 in the entry under 'Trade Creditors'.

(c) The correct answer is **(C)**.

Explanation

The entry for 'Stock' decreases by £1000. At the same time, the entry for 'Bank and cash' increases by £1500. The surplus is shown in the capital section as 'Retained profit' £500.

Chapter 3

Exercise 3.1

The completed cash flow statement is shown in Figure A3.1.

FIGURE A3.1

JONATHAN'S SWEETS:
CASH FLOW STATEMENT 1 MAY TO 31 MAY 199X

		£
	Opening Balance	50
+	Receipts	
	Cash Sales	1100
–	Payments	
	New Supplier	500
	Rent Warehouse	300
	Wages Staff	360
	Salary Director	500
=	Closing Balance	(510)

Exercise 3.2

Stakeholder group	Benefit
Customers	If the business holds sufficient cash, it can make sure there is enough ice cream in stock
	If the business makes sufficient profit, it can invest in developing new exciting flavours
Staff	If the business holds sufficient cash, it can pay staff promptly
	If the business makes sufficient profit, it can offer good benefits, for instance pensions and private health insurance
The wider community	If the business holds sufficient cash, it can meet its bills for rates promptly
	If the business makes sufficient profit, it can afford to support local charities

Exercise 3.3

The completed profit and loss account is shown in Figure A3.2.

FIGURE A3.2

JONATHAN'S SWEETS: PROFIT AND LOSS ACCOUNT 1 MAY TO 31 MAY 199X

		£
	Sales	2600
–	Cost of Goods Sold	1100
=	Gross Profit	1500
–	Expenses	
	Rent	300
	Wages Staff	360
	Salary Director	500
=	Trading Profit	340

Exercise 3.4

(a) The correct answer is **(C)**.

The calculations are shown in Figure A3.3.

FIGURE A3.3

JANINE SWIFT'S DRIVING SCHOOL: CASH FLOW STATEMENT 1 SEPTEMBER TO 3 SEPTEMBER 199X

		£
	Opening Balance	300
+	Receipts	
	Sale of Highway Code	10
	Cash for Lessons	100
–	Payments	
	Purchase of Highway Code	5
	Petrol	55
	Advertisement	15
=	Closing Balance	335

(b) The correct answer is **(B)**.

The calculations are shown in Figure A3.4.

FIGURE A3.4

JANINE SWIFT'S DRIVING SCHOOL:
PROFIT AND LOSS ACCOUNT 1 SEPTEMBER TO 3 SEPTEMBER 199X

		£
	Sales	110
–	Expenses	
	Highway Code	5
	Petrol	25
=	Net Trading Profit	80

Note that the *matching concept* is applied. Only the petrol actually used up to the end of 3 September 199X is included as an expense. Also the advertisement is not yet included as it will only be running the following week, therefore it cannot be matched up with the current week's sales.

Chapter 4

Exercise 4.1

The calculations of cost of goods sold and gross profit are shown in Figures A4.1 and A4.2, respectively.

FIGURE A4.1

'WHITE LION': COST OF GOODS SOLD 1 JULY TO 31 JULY, WORKINGS

		£
	Opening Stock (at valuation)	1100
+	Purchases (at cost)	5640
−	Closing Stock (at valuation)	576
=	Cost of Goods Sold	6164

FIGURE A4.2

'WHITE LION': GROSS PROFIT 1 JULY TO 31 JULY, WORKINGS

		£
	Sales (at selling price)	7520
−	Cost of Goods Sold (Figure A4.1)	6164
=	Gross Profit	1356

Exercise 4.2

Vineleaves Ltd Videos

(a) The closing stock calculations, using FIFO, WAC and LIFO are shown in Tables A4.1, A4.2 and A4.3, respectively.

(b) The impact of the choice of stock valuation method on gross profit is shown in Figure A4.3.

TABLE A4.1

VINELEAVES LTD: FIFO

Month	Purchases (at cost)	Stock issued for sale (at valuation)	Stock after transaction (at valuation)
July	900 @ £6.00		900 @ £6.00
August		700 @ £6.00	200 @ £6.00
September	500 @ £8.00		200 @ £6.00 500 @ £8.00
October		200 @ £6.00 200 @ £8.00	300 @ £8.00

Closing Stock = 300 ∗ £8.00 = £2400

Under the FIFO method, the closing stock is valued at £2400

TABLE A4.2

VINELEAVES LTD: WAC

Month	Purchases (at cost)	Stock issued for sale (at valuation)	Stock after transaction (at valuation)
July	900 @ £6.00		900 @ £6.00
August		700 @ £6.00	200 @ £6.00
September	500 @ £8.00		$700 @ \frac{200*6.00+500*8.00}{700}$ or 700 @ £7.43
October		400 @ £7.43	300 @ £7.43

Closing Stock = 300 ∗ £7.43 = £2229

Under the WAC method, the closing stock is valued at £2229

TABLE A4.3

VINELEAVES LTD: LIFO			
Month	**Purchases (at cost)**	**Stock issued for sale (at valuation)**	**Stock after transaction (at valuation)**
July	900 @ £6.00		900 @ £6.00
August		700 @ £6.00	200 @ £6.00
September	500 @ £8.00		200 @ £6.00 500 @ £8.00
October		400 @ £8.00	200 @ £6.00 100 @ £8.00

Closing Stock = 200 ∗ £6.00 + 100 ∗ £8.00 = £2000

Under the LIFO method, the closing stock is valued at £2000

FIGURE A4.3

VINELEAVES LTD: TRADING ACCOUNT 1 JULY TO 31 OCTOBER 199X		FIFO	WAC	LIFO
		£	£	£
	Sales	18 300	18 300	18 300
	Opening Stock	0	0	0
+	Purchases	9 400	9 400	9 400
−	Closing Stock	2 400	2 229	2 000
=	Cost of Goods Sold	7 000	7 171	7 400
	Gross Profit	11 300	11 129	10 900

Exercise 4.3

(a) The correct answer is **(C)**.
The workings are shown in Table A4.4 and Figure A4.4.

(b) The correct answer is **(A)**.
The workings are shown in Table A4.5.

(c) The correct answer is **(B)**.

TABLE A4.4

CARDSRUS: FIFO STOCK CALCULATIONS			
Date	**Purchases (at cost)**	**Stock issued for sale (at valuation)**	**Stock after transaction (at valuation)**
1 Jan			400 @ £0.50
2 Jan	650 @ £0.65		400 @ £0.50 650 @ £0.65
3 Jan		100 @ £0.50	300 @ £0.50 650 @ £0.65

Closing Stock is valued at
300 ∗ £0.50 + 650 ∗ £0.65 = £572.50

FIGURE A4.4

CARDSRUS: COST OF GOODS SOLD, WORKINGS		
	Opening Stock	£200.00
+	Purchases	£422.50
−	Closing Stock	£572.50
=	Cost of Goods Sold	£ 50.00

TABLE A4.5

CARDSRUS: WAC STOCK CALCULATIONS			
Month	**Purchases (at cost)**	**Stock issued for sale (at valuation)**	**Stock after transaction (at valuation)**
1 Jan			400 @ £0.50
2 Jan	650 @ £0.65		$1050 @ \frac{400*0.5+650*0.65}{1050}$ or 1050 @ £0.59
3 Jan		100 @ £0.59	950 @ £0.59

Closing Stock is valued at 950 ∗ £0.59 = £560.50

Exercise 4.4

The calculations are shown in Table A4.6.

For both methods, the book value at the end of year 6 is accurately reflected as £2000. The slight difference between the two methods is due to rounding error. For the reducing balance method, most of the depreciation is charged during the early years of the asset's life. This seems more appropriate for this kind of asset, as the new technology involved is more likely to give the company a competitive edge during the early years.

TABLE A4.6

BREWERY:
COMPARISON OF DEPRECIATION METHODS

	Straight line		Reducing balance	
	Depreciation Charge to Profit and Loss	**Balance Sheet Entry**	**Depreciation Charge to Profit and Loss**	**Balance Sheet Entry**
Initial	£	£	£	£
Cost		14 000		14 000.00
Year 1	2 000	12 000	3 878.00	10 122.00
Year 2	2 000	10 000	2 803.79	7 318.21
Year 3	2 000	8 000	2 027.14	5 291.07
Year 4	2 000	6 000	1 465.63	3 825.44
Year 5	2 000	4 000	1 059.65	2 765.79
Year 6	2 000	2 000	766.12	1 999.67

Exercise 4.5

The correct answer is **(C)**.

Calculations:

Reducing Balance Method

Depreciation Charge for Year 1: £3000 * 30.1% = £903

Straight Line Method

Depreciation Charge for Year 1: $\frac{£3000 - £500}{5} = £500$

Exercise 4.6

The necessary calculations are shown in Table A4.7 and Figures A4.5–A4.8.

TABLE A4.7

TANIA'S BUSINESS:
FIFO CLOSING STOCK CALCULATIONS

Month	**Purchases (at cost)**	**Stock issued for sale (at valuation)**	**Stock after transaction (at valuation)**
January	1500 @ £3.50		1500 @ £3.50
February	4000 @ £4.00		1500 @ £3.50 4000 @ £4.00
April		1500 @ £3.50 1500 @ £4.00	2500 @ £4.00
July	3500 @ £4.10		2500 @ £4.00 3500 @ £4.10
November		2500 @ £4.00 1500 @ £4.10	2000 @ £4.10

Closing Stock is valued at 2000 * £4.10 = £8200

FIGURE A4.5

TANIA'S BUSINESS:
COST OF GOODS SOLD CALCULATIONS

		£
	Opening Stock	0
+	Purchases	35 600
−	Closing Stock	8 200
=	Cost of Goods Sold	27 400

FIGURE A4.6

TANIA'S BUSINESS: CASH FLOW STATEMENT FOR THE YEAR 1 JANUARY TO 31 DECEMBER 199X

		£
	Opening Balance	20 000
+	Receipts:	
	Sales	52 500
−	Payments:	
	Heat-embossing Machine	3 000
	Purchases of Stock	35 600
	Wages	9 000
	Rent	15 000
=	Closing Balance	9 900

FIGURE A4.7

TANIA'S BUSINESS: PROFIT AND LOSS ACCOUNT FOR THE YEAR 1 JANUARY TO 31 DECEMBER 199X

		£
	Sales	52 500
–	Cost of Goods Sold	27 400
=	Gross Profit	25 100
–	Expenses	
	Depreciation	500
	Wages	9 000
	Rent	15 000
=	Net Trading Profit	600

FIGURE A4.8

TANIA'S BUSINESS: BALANCE SHEET AS AT 31 DECEMBER 199X

	Cost	Depreciation	Net Book Value
	£	£	£
Fixed Assets:			
Heat-embossing Machine	3 000	500	2 500
Current Assets:			
Stock			8 200
Cash			9 900
Net Total Assets			20 600
Capital			20 000
Retained Profit			600
			20 600

Chapter 5

Exercise 5.1

(a) The depreciation charge for the first year is worked out for the two methods as shown in Figure A5.1.

The correct answer therefore is:

(B) £325 higher than under the straight line method

(b) The closing stock calculations are shown in Table A5.1. The cash flow statement, profit and loss account and balance sheet are presented in Figures A5.2–A5.4.

FIGURE A5.1

JOEY'S BUSINESS: DEPRECIATION CALCULATIONS

Straight Line Method:

$$\text{Annual depreciation charge} = \frac{£2500 - £400}{7} = £300$$

Reducing Balance Method:

Depreciation charge for first year

$$= £2500 * 25/100 = £625$$

TABLE A5.1

JOEY'S BUSINESS: CLOSING STOCK CALCULATIONS

FIFO

Month	Purchases	Stock Issued for Sale	Stock After Each Transaction
Jan	1000 @ £3.00		1000 @ £3.00
March	3000 @ £3.30		1000 @ £3.00 3000 @ £3.30
May		1000 @ £3.00 1000 @ £3.30	2000 @ £3.30
Oct	4000 @ £3.20		2000 @ £3.30 4000 @ £3.20
Dec		2000 @ £3.30 1500 @ £3.20	2500 @ £3.20

Closing Stock is valued at 2500 * £3.20 = £8000

FIGURE A5.2

JOEY'S BUSINESS: CASH FLOW STATEMENT FOR THE PERIOD 1 JANUARY TO 31 DECEMBER 199X

		£
	Opening Balance	20 000
+	Receipts:	
	Sales	55 000
–	Payments:	
	Van	2 500
	Stock	25 700
	Wages	10 000
	Rent	9 000
=	Closing Balance	27 800

FIGURE A5.3

JOEY'S BUSINESS: PROFIT AND LOSS ACCOUNT FOR THE PERIOD 1 JANUARY TO 31 DECEMBER 199X

		£
	Sales	55 000
–	Cost of Goods Sold	17 700
=	Gross Profit	37 300
–	Expenses	
	Depreciation	
	Van	300
	Wages	10 000
	Rent	9 000
=	Net Trading Profit	18 000

FIGURE A5.4

JOEY'S BUSINESS: BALANCE SHEET AS AT 31 DECEMBER 199X

	Cost	Depreciation to Date	Net Book Value
	£	£	£
Fixed Assets			
Van	2 500	300	2 200
Current Assets			
Stock			8 000
Cash			27 800
Net Total Assets			38 000
Capital			20 000
Retained Profit			18 000
			38 000

Chapter 6

Exercise 6.1

The final worksheet is shown in Figure A6.1. The version showing the formulae is in Figure A6.2.

It is worth noting that we could have designed the worksheet differently if we had thought there was a possibility that the basic wage might change from £50. It would have been advantageous to allow for this. In setting up the initial table, we entered 50 in cell **D7**. If we move to **D8** and enter =**D7**, whatever is in cell **D7** will appear in **D8**. Initially, the basic wage is 50 so that appears but if the basic wage is changed to 60, all we would need to do is to change the entry in **D7** and the entry in **D8** would automatically be changed as well. We can copy this formula down using the **Edit Fill Down** command or the **Copy** icon.

Exercise 6.2

A print-out of the spreadsheet template is shown in Figure A6.3.

Exercise 6.3

You will need to highlight rows 2, 3, 4 and 5 of Table 6.1 before clicking on the **ChartWizard** icon. Select the **Column** bar chart option 1. Include a legend this time so as to distinguish between the two values each year.

From Figure 6.9, we can see that, overall, turnover increased from 1988 to 1994 but there were setbacks in 1990 and 1993. The highest trading profit was achieved in 1989 with poorer results in 1990, 1991 and 1993.

FIGURE A6.1

FINAL WORKSHEET FOR EXERCISE 6.1 (NUMERICAL VERSION)

FAST FORWARD VIDEO COMPANY				
COMMISSION PAYROLL				
Calculations of gross pay				
EMPLOYEE	SALES (£)	COMMISSION	BASIC PAY(£)	GROSS PAY (£)
		RATE		
Arnold	5,700	3%	60	231.00
Chalmers	7,500	4%	60	360.00
Hobart	6,500	4%	60	320.00
Michaelson	8,500	3%	60	315.00
Pratt	8,000	4%	60	380.00
Smith	7,600	2%	60	212.00
Wilson	4,200	3%	60	186.00
TOTALS	43,800			1818.00

FIGURE A6.2

FINAL WORKSHEET FOR EXERCISE 6.1 (VIEW FORMULA VERSION)

	A	B	C	D	E
1	**FAST FORWARD VIDEO COMPANY**				
2	**COMMISSION PAYROLL**				
3	**Calculations of gross pay**				
4					
5	EMPLOYEE	SALES (£)	COMMISSION	BASIC PAY(£)	GROSS PAY (£)
6			RATE		
7	Arnold	5700	0.03	60	=B7*C7+D7
8	Chalmers	7500	0.04	=$D$7	=B8*C8+D8
9	Hobart	6500	0.04	=$D$7	=B9*C9+D9
10	Michaelson	8500	0.03	=$D$7	=B10*C10+D10
11	Pratt	8000	0.04	=$D$7	=B11*C11+D11
12	Smith	7600	0.02	=$D$7	=B12*C12+D12
13	Wilson	4200	0.03	=$D$7	=B13*C13+D13
14	TOTALS	=SUM(B7:B12)			=SUM(E7:E12)

FIGURE A6.3

TEMPLATE FOR FINANCIAL STATEMENTS CALCULATIONS

	A	B	C	D	E	F	G	H	I	J
1										
2										
3	**Stock Calculations**		**Cash Flow Statement**		**Profit and Loss Account**		Balance Sheet as at End			
4	Opening Stock		Opening Balance		Sales		Fixed Assets	Cost	Depreciation	Net
5	Purchases		Receipts:		Cost of Goods Sold	=b7			to Date	Book Value
6	Closing Stock				Gross Profit	=f4-f5				=h6-i6
7	Cost of Goods Sold	=b4+b5-b6								=h7-i7
8					Expenses:					=h8-i8
9	**Debtors' Calculations**		Total Receipts	=sum(d6:d8)						
10	Opening Balance Debtors		Payments:							=sum(j6:j8)
11	Credit Sales						Current Assets:			
12	Receipts from Debtors						Stock	=b7		
13	Closing Balance Debtors	=b10+b11-b12					Debtors	=b13		
14							Cash and bank	=d20		
15	**Creditors' Calculations**								=sum(h12:h14)	
16	Opening Balance Creditors				Total Expenses	=sum(f9:f15)	Current Liabilities:			
17	Credit Purchases				Net Profit/Loss	=f6-f16	Creditors	=b19		
18	Payments to Creditors								=b19	
19	Closing Balance Creditors	=b15+b16-b17	Total Payments	=sum(d11:d18)			Net Current Assets			=i15-i18
20			Closing Balance	=d4+d9-d19			Net Total Assets			=j10+j19
21										
22							Capital:			
23							Share capital			
24							Retained profit		=f17	
25										=i23+i24

Chapter 7

Exercise 7.1

(a) If the figures are taken at face value, the following comments can be made. The company appears to have succeeded in achieving overall growth in terms of sales. This is made up of a steady growth in Germany, relatively strong year-on-year increases in the UK and initially strong growth in France, but stagnation from Year 2 to Year 3 in this market. In terms of net profit, there was some growth in the German and French market between Year 1 and Year 2, whilst there was a decline in the UK market. Between Year 2 and Year 3, the UK market recovered to its original net profit figure, the German market remained at the same level and net profit in the French market declined slightly.

From this description, the overall impression might be one of a competitive market in which profitability had to be sacrificed to some extent in order to maintain and build sales over the three year period.

(b) Clearly, the above interpretation of the figures is rather limited, and hampered by a lack of additional information. Simply taking the figures at face value would be naive and misleading. If you wished to compile accurate aggregate figures for the company as a whole, you would need to know the appropriate exchange rates to apply. Also, a knowledge of inflation rates would help you assess whether the apparent growth in sales is really due to selling more or whether it is simply a reflection of rising prices. The comparison of the results in the three countries could have been further distorted if different rates of inflation applied in the three markets. Furthermore, a knowledge of gross profit and cost data would help you assess whether the sales growth was brought about by a deliberate penetration strategy, involving dropping prices. Alternatively you might find that the stagnant or falling net profit figures were the result of escalating costs.

Chapter 8

Exercise 8.1

The calculation is:

Calculation of asset turnover

$$\text{Asset turnover} = \frac{£900\,000}{£150\,000} = 6 \text{ times}$$

The asset turnover here means that the value of sales was 6 times the value of net total assets. This tells us that for every £1 invested in the business, £6 worth of sales were generated during the financial year.

Exercise 8.2

The answers for all three parts of this exercise are summarised in Table A8.1.

TABLE A8.1

COMPARISON OF COMPANY LIQUIDITY

Company A	**Company B**	**Company C**
(a)		
Working-capital comparison:		
£1 000	£9 000	£12 000
(b)		
Current ratio comparison:		
Current ratio 1.03	Current ratio 1.75	Current ratio 1.8
Least liquid	Medium	Most liquid
(c)		
Acid test comparison:		
Acid test 0.28	Acid test 0.91	Acid test 0.8
Least liquid	Most liquid	Medium

The ratios in Table A8.1 can be interpreted as follows. All three companies have a positive working capital figure. They are therefore liquid. Should the three companies be forced to pay off all their creditors at once by turning their current assets into cash, for every £1 owed to creditors, Company **C** would be able to raise £1.80, Company **B** £1.75 and Company **A** £1.03.

In terms of the acid test the ranking order is slightly different from that indicated by the current ratios. If the three companies found that they could not sell off their stock, then for every £1 owed to creditors, Company **B** would still be able to raise £0.91, Company **C** £0.8 and Company **A** only £0.28. Clearly not being able to use stock would make quite a difference. This is particularly true for Company **C**, which has more money tied up in stock than Company **B** if seen in relation to the total amount of money invested in current assets. As a result the ranking order has been reversed.

Exercise 8.3

Examples of two advantages of high liquidity, as well as two advantages of low liquidity are noted in Table A8.2.

TABLE A8.2

ADVANTAGES AND DISADVANTAGES OF LIQUIDITY	
High Liquidity	**Low Liquidity**
(1) Cash readily available to meet debts and take up special offers	**(1)** Effective use of trade credit as a source of 'free' short-term business finance
(2) Security and independence from bank and suppliers	**(2)** Valuable resources are freed up and used elsewhere

Exercise 8.4

(a) The ratios for stock turnover, debtors' collection period and creditors' payment period for the two years are shown in Table A8.3.

TABLE A8.3

COMPARISON OF RATIOS OVER TIME		
	Year 1	**Year 2**
Stock turnover	5 times	6.67 times
Debtors' collection period	55 days	61 days
Creditors' payment period	91 days	51 days

The ratios shown in Table A8.3 can be interpreted as follows. Stock control has been improved, resulting in an increase in the stock turnover ratio. However, debtors' collection period has increased by an additional 6 days. This should be monitored to see whether this reflects a genuine industry trend which makes it necessary to offer such long credit periods to debtors in order to remain competitive, or whether it is due to a lack of control. There was also quite a drop in creditors' payment period, by 40 days. Whilst 91 days seems rather long for any industry, the sharp drop does mean a much larger working capital requirement, which may be hard to finance in the short term.

Working-capital calculations are shown in Figure A8.1.

You can see from Figure A8.1 that the overall working capital requirement has increased considerably in year 2. This is the result of a combination of events, partly beyond the control of the business.

FIGURE A8.1

CHANGES IN WORKING CAPITAL OVER TIME			
Extract from Balance Sheet at End of Year 1		**Extract from Balance Sheet at End of Year 2**	
Current Assets	£	Current Assets	£
Stock	2000	Stock	1500
Debtors	150	Debtors	1000
Cash	500	Cash	500
Current Liabilities		Current Liabilities	
Creditors	1500	Creditors	700
Working Capital	1150	Working Capital	2300

(b) Table A8.4 matches the changes in the ratios with the appropriate causes.

TABLE A8.4

INTERPRETATION OF THE RATIOS	
Cause	**Ratio Affected**
Implementation of new sales based ordering system	Stock turnover
Acquisition of large new wholesale account	Debtors' collection period
Unexpected bankruptcy of a key supplier	Creditors' payment period

Exercise 8.5

Figure A8.2 shows an assessment of profitability for the two businesses.

This information can be interpreted as follows. Business **X** is the discounter, achieving a high sales volume through low mark-ups, but implementing excellent cost controls. Overall, the net margin of Business **X** is much lower. Business **Y** has a different pricing policy, as reflected in a mark-up of 50 per cent. However, the maintenance of a high quality image and premium prices also imply higher costs of running the business, and sales volumes have to be sacrificed to a certain extent.

FIGURE A8.2

COMPARISON OF PROFITABILITY

Business X		**Business Y**	
	£000		£000
Sales	800	Sales	600
Cost of Goods Sold	700	Cost of Goods Sold	400
Gross Profit	100	Gross Profit	200
Expenses	80	Expenses	150
Net Profit	20	Net Profit	50

	Business X		Business Y
Net margin	$= \frac{£20}{£800} * 100 = 2.5\%$	Net margin	$= \frac{£50}{£600} * 100 = 8.33\%$
Gross margin	$= \frac{£100}{£800} * 100 = 12.5\%$	Gross margin	$= \frac{£200}{£600} * 100 = 33.33\%$
Mark-up	$= \frac{£100}{£700} * 100 = 14.29\%$	Mark-up	$= \frac{£200}{£400} * 100 = 50\%$

Exercise 8.6

Figure A8.3 provides an assessment of the comparative profitability of the two businesses.

(a) The figures shown in Figure A8.3 indicate that despite the striking differences between the two companies, both yield the same ROCE.

Manufacturer **B** has the higher gross margin and the higher net margin and is therefore more profitable overall.

To answer the question, which firm has the higher capital investment, you need to calculate net total assets which, bearing in mind the balance sheet equation, must equal capital employed. Manufacturer **B** has a higher capital investment.

To assess resource utilisation, the asset turnover ratio must be calculated. Retailer **A** has the higher asset turnover figure which indicates a more effective utilisation of resources.

A comparison of both the current ratio and the acid test indicates that the manufacturer is a lot more liquid than the retailer.

(b) From an investor's point of view, there is little to choose between the two companies, as both achieve the same ROCE, which indicates the same level of overall performance. However, there is a great difference in their respective profitability and resource utilisation ratios, illustrating a typical trade-off between those two areas.

Typically, a manufacturer has to invest quite a lot of capital in plant and machinery. This requirement is less pronounced for a retailer. As a result, the retailer can succeed in generating quite a large amount of sales on the basis of rather more limited resources. The retailer is likely to turn stock round more quickly than the manufacturer and to get generous trade credit terms from suppliers, whilst customers pay cash. On the other hand, the manufacturer has to offer credit terms to customers, and stock will be tied up longer, due to the manufacturing process. This means that the manufacturer has to generate higher margins to make up for these differences. This is normally quite acceptable, as the manufacturer transforms raw materials into complex finished products, whereas the retailer only sells on finished goods purchased elsewhere.

FIGURE A8.3

INTER-FIRM COMPARISON

Retailer A		**Manufacturer B**	
	£		£
Sales	100 000	Sales	100 000
Cost of Goods Sold	80 000	Cost of Goods Sold	50 000
Gross Profit	20 000	Gross Profit	50 000
Expenses	10 000	Expenses	30 000
Net Profit	10 000	Net Profit	20 000

	Retailer A		Manufacturer B
Gross margin	$= \frac{20\,000}{100\,000} = 20\%$	Gross margin	$= \frac{50\,000}{100\,000} = 50\%$
Net margin	$= \frac{10\,000}{100\,000} = 10\%$	Net margin	$= \frac{20\,000}{100\,000} = 20\%$
Net total assets	= £23 000	Net total assets	= £45 000
Asset turnover	$= \frac{100\,000}{23\,000} = 4.35$	Asset turnover	$= \frac{100\,000}{45\,000} = 2.22$
Current ratio	$= \frac{£5\,000}{£7\,000} = 0.71$	Current ratio	$= \frac{£11\,000}{£6\,000} = 1.8$
Acid test	$= \frac{£2\,000}{£7\,000} = 0.28$	Acid test	$= \frac{£6\,000}{£6\,000} = 1$
ROCE = 0.1 * 4.35 = 0.44		ROCE = 0.2 * 2.22 = 0.44	

Chapter 9

Exercise 9.1

Table A9.1 shows the results of the calculations.

TABLE A9.1

PORTFOLIO PERFORMANCE

	Dividend Cover	Dividend Yield	P/E Ratio
Wimpey	1.20	5.4%	15.5
Barratt	1.75	4.2%	13.6
Banner Homes	2.86	2.4%	14.7
Beazer Homes	1.9	4.5%	11.7

Exercise 9.2

(a) Table A9.2 shows the ratios for Sainsbury and Kwik Save.

TABLE A9.2

COMPARISON OF INVESTMENT RATIOS

	Dividend Yield			P/E Ratio			Dividend
	Current	Hi	Lo	Current	Hi	Lo	Cover
Sainsbury	3.4%	3.4	3.7	14.49	14.52	13.3	2.03
Kwik Save	4.2%	4.0	4.7	10.5	10.99	9.3	2.27

(b) The two companies are located at opposite ends of the spectrum of grocery retailing. Sainsbury is a premium priced retailer, increasingly moving towards large out-of-town developments. In contrast, Kwik Save is a UK discount operator with strong historical roots in the field of discounting. As the square footage figures show, both expanded, but Sainsbury more strongly. In 1994, pressures on site values, combined with the rumoured impending saturation of grocery retailing in the UK necessitated some revaluation of property which depressed Sainsbury's EPS and DPS figures.

However, in 1995 Sainsbury's EPS and DPS appeared to have recovered and they even slightly exceeded 1993 values. Kwik Save's performance on those figures was consistently strong, but there was a slight decline in EPS in 1995. Both companies had comparable dividend cover around a level of 2, leaving a strong margin of safety. Market confidence as reflected in the P/E ratio appeared to favour Sainsbury's in May 1995.

Exercise 9.3

(a) Figure A9.1 summarises the calculations.

FIGURE A9.1

IMPACT OF GEARING ON PERFORMANCE

Profit Forecast	Company A	Company B
£20 000		
	$EPS = \frac{£20\,000}{200\,000}$	$EPS = \frac{£20\,000 + £14\,000}{60\,000}$
	$EPS = £0.10$	$EPS = £0.10$
	$ROSF = \frac{£20\,000}{£200\,000}$	$ROSF = \frac{£20\,000 - £14\,000}{£60\,000}$
	$ROSF = 0.10$	$ROSF = 0.10$
£10 000		
	$EPS = \frac{£10\,000}{£200\,000}$	$EPS = \frac{£10\,000 - £14\,000}{60\,000}$
	$EPS = £0.05$	$EPS = (-£0.07)$ (rounded)
	$ROSF = \frac{£10\,000}{£200\,000}$	$ROSF = \frac{£10\,000 - £14\,000}{£60\,000}$
	$ROSF = 0.05$	$ROSF = (-0.07)$
	$Gearing = \frac{£200\,000}{£200\,000}$	$Gearing = \frac{£200\,000}{£60\,000}$
	$= 1$	$= 3.3$ (rounded)

(b), (c) At the higher profit level of £40 000 the higher gearing level for Company **B** resulted in a boost of the returns available to be distributed amongst the shares of the company. The profit forecast of £20 000 reflects the level of profitability at which investors would be indifferent between investing in the two companies. For the pessimistic profit forecast of £10 000, the investors in shares of Company **A** still have a moderate amount of profit to be distributed amongst shareholders, whereas the shareholders of Company **B** are forced to absorb a loss, as the profits are insufficient to cover the interest payments on the long-term loan. This example illustrates the relationship between risk and return: higher gearing implies higher risk, but also potentially greater returns at higher profit levels.

Exercise 9.4

(a) The ratios for this answer are set out in Table A9.3.

TABLE A9.3

COMPARISON OF COMPANIES X AND Y

	Company X	Company Y
Net total assets	£100 000	£100 000
Net margin	0.075	0.10
Asset turnover	1.6	1.5
ROCE	0.12	0.15

Company **Y** has the higher net margin
The companies have the same capital investment
Company **X** has the higher asset turnover
Company **Y** has the higher return on capital employed

(b) Earnings per share = £0.12
Table A9.4 sets out a comparison of projected returns for the three scenarios depending on whether share or loan finance is chosen.

TABLE A9.4

LOAN FINANCE VERSUS SHARE FINANCE

Company X: Use of Share Finance				
	EPS	**Gearing**	**ROCE**	**ROSF**
Recession	0.05	1	0.05	0.05
Indifferent	0.125	1	0.125	0.125
Boom	0.20	1	0.2	0.2
Company X: Use of Loan Finance				
	EPS	**Gearing**	**ROCE**	**ROSF**
Recession	(−0.05)	2	(−0.025)	(−0.05)
Indifferent	0.1	2	0.05	0.1
Boom	0.25	2	0.125	0.25

It becomes clear from the figures in Table A9.4 that the use of loan finance is more risky, as it would result in a loss-making situation in times of recession. However, it also promises potentially greater gains during a boom period. In other words, there is a clear trade-off between risk and potential returns.

Chapter 10

Answers for Exercises 10.1 and 10.2 are provided in the main text.

Exercise 10.3

(a)–(c) Figure A10.1 uses the profit tree model to illustrate the comparison of the 1994 results for Allied Domecq plc and J Sainsbury plc.

As we already know from Exercise 10.2, Sainsbury's 1994 results were depressed because of the devaluation of property and higher depreciation charge for the year. The 1994 Allied Domecq results compare favourably, with a ROSF of 22.4 per cent. This was the result of a ROCE of 13.4 per cent, which was further enhanced by a gearing of 1.68, which is somewhat higher than Sainsbury's figure. An investigation of the branches of the Allied Domecq profit tree illustrates that this is a very different company with a strong manufacturing component to the business. It may help to know that Allied Domecq is the parent company of Carlsberg–Tetley, Dunkin' Donuts and Baskin–Robbins, a large number of UK public houses and a strong wines and spirits division.

The manufacturing element is reflected on the profitability side in a high gross margin of 37.2 per cent, as compared to Sainsbury's 9.5 per cent. This is due to the fact that a manufacturer adds value by making things out of raw materials and can therefore charge for this. The higher costs associated with running a manufacturing operation are reflected in the relatively high level of expenses. As a result net margin, whilst higher than Sainsbury's, is not as far above it as gross margin.

Looking at resource utilisation, Allied Domecq has a substantially lower asset turnover figure than Sainsbury's. This is mostly due to the much lower liquidity of the company, as shown by a current ratio of 1.32 and an acid test of 0.67. Again, this is due to the difference in business focus. A manufacturing company invariably has to be more liquid than a retailer. More money is tied up in stock; stock is harder to sell in the short run, as there are raw materials and work-in-progress as well as finished goods in stock at any one point in time, and it takes time to pass items through the production process. A low stock turnover figure results. Also, manufacturers are expected to give credit to their customers, resulting in a higher debtor figure.

However, in summary, for 1994, the higher profitability of Allied Domecq more than made up for the lower asset turnover and therefore Allied Domecq's performance surpassed that of Sainsbury's. It should be noted that in 1994 Sainsbury's had a high level of exceptional one-off costs which may have distorted the comparative performances for that year.

FIGURE A10.1

THE PROFIT TREE MODEL:
COMPARISON OF THE RESULTS OF J SAINSBURY PLC AND ALLIED DOMECQ PLC 1994

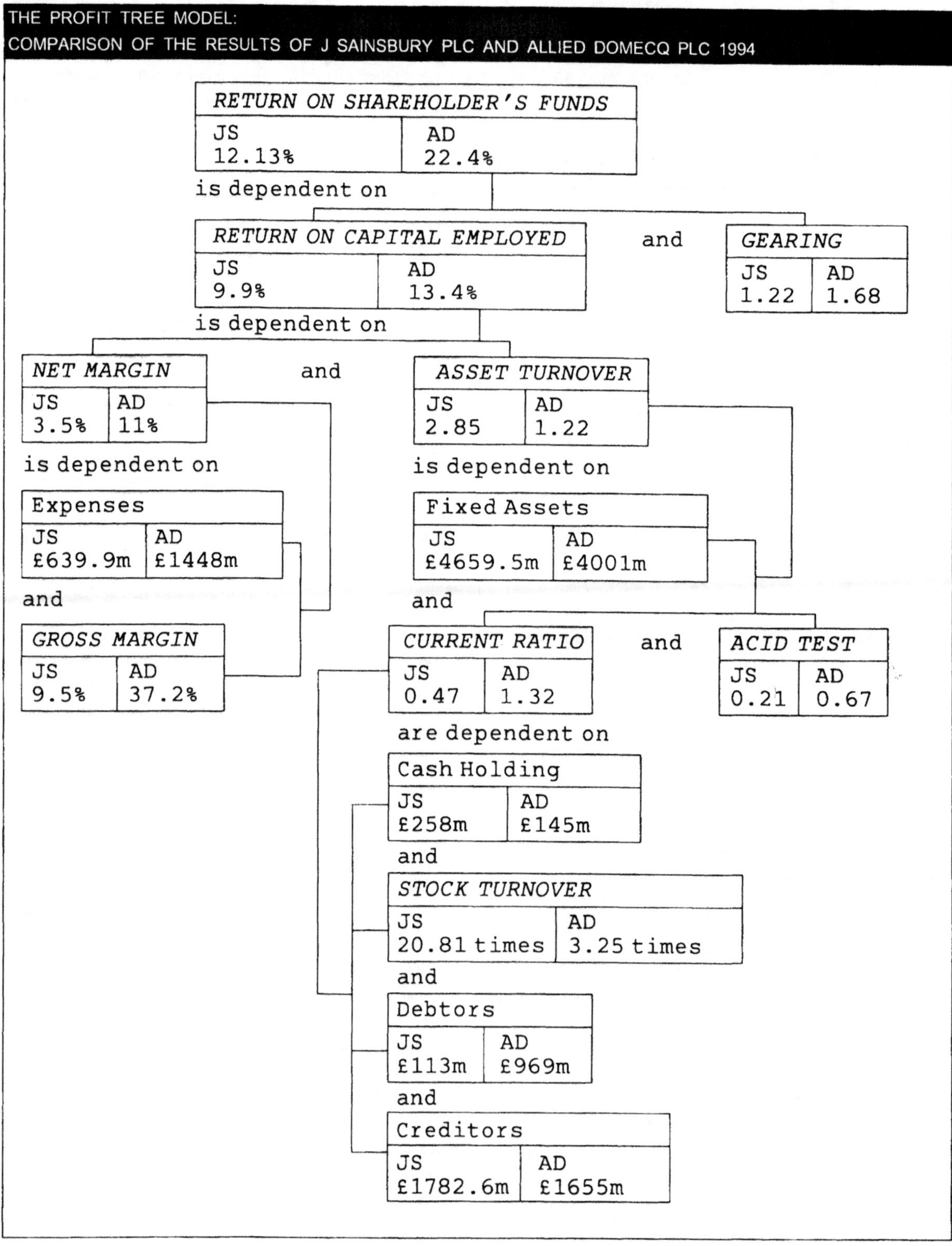

FIGURE A10.2

TEMPLATE FOR PROFIT TREE

	A	B	C	D	E
1					
2	Data Section:				
3	Sales		Fixed assets		
4	Cost of goods sold		Stock		
5	Gross profit		Debtors		
6	Total expenses		Cash		
7	Net profit		Total current assets		
8			Creditors (due within one year)		
9			Net total assets		
10			Share capital		
11			Creditors (due after one year)		
12					
13	Profit Tree Model:				
14		ROSF			
15		=B18*E18*100			
16					
17		ROCE			GEARING
18		=B7/D9*100			=(D10+D11)/D10
19					
20	NET MARGIN		ASSET TURNOVER		
21	=B7/B3*100		=B3/D9*100		
22					
23	Expenses		Fixed assets		
24	=B6		=D3		
25					
26	GROSS MARGIN		CURRENT RATIO	ACID TEST	
27	=B5/B3*100		=D7/D8	=(D7-D4)/D8	
28					
29			Cash holding		
30			=D6		
31					
32			STOCK TURNOVER		
33			=B4/D4		
34					
35			Debtors		
36			=D5		
37					
38			Creditors (due within one year)		
39			=D8		

Exercise 10.4

The answer is shown in Table A10.1.

TABLE A10.1

IMPACT OF DIFFERENT SCENARIOS ON KEY RATIOS

Scenario	Ratio Affected	Increase/Decrease
A key supplier reduces the period for trade credit	Creditors' payment therefore	Decrease
	Asset turnover therefore	Decrease
	ROCE and ROSF	Decrease
The price of raw materials rises, resulting in higher cost of goods sold	Gross margin therefore	Decrease
	Net margin therefore	Decrease
	ROCE and ROSF	Decrease
Stock control is improved, resulting in lower average stock	Stock turnover therefore	Increase
	Asset turnover therefore	Increase
	ROCE and ROSF	Increase

Exercise 10.5

Figure A10.2 is a print-out of the spreadsheet template.

Exercise 10.6

Scenario 1

Result: Gross margin is depressed, which in turn results in a lower net margin and reduced ROCE and ROSF.

Scenario 2

Result: Higher expenses feed into a lower net margin and therefore lower ROCE and ROSF.

Scenario 3

Result: Creditors' payment period increases, resulting in lower liquidity and therefore higher asset turnover. An increase in ROCE and ROSF results.

Scenario 4

Result: There is a trade-off between the two main effects. Higher stock holding means lower stock turnover, which depresses asset turnover. However, the higher gross margin available results in an improved net margin. These two effects more or less balance each other.

Scenario 5

Result: Initially, asset turnover is depressed, as there is a lag between the investment in fixed assets and the sales generated from that investment. Lower ROCE results. However, this illustrates one of the limitations of ratio analysis. It only focuses on the historical performance and current figures. In this sense it encourages a certain amount of short-termism, ignoring potential long-term future returns.

Chapter 11

Exercise 11.1

Reasons why a business needs to forecast demand for its products:

- To reduce uncertainty
- To assist with future planning
- To make the best use of available information
- To keep ahead of the competition
- To estimate what might happen if a particular course of action is taken

Exercise 11.2

Examples are:

- Financial statements
- Sales records
- Industry reports
- Consumer information

Exercise 11.3

The answer is presented in Table A11.1.

TABLE A11.1

PLANNING HORIZONS	
Variable	**Time Period**
Share price of a quoted company	Minute-by-minute End of trading day
Profit	Monthly, annual
Sales	Daily, weekly, monthly, quarterly, annual
Stock levels	Daily, annual

Exercise 11.4

Some of the more striking features in Figure 11.1 are the regular pattern of sales from year to year and the overall upward movement in the sales over the years.

Exercise 11.5

Table A11.2 shows the time series analysis of UK consumers' expenditure on clothing: Some numbers in Table A11.2 are

TABLE A11.2

UK CONSUMERS' EXPENDITURE ON CLOTHING: TIME SERIES ANALYSIS

PERIOD (Yr/Qtr)	EXPENDITURE (£m)	4-QUARTERLY MOVING AVERAGE	ADD IN PAIRS	CENTRED AVERAGE (TREND) £m	EXP/TREND * 100
1988/1	3034				
/2	3284				
/3	3486	3658.75	7328.3	3664.1	95.1
/4	4831	3669.50	7349.8	3674.9	131.5
1989/1	3077	3680.25	7353.5	3676.8	83.7
/2	3327	3673.25	7330.8	3665.4	90.8
/3	3458	3657.50	7312.8	3656.4	94.6
/4	4768	3655.25	7318.3	3659.1	130.3
1990/1	3068	3663.00	7338.3	3669.1	83.6
/2	3358	3675.25	7322.8	3661.4	91.7
/3	3507	3647.50	7288.8	3644.4	96.2
/4	4657	3641.25	7261.5	3630.8	128.3
1991/1	3043	3620.25	7226.8	3613.4	84.2
/2	3274	3606.50	7223.5	3611.8	90.6
/3	3452	3617.00			
/4	4699				

YEAR	QTR 1	QTR 2	QTR 3	QTR 4	
1988			95.1	131.5	
1989	83.7	90.8	94.6	130.3	
1990	83.6	91.7	96.2	128.3	
1991	84.2	90.6			TOTAL
Unadjusted ave	83.8	91.0	95.3	130.0	400.2
Adjusted ave	83.8	91.0	95.3	129.9	400.0

Using Figure A11.1, we can estimate the trend for 1992 by extending the trend line.

	QUARTER 1	QUARTER 2	QUARTER 3	QUARTER 4
Trend £m	3580	3560	3540	3520

Multiplying by the seasonal variation we can predict the actual expenditure in 1992

Seasonal factor %	83.8	91	95.3	129.9
Forecast expenditure £m	3000	3240	3374	4572

Discrepancies between the actual and forecasted expenditure in this instance may be attributed to cyclical variations.

FIGURE A11.1

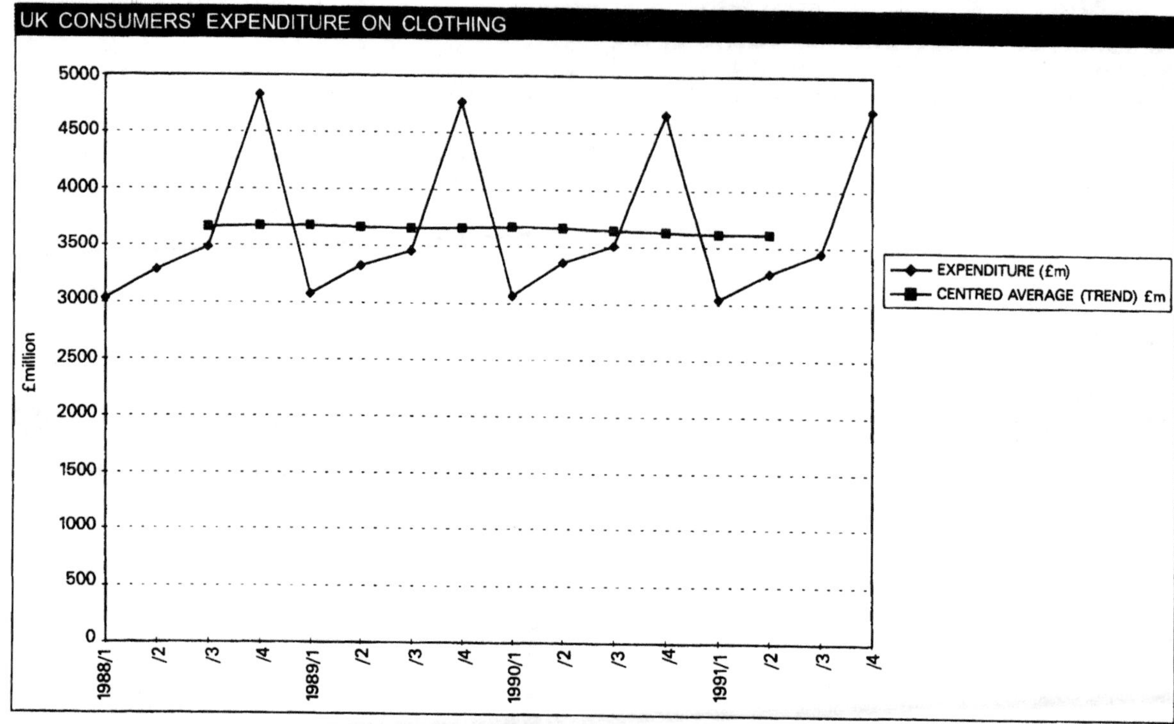

FIGURE A11.2

SCRUMTELLO'S DIY SUPERSTORE: HISTORIGRAM OF SALES

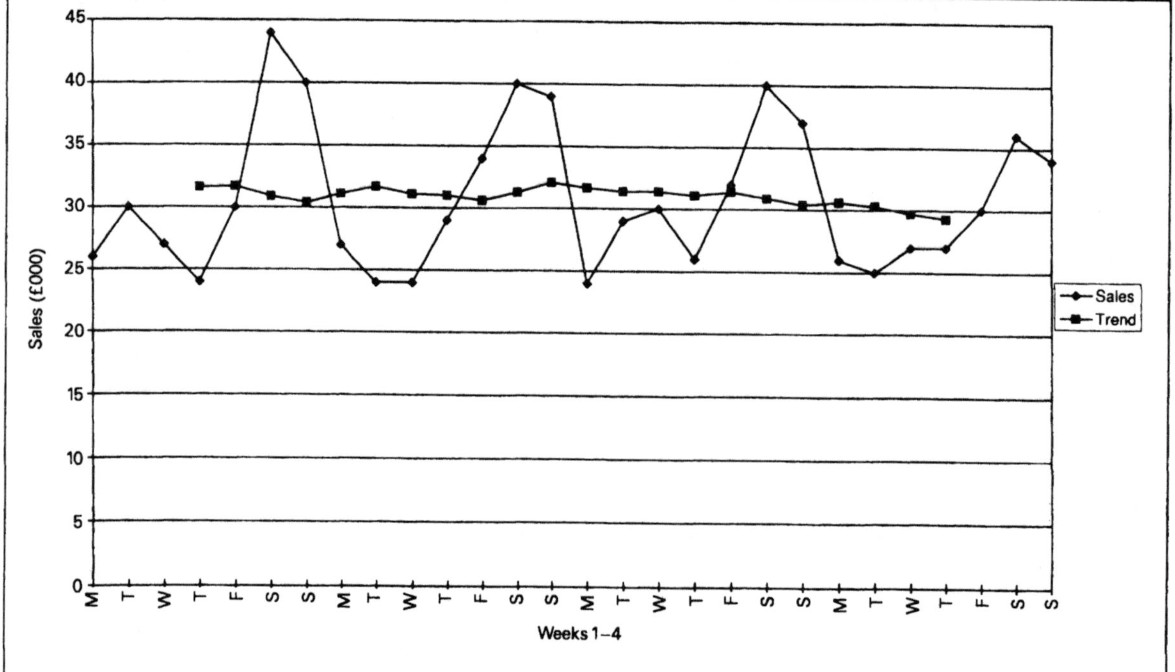

Sales (£000)

Weeks 1–4

Sales

Trend

displayed rounded to one decimal place. Figure A11.1 shows the graph of the trend.

Exercise 11.6

Figure A11.2 shows the historigram. The trend is more or less constant but is tending to move downwards. Predictions are shown in Table A11.3.

TABLE A11.3

SCRUMTELLO'S DIY SUPERSTORE: PREDICTIONS OF TREND (£000) FOR WEEK 5 (TO NEAREST THOUSAND)						
Mon	**Tue**	**Wed**	**Thu**	**Fri**	**Sat**	**Sun**
30	30	30	30	29	29	29

Exercise 11.7

Table A11.4 shows the sales forecast.

TABLE A11.4

SCRUMTELLO'S DIY SUPERSTORE: FORECAST SALES (£000) FOR WEEK 5 (TO NEAREST THOUSAND)	
Mon	$30*82.4\%=25$
Tue	$30*83.4\%=25$
Wed	$30*87.7\%=26$
Thu	$30*86.2\%=26$
Fri	$29*102.4\%=30$
Sat	$29*133.2\%=39$
Sun	$29*124.7\%=36$

Chapter 12

Exercise 12.1

Table A12.1 shows the spreadsheet layout.

Chapter 13

Exercise 13.1

The demand forecast calculation for the off-licence chain is:

Demand forecast for spirits

$$\begin{aligned}\text{Forecast demand} &= 0.7*12+(1-0.7)*14\\ &= 8.4+4.2\\ &= 12.6\end{aligned}$$

This is 13 cases when rounded to the nearest whole case

Of course, when ordering stock, any minimum-order quantities will need to be taken into account but the method indicates the desired order figure.

Exercise 13.2

See Table A13.1. All forecasts have been rounded to the nearest whole number and the rounded value used in the subsequent calculation.

TABLE A13.1

CYCLE SHOP: DEMAND DURING 19X3		
Month	**Actual Demand**	**Forecast Demand**
January	32	32
February	20	32
March	36	28
April	43	30
May	47	34
June	50	38
July	56	42
August	46	46
September	65	46
October	37	52
November	35	48
December	75	44

The exponential smoothing has resulted in a series that fluctuates less than the actual monthly demands. Only in August has it predicted the demand accurately. The exponentially smoothed series shows the trend of sales but it appears likely that there are seasonal variations so a time series analysis might be more helpful to predict the monthly demand.

Exercise 13.3

Mean daily demand

$$= (6+7+7+8+10+10+8)/7 = 56/7 = 8$$

TABLE A12.1

SPREADSHEET LAYOUT WITH FORMULAE FOR EXERCISE 12.1

	A	B	C	D	E	F
1	PERIOD	EXPENDITURE	4-QUARTERLY	ADD IN PAIRS	CENTRED AVERAGE	EXP/TREND*100
2	(Yr/Qtr)	(£m)	MOVING AVERAGE		(TREND) £m	
3						
4	1988/1	3034				
5	/2	3284				
6	/3	3486	=SUM(B4:B7)/4	=C6+C7	=D6/2	=B6/E6*100
7	/4	4831	=SUM(B5:B8)/4	=C7+C8	=D7/2	=B7/E7*100
8	1989/1	3077	=SUM(B6:B9)/4	=C8+C9	=D8/2	=B8/E8*100
9	/2	3327	=SUM(B7:B10)/4	=C9+C10	=D9/2	=B9/E9*100
10	/3	3458	=SUM(B8:B11)/4	=C10+C11	=D10/2	=B10/E10*100
11	/4	4768	=SUM(B9:B12)/4	=C11+C12	=D11/2	=B11/E11*100
12	1990/1	3068	=SUM(B10:B13)/4	=C12+C13	=D12/2	=B12/E12*100
13	/2	3358	=SUM(B11:B14)/4	=C13+C14	=D13/2	=B13/E13*100
14	/3	3507	=SUM(B12:B15)/4	=C14+C15	=D14/2	=B14/E14*100
15	/4	4657	=SUM(B13:B16)/4	=C15+C16	=D15/2	=B15/E15*100
16	1991/1	3043	=SUM(B14:B17)/4	=C16+C17	=D16/2	=B16/E16*100
17	/2	3274	=SUM(B15:B18)/4	=C17+C18	=D17/2	=B17/E17*100
18	/3	3452	=SUM(B16:B19)/4			
19	/4	4699				
20						
21						
22						
23						
24						
25						
26						
27						
28						
29						
30	YEAR	QTR 1	QTR 2	QTR 3	QTR 4	
31	1988			=F6	=F7	
32	1989	=F8	=F9	=F10	=F11	
33	1990	=F12	=F13	=F14	=F15	
34	1991	=F16	=F17			TOTAL
35	Unadjusted ave	=AVERAGE(B32:B34)	=AVERAGE(C32:C34)	=AVERAGE(D31:D33)	=AVERAGE(E31:E33)	=SUM(B35:E35)
36	Adjusted ave	=B35*400/$F$35	=C35*400/$F$35	=D35*400/$F$35	=E35*400/$F$35	=F35*400/$F$35

Exercise 13.4

See Table A13.2. The smoothed mean absolute deviations have been rounded at every stage.

TABLE A13.2

SOFTLIGHT VERTICAL BLINDS: FORECAST ERRORS (α =0.8)

Week	Demand £	Forecast (α =0.8)	Forecast Error	Absolute Deviation	Smoothed MAD
1	9 540	–	–	–	–
2	10 350	9 540	−810	810	810
3	9 760	10 188	+428	428	504
4	9 250	9 846	+596	596	578
5	10 960	9 369	−1 591	1 591	1 388
6	10 650	10 642	−8	8	284
7	10 040	10 648	+608	608	543
8	9 870	10 162	+292	292	342
9	9 890	9 928	+38	38	99
10	9 430	9 898	+468	468	394
11	9 130	9 524	+394	394	394
12	9 980	9 209	−771	771	696

Once again the forecast is above the actual demand in seven weeks and below the actual demand in four weeks but the absolute deviations are much more varied in size. In weeks 6 and 9 the forecasts were very close to the actual values but in week 5 there was a much greater discrepancy than when α equals 0.4.

The smoothed mean absolute deviations are smaller on the whole than for $\alpha = 0.4$ but there is a large value in Week 5. It might be wise to consider an intermediate value of α to see whether that gives a closer fit.

Exercise 13.5

(a) See Table A13.3. $\alpha = 0.3$ gives the most accurate forecast.
The prediction for January 19X4 is 244 cases.

(b) See Table A13.4. The forecasts for $\alpha = 0.5$ and $\alpha = 0.7$ give similar accuracy overall but the higher value responds more rapidly to the sudden increase in July. Using $\alpha = 0.7$, prediction for January 19X4 is 272 cases.

(c) See Table A13.5. None of the forecasts is particularly good as they consistently tend to underestimate this series. $\alpha = 0.7$ is most accurate. Prediction for January 19X4 is 228 cases.

TABLE A13.3

WASHING-UP LIQUID: MONTHLY DEMAND 19X3, DATA SET (a)

		Forecast		
		$\alpha=0.3$	$\alpha=0.5$	$\alpha=0.7$
Jan	242	–	–	–
Feb	215	242	242	242
Mar	215	234	229	223
Apr	257	228	222	217
May	232	237	240	245
Jun	245	236	236	236
Jul	225	239	241	242
Aug	242	235	233	230
Sep	246	237	238	238
Oct	223	240	242	244
Nov	232	235	233	229
Dec	267	234	233	231

TABLE A13.4

WASHING-UP LIQUID: MONTHLY DEMAND 19X3, DATA SET (b)

		Forecast		
		$\alpha=0.3$	$\alpha=0.5$	$\alpha=0.7$
Jan	186	–	–	–
Feb	205	186	186	186
Mar	223	192	196	199
Apr	189	201	210	216
May	175	197	200	197
Jun	208	190	188	182
Jul	296	195	198	200
Aug	279	225	247	267
Sep	260	241	263	275
Oct	285	247	262	265
Nov	276	258	274	279
Dec	270	263	275	277

In **(a)** the demand was fluctuating randomly about a constant mean and a low value of the smoothing constant was adequate. In **(b)** there was a sudden increase in demand and a large value of the smoothing constant was preferred. In **(c)** there appears to be random fluctuations about a rising trend and in this case none of the values suggested for the smoothing constant seems appropriate. In such cases a more elaborate exponential smoothing model is required.

TABLE A13.5

WASHING-UP LIQUID:
MONTHLY DEMAND 19X3, DATA SET (c)

		Forecast		
		$\alpha=0.3$	$\alpha=0.5$	$\alpha=0.7$
Jan	152	–	–	–
Feb	145	152	152	152
Mar	145	150	149	147
Apr	156	149	147	146
May	186	151	152	153
Jun	194	162	169	176
Jul	190	172	182	189
Aug	225	177	186	190
Sep	217	191	206	215
Oct	206	199	212	216
Nov	231	201	209	209
Dec	229	210	220	224

Chapter 14

Exercise 14.1

A glance at the data leaves the impression that larger values of turnover are associated with higher population values. This suggests that as the population numbers in the vicinity of a store increase so does the turnover in the store.

Exercise 14.2

There are unlimited possibilities here. Try collecting data on pairs of variables you think may be related and plot the corresponding scatter diagrams.

FIGURE A14.1

EXERCISE 14.3: SCATTER DIAGRAM

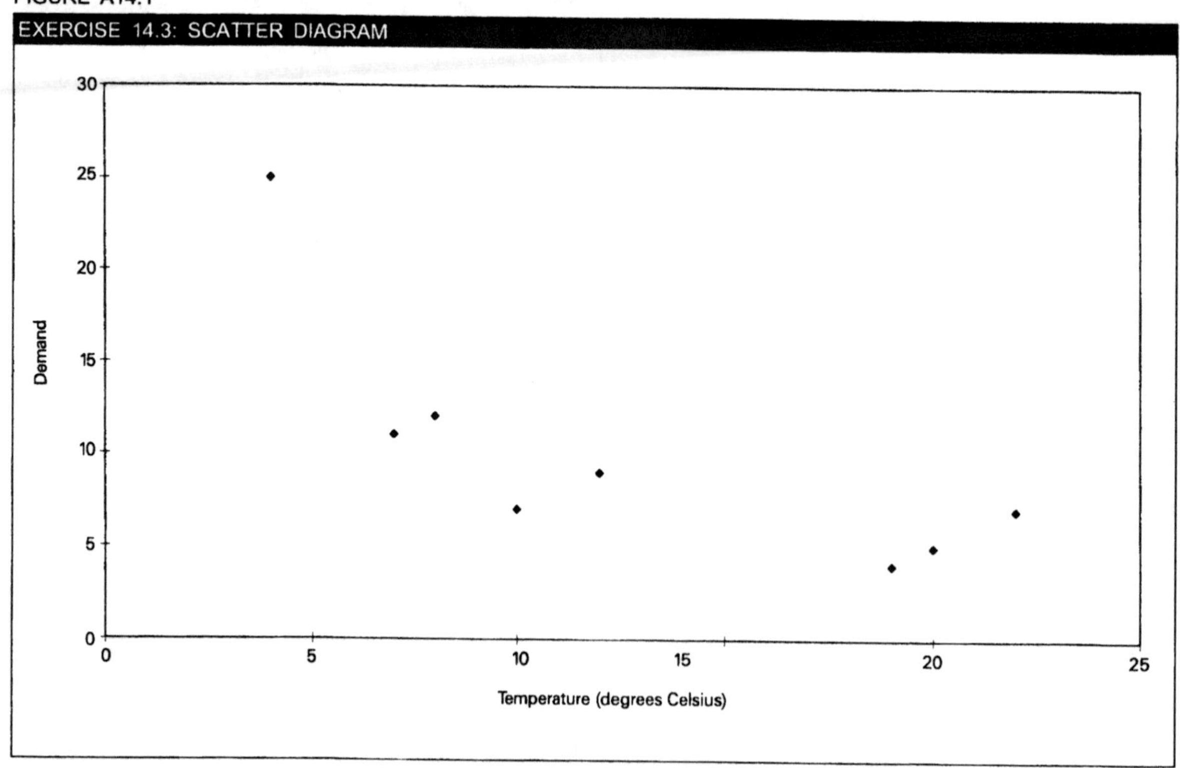

Exercise 14.3

$\Sigma x = 102$ $\Sigma y = 80$ $\Sigma x^2 = 1618$ $\Sigma y^2 = 1110$ $\Sigma xy = 781$

$$r = \frac{n\Sigma xy - \Sigma x \Sigma y}{\sqrt{(n\Sigma x^2 - (\Sigma x)^2)} * \sqrt{(n\Sigma y^2 - (\Sigma y)^2)}}$$

$$= \frac{8 * 781 - 102 * 80}{\sqrt{(8 * 1618 - (102)^2)} * \sqrt{(8 * 1110 - (80)^2)}}$$

$$= \frac{-1912}{\sqrt{2540} * \sqrt{2480}}$$

$$= \frac{-1912}{50.398 * 49.800}$$

$$= \frac{-1912}{2509.82}$$

$$= -0.76.$$

A correlation coefficient **r** $= -0.76$ indicates a strong negative relationship. As the temperature increases, the number of sweaters sold decreases. The scatter diagram is shown in Figure A14.1.

Chapter 15

Exercise 15.1

The answer is shown in Table A15.1 and Figure A15.1.

TABLE A15.1

SLOPE AND INTERCEPT: RESULTS		
(a)	Slope = 3	Intercept = 10
(b)	Slope = −10	Intercept = 250
(c)	Slope = −1	Intercept = 0.256
(d)	Slope = 4	Intercept = 0

Exercise 15.2

(a) Cost = £(150 + 12 * 200) = £(150 + 2400) = £2550

(b) Every extra PCB produced adds £12 to the daily production cost. (This is called a *variable cost* and will be discussed in more detail in Chapter 22.)

(c) The value of the intercept tells us that even if the factory produces nothing, there will be a cost of £150 per day. This cost arises, for example, from providing equipment and utilities regardless of whether these are in use or not. (This is called a *fixed cost* and will be discussed in Chapter 22.)

Exercise 15.3

The equation of the regression line is **y** = 19.6 − 0.753**x**. This tells us that for every degree rise in temperature we can expect the demand for wool sweaters to drop by 0.75. The scatter diagram is shown in Figure A15.2.

Exercise 15.4

(a) When x = 13, y = 9.8

(b) When x = 1, y = 18.8

We would predict sales of 10 sweaters when the temperature is 13 degrees and 19 sweaters when the temperature is 1 degree.

As we found in Exercise 14.3, the correlation coefficient is −0.76 indicating a strong negative relationship for the data. A temperature of 13 degrees is within the range of the data so we can feel reasonably confident about the estimate in **(a)**. On the other hand, a temperature of 1 degree is lower than any of our data values so we should treat the estimate in **(b)** with caution. The weather in this case is so cold that a much larger demand might be expected and this is supported by a demand of 25 sweaters in the coldest week recorded in the data when the temperature was 4 degrees.

FIGURE A15.1(a)

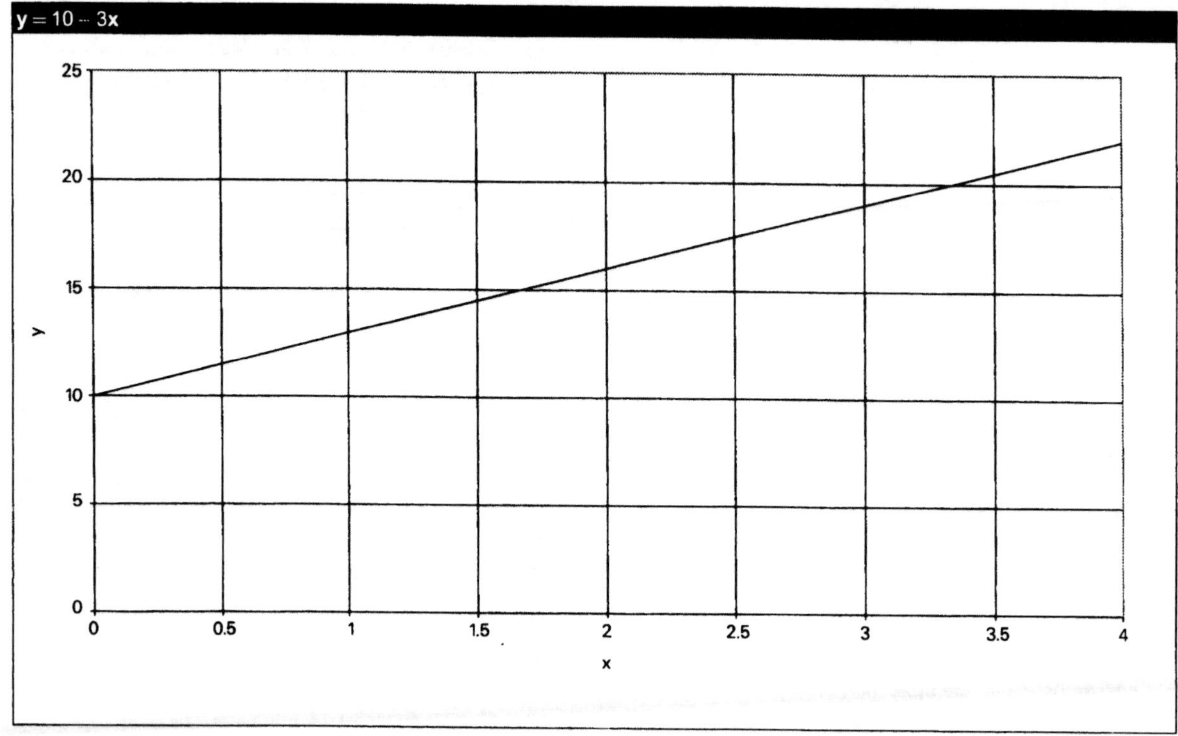

FIGURE A15.1(b)

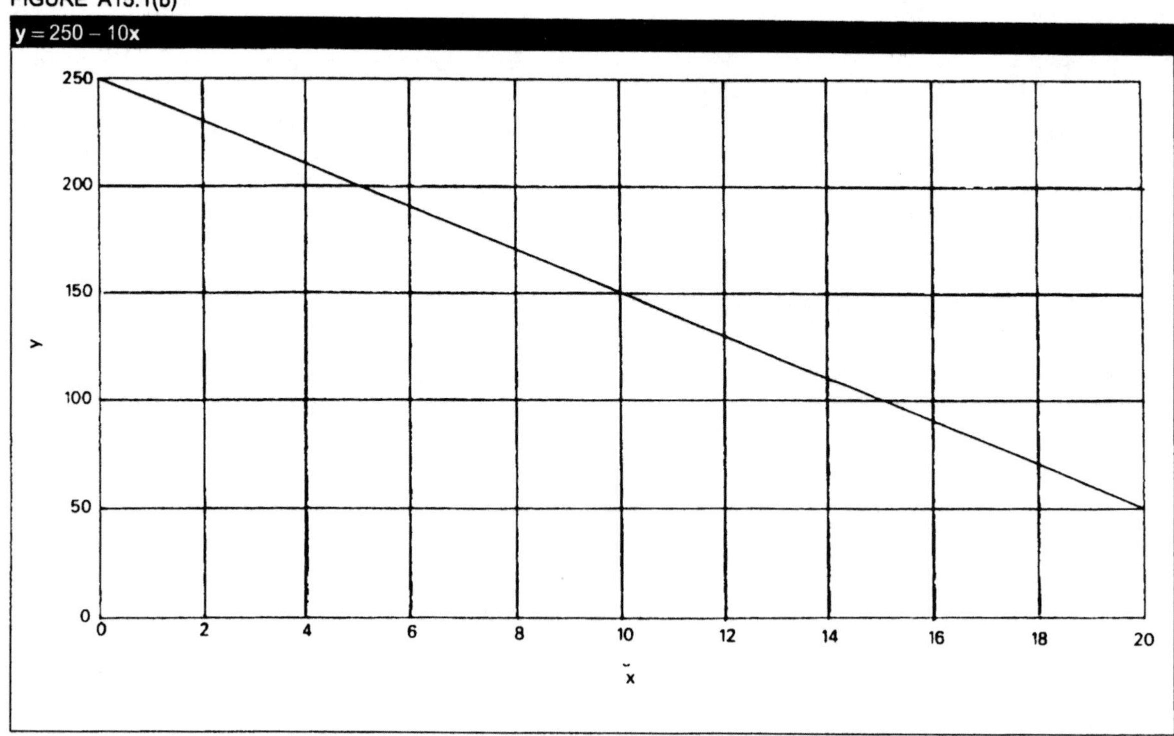

FIGURE A15.1(c)

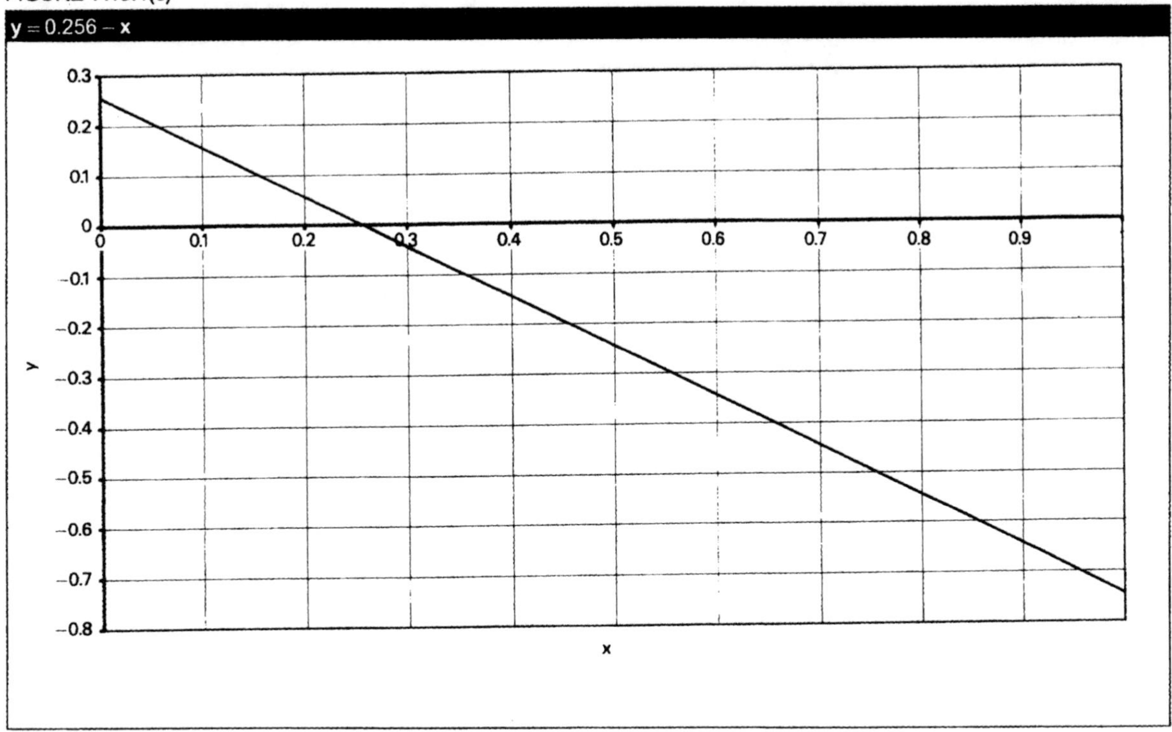

FIGURE A15.1(d)

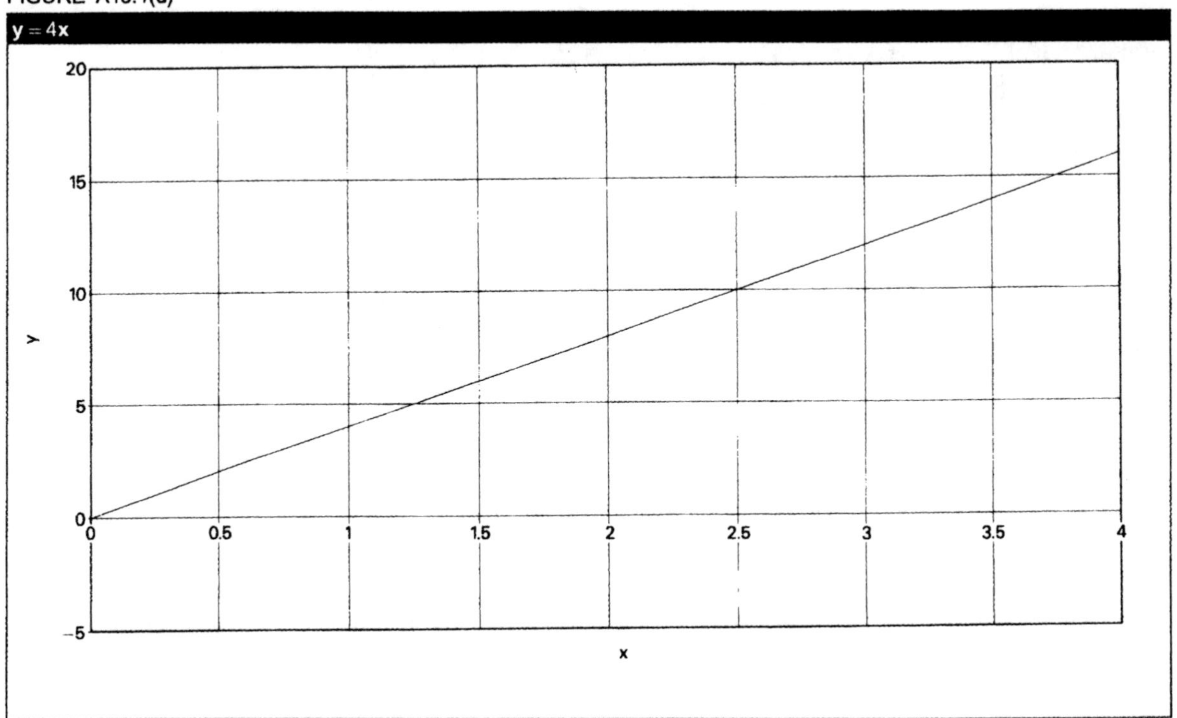

FIGURE A15.2

SCATTER DIAGRAM WITH REGRESSION LINE

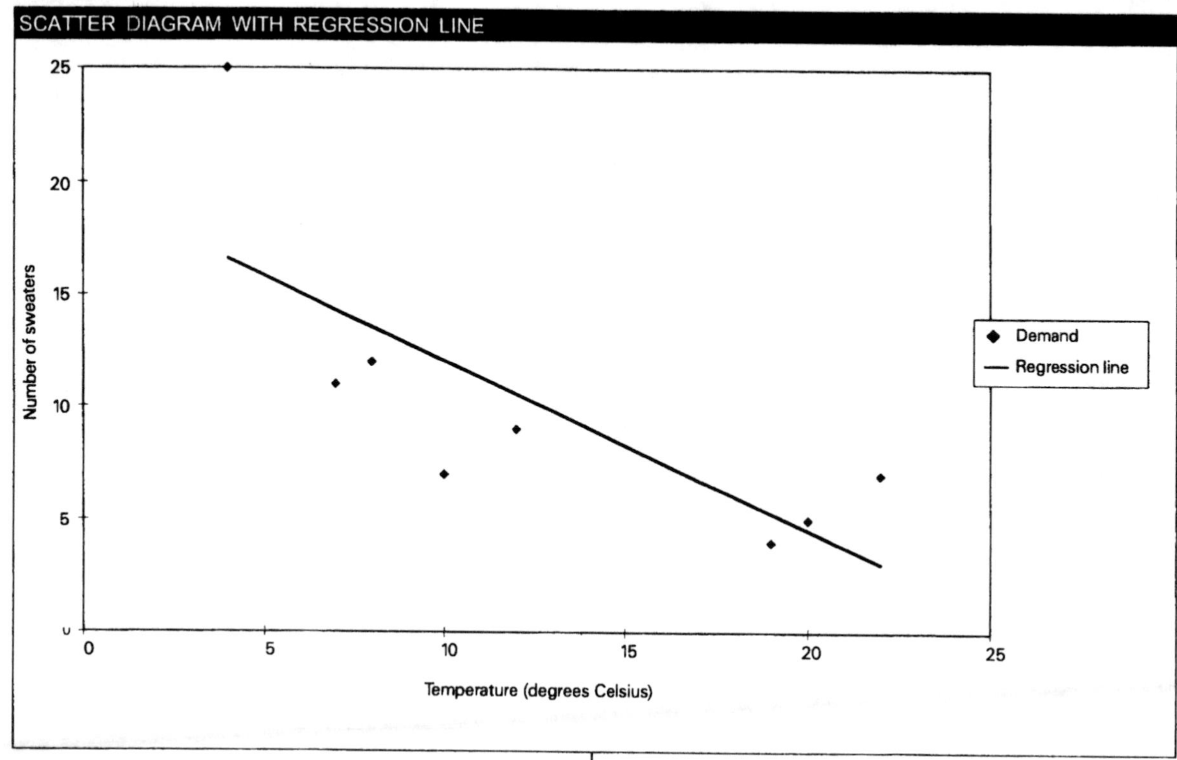

Chapter 16

Exercise 16.1

The finished chart should be similar to Figure 14.1 (p. 114).

Exercise 16.2

We can say that 74.4 per cent of the changes in household expenditure on clothing can be explained by changes in household income but only 54.5 per cent of the changes in household expenditure on clothing can be explained by changes in household size. We conclude that the stronger relationship is the one between expenditure and income.

Exercise 16.3

The regression equation is

$$\mathbf{y} = 16.00 + 0.0154\mathbf{x}$$

where **x** is the floor area in square feet

y is the monthly sales in £000

Correlation coefficient = 0.819
Coefficient of determination = 0.670
P-value of **X Variable 1** = 0.006968

When **x** = 2500, **y** = 16.00 + 0.0154 * 2500 = 54.5
Predicted value of sales = £54 500
Provided there are no sudden changes in sales conditions and coefficient is close to +1, indicating strong positive correlation. The coefficient of determination indicates that 67 per cent of the changes in sales can be explained by the changes in floor area using this regression equation. The sales area in the prediction is within the range of the data.

Exercise 16.4

(a) The regression equation is **y** = 19.6 − 0.753**x**

(b) The correlation coefficient is −0.762. Note that Excel does not give the sign of **r**; you can tell that it is negative correlation from inspection of the scatter diagram or by

FIGURE A16.1

EXERCISE 16.4: REGRESSION PRINT-OUT

SUMMARY OUTPUT						
Regression Statistics						
Multiple R	0.762					
R Square	0.580					
Adjusted R Square	0.510					
Standard Error	4.656					
Observations	8					
ANOVA						
	df	*SS*	*MS*	*F*	*Significance F*	
Regression	1	179.9087	179.9087	8.2976	0.0280	
Residual	6	130.0913	21.6819			
Total	7	310				
	Coefficients	*Standard Error*	*t Stat*	*P-value*	*Lower 95%*	*Upper 95%*
Intercept	19.5976	3.7164	5.2733	0.0019	10.5040	28.6913
X Variable 1	-0.7528	0.2613	-2.8806	0.0280	-1.3922	-0.1133

noting that the **X Variable 1** coefficient in the regression equation is negative

(c) The coefficient of determination is 0.580

(d) The **P**-value corresponding to **X Variable 1** is 0.0280

The regression equation is a good fit because the **P**-value is less than 0.05. The coefficient of determination tells us that 58 per cent of the variation in demand for sweaters can be explained by changes in temperature through this regression equation.

When $\mathbf{x} = 12$, $\mathbf{y} = 19.6 - 0.753 * 12 = 10.564$. We estimate that 10 or 11 sweaters will be sold when the temperature is 12 degrees. The regression print-out is shown in Figure A16.1.

Chapter 17

Exercise 17.1

Your scatter diagram should indicate fairly strong positive correlation; look at Figure A17.1.

Exercise 17.2

Interpreting the output, we see the linear regression model is

$$\mathbf{y} = -49.42 + 24.54\mathbf{x}$$

where $\mathbf{y}$ = Sales (£000) and $\mathbf{x}$ = Number of employees

Alternatively, we can write the model as

Sales (£000) = −49.42 + 24.54 * Number of employees

The other values of interest to us from the output are

the correlation coefficient (multiple **R**)	0.471
the coefficient of determination (**R** square)	0.222
the **X Variable 1** (Employees) **P**-value	0.1698

We conclude that we have fairly weak positive correlation and that only 22.2 per cent of the variation in Sales can be explained by this linear relationship with Number of employees. The **P**-value for the Employees variable is greater than 0.05 so we cannot be confident that there is a linear relationship with Number of employees.

Your diagram should show a wide scatter of points about the regression line.

Exercise 17.3

Sales (£000) = 129.8 + 3.493 * Floorspace (000 sq ft)

When Floorspace = 35 (000 sq ft)

Sales (£000) = 129.8 + 3.493 * 35 = 252.055

Estimated sales = £252 000

Sales (£000) = −49.42 + 24.54 * Number of employees

FIGURE A17.1

RELATIONSHIP BETWEEN SALES AND FLOORSPACE

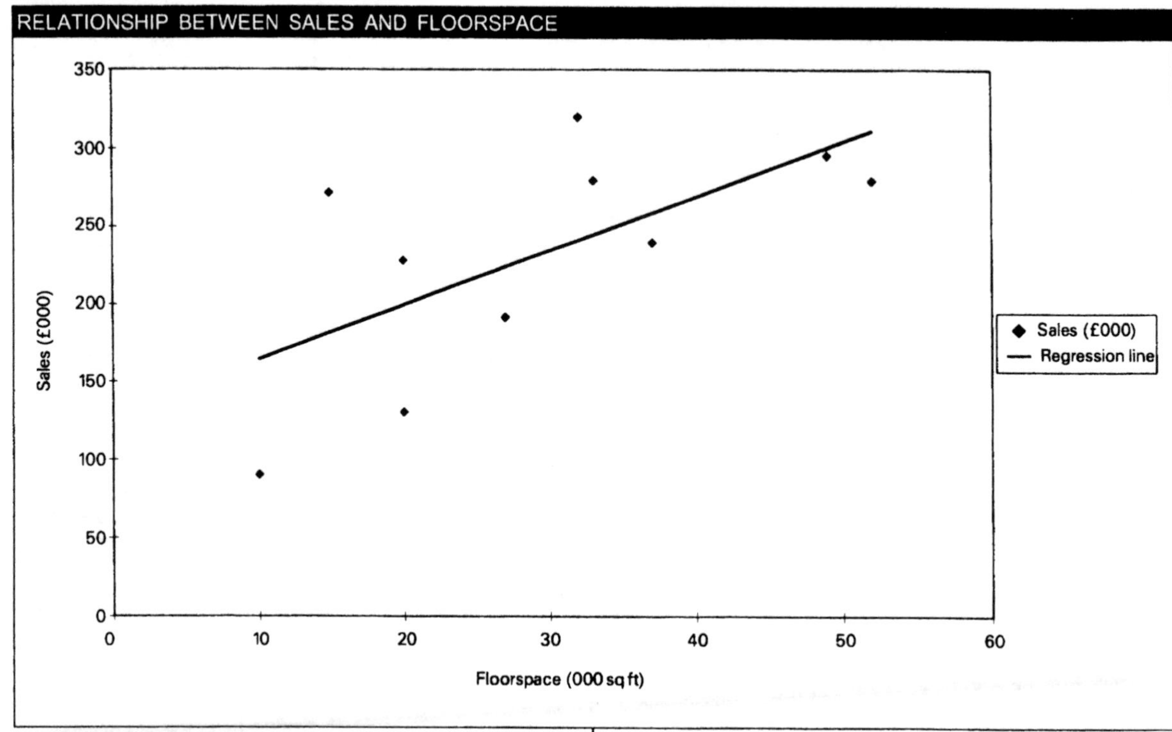

When Number of employees = 14

Sales (£000) = −49.42 + 24.54 * 14 = 294.14

Estimated sales = £294 000

These two estimates are less than the multiple regression estimate. As a test of the model, we should try to find a store of this size and number of employees and see which of the three estimates is closest. If the multiple regression model does perform better than the other two, then this would be additional evidence in its favour.

Exercise 17.4

The regression analysis is given in Figure A17.2.

From the output it can be seen that the best fit is given by the linear regression model of expenditure on income, as this is the only model where the **P**-value is less than 0.05. In this model, however, only 37.6 per cent of the variation in expenditure is explained by the changes in income.The **R** square value in the multiple regression model at 0.473 is higher but the **P**-values and the **Significance F** value are all above 0.05 so we would not have as much confidence in the predictions made with this equation.

The regression equation is

Expenditure (£00) = 24.95 + 0.529 * Income (£000)

When Income = 25 (£000)

Expenditure (£00) = 24.95 + 0.529 * 25 = 38.175

We predict that, if a customer of Lively Oldies Travel Company has an after-tax income of £25 000, their annual expenditure on travel will be approximately £3800.

Chapter 18

The answer to Exercise 18.1 is provided in the text.

Exercise 18.2

Allocate

Counter staff wages, £20 worth of perishable items which have passed their sell-by date, and must be destroyed, Electronic scales, Plastic bags, Set of knives.

Apportion

Rent, Store manager's salary, Cleaner's wage.

FIGURE A17.2

LIVELY OLDIES TRAVEL COMPANY: REGRESSION OUTPUT

SUMMARY REGRESSION OUTPUT

EXPENDITURE on AGE

Regression Statistics	
Multiple R	0.4636
R Square	0.2149
Adjusted R Square	0.1364
Standard Error	8.3790
Observations	12

ANOVA

	df	*SS*	*MS*	*F*	*Significance F*
Regression	1	192.182	192.182	2.737	0.129
Residual	10	702.068	70.207		
Total	11	894.25			

	Coefficients	*Standard Error*	*t Stat*	*P-value*	*Lower 95%*	*Upper 95%*
Intercept	4.1086	21.0770	0.1949	0.8494	-42.8539	51.0710
X Variable 1	0.5222	0.3156	1.6545	0.1290	-0.1811	1.2255

EXPENDITURE on INCOME

Regression Statistics	
Multiple R	0.6130
R Square	0.3758
Adjusted R Square	0.3133
Standard Error	7.4714
Observations	12

ANOVA

	df	*SS*	*MS*	*F*	*Significance F*
Regression	1	336.029	336.029	6.020	0.034
Residual	10	558.221	55.822		
Total	11	894.25			

	Coefficients	*Standard Error*	*t Stat*	*P-value*	*Lower 95%*	*Upper 95%*
Intercept	24.9527	6.0230	4.1429	0.0020	11.5327	38.3727
X Variable 1	0.5290	0.2156	2.4535	0.0341	0.0486	1.0094

EXPENDITURE on AGE and INCOME

Regression Statistics	
Multiple R	0.6877
R Square	0.4730
Adjusted R Square	0.3559
Standard Error	7.2365
Observations	12

ANOVA

	df	*SS*	*MS*	*F*	*Significance F*
Regression	2	422.953	211.476	4.038	0.056
Residual	9	471.297	52.366		
Total	11	894.25			

	Coefficients	*Standard Error*	*t Stat*	*P-value*	*Lower 95%*	*Upper 95%*
Intercept	2.7208	18.2151	0.1494	0.8846	-38.4846	43.9262
X Variable 1	0.3643	0.2828	1.2884	0.2297	-0.2754	1.0041
X Variable 2	0.4547	0.2166	2.0993	0.0652	-0.0353	0.9448

Exercise 18.3

The answer is shown in Figure A18.1.

FIGURE A18.1

PURELY TRAVEL LTD: COST APPORTIONMENT	
Cost	**Base for Apportionment**
Heat and Light	Floor Space
Rates	Floor Space
Clerical Expenses	Turnover
Computer System, Depreciation and Maintenance	Turnover
Canteen	Number of Employees

Exercise 18.4

(a) Grocery, Provisions, Bakery, Wines and Spirits, Kiosk, Produce, Hard Goods, Soft Goods.

Checkouts, Warehouse, Service, Canteen are service cost centres.

(b) This can be done by making broad product groups into cost centres. The ultimate step is to treat each individual product line as a cost centre in its own right.

(c) It enables management to assess the profitability of the different parts of the organisation. This facilitates a rational approach to decision-making. If profit can be assumed to be an important objective of the organisation, then a knowledge of the contribution to profit made by the different parts of the organisation allows you to boost the profitable aspects of the business and to investigate and, if necessary, eliminate the unprofitable ones. In addition, a breakdown of the organisation into profit and cost centres means that the responsibility for cost control can be given to individual managers who are then held accountable.

Exercise 18.5

(a) *Staff Wages* Apportion Base: Sales
Reason: staff switched to busy areas

Salary Cook Allocate
Reason: cook works for coffee shop only

Depreciation Fixtures and Fittings, Rent and Rates, Heat and Light Apportion Base: sq ft
Reason: charges relate to proportion of space used

Bags Apportion Base: Sales
Reason: the more sold, the more wrapped (assuming take-away trade in cafe)

Salary Manager Apportion Base: Gross profit
Reason: manager responsible for profit

(b) Figure A18.2 shows the restated profit and loss accounts.

(c) Based on the approach used above, it would seem that the coffee shop is the more profitable part of the business and shows good potential for expansion. Other considerations to be included are the likely customer demand patterns, expected reactions from the competition and the staff skills and training required if the coffee shop is expanded.

FIGURE A18.2

LORRAINE'S BREAD SHOP AND COFFEE SHOP: PROFIT AND LOSS ACCOUNT 9 OCTOBER TO 15 OCTOBER 199X

	Bread Shop	**Coffee Shop**
	£	£
Sales	6000	4000
Cost of Goods Sold	4500	2000
Gross Profit	1500	2000
Expenses		
Staff Wages	480	320
Salary Cook		150
Depreciation Fixtures and Fittings	54	34
Rent and Rates	314	196
Heat and Light	25	15
Bags	21	14
Salary Manager	122	163
	1016	892
Net Profit	484	1108

Chapter 19

Exercise 19.1

The best match between the cost items and the organisational level at which they can be controlled is **(1)** and **(C)**, **(2)** and **(A)**, **(3)** and **(B)**.

Exercise 19.2

(a) A detailed cash budget is shown in Figure A19.1.

FIGURE A19.1

JOHN BLOGGS:
CASH BUDGET OCTOBER TO DECEMBER

	October	**November**	**December**
	£	£	£
Opening Balance	50 000	(−18 117)	(−8 084)
Cash Receipts			
Bank Loan	10 000		
Cash Sales	12 500	22 500	42 500
Total Receipts	22 500	22 500	42 500
Cash Payments			
Lease Shop	50 000		
Fixtures and Fittings	10 000		
Stock	20 000		
Payments Creditors	0	5 000	9 000
Rent	4 000		
Rates	1 750		
Water	200		
Wages Staff	2 250	4 050	7 650
Salary	1 167	1 167	1 167
Promotions	1 250	2 250	4 250
Total Payments	90 617	12 467	22 067
Closing Balance	(−18 117)	(−8 084)	12 349

(b), (c) Figures A19.2 and A19.3 show summaries of the budgets for the whole three months; for a more detailed approach to monthly planning these can be broken down into monthly budgets.

FIGURE A19.2

JOHN BLOGGS: BUDGETED PROFIT AND LOSS ACCOUNT FOR THE PERIOD OCTOBER TO DECEMBER

	£	£
Sales		77 500
Gross Profit (60% of Sales)		46 500
Expenses:		
Depreciation	1 500	
Rent	4 000	
Rates	1 750	
Water	200	
Promotions	7 750	
Salary	3 501	
Wages	13 950	
		32 651
Net Profit		13 849

FIGURE A19.3

JOHN BLOGGS: BUDGETED BALANCE SHEET FOR END OF DECEMBER

	Cost	**Depreciation**	**Net Book Value**
	£	£	£
Fixed Assets			
Premises	50 000		
Fixtures and Fittings	10 000		
	60 000	1 500	58 500
Current Assets			
Stock	20 000		
Cash	12 349		
		32 349	
Creditors: due within one year			
Trade Creditors		17 000	
Net Current Assets			15 349
Net Total Assets			73 849
Creditors: due after one year			
Long-term Loan Capital			10 000
			63 849
Owner's Capital		50 000	
Retained Profit		13 849	
			63 849

Chapter 20

Exercise 20.1

The answer is presented in Figure A20.1.

FIGURE A20.1

TOY MANUFACTURER: BUDGETED PROFIT AND LOSS STATEMENT FOR THE PERIOD 1 JANUARY 19X5 TO 31 DECEMBER 19X5

		£	£
	Sales		330 000
–	Cost of Goods Sold		220 000
=	Gross Profit		110 000
–	Expenses:		
	Wages	33 000	
	Advertising	33 000	
	Rent and Rates	26 250	
			92 250
=	Net Profit		17 750

Exercise 20.2

(a) *Grocer* – For example, packing customer bags at the checkout, dealing with complaints

(b) *Public house* – For example, organising a darts team, greeting regular customers

(c) *University* – For example, marking dissertations, writing research papers

Exercise 20.3

Figure A20.2 provides the full variance analysis.

FIGURE A20.2

JINX LTD: VARIANCE ANALYSIS

	Budget	**Actual**	**Variance**	**Adverse/ Favourable**
	£	£	£	
Sales	10 000	9 000	(1 000)	**Adverse**
Cost of Goods Sold	6 000	5 800	200	**Favourable**
Gross Profit	4 000	3 200	(800)	**Adverse**
Expenses	3 000	2 800	200	**Favourable**
Net Profit	1 000	400	(600)	**Adverse**

Rule for calculating variances

Sales and Profit:	Actual – Budgeted = Variance
Cost:	Budgeted – Actual = Variance

Exercise 20.4

At a glance it is noticeable that actual sales were considerably lower than planned. The question arises why the sales forecast turned out to be so inaccurate. Maybe there were a lot of unforeseen and unpredictable factors in the environment, which could not have been anticipated. It is also surprising that rent and rates show an adverse variance, as any review in this area should have been anticipated at the time the budget was set.

However, the remainder of the cost variances appear to be favourable. If no further analysis was carried out, this could lead to the erroneous conclusion that all was well. Further calculations quickly show, that whilst the cost items were lower than the budget, this is of course only to be expected in view of the much lower sales level. Unfortunately the costs were not reduced in line with the sales, so that overall a rather large adverse variance on the net profit results.

Exercise 20.5

The full variance analysis is shown in Figure A20.3.

FIGURE A20.3

MARKET TRADER: VARIANCE ANALYSIS FOR FLEXED BUDGETED PROFIT AND LOSS STATEMENT

	Budget Boom	Budget Recession	Actual Recession	Variance
	£	£	£	£
Sales	112 000	56 000	55 500	(500)
Cost of Goods Sold	67 200	33 600	42 180	(8 580)
Gross Profit	44 800	22 400	13 320	(9 080)
Expenses				
Staff	15 680	7 840	5 550	2 290
Wrapping Material	2 240	1 120	832.50	287.50
Storage and Handling	7 840	3 920	4 162.50	(242.50)
Rent	5 000	5 000	5 200	(200)
Depreciation	1 000	1 000	1 000	0
Total Expenses	31 760	18 880	16 745	2 135
Net Profit	13 040	3 520	(3 425)	(6 945)

Exercise 20.6

Figure A20.4 is a print-out of the spreadsheet template.

Chapter 21

Exercise 21.1

Land, labour, machinery, buildings, raw materials, energy, vehicles, capital, and other similar items.

Exercise 21.2

(a) *Fixed factors*:

Head office, aeroplanes, permanent workforce

Variable factors:

In-flight meals, fuel, casual labour

FIGURE A20.4

DIY RETAILER: TEMPLATE FOR BRANCH BUDGETED PROFIT AND LOSS ACCOUNT

	A	B	C	D	E	F
1	Budgeted Profit and	Loss Account				
2		£	%	£	%	£
3		Actual	Sales	Budgeted	Sales	Variance
4	Sales					=B4-D4
5	Cost of Sales		=B5/B$4*100		=D5/D$4*100	=D5-B5
6	Gross Profit	=B4-B5	=B6/B$4*100	=D4-D5	=D6/D$4*100	=B6-D6
7						
8	Selling Expenses:					
9	Wages		=B9/B$4*100		=D9/D$4*100	=D9-B9
10	Heat and light		=B10/B$4*100		=D10/D$4*100	=D10-B10
11	Maintenance		=B11/B$4*100		=D11/D$4*100	=D11-B11
12	Telephone		=B12/B$4*100		=D12/D$4*100	=D12-B12
13	Credit charges		=B13/B$4*100		=D13/D$4*100	=D13-B13
14	Till discrepancies		=B14/B$4*100		=D14/D$4*100	=D14-B14
15	Travel		=B15/B$4*100		=D15/D$4*100	=D15-B15
16	Printing and postage		=B16/B$4*100		=D16/D$4*100	=D16-B16
17	Other		=B17/B$4*100		=D17/D$4*100	=D17-B17
18	Total Selling Expenses	=SUM(B9:B17)	=B18/B$4*100	=SUM(D9:D17)	=D18/D$4*100	=D18-B18
19						
20	Other branch expenses		=B20/B$4*100		=D20/D$4*100	=D20-B20
21	Concession income		=B21/B$4*100		=D21/D$4*100	=B21-D21
22						
23	Store Contribution	=B6-B18-B20+B21	=B23/B$4*100	=D6-D18-D20+D21	=D23/D$4*100	=B23-D23

(b) *Fixed factors*:
Premises, tables, chairs, crockery, permanent workforce, kitchen equipment
Variable factors:
Food, drink, energy for cooking, paper goods, casual labour

(c) *Fixed factors*:
Premises, fixtures and fittings, heat and light
Variable factors:
Sales wrapping

(d) *Fixed factors*:
Factory, canning machinery, permanent workforce
Variable factors:
Fruit, sugar, metal for cans, casual labour, power for operating production line

Exercise 21.3

(a) *Fixed costs*:
Rent or mortgage repayments on premises, rates, depreciation of fixtures, insurance, wages of permanent workforce
Variable costs:
Wrapping materials, purchase of shoes for re-sale
Semi-variable costs:
Telephone bill, electricity bill, cleaning and maintenance

(b) *Fixed costs:*
Rent or loan repayments on premises, rates, depreciation of machinery, insurance, wages of permanent workforce
Variable costs:
Purchase of fruit and other ingredients, metal for cans, labels, cartons for packaging, wages of casual labour
Semi-variable costs:
Gas or electricity bill, cleaning and maintenance

Exercise 21.4

(a) Current operation
Fixed factors:
Large number of highly skilled staff, relatively cheap ovens
Variable factors:
Ingredients, fuel for ovens in store

Proposed operation
Fixed factors:
Very small number of highly skilled staff (in the central production unit), expensive central ovens, chilled distribution, chilled storage in each store
Variable factors:
Large number of semi-skilled staff, fuel for ovens in store.

(b) In both situations there is high dependence on fixed factors, namely highly skilled staff and cheap ovens in the current method or expensive central oven and chilled distribution in the proposed method. In the proposed method, the majority of labour costs are variable.

(c) The central ovens allow for economies of scale because very large batches will be able to be processed together before being despatched to the separate stores. This will reduce setting-up times and minimise down-time between processing different products. There may be diseconomies of scale if the distribution system cannot operate efficiently due to congested roads or poor siting of central bakery.

Exercise 21.5

The customer perceives all the outlets as part of the same organisation and the franchisee gains the benefit of nationwide and international advertising campaigns (and their attendant publicity).

The franchisor can negotiate bulk-discounts from manufacturers resulting in lower prices to the franchisee.

Because the franchisor is well known and respected, there is less risk to the franchisee when the outlet opens. Financial institutions may be more willing to make funds available to potential franchisees and on better terms.

Exercise 21.6

The major supermarket chains use information technology in many ways: electronic point of sale (EPOS), electronic funds transfer at point of sale (EFTPOS), electronic data interchange (EDI) to order from suppliers, electronic mail to communicate with employees within the organisation, electronic stock control.

These all involve high fixed costs at installation but once in place allow for economies of scale such as greater speed at checkouts, paperless transactions, instantaneous transfer of funds, analysis of performance by product group or by product line, knowledge of customer buying habits, less wastage of produce, greater ability to meet demand and many more advantages like these.

Chapter 22

Exercise 22.1

The calculations are:

Bracken Ltd: Calculation of break-even point

Total fixed costs = £5000 per year
Total variable costs = £2.50 per unit
Unit contribution = £4 − £2.50 = £1.50

Break-even point (units) = £5000/£1.50 = 3333.33

Break-even point (£) = 3334 * £4 = £13 336

Bracken Ltd needs to sell 3334 gnomes each year to break even. This represents a sales revenue of £13 336. Note that rather than dealing with a fraction of a gnome, we have rounded up to the next whole number.

Exercise 22.2

(a) If Maria recruits only 250 members, she will be 40 contributions short of her break-even level; she will suffer a loss of 40 * £50 or £2000

(b) The most likely scenario is a membership of 400 giving a profit of (400 − 290) * £50 = £5500

Exercise 22.3

For the break-even chart (Figure A22.1), observe the following workings.

- The **X**-scale goes from 0 to 6000 units.
- The points on the revenue line are worked out like this:

  When sales volume = 0, sales revenue = 0
  When sales volume = 6000 units,
  sales revenue = 6000 * £4 = £24 000

- The **Y**-scale goes from 0 to £24 000.
- The fixed cost line is at £5000 regardless of the sales volume.

FIGURE A22.1

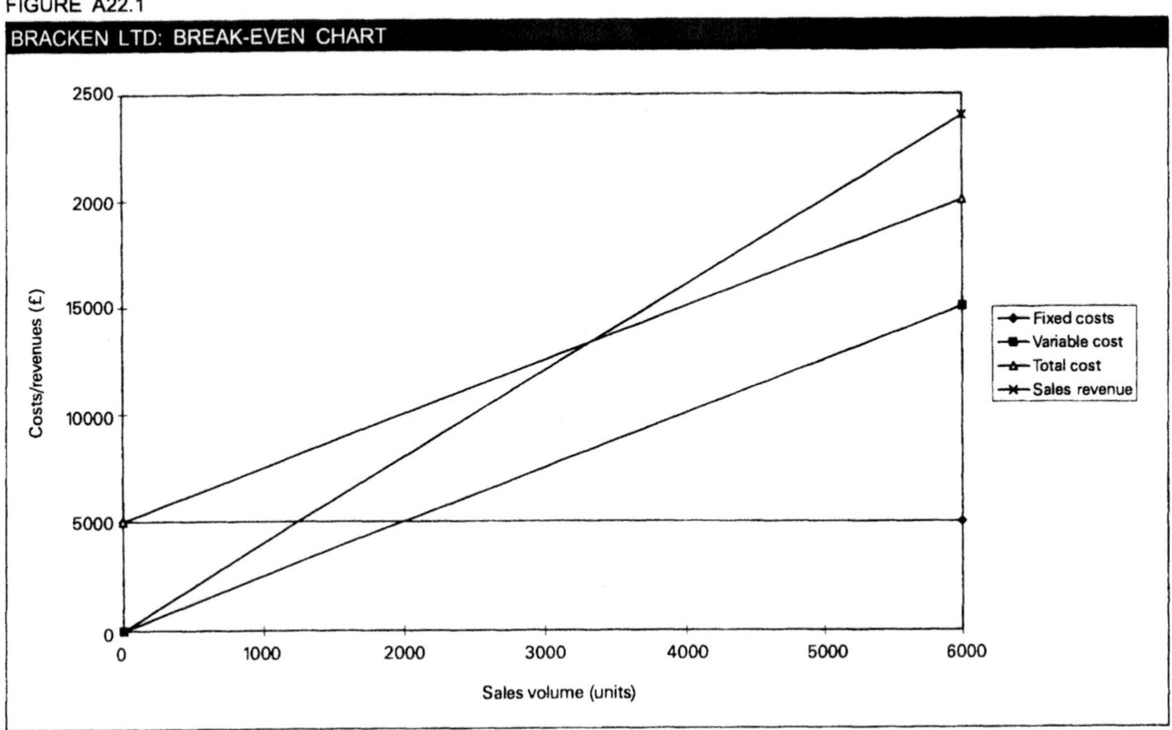

- The points on the variable cost line are worked out as follows:

  When sales volume = 0, variable cost = 0
  When sales volume = 6000 units,
  variable cost = 6000 * £2.50 = £15 000

- Finally, the total cost is computed by adding the fixed and variable cost together at the different sales volumes:

  When sales volume = 0, total cost = £5000
  When sales volume = 6000, total cost = £20 000

Drawing these revenue and cost lines on the graph enables the break-even point to be found. You will be able to obtain an approximate value only from your graph, about 3300 gnomes giving a sales revenue of around £13 400.

Profit at 5000 gnomes = £2500
Loss at 3000 gnomes = £500

Exercise 22.4

The calculations are:

Calculations for Exercise 22.4

Unit contribution = £120 − £100 = £20

Break-even point = £14 500/20 = 725 units

This corresponds to a sales revenue of £87 000

Profit if there are 750 members = 25 * £20 = £500

The break-even chart is shown in Figure A22.2.

Maria does not make as much profit as before. She is better keeping the membership fee at £150 and looking after her current 400 members well so that there is no fall off in membership.

FIGURE A22.2

MARIA'S STUDIO: NEW BREAK-EVEN CHART

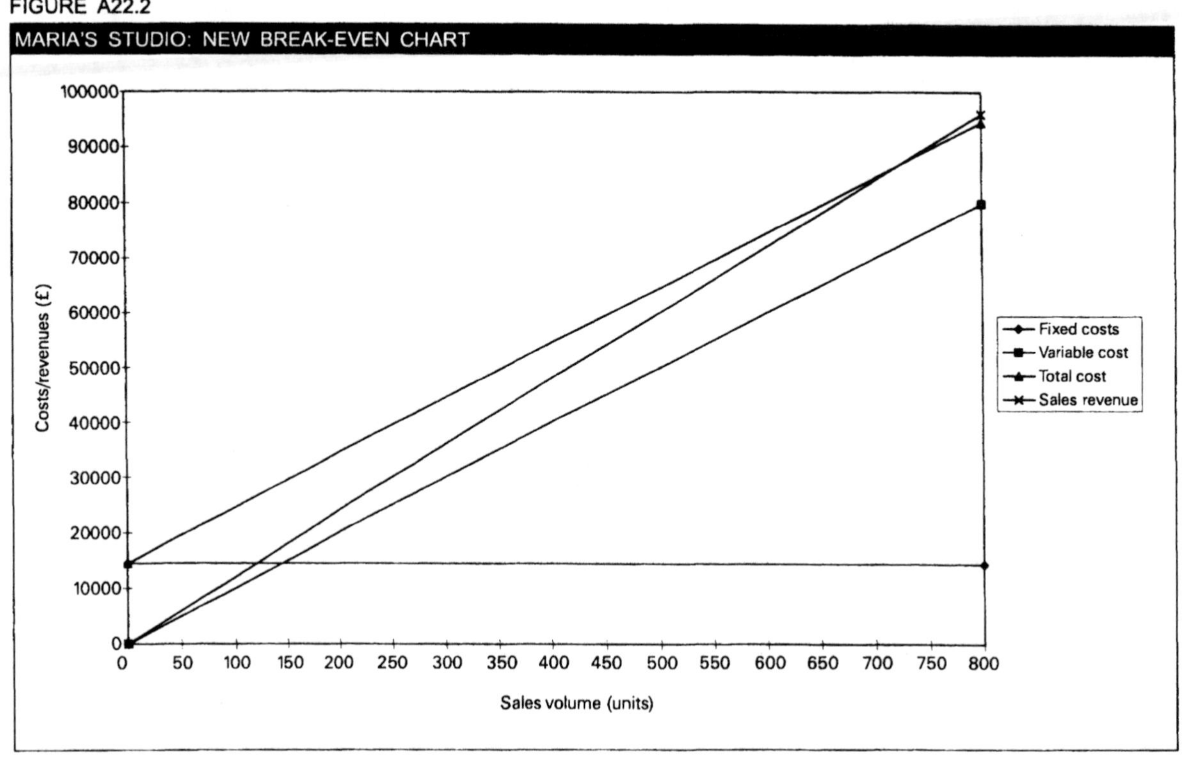

Exercise 22.5

The calculation is:

Kevin's Gym: Calculations for Exercise 22.5

Fixed Annual Costs

Depreciation Charge £150 000/6	= £25 000
Maintenance	= £ 4 000
Insurance	= £ 4 000
Total	= £33 000

Variable costs = £56 per member per year
Selling price = £150 per member per year

Unit contribution = £150 − 56 = £94

Break-even point (BEP) = £33 000/£94 = 351.1 members or £52 660 in revenue.

We can see that Kevin needs a considerably higher membership than Maria in order to break even. This is to pay for his higher fixed costs. However, once he has broken even, every new member brings him £94 extra profit as compared to the £50 that Maria gains. If Kevin's membership stabilises at 400, the same value as Maria, his profit will be (400 − BEP) * £94 = £4600. We saw in Section 22.3 that Maria's profit was £5500 at this membership level.

Exercise 22.6

The calculations are:

Maria's Studio: Comparison of alternative projects

Slendertone consultant

Extra income = 50 * £150 = £7500 per year

Massage parlour:
Annual fixed costs

Depreciation charge = £1800/6 = £300
Staff = £9000

Total fixed costs = £9300
Variable costs = £1.50 per customer
Selling price = £10 per customer
Unit contribution = £8.50
Break-even point = £9300/£8.50 = 1 094 sessions per year
This equates to 1094/50 = 22 sessions per week

Float tank:
Annual fixed costs

Depreciation charge = £30 000/6 = £5000
Staffing and cleaning = £100 * 50 = £5000

Total fixed costs = £10 000
Variable costs = £2.50 per customer
Selling price = £20 per customer
Unit contribution = £17.50
Break-even point = £10 000/£17.50 = 571.4 sessions per year
This equates to 571.4/50 = 11.4 sessions per week

The float tank has a lower break-even point. There are 320 members at present. It seems likely that as the facilities are open for a maximum of 60 sessions per week that they would be fully utilised. Based on this assumption, a comparison of potential annual profits can be carried out:

Maria's Studio: Comparison of projected profits

Annual profit from massage parlour
= (60 * 50 − 1094) * £8.50
= £16 200

Annual profit from float tank
= (60 * 50 − 571.4) * £17.50
= £42 500

Both these profits are much higher than the slendertone concession income. The float tank appears to be the best option. However, naturally other factors, such as the initial capital investment and the risk associated with the options should also be taken into consideration before making a final decision.

Chapter 23

Exercise 23.1

This answer is discussed in the text.

Exercise 23.2

The sensitivity analysis is shown in Figure A23.1.

FIGURE A23.1

KUMFEE BED COMPANY: SENSITIVITY ANALYSIS

INPUT	Bunkee	Luxuree	Sofee	Foldee
Fixed costs	23000	75000	45000	15000
Variable cost per unit	54	120	62	40
Selling price per unit	350	1650	750	120
Minimum sales volume(units)	100	50	200	300
Maximum sales volume(units)	400	250	400	800
Most likely sales volume(units)	300	150	350	600

SENSITIVITY ANALYSIS	SCENARIO 0			
Description of change	No change			
Adjusted input	Bunkee	Luxuree	Sofee	Foldee
Fixed costs	23000	75000	45000	15000
Variable cost per unit	54	120	62	40
Selling price per unit	350	1650	750	120
Minimum sales volume(units)	100	50	200	300
Maximum sales volume(units)	400	250	400	800
Most likely sales volume(units)	300	150	350	600
OUTPUT				
Unit contribution	296	1530	688	80
Break-even point (units)	77.70	49.02	65.41	187.50
Break-even point (£)	27195.95	80882.35	49055.23	22500.00
Profit/loss at minimum sales volume	6600	1500	92600	9000
Profit/loss at maximum sales volume	95400	307500	230200	49000
Profit/loss at most likely sales volume	65800	154500	195800	33000

SENSITIVITY ANALYSIS	SCENARIO 1			
Description of change	Demand down by 15%			
Adjusted input	Bunkee	Luxuree	Sofee	Foldee
Fixed costs	23000	75000	45000	15000
Variable cost per unit	54	120	62	40
Selling price per unit	350	1650	750	120
Minimum sales volume(units)	85	42.5	170	255
Maximum sales volume(units)	340	212.5	340	680
Most likely sales volume(units)	255	127.5	297.5	510
OUTPUT				
Unit contribution	296	1530	688	80
Break-even point (units)	77.70	49.02	65.41	187.50
Break-even point (£)	27195.95	80882.35	49055.23	22500.00
Profit/loss at minimum sales volume	2160	-9975	71960	5400
Profit/loss at maximum sales volume	77640	250125	188920	39400
Profit/loss at most likely sales volume	52480	120075	159680	25800

SENSITIVITY ANALYSIS	SCENARIO 2			
Description of change	Variable costs up by 20%			
Adjusted input	Bunkee	Luxuree	Sofee	Foldee
Fixed costs	23000	75000	45000	15000
Variable cost per unit	64.8	144	74.4	48
Selling price per unit	350	1650	750	120
Minimum sales volume(units)	100	50	200	300
Maximum sales volume(units)	400	250	400	800
Most likely sales volume(units)	300	150	350	600
OUTPUT				
Unit contribution	285.2	1506	675.6	72
Break-even point (units)	80.65	49.80	66.61	208.33
Break-even point (£)	28225.81	82171.31	49955.60	25000.00
Profit/loss at minimum sales volume	5520	300	90120	6600
Profit/loss at maximum sales volume	91080	301500	225240	42600
Profit/loss at most likely sales volume	62560	150900	191460	28200

SENSITIVITY ANALYSIS	SCENARIO 3			
Description of change	Selling price down by 5%			
Adjusted input	Bunkee	Luxuree	Sofee	Foldee
Fixed costs	23000	75000	45000	15000
Variable cost per unit	54	120	62	40
Selling price per unit	332.5	1567.5	712.5	114
Minimum sales volume(units)	100	50	200	300
Maximum sales volume(units)	400	250	400	800
Most likely sales volume(units)	300	150	350	600
OUTPUT				
Unit contribution	278.5	1447.5	650.5	74
Break-even point (units)	82.59	51.81	69.18	202.70
Break-even point (£)	27459.61	81217.62	49289.01	23108.11
Profit/loss at minimum sales volume	4850	-2625	85100	7200
Profit/loss at maximum sales volume	88400	286875	215200	44200
Profit/loss at most likely sales volume	60550	142125	182675	29400

SENSITIVITY ANALYSIS	SCENARIO 4			
Description of change	Fixed costs up by 5%			
Adjusted input	Bunkee	Luxuree	Sofee	Foldee
Fixed costs	24150	78750	47250	15750
Variable cost per unit	54	120	62	40
Selling price per unit	350	1650	750	120
Minimum sales volume(units)	100	50	200	300
Maximum sales volume(units)	400	250	400	800
Most likely sales volume(units)	300	150	350	600
OUTPUT				
Unit contribution	296	1530	688	80
Break-even point (units)	81.59	51.47	68.68	196.88
Break-even point (£)	28555.74	84926.47	51507.99	23625.00
Profit/loss at minimum sales volume	5450	-2250	90350	8250
Profit/loss at maximum sales volume	94250	303750	227950	48250
Profit/loss at most likely sales volume	64650	150750	193550	32250

All the beds are profitable at the most likely sales volumes. Luxuree is vulnerable to all scenarios, making a loss at lower sales volumes, except in the case of increased variable costs. Luxuree has a high selling price and the highest unit contribution, so if it were possible to stimulate demand to the high end of the range, it would offer very high profits.

Although Bunkee and Foldee have lower fixed costs, they fail to deliver high profits because the selling price is relatively low, resulting in low unit contribution. Their sales would need to be unrealistically high before their profits approached those of Sofee. If the company is confident of its demand predictions, it should choose Sofee. It has moderately high fixed costs and a mid-range price but sells reasonably well.

Exercise 23.3

Looking at Figure 23.6, we see that the video offering is a high fixed cost, low variable cost, low selling price and high sales volume operation as compared with the telephone option which, in relative terms, has a low fixed cost, high variable cost, high selling price and low sales volume.

In Scenario 0, at the most likely sales levels, the profits in the video and telephone options are £380 000 and £317 500 respectively. Although the telephone option has a higher unit contribution, the much higher sales volume of the video option pulls up the profit.

If the selling price has to be reduced, as in Scenario 1, the telephone offering is more severely affected. The two options now have a similar unit contribution but the video option generates a higher sales volume.

Again, if variable costs increase, Scenario 2, the telephone option, with its highly qualified staff is affected more.

If the demand falls off, Scenario 3, both are relatively little affected. The video profit is reduced by a greater money amount than the telephone but is still higher.

A change in fixed costs, Scenario 4, also has relatively little effect because of the high sales volumes.

It appears that the video option is the more profitable, whatever the scenario but it is vulnerable to a lower selling price. A reduction of 5 per cent in the selling price, leads to a 16 per cent decrease in profit. Provided the store is not forced into price-cutting by competitors, it should generate good profits from the video option.

Chapter 24

The answers to Exercises 24.1 and 24.2 are dealt with in the text.

Exercise 24.3

(a) The £1000 contributed to the brewery's campaign is a sunk cost and therefore does not come into this decision.

The same goes for the £150 for damages.

The £80 per week for additional bar staff is a differential cost and should be considered when taking this decision. It must be offset against the additional gross profit.

The workings for finding the additional gross profit are:

'Spread Eagle': Workings for Exercise 24.3

Extra Sales = £400 per week

$$\text{Average gross margin} = \frac{1900}{4500} = 42\%$$

Additional gross profit generated = £400 * 42% = £168

Additional net profit = £168 − £80 = £88

From a purely financial point of view it is worth keeping the pub open in the afternoon, but only just.

(b) The fact that the afternoon opening seems to have attracted undesirable clientele must be taken seriously, as it could affect the overall customer profile in the long run and down-grade the pub.

The landlord and landlady should evaluate what the overall customer profile they are aiming to attract actually is. Is there anything they can do to make the pub more attractive to families and shoppers, for instance?

It is also worth investigating whether the above calculations include any reward for the extra time spent by the landlady supervising activities from the flat above the pub premises. Often landladies are only paid a token amount and it is taken for granted that they will not object to changes in opening hours such as this, even though it could imply extra work.

Exercise 24.4

The relevant costs for taking this decision are:

Car Manufacturer: Relevant costs

	£
Raw Materials	20
Direct Labour	15
Additional Overhead	5
Opportunity Cost	60
	100

This compares favourably to the supplier's quote of £110 each

Exercise 24.5

(a) *Ignore*

Cost of rent and rates = Common costs

Cost of advertisement = Sunk cost

(b) *Relevant costs*, to be taken into account when making the decision are:

Johnson's: Relevant costs and revenues

Additional fixed cost £100

Additional revenue per week £200
Additional variable cost per week £80 = *Differential cost*
Marginal gain £120

Loss of weekly revenue £90
Loss of weekly variable cost £40 = *Opportunity cost*
Marginal loss £50

The introduction of the new product line appears to be a good idea, provided it remains popular for more than one week.

Chapter 25

Exercise 25.1

(a) Reasons for choice of pricing strategies are given in Table A25.1.

TABLE A25.1

OWN BRAND PRODUCT LINES: COMPARISON OF STRATEGIC OBJECTIVES		
	ALDI	**J Sainsbury**
(1)	Inexpensive image	High quality image
(2)	Market penetration	Very large product range
(3)	Very high stock turnover	Investment in service and technology

In your discussion of the most important influences, you have probably argued that ALDI is aiming for a high market share in the grocery discount sector and is therefore selling a limited product range and keeping prices as low as possible. In contrast, J Sainsbury plc is aiming to provide a much broader product range to a consumer from the higher socio–economic groups who is likely to have a preference for completing the full weekly shopping trip under one roof and who is therefore prepared to pay a little extra in exchange.

(b) Both companies are constrained by the costs of operations. In the long run, all costs must be recovered, otherwise the business is not viable and will go into liquidation. However, in other respects the two retailers are very different. The management of J Sainsbury plc not only have to recover costs, but they also have to achieve adequate profits which will be in line with shareholder expectations. If they fail to do so, the shareholders will take their money elsewhere. By comparison, ALDI has no shareholders but is financed through a trust fund. It is the stated objective of the fund to pursue the long-term wealth of the company. The management of the trust fund can therefore be very patient, whereas the management of J Sainsbury plc have to satisfy often impatient shareholders. This means that in the short run, a much lower ROCE is acceptable to ALDI than to J Sainsbury.

Exercise 25.2

The answer is summarised in Table A25.2.

TABLE A25.2

EVALUATION OF COST-PLUS PRICING	
Strengths	**Weaknesses**
All costs are recovered	Inaccurate
Easy to use	Potentially profitable opportunities may be forgone

The answer to Exercise 25.3 is provided in the main text.

Exercise 25.4

First of all, do not worry if you found it quite difficult to decide how to approach this exercise. So far, most of the other exercises were very specific, only requiring the use of one technique at a time – this one is complex and requires the use of several techniques to illuminate the different angles of the problem.

(1) Break-even analysis

Rather than determining the BEP for an annual set of costs and revenues, here the objective is to find out how many units need to be sold for the project to break even and to see

TABLE A25.3

DELANEY'S: BREAK-EVEN ANALYSIS BASED ON PROJECTION	
Project fixed costs	
	£
Cold Storage	650
Display Cabinet	1 800
Advertising	500
Survey	400
Promotion	500
Total	3 850
Variable Costs	£1.20/unit
Mark-up	25%
Selling Price	£1.50/unit
Contribution	£0.30/unit

$$\text{BEP} = \frac{£3850}{£0.30} = 12\ 833 \text{ units}$$

whether break-even has actually been achieved and a contribution to profit been made.

The calculations are set out in Table A25.3.

If the target mark-up had been achieved, break-even would have been reached once 12 833 units had been sold. As the forecast for the first six months only comes to 4250 units, the project still has some way to go before it breaks even.

Using the actual figures, the margins really achieved are summarised in Table A25.4.

TABLE A25.4

DELANEY'S: ACTUAL GROSS MARGINS

Month	**1**	**2**	**3**	**4**	**5**	**6**
Gross Margin	13.3%	8.5%	14.1%	8.4%	8.9%	14.9%

In other words, the average gross margin achieved was 11.35 per cent. Assuming, that a price of £1.50 per unit was charged as planned, and that the only variable costs are the purchase price, mark-downs and wastage, the actual unit contribution can be calculated and the break-even point computed on that basis, as shown in Table A25.5.

TABLE A25.5

DELANEY'S: BREAK-EVEN ANALYSIS BASED ON ACTUAL RESULTS

$$\text{Contribution} = £1.50 * 11.35\% = £0.17$$

$$\text{BEP} = \frac{£3850}{£0.17} = 22\,647 \text{ units}$$

This means that as a result of the higher variable costs, and therefore lower unit contribution, the BEP in units has nearly doubled. This is indeed cause for concern, especially since during the first six months only 1001 units have been sold (**calculation**: sum of sales revenue for the first six months divided by selling price, which was £1.50).

If the current trend continues it will take more than 10 years before the project breaks even.

(2) Short-term decision-making

Should the project be discontinued then?

An evaluation from the viewpoint of short-term decision-making is based on the figures set out in Table A25.6.

Unfortunately, if looked at from a short-term decision-making point of view, all the above costs are *sunk costs*, with the possible exception of that part of the cost of the cold storage and display equipment which could still be recovered if the equipment were sold now (or transferred to another department – that would have much the same effect, as far as this decision is concerned). As the equipment is relatively new, it seems reasonable to assume that some of this cost can be recovered – this is something that needs investigating immediately.

TABLE A25.6

DELANEY'S: PROJECT COSTS AFFECTING SHORT-TERM DECISIONS	
	£
Cold Storage	650
Display Cabinet	1 800
Advertising	500
Survey	400
Promotion	500
Total	3 850

(3) Marginal costing

Clearly the target margins have not been achieved. However, in each of the six months, the project has made a contribution to fixed costs. It should therefore not be discontinued unless it can be replaced with an alternative which guarantees a higher contribution.

(4) Variance analysis and responsibility accounting

When working through this exercise, it may also be useful to do a cash budget and a variance analysis.

This is shown in Figure A25.1.

FIGURE A25.1

DELANEY'S: CASH BUDGET AND VARIANCE ANALYSIS			
	Budget	**Actual**	**Variance**
	£	£	£
Opening Balance	0	0	0
Receipts			
Sales	6375	1502	−4873
Payments			
Cold Storage	650	650	0
Display Cabinet	1800	1800	0
Advertising	500	500	0
Survey	400	400	0
Promotions	500	500	0
Cost of Goods Sold			
Mark-downs and Wastage	5100	1336	3764
Closing Balance	−2575	−3684	−1109

This information can be used as a starting point in any discussion with the project manager. The next step would be to treat it as a *flexible budget* and adjust the budgeted figures for the actual sales volume, this would once again highlight the real problem area, which is lack of demand and resulting waste. This should then lead to an analysis including other areas of expertise.

Further analysis may assess the results of the advertising campaign and the in-store promotion, trying to get some clues as to what went wrong. Clearly Delaney's management are none too sure which niche of the market their product is aimed at and what demand, if any, exists. Further research is needed, if this project is to have a future.

Rather than carrying out some more original research in a half-hearted and ill-informed manner (and it is impossible to get any findings of real value for £400), it might be a useful starting point to look at the secondary literature and see whether there are any MINTEL or Key Note reports on this market.

Also Delaney's need to give some thought to who their customers really are, and bearing this in mind, decide what their long-term objectives for this product range should be (or alternatively whether the product range should be replaced).

Chapter 26

Exercise 26.1

The calculations are:

Calculations for Exercise 26.1

(a) Time period for compounding is 1 year

i = interest rate per year = 5% = 0.05

n = number of years = 2

Future Value = £5000 ∗ $(1+0.05)^2$ = £5000 ∗ $(1.05)^2$

= £5000 ∗ 1.1025 = £5512.50

(b) Time period for compounding is 6 months

i = interest rate per 6 months = 5%/2 = 2.5% = 0.025

n = number of 6 months = 4

Future Value = £5000 ∗ $(1+0.025)^4$ = £5000 ∗ $(1.025)^4$

= £5000 ∗ 1.10381289 = £5519.06 to the nearest penny

(c) Time period for compounding is 1 quarter

i = interest rate per quarter = 5%/4 = 1.25% = 0.0125

n = number of quarters = 8

Future Value

= £5000 ∗ $(1+0.0125)^8$ = £5000 ∗ $(1.0125)^8$

= £5000 ∗ 1.104486 = £5522.43 to the nearest penny

Exercise 26.2

(a) Option 1

Present value = £200 000

(b) Option 2

See Table A26.1

TABLE A26.1

BRIGHT OFFICE COMPANY: SCHEDULE OF PAYMENTS		
Time	**Payment**	**Present Value**
	£	£
Now	50 000	50 000
End Year 1	60 000	56 075
End Year 2	70 000	61 141
End Year 3	80 000	65 304
	Total	232 520

Present value = £232 520

The present values are worked out using the formula, as follows:

- Present value of £60 000 after 1 year = £60 000/(1 + 0.07)
- Present value of £70 000 after 2 years = £70 000/$(1+0.07)^2$

- Present value of £80 000 after 3 years $= £80\,000/(1+0.07)^3$

(c) Option 3

Present value $= £290\,000/(1+0.07)^3 = £236\,726$

The cheapest option is Option 1, which is to pay £200 000 now, but Bright Office would have to be convinced that the property company would still be around in three years' time to do the job.

Exercise 26.3

(a) Option 1
Present value = £200 000

(b) Option 2
See Table A26.2
Present value = £232 500 (to 4 significant figures)

TABLE A26.2

BRIGHT OFFICE COMPANY: SCHEDULE OF PAYMENTS USING PRESENT VALUE TABLES

Time	Payment £	Discount Factor (from Table 26.2)	Present Value £
Now	50 000	1	50 000
End Year 1	60 000	0.9346	56 076
End Year 2	70 000	0.8734	61 138
End Year 3	80 000	0.8163	65 304
		Total	232 518

(c) Option 3
Present value $= £290\,000 * 0.8163 = £236\,727 = £236\,700$ (to 4 significant figures)

Note that the answers have been rounded to 4 significant figures because the discount factors in the present value table are given to only 4 decimal places, so these answers are not as precise as using the formula. We still conclude that the cheapest option is Option 1.

Exercise 26.4

See Table A26.3

TABLE A26.3

DANNY: DCF CALCULATION

Time	Cash Flow £	Discount Factor	Present Value £
Now	−100 000	1	−100 000
End Year 1	15 000	0.9346	14 019
End Year 2	15 000	0.8734	13 101
End Year 3	30 000	0.8163	24 489
End Year 4	30 000	0.7629	22 887
End Year 5	30 000	0.7130	21 390
		Net Present Value (NPV)	−4 114

The NPV is negative. The investment is not profitable at a discount rate of 7 per cent.

Exercise 26.5

Work out the net cash flows each year and then perform a discounted cash flow calculation using a rate of 12 per cent per annum as shown in Table A26.4.

TABLE A26.4

AHMAD: DCF CALCULATION

Time	Net Cash Flow £	Discount Factor	Present Value £
Now	−70 000	1	−70 000
End Year 1	15 000	0.8929	13 394
End Year 2	35 000	0.7972	27 902
End Year 3	45 000	0.7118	32 031
		Net Present Value (NPV)	3 327

The NPV is positive so Ahmad is getting more than 12 per cent per annum. He should buy the shop.

Exercise 26.6

The NPV calculation is shown in Table A26.5.

TABLE A26.5

EXERCISE 26.6: NPV CALCULATIONS (RATE = 10%)			
Time	**Net Cash Flow £**	**Discount Factor**	**Present Value £**
Now	−450 000	1	−450 000
End Year 1	115 000	0.9091	104 547
End Year 2	135 000	0.8264	111 564
End Year 3	145 000	0.7513	108 939
End Year 4	160 000	0.6830	109 280
		Net Present Value (NPV)	−15 670

The NPV is negative so the IRR must be between 8 per cent and 10 per cent.

We can perform the calculation using a rate of 9 per cent as shown in Table A26.6.

TABLE A26.6

EXERCISE 26.6: NPV CALCULATIONS (RATE = 9%)			
Time	**Net Cash Flow £**	**Discount Factor**	**Present Value £**
Now	−450 000	1	−450 000
End Year 1	115 000	0.9174	105 501
End Year 2	135 000	0.8417	113 630
End Year 3	145 000	0.7722	111 969
End Year 4	160 000	0.7084	113 344
		Net Present Value (NPV)	−5 556

The NPV is negative so the IRR must be between 8 per cent and 9 per cent, but from the size of the NPV we conclude that the internal rate of return is approximately 8.5 per cent.

Chapter 27

Exercise 27.1

Expected receipts per throw are

$$40 * 1/6 + 10 * 1/3 + 0*1/2 = 10\text{p}$$

This is exactly the same amount as he has to pay to join the game so now the game is fair. In other words Jim's expected winnings are zero and the banker's expected winnings are zero. Jim can now join the game in the knowledge that he is not getting ripped off by the banker.

Exercise 27.2

Weather fine Income = 750 * £5 = £3750

Weather wet Income = 50 * £5 = £250

Expected income per concert

= (£3750 * 70%) + (£250 * 30%) = £2700

Average cost for performers per concert = £500

Expected net income per concert = 2200

This is well in excess of the £200 per concert proposed by the council. The society can afford to continue with the concerts. Although it will lose money on wet nights, this is more than offset by the gain on fine evenings.

Exercise 27.3

First location:

Expected net profit

= £80 000 * 0.7 + (−£5000) * 0.3

= £56 000 − £1500 = £54 500

Second location:

Expected net profit

= £120 000 * 0.6 + (−£10 000) * 0.4

= £72 000 − £4000 = £68 000

The second location gives the higher expected net profit and would be selected on those grounds. Note that there is a 40 per cent chance of a loss of £10 000 using this strategy. Other strategies are possible. An optimist would always select the option that will bring in the most money if all goes well so this would be the second location with its chance of £120 000 in profits. A pessimist would always choose the option that minimises losses if everything turned out badly. Here, he would select the first location as the most to be lost is £5000.

Exercise 27.4

(a) Stock 200 dozen biscuits:

If demand is 160, gross profit =

160 * £0.70 − 160 * £0.40 − 40 * £0.40 = £32

If demand is 180, gross profit =

180 * £0.70 − 180 * £0.40 − 20 * £0.40 = £46

If demand is 200 or 220, gross profit =

200 * £0.70 − 200 * £0.40 = £60

(b) Stock 220 dozen biscuits

If demand is 160, gross profit =
$160 * £0.70 - 160 * £0.40 - 60 * £0.40 = £24$

If demand is 180, gross profit =
$180 * £0.70 - 180 * £0.40 - 40 * £0.40 = £38$

If demand is 200, gross profit =
$200 * £0.70 - 200 * £0.40 - 20 * £0.40 = £52$

If demand is 220, gross profit =
$220 * £0.70 - 220 * £0.40 = £66$

Exercise 27.5

Build small factory:

$$EMV = 200 * 0.5 + 200 * 0.3 + 150 * 0.2$$
= 190 thousand pounds

Build large factory:

$$EMV = 350 * 0.5 + 175 * 0.3 + 100 * 0.2$$
= 247.5 thousand pounds

Based on expected monetary values, the company should choose to build the large factory.

Exercise 27.6

The payoff matrix is shown in Table A27.1.

TABLE A27.1

'BROWN BEAR' PUB: PAYOFF MATRIX (PAYOFFS IN £)

	Decision Options		
State of Nature	**Stock 30**	**Stock 40**	**Stock 50**
Level of Demand			
30	21	16	11
40	23	28	23
50	25	30	35

Stock 30

$$EMV = £21 * 0.25 + 23 * 0.5 + 25 * 0.25 = £23$$

Stock 40

$$EMV = £16 * 0.25 + 28 * 0.5 + 30 * 0.25 = £25.50$$

Stock 50

$$EMV = £11 * 0.25 + 23 * 0.5 + 35 * 0.25 = £23$$

The best option based on expected monetary value is to stock 40 and buy in extra supplies on days when demand is above this level.

Exercise 27.7

Referring to Table A27.1, we calculate:

Expected profit with perfect information =
$£21 * 0.25 + £28 * 0.5 + £35 * 0.25 = £28$

EVPI = £28 − £25.50 = £2.50 per day

The landlord could ask customers to phone in with orders or to let him know the previous day if they are not going to be having a sandwich the following lunchtime.

Chapter 28

Exercise 28.1

See answers to Exercises 26.4, 26.5 and 26.6.

Exercise 28.2

See Table A28.1.

TABLE A28.1

PREMIER PUB COMPANY: EXPECTED CASH FLOWS

Scenario	**Buying**		**Renting**	
	NPV	**IRR**	**NPV**	**IRR**
Original	−£166 197	0%	£117 248	23%
Sales +£60 000	£42 104	7%	£325 548	48%
Sales −£40 000	−£305 064	−7%	−£21 620	2%
Slower Growth	−£225 877	−3%	£57 568	15%
Cost of Goods Sold 45%	−£274 205	−5%	£9 240	7%
Cost of Goods Sold 35%	−£58 189	4%	£225 255	36%

Studying the results in Table A28.1, it appears that the renting option is superior to the buying option in every scenario. The renting option is vulnerable if sales are only £240 000. Before it goes ahead with the project, the Premier Pub Company must be confident that it can achieve the projected sales level of £280 000. If the cost of goods sold rises to 45 per cent of sales revenue, the company will achieve only a 7 per cent rate of return, so it is vital for them to keep costs under control.

Further Reading

Dickey, T. (1992). *Budgeting*, Kogan Page, London.

Doyle, P. (1994). *Marketing Management and Strategy*, Prentice Hall International, London.

Drury, C. (1994). *Costing* (3/e), Chapman & Hall, London.

Emmanuel, C., Otley, D. and Merchant, K. (1990). *Accounting for Management Control* (2/e), Chapman & Hall, London.

Gazely, A.M. (1993). *Drury's Management and Cost Accounting* (3/e) Spreadsheet Applications Manual, Chapman & Hall, London.

Glautier, M.W.E. and Underdown, B. (1991). *Accounting Theory and Practice* (5/e), Pitman, London.

Guiltinan, J.P. (1989). 'A Conceptual Framework for Pricing Consumer Services', in M.J. Bitur and L.A. Crosby, eds, *Proceedings: AMA Services Marketing Conference*.

Horngren, C.T. and Sundem, G.L. (1993). *Management Accounting* (9/e), Englewood Cliffs, New Jersey, Prentice-Hall.

Knight, J. (1995). *Personal Computing for Business*, Pitman, London.

Lucey, T. (1993). *Costing* (4/e), DP Publications Ltd, London.

Lucey, T. (1992). *Management Accounting* (3/e), DP Publications Ltd, London.

McKenzie, E. (1978). 'The Monitoring of Exponentially Weighted Forecasts', *Journal of the Operational Research Society*, **29** (5), 449–58.

McKenzie, W. *Using and Interpreting Company Accounts*, *Financial Times*/Pitman, London.

Moran, K. (1995). *Investment Appraisal for Non-Financial Managers*, Pitman, London.

Smith, T. (1992). *Accounting for Growth*, Century Business, London.

Shearer, P. (1994). *Business Forecasting*, Prentice-Hall International, Hemel Hempstead.

Stoodley, K.D.C, Lewis, T. and Stainton, C.L.S. (1980). *Applied Statistical Techniques*, Ellis Horwood, Chichester.

Waddell, D. and Sohal, A.S. (1994). 'Forecasting: The Key to Managerial Decision Making', *Management Decision*, **32** (1), 41–9.

Ward, K. (1989). *Financial Aspects of Marketing*, Heinemann, Oxford.

Wood, F. (1993). *Business Accounting Volumes 1 and 2* (6/e), Pitman, London.

Glossary of Terms

ABSOLUTE CELL REFERENCE
In a *SPREADSHEET*, a cell reference which does not change when copied. This is achieved by typing a $ symbol before the column label and the row number of the cell (*see* **RELATIVE CELL REFERENCE**).

ABSOLUTE DEVIATION
The positive difference between the forecasted and actual values disregarding any negative signs.

ABSORPTION COSTING
A system which attempts to track and record the full *COST* of producing, distributing and selling each product and which relates this cost to the product via a series of *COST CENTRES*. The full cost is used as the basis for *PRICING* and decision-making (*see* **COST-PLUS PRICING, FULL COST PRICING**).

ACID TEST
A *RATIO* measuring the immediate *LIQUIDITY* of an organisation if it does not rely on selling its stock in order to pay creditors.

$$\text{Acid Test} = \frac{\text{Current assets} - \text{Stock}}{\text{Current liabilities}}$$

For example, an acid test ratio of 0.4 means that for every £1 owed to creditors in the short term the business can raise £0.40 without having to sell off any stock. This ratio is particularly relevant when analysing the accounts of manufacturing organisations, as they may find it difficult to sell their stock quickly.

ACTUAL COST
The exact historical costs actually incurred during the *BUDGET* period. These are compared to *STANDARD COSTS* to determine the *VARIANCE*.

ADVERSE
A variance arising from *ACTUAL COSTS* which are higher than the *STANDARD COSTS* budgeted for. The principles of *RESPONSIBILITY ACCOUNTING* and *MANAGEMENT BY EXCEPTION* dictate that this should be investigated and if the cost is a *CONTROLLABLE COST*, remedial action should be taken (*see* **VARIANCE, VARIANCE ANALYSIS**).

ALLOCATION
The process of directly identifying *COSTS* with the *COST CENTRES* where they are incurred.

APPORTIONMENT
The division of unallocated *COST* (*OVERHEAD*) among a number of *COST CENTRES* in proportion to the benefits received, using an appropriate base, such as turnover, number of employees.

ASSET
A right (for example, a patent) or property (for example, shop premises, stock) acquired for use in the business; depending on its nature it can be a *FIXED ASSET* or a *CURRENT ASSET*.

ASSET TURNOVER

A *RATIO* showing the relationship between the capital invested in the business and the sales revenue generated on that basis.

$$\text{Asset turnover} = \frac{\text{Sales}}{\text{Net total assets}}$$

For example, an asset turnover figure of 3.7 means that in the accounting period under scrutiny the value of sales was 3.7 times that of the value of the net total assets of the business.

ATTAINABLE STANDARD

A *STANDARD COST* based on historical average *COST* data and on realistic assumptions about what is achievable in future periods.

AVERAGE COST

The share of the total cost attributed to each unit sold.

$$\text{Average cost} = \frac{\text{Total cost}}{\text{Number of units sold}}$$

BALANCE SHEET

An accounting statement showing the financial position of a business at a particular point in time. It draws on the records kept by the business and communicates information concerning those aspects of the business which can be given an objective monetary value. The balance sheet is based on the *BALANCE SHEET EQUATION.*

BALANCE SHEET EQUATION

The *BALANCE SHEET* is based on the equation:

$$\text{Assets} = \text{Capital} + \text{Liabilities}$$

This means that management is accountable for every penny that has been invested in the business and must disclose what the business has got to show for the investment in terms of *ASSETS.*

BAR CHART

A chart that consists of a series of horizontal or vertical bars representing the frequency in different categories.

BOTTOM UP

An approach to drawing up a *BUDGET* which starts from the grass roots, involving line management in compiling budgets for their own areas of responsibility. This approach is often used in combination with the *TOP DOWN* approach. The budgets for the individual *COST CENTRES* and *PROFIT CENTRES* are brought together in the *MASTER BUDGETS* (*see* **ZERO-BASE BUDGETING**).

BREAK-EVEN ANALYSIS

A technique for analysing the relationship between *COST*, sales volume and *PROFIT* which is used to assess the potential viability of projects and to find the most profitable combination of resources and prices (*see* **BREAK-EVEN CHART, BREAK-EVEN POINT**).

BREAK-EVEN CHART

A diagram showing the relationship between *COST*, sales volume and *PROFIT* and the *BREAK-EVEN POINT.*

BREAK-EVEN POINT

The point at which neither profit nor loss is made for a given combination of costs and selling price

$$\text{Break-even point in units} = \frac{\text{Total fixed costs}}{\text{Unit contribution}}$$

Break-even point in £ =

$$\text{Break-even point in units} * \text{Selling price/Unit}$$

(*see* **BREAK-EVEN ANALYSIS, BREAK-EVEN CHART, CONTRIBUTION, UNIT CONTRIBUTION, MARGINAL COSTING**).

BUDGET

A detailed plan of the activities of a business for a specific future time period, concerning the allocation of physical resources, expressed in money terms. This plan is based on *STANDARDS* and serves as a yardstick against which actual performance can be compared. It can act as a motivating tool for line management by devolving responsibility, improving communication and control (*see* **BOTTOM UP, BUDGET, FIXED BUDGET, FLEXIBLE BUDGET, MANAGEMENT BY EXCEPTION, MANAGEMENT BY OBJECTIVES, MASTER BUDGET, TOP DOWN, VARIANCE ANALYSIS, ZERO-BASE BUDGETING**).

BUDGETED BALANCE SHEET

A forecast of the balance sheet as it would look at the end of the budgetary period if everything went according to plan. This is part of the *MASTER BUDGET.*

BUDGETED INCOME STATEMENT (*see* **BUDGETED PROFIT AND LOSS ACCOUNT**).

BUDGETED PROFIT AND LOSS ACCOUNT

A detailed plan of the expected revenues and expenditure of the business for the budgetary period. This is part of the *MASTER BUDGET.*

BUDGETED PROFIT AND LOSS STATEMENT (*see* **BUDGETED PROFIT AND LOSS ACCOUNT**).

BUSINESS CYCLE (*see* **ECONOMIC CYCLE**).

BUSINESS ENTITY
For accounting purposes the business's affairs are treated as separate from the private affairs of the owner, even in the case of unincorporated businesses, where legally there is no such distinction.

CAPITAL
The value of the original investment made by the owner of the business, plus any long-term loans taken out, plus any *RETAINED PROFITS* reinvested in the organisation over time. The capital of most large incorporated businesses consists of a mixture of *SHARE FINANCE* and *LOAN FINANCE*. Because of the *DUALITY* rule, the *BALANCE SHEET* total for the capital section must equal the balance sheet figure for net total assets.

CAPITAL GAIN
The gain in the market price of shares due to the success of the business, changes in market confidence or general stock market fluctuations.

CAPITAL STRUCTURE
The combination of long-term sources of finance used to resource the business (*see* **GEARING**).

CASH BUDGET
A detailed forecast of the cash flows for the budgetary period, showing cash payments and receipts and their timing. This is part of the *MASTER BUDGET*.

CASH FLOW
The physical movement of cash over time.

CASH FLOW STATEMENT
An accounting statement based on the organisation's records of the physical cash *RECEIPTS* and *PAYMENTS* which take place in the course of business activities.

CATASTROPHIC VARIATION
An abnormal large movement of a *TIME SERIES* affecting the value of the variable in a single time period (*see* **RESIDUAL VARIATION**).

CELL
The element of a *SPREADSHEET* where entry of *TEXT*, *NUMBER* or a *FORMULA* can be made.

CENTRED AVERAGE
A procedure used in the method of *MOVING AVERAGES* to ensure that the *TREND* values are calculated for exactly the same points in time as the data values. This procedure needs to be used only when the moving average is calculated over an even number of time periods such as the four quarters of a year. Each consecutive pair of moving averages is added and divided by two.

CLOSING BALANCE
The value of a resource (such as cash or stock) held by the business at the end of the accounting period.

COEFFICIENT OF DETERMINATION
This is also called **R** square. In both *LINEAR REGRESSION* and *MULTIPLE REGRESSION*, it is the proportion or percentage of the variation in the *DEPENDENT VARIABLE*, **Y**, that is explained by changes in the *EXPLANATORY VARIABLE(S)* through the regression equation. The closer the coefficient is to one or 100 per cent, the better the fit of the equation to the data.

COMMON COST
A *COST* which does not differ between alternatives. In the context of short-term decision-making this type of cost can be disregarded, as it is not affected by the decision.

COMPOUND INTEREST
A charge resulting from the application of a predetermined percentage rate to cumulative funds consisting of the *PRINCIPAL* plus the interest of previous periods added to it.

CONTRIBUTION
That part of the selling price which is left after all variable *COSTS* have been paid for. This initially is used to pay for fixed costs; once all fixed costs have been paid for, this is *PROFIT*.

CONTROLLABLE COST
A *COST* which can be influenced by the manager in charge of the relevant *COST CENTRE*. The manager can therefore be made accountable for this cost and charged with the responsibility of controlling it (*see* **RESPONSIBILITY ACCOUNTING, VARIANCE ANALYSIS**).

CORRELATION
The degree of linear relationship between two variables, as established through *CORRELATION ANALYSIS* and expressed by the *CORRELATION COEFFICIENT*.

CORRELATION ANALYSIS
A technique for calculating and examining the degree of *CORRELATION* between two variables.

CORRELATION COEFFICIENT

A measure of the strength and direction of the *CORRELATION* between two variables. It is denoted by the symbol **r**. Its value is +1 in the case of *perfect POSITIVE CORRELATION*. In the case of *perfect NEGATIVE CORRELATION* its value is −1.

COST

The amount of financial resource used up in relation to a specified thing, product or activity (*see* **CONTROLLABLE COSTS, UNCONTROLLABLE COSTS, COSTING SYSTEM, COST CENTRE**).

COST CENTRE

A location, function, item of equipment or product line to which direct *COSTS* can be allocated and *OVERHEAD* apportioned for planning and control purposes.

COST OF GOODS SOLD

The *MATCHING CONCEPT* implies that in order to calculate *GROSS PROFIT* in the *TRADING ACCOUNT*, the selling and purchase prices must be matched for the same goods, which are the goods actually sold during the accounting period. The sales figure can be obtained from till records. The cost of goods sold figure must be calculated to eliminate the distorting influence of differences in stock holding at the beginning and the end of the accounting period. The calculation is carried out using the formula:

$$\text{Opening stock} + \text{Purchases} - \text{Closing stock}$$

$$= \text{Cost of goods sold}$$

COSTING SYSTEM

A methodical approach towards determining *COSTS* and relating them to business activities (*see* **ABSORPTION COSTING, DIRECT PRODUCT PROFITABILITY**)

COST-PLUS PRICING

A technique which uses the total *COST* of producing, distributing and merchandising a product as the basis for *PRICING*. Total cost is established through a system of *ABSORPTION COSTING* or *DIRECT PRODUCT COSTING* and the price is calculated by adding a predetermined *MARK-UP* to the cost.

CREDITOR

A person or organisation to which the business owes money (*see* **CURRENT LIABILITY, LONG-TERM LIABILITY**).

CREDITORS: DUE AFTER ONE YEAR (*see* **LONG-TERM LIABILITY**).

CREDITORS: DUE WITHIN ONE YEAR (*see* **CURRENT LIABILITY**).

CREDITORS' PAYMENT PERIOD

A *RATIO* which shows how many days it takes the business (on average) to pay its suppliers.

$$\text{Creditors' payment period (in days)}$$

$$= \frac{\text{Creditors}}{\text{Credit purchases}} * 365$$

This ratio gives an indication as to the credit terms the business is obtaining. A figure of 47 would mean that on average it takes 47 days after delivery before suppliers are paid.

CURRENT ASSET

An *ASSET* which is in the form of cash or will be turned into cash within the next accounting period (usually one year). This includes the cash in the tills, money outstanding from *DEBTORS* and stock to be sold to customers.

CURRENT LIABILITY

Those amounts which the business owes to outsiders at the *BALANCE SHEET* date and which it reasonably expects to have to pay out within the next accounting period (usually one year). These include, for example, *TRADE CREDITORS* and bank overdrafts.

CURRENT RATIO

A *RATIO* measuring the *LIQUIDITY* of a business.

$$\text{Current ratio} = \frac{\text{Current assets}}{\text{Current liabilities}}$$

A current ratio of, for instance, 0.3 means that for every £1 owed to creditors in the short run £0.3 can be raised by turning current assets into cash.

CYCLICAL VARIATIONS

The fluctuations in economic variables reflecting the movement of the economy through boom and recession. The impact of the business cycle on the individual organisation is of a long-term and gradual nature and can therefore not be taken into account when making short-term forecasts (*see* **TIME SERIES ANALYSIS**)

DEBTOR

A person or organisation owing money to the business (*see* **CURRENT ASSET**).

DEBTORS' COLLECTION PERIOD

A *RATIO* measuring the time it takes for *DEBTORS* to settle their accounts.

$$\text{Debtors' collection period (days)} = \frac{\text{Debtors}}{\text{Credit sales}} * 365.$$

DEPENDENT VARIABLE

The variable the values of which are to be predicted in the context of forecasting using *LINEAR REGRESSION* and *MULTIPLE REGRESSION.*

DEPRECIATION

The matching of the *COST minus* the salvage value of a *FIXED ASSET* to the accounting periods during which the business has the use of that *ASSET*, in a systematic and rational manner. Two main depreciation methods have been examined, the *STRAIGHT LINE* method and the *REDUCING BALANCE* method. The method should be chosen which most closely reflects the pattern of the asset's usefulness to the business.

DIFFERENTIAL COST

The *COST* of selling a number of additional units as a direct result of a short-term decision (*see* **INCREMENTAL, RELEVANT COST**).

DIRECT PRODUCT COST (DPC)

A *COST* which can be allocated to an individual product and which is affected by variations in the storing and handling of the product. Direct product costing is a system of cost accounting which is based on the detailed *ALLOCATION* of all those costs which can be directly identified with the handling, distribution and selling of a product to the product.

DIRECT PRODUCT PROFIT (DPP)

The *CONTRIBUTION* to *PROFIT* and unallocated *COSTS* made by an individual product after all the *DIRECT PRODUCT COSTS* have been accounted for.

DIRECT PRODUCT PROFITABILITY

A system which uses *DIRECT PRODUCT COSTING* as the basis for making decisions concerning the choice of distribution channels, pricing and space management.

DISCOUNT FACTOR

The factor $1/(1+\mathbf{i})^{\mathbf{n}}$ used in *PRESENT VALUE* calculations, where $\mathbf{i}$ is the *DISCOUNT RATE*. The present value of a future sum is calculated by multiplying the *FUTURE VALUE* by the discount factor.

DISCOUNT RATE

The interest rate used when computing the *DISCOUNT FACTOR* in *PRESENT VALUE* calculations.

DISCOUNTED CASH FLOW (DCF) TECHNIQUE

A forecast of the capital expenditure and annual revenues associated with a capital investment project, expressed in terms of *PRESENT VALUES*. This can be used to compare and decide between mutually exclusive projects (*see* **DISCOUNTING, INTERNAL RATE OF RETURN, NET PRESENT VALUE, PRESENT VALUE, PRESENT VALUE TABLE**).

DISCOUNTING

Calculating the *PRESENT VALUE* of a sum of money expected to be received at a future point in time through the application of a pre-determined percentage rate, which usually reflects the *OPPORTUNITY COST.*

DIVIDEND

A slice of the *PROFIT* of an accounting period which is distributed to the shareholders. The amount of dividend to be paid on each share depends on the profits made by the business.

DIVIDEND COVER

A *RATIO* measuring the extent to which the business can afford to pay out current levels of *DIVIDEND*

$$\text{Dividend cover} = \frac{\text{Earnings per share}}{\text{Dividend per share}}$$

To give an example, a dividend cover of 3 implies that net profit after tax is three times the amount of the total dividends paid out.

DIVIDEND PER SHARE (DPS)

A *RATIO* measuring the relationship of the total *DIVIDEND* paid out and the number of shares over which this is distributed.

$$\text{Dividend per share} = \frac{\text{Total dividend}}{\text{Number of ordinary shares}}$$

DIVIDEND YIELD

A *RATIO* measuring the relationship of the *DIVIDEND* received and the current market price of a share. This ratio fluctuates with the market price of the share. It can be used to compare the returns the shareholder receives in form of dividends to those which could be obtained by investing the money tied up in shares in some other manner

$$\text{Dividend yield} = \frac{\text{Dividend per share}}{\text{Share price}} * 100.$$

DUALITY

The principle that every business transaction has at least two effects on the *BALANCE SHEET*. Any form of business activity entails turning the resources of the business from one form into another, for example cash into stock and stock back into more cash via sales to customers. To give an example, imagine a business acquires stock from a supplier for £1000 cash. As a result of this transaction the balance sheet entry *CURRENT ASSETS*: 'cash' would decrease by that amount, whereas the entry under Current assets: 'stock' would increase by the same amount: the resource 'cash' has been turned into the resource 'stock'.

EARNINGS PER SHARE (EPS)

A *RATIO* measuring the relationship of the profits generated over an accounting period to the number of ordinary shares issued

$$\text{Earnings per share} = \frac{\text{Net profit after tax}}{\text{Number of ordinary shares}}.$$

ECONOMIC CYCLE

The long-term fluctuations in the economy as it passes through boom, recession, depression, expansion and returns to boom.

ECONOMIES OF SCALE

Cost savings arising with increases in sales volume as *OVERHEAD* can be *APPORTIONED* to a larger number of units sold and therefore spread more thinly. For example, a large multiple retailer with a high annual turnover is more likely to enjoy savings from bulk buying and will find it easier to afford the cost of investing in equipment than an independent competitor who has only a small sales volume.

EQUATION OF A STRAIGHT LINE

This is of the form $\mathbf{y} = \mathbf{a} + \mathbf{b} * \mathbf{x}$, where $\mathbf{x}$ represents values of the *EXPLANATORY VARIABLE* and $\mathbf{y}$ represents values of the *DEPENDENT VARIABLE* in a *LINEAR RELATIONSHIP*. The *INTERCEPT* is represented by the symbol $\mathbf{a}$. The *SLOPE* is represented by the symbol $\mathbf{b}$.

EXPECTED MONETARY VALUE (EMV)

In conditions of risk when different possible outcomes may occur with known probabilities, the expected monetary value is the sum of the *PAYOFF* associated with each outcome multiplied by its probability of occurrence.

EXPECTED VALUE OF PERFECT INFORMATION (EVPI)

The difference between the *EXPECTED MONETARY VALUES* under conditions of risk and conditions of certainty. It is the maximum amount we would be prepared to pay to obtain perfect knowledge of the market.

EXPENSE

The *COST* of generating the *SALES REVENUE* of an accounting period.

EXPLANATORY VARIABLE

A variable which is used as the basis for predicting future values of the *DEPENDENT VARIABLE*.

EXPONENTIAL SMOOTHING

A *SHORT-TERM FORECASTING* technique which attaches differing weight to more recent data than to older data through the application of a *SMOOTHING CONSTANT* α (alpha). The procedure is monitored through the calculation of the *SMOOTHED MEAN ABSOLUTE DEVIATION*.

EXTRAPOLATION

Estimating the *DEPENDENT VARIABLE* in *LINEAR REGRESSION* and *MULTIPLE REGRESSION*, for **X**-values outside the range of the given data (*see* **INTERPOLATION**).

FACTOR

An element of resource which is needed to make up a business. Such elements can be divided into *FIXED FACTORS* and *VARIABLE FACTORS*.

FAVOURABLE

A *VARIANCE* arising from *ACTUAL COSTS* which are lower than the *STANDARD COSTS* budgeted for.

FIRST IN FIRST OUT (FIFO)

A method of stock valuation. For accounting purposes the assumption is made that the goods first purchased are the first to be sold. In this sense the method matches the physical flow of goods. In times of inflation FIFO assigns a realistic value to stock in the *BALANCE SHEET*. However, this implies lower accuracy in matching current *SALES REVENUE* with current purchase costs in the *PROFIT AND LOSS ACCOUNT*, which on paper results in higher *GROSS PROFIT* figures than would be obtained using the *LAST IN FIRST OUT* (*LIFO*) or the

WEIGHTED AVERAGE COST (*WAC*) method of stock valuation. The FIFO method is legally acceptable in the UK. It is most appropriate for businesses selling goods of considerable value per item.

FIXED ASSET
An *ASSET* which has been acquired of relatively permanent use in the business, at some considerable cost. As the asset will be useful for a number of accounting periods, the *MATCHING CONCEPT* implies that *DEPRECIATION* must be charged.

FIXED ASSET RATIO
A *RATIO* measuring the relationship of *SALES REVENUE* generated and the monetary value of a business's investment in *FIXED ASSETS*.

FIXED BUDGET
A *BUDGET* which is based on only one sales level.

FIXED COST
A *COST* which does not vary with the level of output or sales.

FIXED FACTOR
A resource element of a relatively inflexible and permanent nature. The amount of this kind of resource used in the business can only be changed in the long run. Examples are land and capital. (For contrast, *see* **VARIABLE FACTOR**.)

FLEXIBLE BUDGET
A *BUDGET* which is adjustable according to sales volume.

FORECASTING
Estimating the value of future variables such as revenue, stock or number of employees. Techniques for making such forecasts include *LINEAR REGRESSION*, *EXPONENTIAL SMOOTHING* and *TIME SERIES ANALYSIS* (*see* **SHORT-TERM** and **LONG-TERM FORECASTING**).

FORECAST ERROR
The difference between the value of a variable predicted for a time period and the actual value of that variable. In the context of *EXPONENTIAL SMOOTHING*, this is monitored by calculating the *SMOOTHED MEAN ABSOLUTE DEVIATION*.

FORMULA
An algebraic expression for working out the value of a calculation. In a *SPREADSHEET* it consists of a sequence of numbers, cell addresses and *OPERATORS*, prefixed by an = sign.

FULL COST PRICING (*see* **COST-PLUS PRICING**).

FUNCTION
In a *SPREADSHEET*, a built-in *FORMULA* for commonly used procedures such as summation.

FUTURE VALUE
The future equivalent of an amount of money currently held. This is calculated by applying a pre-determined interest rate which reflects the *OPPORTUNITY COST* of the money.

GEARING
A *RATIO* showing the long-term *CAPITAL STRUCTURE* of the business expressed as the relation of *SHARE FINANCE* to the total capital of the business. It is calculated using the formula:

$$\text{Gearing} = \frac{\text{Share capital} + \text{Long-term loan capital}}{\text{Share capital}}$$

For example, if a business has £100 000 worth of share finance and £50 000 loan finance, then the gearing is 1.5.

GROSS MARGIN
A *RATIO* providing a measure of *PROFITABILITY* which relates the level of profit before expenses to the sales level achieved by the business

$$\text{Gross margin} = \frac{\text{Gross profit}}{\text{Sales}} * 100$$

A gross margin of, for instance, 18 per cent means that for every £1 of sales achieved by the business, £0.18 is gross profit.

GROSS PROFIT
The difference between selling prices and purchase prices, applied to the same goods, which have been sold to customers during an accounting period. Gross profit is calculated in the *TRADING ACCOUNT* using the formula

$$\text{Sales} - \text{Cost of goods sold} = \text{Gross profit.}$$

HISTORIGRAM
A *LINE CHART* depicting a *TIME SERIES*.

IDEAL STANDARDS
Those *STANDARD COST* levels which might be achieved if all aspects of the business could be guaranteed to operate to perfection and under conditions of

certainty. Whilst it is useful to have ideals and to aim for them, staff can be de-motivated if standards are always set too high.

INCREMENTAL

Additional, in a step-wise fashion. Management accounting makes use of this concept in a number of ways:

(a) An incremental approach to budgeting bases the *BUDGET* on historical *COST* and sales data, plus a certain percentage increase which reflects inflation

(b) An incremental volume consists of a number of additional units, rather than just one; in the context of short-term decision-making this concept is used to establish the *DIFFERENTIAL COST* of undertaking a project.

INTERCEPT

The point where a straight line cuts through the vertical (or **Y**) axis. In the *EQUATION* of a *STRAIGHT LINE*, it is the value of **Y** when **X** equals zero.

INTERNAL RATE OF RETURN (IRR)

A *DISCOUNTED CASH FLOW* technique which determines that percentage rate which results in the *NET PRESENT VALUE* of zero when applied to discount the cash flows of a given capital investment project. This is the rate for which the project breaks even.

INTERPOLATION

Estimating the *DEPENDENT VARIABLE* in *LINEAR REGRESSION* and *MULTIPLE REGRESSION*, for **X** values within the range of the given data (*see* **EXTRAPOLATION**).

LAST IN FIRST OUT (LIFO)

A method of stock valuation. For accounting purposes, the assumption is made that the goods last purchased are the first ones to be sold. (**Note**: Accounting methods of stock valuation do not have to reflect the physical flow of goods.) In times of inflation the LIFO method is accurate in matching current *COSTS* and *SALES REVENUES*, thereby resulting in a lower *GROSS PROFIT* figure than FIFO or WAC. However, in the *BALANCE SHEET* an unrealistically low figure is assigned to stock as a result. This method is legally acceptable in the USA.

LEARNING CURVE

A graphic representation of the fact that efficiency improves and cost savings are achieved as an initially new task becomes familiar.

LEAST SQUARES REGRESSION LINE

In a *SCATTER DIAGRAM*, the line that minimises the sum of the squares of the vertical deviations of the points from the line (*see* **LINEAR REGRESSION**).

LIABILITY

An amount owed by the business to an outsider at the *BALANCE SHEET* date. Depending on how soon it will become due, this can be classed as a *CURRENT LIABILITY* or as a *LONG-TERM LIABILITY*.

LINE CHART

A chart consisting of one or more series of points joined with straight lines. It is often used to show changes over time (*see* **HISTORIGRAM**).

LINEAR REGRESSION

A technique which is used to calculate the *EQUATION* of the *STRAIGHT LINE* which provides the 'best fit' for a given set of data for two variables. This can be used to make a forecast by extending the line to cover other values of the variables (*see* **LEAST SQUARES REGRESSION LINE**).

LINEAR RELATIONSHIP

An association between two variables which can be diagrammatically represented in the form of a straight line.

LIQUIDITY

The short-term ability to repay creditors falling due within the next 12 months by turning *CURRENT ASSETS* into cash, as measured by the *CURRENT RATIO* and the *ACID TEST*.

LOAN FINANCE

Finance borrowed from the financial institutions on a long-term basis, at an agreed interest rate and with a fixed repayment date (*see* **CAPITAL STRUCTURE**).

LONG-TERM FORECASTING

A technique for estimating the value of a variable several periods of time ahead (*see* **TIME SERIES ANALYSIS**).

LONG-TERM LIABILITY (*see* **LOAN FINANCE**).

MANAGEMENT BY EXCEPTION (MBE)

A management style which concentrates on identifying those areas of the business where things are going wrong and intervention is needed, leaving well enough alone in other areas. *VARIANCE ANALYSIS* and *RESPONSIBILITY ACCOUNTING* are used as management tools in this context.

MANAGEMENT BY OBJECTIVES (MBO)
The translation of organisational objectives into individualised objectives and targets for line management. This is an aspect of *RESPONSIBILITY ACCOUNTING*. Individual objectives, expressed in money terms, are set as part of the *BUDGET*ing process; these serve as a yardstick against which actual results can be evaluated (*see* **BOTTOM UP, MANAGEMENT BY EXCEPTION, TOP DOWN, VARIANCE ANALYSIS**).

MARGINAL COST
The additional *COST* incurred as a result of selling one extra unit.

MARGINAL COST PRICING
A technique which uses the *MARGINAL COST* as the basis for pricing goods which are sold in the course of borderline activities. (For comparison, *see* **FULL COST PRICING**.)

MARKET PENETRATION
A *PRICING* strategy which aims for rapid gains of market share through low prices.

MARK-UP
A *RATIO* used in the context of *PRICING*. Here the cost price of goods is used as the basis, to which a predetermined percentage is added to calculate the selling price to be charged for the goods. This percentage is the target gross profit

$$\text{Mark-up} = \frac{\text{Gross profit}}{\text{Cost of goods sold}}$$

For example, a mark-up of 0.35 means that the selling price of goods is worked out by adding 35 per cent of the cost price to it.

MASTER BUDGET
An integrated *BUDGET* bringing together all aspects of the business in a master plan, consisting of

- a *CASH BUDGET*
- a *BUDGETED PROFIT AND LOSS ACCOUNT*
- a *BUDGETED BALANCE SHEET*.

MATCHING CONCEPT (*see* **MATCHING PRINCIPLE**).

MATCHING PRINCIPLE
In the calculation of *PROFIT* the *SALES REVENUE* for an accounting period must be set off against the *EXPENSES* incurred in bringing about these sales. This principle is reflected in the application of *DEPRECIATION* and stock valuation methods.

MEAN
The average of a set of values calculated by summing them and dividing by the number of values.

MOVING AVERAGES
A technique for calculating the *TREND*, in the context of *TIME SERIES ANALYSIS*, which bases forecasts on the average figures of a number of previous periods. This smooths out the peaks and troughs caused by *SEASONAL VARIATIONS*.

MULTIPLE REGRESSION
A statistical technique for constructing a forecasting equation which is used to forecast the values of a *DEPENDENT VARIABLE* based on the values of a number of *EXPLANATORY VARIABLES*. For each additional explanatory variable the *COEFFICIENT OF DETERMINATION* is calculated to indicate the degree of additional explanation provided by introducing this variable. The multiple regression model is

$$\mathbf{y} = \mathbf{a} + \mathbf{b}_1\mathbf{x}_1 + \mathbf{b}_2\mathbf{x}_2 + \mathbf{b}_3\mathbf{x}_3 + \cdots$$

where $\mathbf{y}$ represents values of the dependent variable and $\mathbf{x}_1, \mathbf{x}_2, \mathbf{x}_3, \ldots$ represent values of the explanatory variables (*see* **LINEAR REGRESSION**).

MULTIPLICATIVE MODEL
A model used to combine the different components of a *TIME SERIES ANALYSIS*.

$$\text{Value of variable} = \text{Trend} * \text{Seasonal variation} * \text{Residual variation}$$

NEGATIVE CORRELATION
Linear association between two variables, for which an increase in the values of the *EXPLANATORY VARIABLE* goes with a decrease in the values of the *DEPENDENT VARIABLE*.

NET MARGIN
A *RATIO* providing a measure of *PROFITABILITY* which relates the level of *PROFIT* after *EXPENSES* to the sales level achieved by the business

$$\text{Net margin} = \frac{\text{Net profit}}{\text{Sales}} * 100$$

A net margin of, for example, 7 per cent means that after all expenses have been paid for every £1 worth of sales achieved by the business, £0.07 are left in the business.

NET PRESENT VALUE (NPV)

A *DISCOUNTED CASH FLOW* technique, used to determine the *PRESENT VALUE* of the cash flows associated with a capital investment project, expressed in current prices, by *DISCOUNTING* them, making use of an appropriate percentage rate.

NUMBER

In a *SPREADSHEET*, any entry that is not *TEXT* or a *FORMULA*.

OPENING BALANCE

The value of a resource, such as stock or cash, held by the business at the beginning of the accounting period.

OPERATOR

A mathematical symbol to denote a procedure such as addition (+) (*see* **SPREADSHEET**).

OPPORTUNITY COST

The benefits forgone as a result of undertaking one course of action as opposed to another. This is measured in terms of the likely *PROFITS* from the most promising alternative course of action.

ORDINARY SHARE

Dominant type of share (*see* **SHARE FINANCE**).

OVERHEAD

A *COST* which cannot be directly allocated to a *COST CENTRE*, but must be apportioned.

P-VALUE

A value that is calculated as part of the regression output from a *SPREADSHEET*, reflecting the degree to which a particular *EXPLANATORY VARIABLE* contributes to a regression equation. If the **P**-value for a variable is less than 0.05, that variable makes a significant contribution to the regression equation and we can have confidence in using it for forecasting purposes (*see* **LINEAR REGRESSION, MULTIPLE REGRESSION**).

PAYMENT

A physical transfer of an amount of cash from the business to an outside party, for example a supplier.

PAYOFF

The monetary value associated with the occurrence of a *STATE OF NATURE*.

PAYOFF MATRIX

A table showing the different possible *PAYOFFS* dependent on which option is chosen and on the *STATE OF NATURE* that occurs.

PERFORMANCE

The ability of the business to generate *PROFITS* in relation to the value of the resources invested in it. This is measured through the *RETURN ON CAPITAL EMPLOYED* (*ROCE*) ratio (*see* **RATIO ANALYSIS**).

PIE CHART

A circular chart divided into sectors showing the proportion or percentage of items in different categories.

POSITIVE CORRELATION

Linear association between two variables, for which an increase in the values of the *EXPLANATORY VARIABLE* goes with a increase in the values of the *DEPENDENT VARIABLE*.

PRESENT VALUE

The current equivalent of an amount of money expected to be held at a future point in time. This is calculated by *DISCOUNTING* the future amount through the application of a pre-determined *DISCOUNT RATE*, chosen to reflect the *OPPORTUNITY COST* of money.

PRESENT VALUE TABLES

Tables listing the *DISCOUNT FACTORS* used in calculating the *NET PRESENT VALUE* of a capital investment project for a number of combinations of years and *DISCOUNT RATES*.

PRICE EARNINGS RATIO (P/E)

A *RATIO* which measures the relationship of the current market price of a share and the business's earnings attributable to it. This ratio fluctuates with the market price of the share

$$\text{Price earnings ratio} = \frac{\text{Share price}}{\text{Earnings per share}}.$$

PRICING

The process of establishing selling prices (*see* **COST-PLUS PRICING, MARGINAL COST PRICING, MARKET PENETRATION, SKIMMING**).

PRINCIPAL

Initial amount invested (in the context of the calculation of *COMPOUND INTEREST*).

PROFIT

The amount of financial surplus generated by the business activities of an accounting period. Profit is calculated in the *PROFIT AND LOSS ACCOUNT* by matching the *COSTS* and *SALES REVENUE* of the accounting period. This is done in stages, from *GROSS PROFIT*, through *TRADING PROFIT* to *RETAINED PROFIT*.

PROFIT AND LOSS ACCOUNT
An accounting statement which shows the *SALES REVENUE* and *EXPENSE* transactions which have taken place between two *BALANCE SHEET* dates. It reports the *PROFIT* or loss made by the business in the course of the accounting period.

PROFIT CENTRE
A *COST CENTRE* which directly generates *SALES REVENUE* for the business.

PROFIT TREE
A model of structured *RATIO ANALYSIS*, taking the *RETURN ON SHAREHOLDERS' FUNDS* as the starting point and showing the relationship between key ratios, thus facilitating interpretation.

PROFITABILITY
The relationship between the volume of business activity and the *PROFITS* generated, as measured by the *RATIOS*: *GROSS MARGIN* and *NET MARGIN*.

PUBLIC LIMITED COMPANY (PLC)
The legal format of a large incorporated business, whose shares are publicly sold and quoted on the Stock Exchange.

RANDOM VARIATION
In *TIME SERIES ANALYSIS*, small variations that cannot be predicted and which are equally likely in the long run to push up the value of the time series as to lower it (*see* **RESIDUAL VARIATION**).

RATIO
A quantitative relation between two figures, determined by the number of times one contains the other (*see* **RATIO ANALYSIS**).

RATIO ANALYSIS
A tool of financial control which uses *RATIOS* to plan and monitor changes in company performance over time, as well as in comparison to industry average performance.

RECEIPT
The physical transfer of an amount of cash from an outside party, for example a customer, to the business.

REDUCING BALANCE
A method of calculating the annual amount of *DEPRECIATION* to be charged to the *PROFIT AND LOSS ACCOUNT* through the repeated application of a certain percentage rate. In the first year this rate is applied to the historic *COST* of the *FIXED ASSET* to calculate the charge. This charge is treated as an *EXPENSE* in the profit and loss account. To find the depreciation charge for year 2, first the depreciation charge applied in year 1 is deducted from the historic cost. This gives the book value at the end of year 1. This book value is the figure which goes into the *BALANCE SHEET* at the end of year 1.

To find the depreciation charge of year 2, the same percentage rate is applied to this book value at the end of year 1. The same procedure as for year 1 is carried out again. This is repeated for as many years as the asset is to be depreciated over.

The percentage rate to use can be found through the formula:

$$\text{Percentage depreciation rate} = (1 - \sqrt[n]{(\text{Scrap value}/\text{Cost})}) * 100$$

with **n** = number of years expected life of asset.

This method allocates a higher depreciation charge to the earlier accounting periods. It is therefore the appropriate method to use where the asset is most useful to the organisation in the earlier years of its life, for instance, assets using the latest technology and becoming obsolete quickly, such as computer equipment (*see* **DEPRECIATION**).

RELATIVE CELL REFERENCE
The default procedure used in a spreadsheet package to label a *CELL* so that, when copying takes place, the cell address in a formula is modified automatically to take account of the number of rows and columns between the source and the destination cells (*see* **ABSOLUTE CELL REFERENCE**).

RELEVANT COST
In the context of short-term decision-making, a *COST* is relevant if it is affected by the decision. Relevant costs include *DIFFERENTIAL COSTS* and *OPPORTUNITY COSTS*. These types of costs must be taken into consideration when making the decision.

RELEVANT RANGE
The range of sales volumes for which the level of *FIXED COSTS* remains unaltered.

RESIDUAL VARIATION
In *TIME SERIES ANALYSIS*, any variation that cannot be attributed to *TREND*, *CYCLICAL VARIATION* or *SEASONAL VARIATION*. It may be *CATASTROPHIC VARIATION* or *RANDOM VARIATION*.

RESOURCE UTILISATION

The value of *SALES REVENUE* generated on the basis of a capital investment made in a business. This is measured by the *ASSET TURNOVER* ratio.

RESPONSIBILITY ACCOUNTING

A managerial control system based on the principles of *MANAGEMENT BY OBJECTIVES*, by which corporate objectives are translated into individual objectives for line management. In parallel, responsibility for controlling *COST* items is identified with line managers who are held responsible for the monitoring and control of these items.

RETAINED PROFIT

The amount of *PROFIT* reinvested in the business.

RETURN ON CAPITAL EMPLOYED (ROCE)

A *RATIO* measuring business *PERFORMANCE* by relating the profits generated by the business to the value of the resources invested in it

$$\text{ROCE} = \frac{\text{Net profit}}{\text{Net total assets}}$$

For example, a ROCE figure of 0.14 means that for every £1 invested in the business, a net profit of £0.14 has been generated during the accounting period in question. The *PROFIT TREE* model relates the ROCE to the *ASSET TURNOVER* and *NET MARGIN*, facilitating interpretation.

RETURN ON SHAREHOLDERS' FUNDS (ROSF)

A *RATIO* relating the *PROFIT* generated to the money invested in the *SHARE FINANCE* of the business

$$\text{Return on Shareholders' Funds} = \frac{\text{Net profit } (\textit{minus} \text{ loan interest})}{\text{Share finance}}$$

The *PROFIT TREE* model links this ratio to *RETURN ON CAPITAL EMPLOYED* on one hand and *GEARING* on the other.

SALES PER EMPLOYEE

A *RATIO* measuring the relationship of the *SALES REVENUE* generated to the number of staff members employed by a business.

SALES PER SQUARE FOOT

A *RATIO* measuring the relationship of the *SALES REVENUE* generated to the space occupied by a branch of a business.

SALES REVENUE

The monetary value of the business an organisation has generated from its customers over an accounting period. This includes cash and credit sales.

SCATTER DIAGRAM

A graphical presentation of the relationship between two variables. The convention is to plot the *DEPENDENT VARIABLE* on the vertical (or **Y**) axis and the *EXPLANATORY VARIABLE* along the horizontal (or **X**) axis so that each pair of values (**X**, **Y**) corresponds to one point on the diagram. This is used to gain a visual impression of the nature of the relationship between the two variables, in the context of *CORRELATION* and *LINEAR REGRESSION ANALYSIS*.

SEASONAL ADJUSTMENT FACTOR

A percentage to indicate how much the value of a *TIME SERIES* is typically above or below the *TREND* figure for a particular season. In the context of *TIME SERIES ANALYSIS*, this is used to adjust the trend for seasonal effects in order to assist accurate *FORECASTING*.

SEASONAL VARIATIONS

Short-term regular fluctuations in variables due to predictably recurring events such as pay days, festivities, holidays and types of weather. When making sales forecasts, the seasonality must be taken into account. In the context of *TIME SERIES ANALYSIS* this is done by applying a *SEASONAL ADJUSTMENT FACTOR* to the *TREND*.

SEMI-VARIABLE COST

A cost which has a *FIXED COST* element as well as a *VARIABLE COST* aspect. For example, a telephone bill consists of a basic charge (the fixed cost part) and an itemised unit cost which varies directly with the number of telephone calls (the variable part). For cost accounting purposes this type of cost is split into its fixed and variable elements.

SENSITIVITY ANALYSIS

A thorough examination of the degree of potential vulnerability of an organisation to changes in a number of internal and external factors. The focus is on the question 'What if...?' with the objective of identifying and minimising risk exposure. On the basis of the outcomes of such an analysis, a number of contingency plans can be made for alternative sets of circumstances, taking into account uncertainty. This allows the planner to switch to that plan which most closely matches reality. A much quicker response to changing circumstances is possible than there would have been if only one plan had been made.

SHARE FINANCE
The risk *CAPITAL* investment in a company. Shareholders are the owners of the business. They gain from the investment in shares in two forms: through the receipt of *DIVIDENDS* and *CAPITAL GAIN*. For *ORDINARY SHARES*, shareholders are not legally entitled to dividends, and the amount of dividends, will vary depending on the *PROFITABILITY* of the business. Capital gains arise as the business prospers and the market value of the shares increases. Unlike *LOAN FINANCE*, shares are irredeemable. However, they are transferable and a large and active market exists in the form of the Stock Exchange.

SHORT-TERM FORECASTING
A technique for making accurate predictions of the value of a variable just one period of time ahead. An example of such a technique is *EXPONENTIAL SMOOTHING*.

SKIMMING
A *PRICING* strategy which aims to exploit early opportunities in a new product market by charging high prices.

SLOPE
In the *EQUATION OF A STRAIGHT LINE*, the amount by which the *DEPENDENT VARIABLE*, **Y**, changes when the *EXPLANATORY VARIABLE*, **X**, increases in value by one unit.

SMOOTHING CONSTANT, α
The Greek letter α is used in the context of *EXPONENTIAL SMOOTHING*, to represent the smoothing constant. This constant assumes a value between 0 and 1, chosen by the forecaster, depending on the relative weighting he/she wishes to give to the most recent data. A high value of α gives a lot of weight to the most recent data; a low value of α gives a smoother series. A high value is normally chosen where recent changes and events are likely to have a very strong impact on future data.

SMOOTHED MEAN ABSOLUTE DEVIATION
A system for monitoring the general trend in forecasting errors for an *EXPONENTIAL SMOOTHING* system of *SHORT-TERM FORECASTING*. This system gives greater weight to more recent *FORECAST ERRORS* through the application of a *SMOOTHING CONSTANT*.

SPREADSHEET
A computer package that displays words and numbers in rows and columns and enables calculations to be performed.

STANDARD
An average based on historical data from a number of accounting periods, used to draw up a *BUDGET* for a future period (*see* **ATTAINABLE STANDARD, IDEAL STANDARD**).

STANDARD COST
An average *COST* based on historical data, used to draw up a *BUDGET* for a future period. *VARIANCE ANALYSIS* compares standard costs and *ACTUAL COSTS*.

STATE OF NATURE
A happening over which we have no control.

STOCK
Goods held for sale to customers (*see* **CURRENT ASSET**).

STOCK TURNOVER
A *RATIO* showing the number of times the average stock of a business is sold in one accounting period

$$\text{Stock turnover} = \frac{\text{Cost of goods sold}}{\text{Average stock}}$$

A stock turnover of 18 means that in one accounting period the business would sell stock to the value of 18 times that normally held in the business at any one point in time. Stock turnover can vary greatly between industries.

STRAIGHT LINE
A method of calculating the annual amount of *DEPRECIATION* to be charged to the *PROFIT AND LOSS ACCOUNT* by using the formula

$$\text{Annual depreciation charge} = \frac{\text{Historic cost} - \text{Scrap value}}{\text{Number of years of expected life of asset}}$$

The cost of the *ASSET* is spread over its useful life in equal parts. This method is therefore appropriate where the business is getting the same amount of use of the asset in each accounting period, as in the case of office furniture (*see* **DEPRECIATION**).

SUNK COST
A *COST* which cannot be recovered. In the context of short-term decision-making this type of cost is ignored as it is not affected by the decision.

TEMPLATE
A standard, generalised spreadsheet layout, which can be re-used an unlimited number of times for different problems requiring the application of the same technique.

TEXT
In a *SPREADSHEET*, any entry of words or a string of keyboard characters that is not a *NUMBER* or a *FORMULA*.

TIME SERIES
A table of figures showing the values of a variable at regular intervals in time. This can be used to make forecasts through *TIME SERIES ANALYSIS*.

TIME SERIES ANALYSIS
A technique for making forecasts based on the analysis of historical figures in the form of a *TIME SERIES*. This technique separates out the *SEASONAL VARIATIONS* and the overall *TREND*, facilitating predictions for the future movement of the series, provided the underlying assumptions remain unchanged.

TIME VALUE
In the context of *COMPOUND INTEREST* calculations, the fact that the earlier we receive a sum of money, the greater its value to us as it can be invested at the current discount rate and earn interest.

TOP DOWN
An approach to budgeting which takes the views of top management as the starting point for drawing up a *BUDGET*. This is based on the idea that there are considerable *ECONOMIES OF SCALE* to be derived from centralised information gathering and evaluation. A head office view of the economy, the industry and the company is therefore necessarily more accurate than a branch view. However, since branch managers are more aware of local preferences and peculiarities, this is often combined with a *BOTTOM UP* approach.

TOTAL COST
The sum of all *FIXED COSTS*, *SEMI-VARIABLE COSTS* and *VARIABLE COSTS*.

TRADE CREDITOR (*see* **CURRENT LIABILITY**).

TRADING ACCOUNT
The part of the *PROFIT AND LOSS ACCOUNT* which sets the *COST OF GOODS SOLD* against the *SALES REVENUE* of the accounting period to calculate *GROSS PROFIT*.

TRADING PROFIT
The financial surplus calculated by deducting the business *EXPENSES* of an accounting period from the *GROSS PROFIT* for that period.

TREND
The long-run component of a *TIME SERIES*. In the context of *TIME SERIES ANALYSIS* this can be estimated by filtering out the impact of *SEASONAL VARIATIONS*.

UNCONTROLLABLE COST
A *COST* which cannot be influenced by the manager in charge of the relevant cost centre. The manager can therefore not be held responsible for any *ADVERSE VARIANCES* in this type of cost (*see* **RESPONSIBILITY ACCOUNTING**).

UNIT CONTRIBUTION
That part of the selling price charged for each unit which is left after all unit *VARIABLE COSTS* have been paid for. This initially is used to pay for *FIXED COSTS*; once all fixed costs have been paid for, this is the profit made on the sale of each additional unit.

Unit contribution

= Selling price/Unit – Variable cost/Unit

(*see* **CONTRIBUTION**).

VARIABLE COST
A *COST* which varies in proportion to the level of sales or output of the business.

VARIABLE FACTOR
A resource element of a flexible and easily adjustable nature. The amount of this kind of resource used in the business can be changed in the short run. An example is labour. (For contrast, see **FIXED FACTOR**).

VARIANCE
The difference between *ACTUAL COST* and *STANDARD COST* for a budgetary period. This can be *ADVERSE* or *FAVOURABLE* and is investigated in the process of *VARIANCE ANALYSIS* (*see* **VARIANCE ANALYSIS**).

VARIANCE ANALYSIS
The process of calculating *VARIANCES*, identifying responsibility for *COST* control, investigating reasons behind *ADVERSE* variances, and taking remedial action.

WEIGHTED AVERAGE COST (WAC)
A method of stock valuation. Under this method the average cost of all goods in stock is calculated every time a purchase of stock is made. In this calculation a

weighting is given to the quantities purchased at the different cost prices, using the formula

WAC

$$= \frac{\text{Quantity } \mathbf{A} * \text{Price } \mathbf{A} + \cdots + \text{Quantity } \mathbf{N} * \text{Price } \mathbf{N}}{\text{Quantity } \mathbf{A} + \cdots + \text{Quantity } \mathbf{N}}$$

In times of inflation or deflation, the use of WAC will result in a *GROSS PROFIT* figure in between those resulting from the use of LIFO or FIFO. The use of this method is legal in the UK. WAC is mostly used by businesses selling large quantities of small and indistinguishable items.

XY CHART
A chart showing the relationship between two variables (*See* **SCATTER DIAGRAM**).

ZERO-BASE BUDGETING
A form of *BOTTOM UP* budgeting by which line managers are required to compete with each other for resources as part of the budgeting process. To claim resources they have to submit detailed requests, justifying future expenditure plans. These are evaluated (and approved or rejected) in the light of the comparative benefits to the organisation.

Index